The Films
of Tennessee Williams

The Films
of Tennessee Williams

Gene D. Phillips

Philadelphia
Art Alliance Press
London and Toronto: Associated University Presses

Associated University Presses, Inc.
4 Cornwall Drive
East Brunswick, N. J. 08816

Associated University Presses
69 Fleet Street
London EC4Y 1EU, England

Associated University Presses
Toronto M5E 1A7, Canada

Library of Congress Cataloging in Publication Data

Phillips, Gene D
   The films of Tennessee Williams.

   Filmography: p.
   Bibliography: p.
   Includes index.
   1. Williams, Tennessee, 1911-   —Film adaptations.
I. Title.
PS3545.I5365Z823   812'.5'4   76-50204
ISBN 0-87982-025-X

PRINTED IN THE UNITED STATES OF AMERICA

For
Robert and Kevin,
who understood

Contents

Contents

Foreword
Tennessee Williams and the Theater

Catharine Hughes, drama critic of *America*

THE 1975–76 THEATRE SEASON (and, for that matter, the 1975–76 book publishing year) was a big one for Tennessee Williams. There were major New York revivals of *The Glass Menagerie, Sweet Bird of Youth, Summer and Smoke, 27 Wagons Full of Cotton* and a number of lesser productions and plays off-Off Broadway. His first "full length" novel, *Moise and the World of Reason,* was published in May, 1975, and, although it received what are often euphemistically referred to as "mixed notices," it contained some passages of great and revealing lyricism and insight. His *Memoirs,* published the following November, are in many ways a remarkable document and, remarkable or not, took up residence on the best-seller list, albeit in its nether regions.

Although occasional claims are made for Arthur Miller, Williams is by all odds the most significant American playwright to emerge during the period that began roughly at the end of World War II. He may even be the most significant American playwright thus far. Yet it has been fifteen or more years since his last major critical and popular success, *The Night of the Iguana,* won the New York Drama Critics Circle Award in 1961. In more recent years, such theoretically major works as *Kingdom of Earth* and *Out Cry* have been deserved critical and box office failures, while *In the Bar of a Tokyo Hotel* and *Small Craft Warnings,* both produced Off Broadway, have fallen far short of the early plays that established Williams's reputation. It hardly lessens the conundrum to note that his first Broadway play and first success, *The Glass Menagerie,* remains, arguably, his best play. And it was produced in 1945.

Williams's career has, as it happens, followed a pattern similar to that of

9

many, perhaps most, of the American dramatists and novelists of the past three decades: the initial great success and great expectations, the subsequent critical and public disenchantment, the repeated suggestion over the past decade that he is "written out," though *Menagerie, A Streetcar Named Desire* and *Cat on a Hot Tin Roof* cannot themselves be written off. It remains for the social scientists to explore Scott Fitzgerald's contention that there are no "second acts" in American life, at least in the life of the American artist. America's writers frequently tend to confirm it. Williams's more recent activities bring it into question.

His career is in many ways a remarkable one, even if he were never again to write another word. Born Thomas Lanier Williams (he adopted the "Tennessee" years later) in Columbus, Mississippi, on March 26, 1911, he graduated from the University of Iowa in 1938. (Among other things, he had, like the narrator of *Menagerie,* worked in between for a shoe company, which Tom Wingfield in that play calls a "living death.") He achieved limited national recognition with an award from the Group Theatre in 1939, and his first major production came with *Battle of Angels,* which closed in Boston during a pre-Broadway tryout run in 1940. It was subsequently rewritten as *Orpheus Descending,* 1957.

It was, however, with *The Glass Menagerie,* which one critic, with some exaggeration but considerable validity, has asserted was "the beginning of a new epoch in Western theater history," that Williams was established as a significant figure in the postwar American theater. Not surprisingly, it displayed many of the themes and preoccupations that were to absorb him over the next thirty years. In a preface to the published version, Williams refers to it as initiating "a new, plastic theater which must take the place of the exhausted theater of realistic conventions if the theater is to resume vitality as part of our culture." Whether it was that is dubious; that it was the first major and enduring postwar American play is beyond challenge.

Say what one will about its maudlin moments and its occasional sentimentality, *The Glass Menagerie* is a work of poignance and poetry. Its characters—at least Tom and Laura—have the sensitivity that Williams, too often mistakenly, equates with the poetic or artistic. They are "different," and "difference"— abnormality in any form—would seem for Williams to be the hallmark of the potential hero, the potential saint, and normality its antithesis.

This is equally so in Williams's second major play, *A Streetcar Named Desire* (1947), which received both the New York Drama Critics Circle Award and the Pulitzer Prize. Williams has said that *Streetcar's* meaning is "the ravishment of the tender, the sensitive, the delicate by the savage and brutal forces of modern society," and that is surely one interpretation that can be placed upon it. It is, however, an oversimplification that denies Blanche's complexity, for she has her cruel aspect, her mendacity, to go hand in hand with her fragile vulnerability. Her role in the Kowalski household is threatening and destructive, and it is only the fact that Stella and Stanley genuinely do love each other, despite their disparate backgrounds and personalities, that enables their marriage to endure her presence.

Yet, Blanche is almost the Tennessee Williams archetype. She tells Mitch: "I don't want realism. I want magic! . . . I don't tell truth, I tell what *ought* to be truth," a line that could be spoken by at least one character in virtually every ~ting of the wounded, the fugitive and the mutilated, the ~ lonely, he suggests a world at once recognizable and his characters, he writes of them with a compassion naudlin. With Blanche, however, the artist's hand ~ characterization and the play as a whole are far the case in most of the works that have es to rework his plays long after they ~metimes they do not. With the "new" in 1974, his decision was clearly a good ~ms, however, for Williams attempts to ~, even now, to be completely successful. ~uy, who tragically and too late has discovered wife for years and now wants both a final fling, which he ~ave, and an heir from his son Brick. Then there is the guilt-~ ~ck, asserting the purity of his friendship with the dead Skipper, refusing to acknowledge it for what it was—for at least one of them—and because of that refusing also to go to bed with his wife. And what of Maggie herself, Maggie the Cat? Are her intensity and passion prompted more by a craving for wealth or a craving for Brick, even at the moment at the end of the play when she denies him his liquor, telling the hobbling, crutch-bound man that she will return it only after he impregnates her, after which they'll "get drunk together"?

Holding it all together should be two factors: the theme of "mendacity," the curse that Brick tells his father is responsible for his alcoholism, and Brick himself. The mendacity theme emerges with considerably greater effect in the 1974 version, but Brick does not. The audience is still required to take on faith whatever it is that Maggie, Big Daddy and Big Mama find so attractive, so worthy of love, even of admiration, in Brick. The character is far too sketchily written. It is not sufficient to have Maggie recall that Brick is one of those "weak, beautiful people who give up with such grace"—especially when the grace is not on view—and to witness instead only his ironically polite indifference. Brick is far too pivotal to everyone else's actions for that. Even so, the play holds up remarkably well after two decades.

In *Orpheus Descending*, Val Xavier, who functions as both Orpheus and Christ, another of Williams's symbolic, semimythical figures, observes: "Nobody ever gets to know no body! We're all of us sentenced to solitary confinement inside our own skins, for life!" In *The Eccentricities of a Nightingale*, a revision of *Summer and Smoke*, Alma refers to "my little company of the faded and frightened and difficult and odd and lonely." Whether they be failed artists or poets, priapic young men or people of "refinement" (Blanche, for instance), "mad" (as most of Williams's heroines to some extent are) or mutilated, they are outsiders, struggling against a world that fails to recognize their vision or their "talent." They are attempting to escape that very "world of reality" from which, at 14, Williams wrote in the foreword to *Sweet Bird of Youth*, he was attempting to escape, although they seldom if ever succeed. They are offered, not as victims of their private illusions, but as victims of that world in which "normality, triumphant, is nonetheless somehow damnable." When Williams successfully presents their pain as people rather than as symbols, as he did in several of the early plays, he is a dramatist of poignance and power.

But what of the present? What of Tennessee Williams now?

The Red Devil Battery Sign, a play set in Dallas immediately after the assassination of John F. Kennedy, closed in Boston during a tryout run in the summer of 1975. Even Williams concedes that the play was not yet ready for public presentation. A revised version was produced in Vienna the following winter and was well received. Another new work, *This is (An Entertainment)*, premiered in San Francisco in 1976, and still another, *Vieux Carre*, opened on Broadway in May, 1977.

Whatever else it may prove, the fact that Williams has produced two books and three plays in two years clearly gives the lie to the numerous claims that he is in any sense "written out." In the *Memoirs*, he says: "I have made a covenant with myself to continue to write, since I have no choice, it is so deeply rooted as a way of existence and a form of flight."

We are prone to refer to Williams as the foremost American playwright "since O'Neill." Now in his sixties and still enormously productive, he may yet prove that there is no need for that qualifying phrase.

Acknowledgments

FIRST OF ALL, I am most grateful to Tennessee Williams who gave me his personal impressions on the films made of his work and his encouragment in preparing this book.

Of the many others who helped me I would like to mention:

Dakin Williams, brother of the playwright: film directors Elia Kazan, Richard Brooks, Joseph Losey, John Huston, Sidney Lumet, and cinematographer James Wong Howe, all of whom spoke with me about their Williams films over the long period in which I was engaged in remote preparation for this study; stage director Herbert Machiz and actor Donald Madden, both of whom have known Williams for many years; writer Gore Vidal; film producers Louis de Rochemont and Lothar Wolff; and Rev. Joseph LeRoy, S.J., who knew Williams when he converted to Catholicism.

Patrick Sheehan, of the Motion Picture Section of the Library of Congress; Holly Hall, Chief of the Special Collections of Washington University Library; Mary Lee Sweat, Reference Librarian of the Library of Loyola University of New Orleans; Thomas Quinn Curtiss, film critic of *The International Herald Tribune*; my colleagues at Loyola University of Chicago who provided me with special materials: Anne Callahan of Modern Languages, Margaret Dagenais of Fine Arts, Benjamin Llamzon of Philosophy, and Arthur Bloom and Raoul Johnson of Theater; Loyola University of Chicago for granting me a sabbatical leave in order to finish this book; and Kevin H. Flaherty, S.J., who shared his insights with me about a psychological approach to Williams's characters, especially Blanche DuBois.

Acknowledgment is made for permission to quote from the works of Tennessee Williams copyrighted as follows:

New Directions, New York, and Secker and Warburg, London: *Battle of Angels* © 1940, 1945, 1971 by Tennessee Williams. *The Glass Menagerie* ©

1945, 1948, 1971 by Tennessee Williams. *Twenty-Seven Wagons Full of Cotton and Other One-Act Plays* © 1945, 1953, 1966 by Tennessee Williams. *A Streetcar Named Desire* © 1947, 1953, 1971 by Tennessee Williams. *One Arm and Other Stories* © 1948, 1957, 1967 by Tennessee Williams. *Summer and Smoke* © 1948, 1950, 1971 by Tennessee Williams. *The Roman Spring of Mrs. Stone* © 1950, 1969 by Tennessee Williams. *The Rose Tattoo* © 1951, 1971 by Tennessee Williams. *Baby Doll* © 1957 by Tennessee Williams. *Orpheus Descending* © 1955, 1958, 1971 by Tennessee Williams. *Suddenly Last Summer* © 1958, 1971 by Tennessee Williams. *Sweet Bird of Youth* © 1959, 1962, 1972 by Tennessee Williams. *Period of Adjustment* © 1960, 1972 by Tennessee Williams.. *The Night of the Iguana* © 1961, 1963, 1972 by Tennessee Williams. *The Milk Train Doesn't Stop Here Anymore* © 1963, 1964, 1976 by Tennessee Williams. *Kingdom of Earth* © 1967, 1969, 1976 by Tennessee Williams. *The Knightly Quest: A Novella and Four Short Stories* © 1966 by Tennessee Williams.

Doubleday, Garden City, N.Y., and Secker and Warburg, London: *Memoirs* © 1972, 1975 by Tennessee Williams.

Acknowledgment is made for the use of Catharine Hughes's essay on Tennessee Williams which appears as the preface of this book. It is reprinted with permission of *America* © 1976 by America Press, 106 West 56th Street, New York, N.Y.—10019. All rights reserved. Acknowledgment is made for permission to quote from Dakin Williams's biography-in-progress of Tennessee Williams, entitled *My Brother's Keeper*.

Acknowledgment is made to Jac Tharpe of the University of Southern Mississippi for allowing me to have an early copy of the monumental collection of essays which he has edited for the University Press of Mississippi, *Tennessee Williams: A Tribute*, enabling me to have access to this material while preparing my own present volume.

Introduction
Tennessee Williams and the Movies

> Concerning the movies of my plays let me say in general that there are no unmixed
> blessings or afflictions that I know of.
> —Tennessee Williams to the author

IN HIS AUTOBIOGRAPHY, *Fun in a Chinese Laundry*, film maker Josef Von
Sternberg remarks that "both the stage and the screen have chewed on the same
breast." This is Sternberg's rather picturesque way of noting how often film
studios have turned to the stage for material, "despite the complete difference in
technique, the appeal of one being to the eye, the other to the ear." With that
very simple observation, Sternberg has articulated for me in equally simple
terms the basic thrust of this book, which is an examination of the relationship of
the motion picture and theater media as reflected in the screen versions of the
work of one playwright, Tennessee Williams.

This book is meant to be a companion volume to my earlier study of the
relation of fiction and film which centered on the movies made from the fiction of
Graham Greene. The two books obviously have a great deal in common, just as
the two subjects, Graham Greene and Tennessee Williams, have a great deal in
common. For one thing, both Greene and Williams are among the very few
major literary talents of our time to show serious interest in the motion picture
medium. For another, both men have had all of their major works committed to
celluloid and have, moreover, often served as consultants on the film versions of
their work, and at times have scripted or co-scripted the screenplays themselves. Hence Williams is the perfect subject for a book about film and drama,
just as Greene was the ideal subject for a book about film and fiction.

Much has been written on the theoretical level about the relationship of film
and drama, ranging from Allardyce Nicoll's groundbreaking *Film and Theater*

Tennessee Williams on the set of *Night of the Iguana* with Sue Lyon.

to James Hurt's collection of essays, *Focus on Film and Theater*. The purpose of my present study is to show how the wedding of drama and film works out concretely in an analysis that is based on literary and cinematic theory about the nature of the two media, but which focuses on the screen versions of the plays of a single dramatist.

Later in these introductory remarks, therefore, I shall briefly analyze the nature of drama and of film as two separate media in order to show how they are different and how they are similar. The succeeding chapters will examine the motion pictures based on Williams's work in the context of the critical theory developed at the beginning of the book. In taking up each of Williams's works that has been filmed, I first consider it as a literary and dramatic work in its own right, independent of the fact that it was later filmed; for it is only in understanding the significance of each play in itself as Williams originally conceived it for the stage that we can judge the relative artistic merits of the subsequent screen version, and consequently come to a firmer grasp of the relationship of the motion picture medium to the theater.

I should mention at this point that one of the Williams films treated in these pages was based not on a play but on a novella called *The Roman Spring of Mrs. Stone*. I include it not only in the interest of completeness but also because of Williams's high regard for the film.

My interest in the films of Tennessee Williams was first stirred more than a decade agon when I ran across a program for a film series held at Notre Dame University in the summer of 1965. It included a brief essay by Robert Haller entitled "Tennessee Williams: The American Dream." He began by acknowledging the apparent anomaly of including an article on Williams in a booklet devoted to film directors, but the anomaly was quickly explained:

"His plays, even when transposed to the screen without his assistance, possess a continuity and quality rare for anyone—be he a director, writer, or actor. John Huston, Elia Kazan, Sidney Lumet, and Richard Brooks have all turned their formidable talents to the task of filming Williams and it is remarkable how little of their personal style and how much that of the playwright has persisted."

This is not to suggest that the personal style of the director is not important to the artistic success of a film, as Richard Corliss reminds us in *Talking Pictures: Screenwriters in the American Cinema:* "The importance of a director's personal—or even visual—style is not in question here, only the assumption that he creates a style out of thin air" instead of adapting it to the exigencies of the story which he is filming. While it is true that the director is ultimately responsible *for* the overall quality and artistic unity of a motion picture, it is also true, says Corliss, that "he must be responsible *to* something: the screenplay." As writer-director Richard Brooks says, "You having nothing to direct until you have a story."

Foster Hirsch has written in *Cinema* magazine in a vein similar to that of Haller about the critical problems associated with filming Williams's plays, and a single quotation from Hirsch's piece is enough to indicate the rich field to be mined from an examination of these films. The plays of Tennessee Williams are deeply theatrical, says Hirsch, "because of their lush and literary imagery, cascading set speeches, concentrated time spans, limited setting, and confined action." And yet, he continues, these unmistakably stage-bound works have been translated into "eminently successful movies that challenge rigid preconceptions of 'theatrical' and 'cinematic' formats. The Williams films retain the spirit of the original plays, so that even when Williams did not work on the screenplays, his personality still dominates them. A movie based on a Tennessee Williams play is a Tennessee Williams film because its chief nourishment comes from the playwright himself."

Mr. Hirsch's challenging remarks serve as a focus for the present book in that he has provided a useful yardstick by which one can measure the stature of the various screen adaptations of Williams's plays: for it is only in ascertaining to what extent a given film has preserved intact the spirit of the Williams play on which it was based that we can judge the validity of the movie as a faithful adaptation of the Williams original. Furthermore, because some of Williams's works have also been produced on television, I shall refer to these productions when the occasion arises, particularly in the epilogue, in order to see whether Williams has fared better on the big screen or on the little screen.

Williams's plays have proved easily adaptable both to movies and television for several reasons: his loosely constructed plots are easily modified; his central characters are boldly drawn figures experiencing an emotional crisis with which audiences can easily identify; and his stories are melodramatic enough to grip an audience's attention.

A persistent problem that has made it difficult in one respect to create genuine film and television versions of Williams works, however, is that posed by censorship. Many of the movies in particular were made when the screen did not enjoy the same freedom as that of the legitimate theater. Hence themes and situations which Williams treated frankly on stage were a source of controversy when these same elements found their way into a Williams film. Williams has told me that he sympathizes with the film makers who were "engaged in making films of plays that were not really suitable, at the time that they were filmed, for treatment on the screen with that degree of honesty which I think is necessary to an art form."

For example, Williams has often dealt with homosexuality in his plays and it is interesting to see how this theme was only allowed to intrude gradually into the film versions: from the reticent remarks of Blanche DuBois with her late husband's homosexuality in *A Streetcar Named Desire* to the unvarnished treatment of the homosexual Sebastian in *Suddenly, Last Summer* less than a decade later.

I shall, of course, have more to say later in the book about the concessions to the moral standards of motion picture morality which film makers had to make in adapting Williams's plays to the cinema, in order to seek to understand how these concessions may have altered in some degree the intent of Williams's original work. Suffice it to say at this point that Williams, like D. H. Lawrence before him, has been pilloried by some as a cynical purveyor of corrupt stories about human degradation and has likewise been praised by others as a serious moralist akin to Lawrence himself. It is as the latter that I believe he comes through in both the plays and their movie counterparts, as I hope to demonstrate in analyzing each in turn.

Concerning what some consider to be his rather lurid subject matter Williams has said, "All my life I have been haunted by the obsession that to desire a thing or to love a thing intensely is to place yourself in a vulnerable position, to be a possible, if not a probable loser of what you most want. . . . Having always to contend with this adversary of fear, which was sometimes terror, gave me a certain tendency toward an atmosphere of hysteria and violence in my writing, an atmosphere that has existed since the beginning." In addition, Williams believes that since we live in a hostile world, violence has a place in art. "I feel that so much of contemporary life is a shocking matter, and one is obliged to catch the quality that prevails in contemporary life. If you just read the newspapers in America, you'll see that my plays are far from exaggerations." In any case, the violence in a Williams play almost always takes place offstage, as he himself attests at the beginning of the first chapter, something his critics often forget, just as they forget that he has been critical of films of his plays that bring his offstage violence on-screen, as happened in the case of *Suddenly, Last Summer*.

Since my method of procedure will be similar in this book to that which I followed in my previous book on the films of Graham Greene, I would like to take the liberty of quoting the review of that book by Michael Desilets in *Filmograph*. Desilets notes that my manner of writing the Greene study "seems simple enough." The author, he says, "has read the books and the scripts, interviewed people connected with each film; weighed other evaluations with his own to arrive at a consensus. In other words his book is not instant criticism." The goal of the present book, then, is to follow the same format which Desilets outlined above as having been my approach in the Greene volume in order to promote further dialogue about the relationship of literature and film.

That the nature of this relationship is still a live issue has been reflected in the comments prompted by discussion of my Greene book in printed reviews and in round table discussions at various conventions. There are those, I have learned, that believe very strongly that literature and film should preserve their own respective turfs and be studied separately, without any attempt to understand one in the light of the other. My own conviction is that what one learns about the integration of literature and film as complementary media enhances one's appreciation of both.

Let us spend a little time, therefore, sketching the relationship of film and theater so that we can better appreciate the films made from Williams's work in the chapters to come.

First of all, let me point out that in general cinema has more in common with fiction than with any other form of literature. One might be tempted to suppose that film is closer to drama than to fiction since a play, like a motion picture, is acted out before an audience. But the similarity really ends there. Both a novel and a film depend more on description and narration than on dialogue, while in a play the emphasis is reversed. Novelist Robert Nathan, in affirming that film is closer to fiction than to drama, calls a movie "a novel to be seen instead of told," because a motion picture, like a novel, "ranges where it pleases, it studies the reactions of single characters, it deals in description and mood, it follows, by means of the camera, the single, unique vision of the writer."

Precisely because the drama is literally stage-bound and does not possess the mobility of the movie camera, the dramatist, to a much greater degree than the screen writer, must rely on words to convey the burden of his story and its theme to his audience. For the bulk of the audience in a theater is simply too far from the stage to see the telling gestures and facial expressions that can communicate wordlessly a great deal to an audience watching the images at close range on a screen.

Nevertheless, because both movies and plays are designed to be performed before an audience, movie makers from the very dawn of cinema history have turned to the stage for source material for films, as Josef Von Sternberg noted at the beginning of this prologue. The earliest silent films based on stage plays were merely condensed versions of the original plays, sometimes photographed on the original set used in the stage production. As early as 1912 Sarah Bernhardt appeared in a silent film based on her Paris stage production of *Queen Elizabeth*. Each scene in the film approximated one scene in the play, with the static camera simply recording each scene acted out before it in a single long shot. The "curtain call" at the end of the movie which had the star bowing to the camera as to an audience left little doubt that the purpose of the picture was to preserve for posterity a record of Ms. Bernhardt's stage performance on film.

Indeed Ms. Bernhardt herself looked upon the film medium as her one chance for immortality. The American distribution company of the movie was called "Famous Players in Famous Plays" as an additional indication that her film and others like it pretended to be no more than photographed stage plays which would allow audiences beyond the ambit of touring companies to see "famous players in famous plays." When George Bernard Shaw saw the Bernhardt film, he commented in *Metropolitan Magazine* that the cinema could make available to the mass audience stage productions of important plays—but only after it had found its voice.

With the advent of sound in the late Twenties the movies learned to talk and, as Shaw predicted, the motion picture industry turned more than ever to the stage for new properties to film. Hollywood imported playwrights, directors, and stars from Broadway to put the plays on the screen. It is not surprising that the

George Cukor, veteran movie director, who was called to Hollywood, like other Broadway stage directors, at the coming of sound.

influence of these theater-oriented artists, combined with the tyranny of the new sound equipment (which dictated that the camera he immobilized in a soundproof box resembling a telephone booth), produced movies that differed little from the stage originals on which they were so obviously based. George Bluestone sums up the situation in *Novels into Film* this way: Just as the early silent films erred by imitating the fixed frame of the stage, so the early sound films erred by reproducing theatrical dialogue.

George Cukor, one of the Broadway directors brought out to Hollywood in the wake of the birth of the talkies, recalls, "The studios were all terrified when sound came in. Directors were abandoning all that they had learned about camera movement in the days of silent pictures. The camera was quarantined inside a soundproof booth so that the mechanical noises would not be picked up on the sound track, and had to remain stationary throughout each take. Gradually, however, the techniques of making sound films were perfected." For one thing, noiseless cameras were developed so that the camera was liberated from its confinement and could once more move freely among the actors. For another, actors began feeling more and more at home in the new medium of talking pictures, so that their performances became less self-conscious, less theatrical, just as directors like Cukor were beginning to feel more comfortable behind the camera.

"It took directors like myself three or four years to cotton up to screen directing after coming from the theater," Cukor told me. "In films you are working in very close quarters; in the theater the actors have to act with their voices in order to project to the back of the balcony. The director has to keep in mind when making a film that what would be a good performance on the stage would be overacting on the screen." This last point was, unfortunately, often forgotten in making the early sound movies.

While Cukor and others were learning how to cope with sound in the first years of the talkies, Hollywood turned out many films based on Broadway stage successes which amounted to little more than putting the play on the screen almost as it had been put on in the theater. The only gestures made in the direction of making the film look a little less stagey than the play was to show a character entering the building where the scene was set. Once inside, however, the action would proceed as it did on the stage. Shaw satirized this approach to filming plays when he said that a certain portion of every film must consist of "going up and down stairs and getting in and out of motor cars. . . . My plays do not depend on staircases for their interest. I am, therefore, told that I do not understand the art of the screen."

Looking back on the birth of the sound era in his article on film production in *The Encyclopedia Britannica,* Alfred Hitchcock writes that the introduction of spoken dialogue constituted the final touch of realism needed by the film medium; but in pure cinema dialogue would always be designed as a

Alfred Hitchcock, who deplored that the coming of sound brought with it a proliferation of photographed stage plays.

complement to the visual images, and a good director would never rely too heavily on the spoken word. "That is what happened at the appearance of sound," when screen directors filmed stage plays straight, and moving pictures temporarily ceased to move, writes Hitchcock. These films were "just photographs of people talking. . . . The consequence was a loss of the art of reproducing life in pictures." One of the most basic elements of the cinema,

Hitchcock insists, is the telling of a story as visually as possible: "to embody the action in the juxtaposition of images that have their own specific language and emotional impact—that is cinema."

The radical differences between theater and film, as Hitchcock has expressed it above, is that drama relies primarily on dialogue to tell its story while a movie depends primarily on images. Surely some of the spoken exposition that could not be shown on a stage can be depicted directly on the screen; surely some of the characters' feelings, which had to be verbalized on a stage, can be portrayed in close shots of facial expressions and gestures on the screen. As A. R. Fulton writes in *Motion Pictures: The Development of an Art,* now that the camera has become flexible once more, plays adapted to the screen should be less theater-like than they were in the early days of movie history. "The camera, moving about freely, gives the spectator the impression that he is not confined to his seat in the theater but can come closer to the scene, and watch it from all sides, even from above and below."

We accept the conventions of the stage when we see a play, but we reject these very same conventions when they are slavishly carried over to the screen because movies need not—and therefore should not—be bound to them. As Lazlo Benedek reflected about his directing the film of *Death of a Salesman,* "It is a curious psychological phenomenon that the people who make up a theater audience will for two or three hours watch contentedly as actors on a stage talk to each other; but when these same people go to a film they will get restless after more than five minutes of straight dialogue." The reason is simple: when people go to a movie they do not want to see a play.

To what extent, then, should a play be opened out spatially to include more settings than were possible in the theater in order to exploit the greater flexibility of the motion picture medium? Asked this question, veteran director Billy Wilder replied, "It depends on the play. Certain plays call for being opened out more than others. Indeed the playwright himself might have opened up his play more had he not been straightjacketed by the format of the stage. That was the case with *The Front Page* (1975), which we opened out much more than the 1930 movie did; we added a chase scene and other things. On the other hand, sometimes opening up a play for the screen can ruin it. When I made *Stalag 17* (1953), I wanted the audience to experience the confinement of a prisoner of war camp and therefore we shot no scenes outside of the camp. If we lost that sense of isolation that was in the play, the intensity of the whole story would have to some extent been dissipated."

Another veteran director, William Wyler, who has adapted countless plays to the screen, agrees with Wilder, and he is worth quoting on this point at some length:

"I have never been overly concerned about opening up a play for the screen," he told me, "because you can alter a play for the cinema to the point of obliterating the qualities that made it a good property in the first place. Just because the film director has the facilities to carry the action outside of the relatively few sets where the play took place, it doesn't follow that he should automatically exercise that freedom. The playwright had to discipline himself to concentrate his action in a circumscribed area, and this often serves to tighten the play's construction and make for a fast-moving story. Opening up the play too much for the screen can, therefore, cause the pace of the story to slacken. Conversely, the film director also wants to avoid making a photographed stageplay.

"My approach to filming a play, consequently, has been to retain the basic construction of the original, while at the same time lending the story the illusion of more movement than took place on the stage. For example, *Detective Story*, which I filmed in 1951, originally was staged in a couple of rooms in a police station. I extended the action in the film by playing it throughout the two-story building, from the basement to the roof. The constant movement back and forth among these various playing areas kept the film from becoming static, while retaining at the same time the tight construction of the play."

While he was collaborating on the screenplay for *Detective Story*, Wyler toyed with the idea of creating a scene in the home of the detective (Kirk Douglas), to show the kind of atmosphere in which he lived, but finally discarded the idea entirely. "Taking the detective home and then back to the station slowed down the action and it didn't really contribute much to the film's background anyhow. If you introduce a lot of spurious scene shifting into a film just to prove you're not reproducing the play, you run the risk of opening up the play to the point where you close down the viewer's interest in the story you are trying to tell."

As playwright Mart Crowley, who adapted his own *Boys of the Band* to the screen in 1970, puts it, "A film does not add variety to a scene simply by breaking up the dialogue from the play with shots of the Seagram Building and three or four other location backgrounds. The variety must come within the scene by photographing the action from different points of view."

Since the advent of widescreen motion pictures in the early fifties, the movie screen can have the same dimensions as the proscenium arch of a theater stage. As a result a film director can encompass more of a setting and of the action of a scene in a single shot than he can when shooting for the dimensions of the conventional "square" screen, for which he must use several successive shots to cover all of the aspects of the set and the action. Since the widescreen approximates the dimensions of the proscenium arch, a lazy movie maker can be tempted to compose his shots with little camera movement, as if he were directing a stage play rather than a film, thus taking a decided step backwards in the development of the art of the motion picture; and there are widescreen movies which exemplify how a director can succumb to this temptation.

Given the risks that a playwright like Tennessee Williams runs in entrusting his work to a film studio for adaptation to the screen, why do so many dramatists willingly allow their cherished works to be filmed? The most obvious answer is the considerable amount of income which a writer derives from selling his plays to the movies. Though, as we shall see in the ensuing chapters, Williams is not happy with some of the films of his plays, he is the first to admit that "I could not easily have lived without the movie sales. . . . There are no unmixed blessing or afflictions that I know of."

Secondly, just as Sarah Bernhardt saw the movies as a way not only to reach a world-wide audience but also to immortalize her performances for future generations, so too a playwright like Williams sees the cinema as a way of making his plays more available to present and future audiences that far exceed in number those which will ever see his work in the theater. "When I decided to film Arthur Miller's *Death of a Salesman*," Lazlo Benedek recalls, "I felt it was my chance to make available a very important and thought-provoking play about the false values in the commercialized life style in the United States to a larger audience without changing or in any way diminishing its thematic impact. The controvery which surrounded the film when it opened in 1951 indicates that the thematic strength of the play was carried over into the film. In other words we had been faithful to the spirit of the original play, and not just to its plot."

The third and possibly most important reason why a playwright will allow his stage work to see the light of the silver screen, then, is that it is just possible that the film will remain faithful to the spirit of his original play and that he can recognize the movie as a reflection of his work just as much as he recognized the play to be his own. In the last analysis, George Bluestone contends, what a conscientious screen writer is doing when he adapts a literary work to the movie medium is composing a cinematic paraphrase of the original work. The resulting film can never be a replica of the novel or play from which it is dervied, for a work of art conceived in terms of the techniques of one medium always to some extent resists conversion into another medium; but the adapter telling the story in the new medium can, for all of that, preserve the original writer's thematic intent and personal vision while at the same time translating that theme and vision as much as possible into the visual terms of the screen.

Unquestionably, then, a play must undergo many superficial alterations when it is adapted to the motion picture screen. What must be preserved throughout the transition from stage to screen is, as I have mentioned, the spirit and theme of the original work. If the fundamental intent of the original play is somehow mislaid between stage and screen, then the author of the source work has just grounds for complaint. In the preface to his *Three Plays*, Graham Greene pictures the author of a work that is filmed as the "forgotten man" in the movie business, a bewildered figure who materializes at the studio to watch the rough cut of a film drawn from his writings, clearing his throat nervously at hearing lines that are not his, but for which he will probably bear the critics' blame. The excitement of his original creation, he finds, has been lost in the many rewritings of the screenplay and now he is the only one of the spectators who fondly remembers how it all began in his typewriter.

Tennessee Williams, as much as Graham Greene, has just cause for complaint about some of the films of his work. Nevertheless, once we have examined the many movies of his plays, I am confident that it will become clear that every one of them retains at least some moments that reflect Williams's original work and that at least some of them rank as examples of superior cinema just as the plays from which they were adapted rank as superior dramas.

Before turning to our survey of the individual films, let me end this general introduction about the relationship of film and theater by citing Pauline Kael's valentine to filmed theater in *Going Steady:*

"A play gives an actor a role he can work up and make his own, and this is usually still the case when the play is filmed—something that is rarely possible in movies derived from other material. . . . Some of the most enjoyable movies ever made—such as George Cukor's *Dinner at Eight*—are well-made adaptations of plays. I *like* filmed theater; I think there is a charge and a glamour about filmed plays . . . that one rarely gets from adaptations of novels or from those few screen 'originals.' Filmed plays are often denigrated, somewhat dishonestly, by people who learn a little about what is said to be proper to the film medium and forget about the pleasure they've been getting from filmed plays all their lives."

No small measure of that pleasure has been provided by the films of Tennessee Williams's plays, to which we now turn.

The Films
of Tennessee Williams

What's straight? A line can be straight or a street. But the heart of a human being?
—Blanche DuBois

1
Irving Rapper:
The Glass Menagerie

A SLEEK LIMOUSINE pulls up to the curb in front of the Festival Palace in Cannes and the door swings open. It is the opening night of the 1976 Cannes International Film Festival and the president of the jury has just arrived to participate in the festivities. He is wearing formal evening dress and a broad smile. Although he is somewhat short of stature, he is nonetheless an imposing figure; and the people crowding the curb strain to get a good look at the most famous playwright in the English speaking world: Tennessee Williams.

Since the festival jury is usually composed of film directors, movie stars, and others connected closely with the motion picture industry around the world, there has been some speculation among my colleagues in the international press corps as to why an American playwright was chosen to head the film festival jury. The answer, I tell them, is quite simple: not only have all of Williams's major works been committed to celluloid, but he has been involved in varying degrees in the making of all of these films.

Of course Williams's presence at Cannes was an enormous piece of good luck for me, since it enabled me to get some additional data from him for the present work. I had initially discussed this project with him by phone some months earlier and found him cordial and cooperative. He very graciously followed up our phone conversation about the films of his work a few days later with a detailed letter in which he gave his further reflections about the individual movies. This material, coupled with the additional things which he told me in Cannes when I met him at the time of his press conference with the attending journalists, has given me a fairly complete picture of how Williams himself feels

Tennessee Williams on the terrace of the Festival Palace at the Cannes Film Festival, where he was president of the 1976 international jury.

about the way in which his work has fared in its various screen incarnations. His reaction to individual movies will be found spread throughout this book as each film is taken up in turn. But it would be good at the outset, before going on to the first of the movies, to examine his overall reactions to the movie adaptations of his plays.

To begin with, Williams finds the whole subject distressing and does not like to talk about it at any length because most of what he has to say "could only give unnecessary offense to the artists who were engaged in making films of plays which were not really suitable, at the time that they were filmed, for treatment on the screen with that degree of honesty which I think is necessary to an art form. Almost invariably some concessions had to be made to the censors of the Motion Picture Association of America who were in command at the time." Their function, as far as he could see, was to protect the American public from "the frightful contagion of truth," which was acceptable on the stage, but not on the screen.

There is a certain irony about movie producers posing as protectors of public morality, Williams feels. In actual fact they believed that they knew what various pressure groups would accept as moral film fare as well as what the critics and the public would accept as entertainment; and that is what the producers gave them for their price of admission. When Williams's work did not fit the producers' preconceived notions of the temper of the times, the film versions were altered accordingly.

"Fortunately," he told me, "this falsely moral sort of censorship has now collapsed. You might say that the sky is the limit—or the taste of the artists involved." The public is no longer dismayed by films that deal honestly with the realities of ordinary life, he believes.

Given this new climate in the movie industry, I thought it proper to ask Williams if there are any of the movies of his plays that he would like to see

Scenes from four Williams films: *Last of the Mobile Hotshots, Baby Doll, Cat on a Hot Tin Roof,* and *Night of the Iguana.*

remade. "In a way I wish that almost all of my films could be remade now that there is greater freedom of the screen," he replied. "Although really if they just changed the endings of most of the films back to what they were in the original plays, that alone would suffice to bring the movies more into line with their source material. In most cases it was the ending of each film that was noticeably altered. The movie would go along fairly well up to the very end when the whole picture would be marred by a false denouement. The directors and actors in each case didn't like this any more than I did. But these compromises had to be made because of the inhibiting pressure applied by the strong censorship system of the time. In fact, upon looking back on those days, I count myself fortunate that those compromises were not greater than they were."

The thought that seems to nag Williams most about this whole question of the movies of his work is that more people have seen the films than have—or ever will—see the plays from which they were derived. Thus, when people discuss his plays with him, he finds that they are usually referring to the film adaptations, which they always seem to assume are accurate representations of the original works: "When some well-intentioned admirer says to me that they were delighted to find that the movie of *Sweet Bird of Youth* ends with the two young lovers getting together instead of their morbidly being kept apart, I confess I don't know what to reply, since the latter ending is precisely the one which I wrote in the play!"

Another irony that Williams finds involved in the whole question of the censorship of his films was brought into sharp focus at Cannes. "I found while being president of the jury at Cannes that my films are quite mild when compared to the movies being made today, of which I have seen quite a cross section during the festival. There are those who think my plays deal with violence. It is true that as a writer I have sometimes found it necessary to represent the existence of pain and terror in my plays by dealing with violent behavior. But those who know my work also know that the violence usually occurs offstage. I have been criticized for writing about cannibalism and castration and other terrifying topics, but I have not portrayed them directly before the audience."

When Williams elaborated these remarks in his press conference in Cannes, he unwittingly earned himself sensational headlines in subsequent newspaper accounts of the conference, such as the one which appeared the very next day in *Film Today:* "Jury chief attacks screen violence at Cannes Festival!" Nevertheless, his very sensible remarks reflect his general feeling about the depiction of graphic realism on stage and screen, and will be worth remembering when we take up his films.

"Personally I find it difficult to watch a great deal of violence either on the stage or on the screen," he explained. "I think it is artistically valid to suggest it because violence is certainly a significant part of the times in which we live. But

I don't think the camera should linger on terrible brutalities because I think that this can ultimately have a brutalizing effect on the spectators. Producers who say that violent movies teach the public that violence is evil are really using this argument merely as an excuse to make shocking films. Violence doesn't improve anyone's moral character, and all of us need our moral character improved—including myself.

"I think it is necessary, if one is to have an honest stage and screen, to deal with the harsher realities of life; but that does not mean that one should derive a voluptuous pleasure from viewing a succession of bloody spectacles, as if one were at the old Roman Coliseum watching people being devoured by lions. I don't think that such gore enhances the appeal of movies for most people, whether they are sophisticated or not. By the same token I don't believe that films should seek to appeal to the moviegoer on a political level, since that makes the film incline one toward one faction rather than another—and partisanship in my opinion has no place in an art form."

Williams also expressed his opinion in Cannes that the new freedom of the screen was being exploited in the portrayal of sex as well as of violence. "Some of it is only classy porn," he commented. "I have seen some films in which nudity was depicted in a beautiful fashion; but when it is not—which is more often the case—I find it crude and offensive. Making love should be depicted as a thing of magic and moonlight and not shown in gross detail.

"As a writer grows older, he develops a greater interest in representing tenderness, friendship, love, and romance in what he writes. I have been often frightened by what I have seen on the screen in the Festival Hall, and as a result when I go home I will take with me a clearer and more intense appreciation of those things which are the opposite of cruelty and violence. Indeed, the film medium is ideally suited to a lyrical style of expression, and this lyricism can be badly damaged by political partisanship and voluptuous cruelty."

The choice of Tennessee Williams as president of the jury of the largest and most important film festival in the world might be called the apotheosis of his association with the cinema. This long association really began in childhood with his first exposure to the movies. "When I was young," he remembers, "I was obsessed with the screen. I went to the movies all the time. I used to want to climb into the movie screen and join the action. My mother had to hold me down." Gilbert Maxwell, a friend of Williams's from boyhood, recalls in his biography of Williams that the latter was too weak, timid, and introspective to join in games with boys his own age, and gradually retreated into the make-believe world of books and movies.

The first films which Williams can recall seeing as a lad were the slapstick comedies of Fatty Arbuckle and of Charlie Chaplin, and somewhat later, romantic costume epics like *The Scarlet Pimpernel* with Leslie Howard. "All through childhood and adolescence," Maxwell writes, "Williams sought escape in movie houses from a world of poverty and misunderstanding" that seemed less real than the fanciful world of the silver screen. (Tom Wingfield, the hero of *Glass Menagerie*, has the same affinity for movies as his creator, and for the same reason.)

Although this book does not purport to be a full-dress biography of Tennessee Williams, it is appropriate to take a brief look at the private world in which he grew up. For, as one of his characters says, a writer's life is his work and his work is his life; and Williams notes in his *Memoirs* that there is a great deal of similarity between his plays and his life. He has often drawn on his personal experiences and observations of others in order to create characters and situations in his plays, as I shall often have occasion to point out throughout this book. His very first Broadway play, *The Glass Menagerie*, which was also his first film, was a picture of his own family situation before he left home to seek his fortune in the world at large. Hence a sketch of his early life is very much in order before taking up *The Glass Menagerie* a little later in this chapter.

Thomas Lanier Williams was born in his grandfather's Episcopal rectory in Columbus, Mississippi, on Palm Sunday, March 26, 1911, to Cornelius Coffin Williams and Edwina Dakin Williams. His father (known as "C.C.") was a travelling salesman often on the road, and so his family lived with his wife's parents. This rather staid, not to say starchy, environment was very pleasant for Tom and his older sister Rose, to whom he became very attached during their serene childhood days in a peaceful Southern town. C.C.'s family were of pioneer stock, frontiersmen and Indian fighters who came from Tennessee. Hence Tom's pen name: "I took Tennessee as my professional name mainly because the Williamses had fought the Indians in Tennessee, and I discovered that the life of a young writer was going to be something similar to the defense of a stockade against a band of savages."

His mother's people, on the other hand, had an austere Quaker strain in their ancestry. "Roughly there was a combination of Cavalier and Puritan strains in my blood," Williams explains, "which may be accountable for the conflicting impulses I often represent in the people I write about."

Tom's father, often absent during these early formative years, had little influence on the lad's early growth. As a result little Tom's world took on the decidedly feminine frame of reference of his mother and sister, and he looked upon his boisterous and blustering father—and the masculine world which he represented—as crude and unpleasant by comparison. (Tom's younger brother Dakin, born after the family moved to St. Louis and C.C. had settled into an office job, grew up closer to his father.)

Williams remembers those early days in Mississippi as pleasant and gracious. He and Rose played together in their own background. "We were exclusive, so close to each other that we had no need of others." In an autobiographical sketch which he once prepared for his agent as a press release, he tells how this blissful, idyllic, insulated world of childhood was shattered by his father's transfer in 1918 to a job in the St. Louis branch of the shoe firm for which he worked.

"It was a tragic move. Neither my sister nor I could adjust ourselves to life in a Midwestern city. The school children made fun of our Southern speech and manners. I remember a gang of kids following me home yelling 'Sissy!'; and home was not a pleasant refuge. It was a perpetually dim little apartment in a wilderness of identical brick and concrete structures the color of dried blood and mustard, with no grass and no trees nearer than the park. In the South we had never been conscious of the fact that we were economically less fortunate than others. We lived as well as anyone else," and enjoyed the instant acceptance that came from being related to the local Episcopal pastor.

"But in St. Louis we suddenly discovered that there were two kinds of people, the rich and the poor, and that we belonged more to the latter. . . . If I had been born to this situation, I might not have resented it so deeply. But it was forced on my consciousness at the most sensitive age of childhood. It produced a shock and rebellion that has grown into an inherent part of my work. . . . I am glad that I received this bitter education, for I don't think any writer has much purpose back of him unless he feels bitterly the inequities of the society he lives in."

Now that his father had an office job and was home more often, he had a chance to monitor the way in which his son Tom was growing up; and he was very displeased to find that Tom had more of the refined sensibilities of his mother than the virile, masculine traits of his father. "Our father, C.C., generally hated and abused Tom during his childhood and adolescence," writes Dakin Williams in his biography-in-progress of his brother, which he has kindly allowed me to quote in these pages. "C.C. called Tom a sissy, a 'Miss Nancy.' During this period my mother sheltered Tom from his father's wrath and fought monthly battles with C.C. over the bills occasioned by any expenditures for Tom's clothing or education. My grandmother, generally conceded to be a saint on earth, was of great assistance in scraping together the funds necessary to keep Tom afloat in college."

It is no wonder that Tennessee Williams was later to base two domineering father figures, Big Daddy Pollitt in *Cat on a Hot Tin Roof* and Boss Finley in *Sweet Bird of Youth*, on C.C. Williams. (Williams even refers to C.C. as "Big Daddy" in his autobiography.) Like Big Daddy's and Boss Finley's sons, Tom Williams harbored feelings that were a mixture of love and hate toward his father. As he grew older and began to chafe under the influence of his strong-willed mother, however, he began to sympathize more and more with his father's taking refuge in liquor and cards to escape confrontations with his wife.

"Tom actually felt that it was my mother, Edwina, who was to blame for my father's unhappy domestic situation," comments Dakin, who once received a letter from his older brother "detailing his accusations against Mother, saying in essence that C.C. was a completely normal, sex-loving male who had fallen into a hothouse of Victorian prudishness. According to Tom, Dad would have been completely justified in doing to Edwina exactly what the father had done to the mother in *The Glass Menagerie,*" i.e., walk out on her. In point of fact, C.C. and Edwina Williams eventually separated.

The unpleasant atmosphere of the Williams household caused the excessively sensitive and vulnerable Rose to withdraw gradually from the bleak world of reality into a private world of her own. Eventually she was committed to an institution and in 1937 was lobotomized. The tragedy of his sister's mental illness unquestionably constitutes the most traumatic experience of William's entire life, and he has sought to come to terms with it not only in his delicate depiction of Rose in *Menagerie* but also in his treatment of psychosurgery in *Suddenly, Last Summer,* as we shall see.

Tom was, like Rose, a sensitive and vulnerable youngster, and the upshot of his alienation from his father in his early years, along with his corresponding identification with the female members of his family, was that he grew up homosexual. Although this discovery about his personal psychology caused him considerable emotional conflict for a long time, he has in recent years become increasingly more candid in talking about his sexual identity when it is relevant to a discussion of his work. "I have never considered my homosexuality as anything to be disguised," he says today; "neither did I consider it a matter to be overemphasized. I consider it an accident of nature."

Like his sister, Tom Williams sought solace from the unpleasant world of reality, and from his school days onward he looked more and more to writing as an escape from loneliness. Writing became "my retreat, my cave, my refuge." He published his first story when he was sixteen and still in high school, and won a ten dollar prize in a contest conducted by the Loew's State Theater in St. Louis for the review he submitted of the silent film *Stella Dallas* starring Belle Bennett and Lois Moran.

Williams entered the University of Missouri in 1929 during the Depression years and could not afford to finish. So in 1931 his father, who had little interest in his son's higher education anyway, got him a job as a clerk-typist with his own firm, the International Shoe Company in St. Louis, at $65 a month. Williams refers to this three-year stint as his "season in hell," but he found that this term of "indescribable torment" was also of immense value to him as a writer, for it gave him a firsthand knowledge of what it means to be a small wage earner in a hopelessly routine job, and he later poured this experience into the character of Tom, the autobiographical hero of *The Glass Menagerie*.

Tom continued to write in his spare time: "When I came home from work I would tank up on black coffee so I would remain awake most of the night, writing short stories which I could not sell. Gradually my health broke down. One day, coming home from work, I collapsed and was removed to a hospital. The doctor said I couldn't go back to the shoe company." That welcome news accelerated Williams's recuperation, and marked the beginning of his advance from "shoe biz to show biz," as he puts it. Tom went to visit his beloved grandparents in Memphis, where they had moved after his grandfather's retirement from the ministry.

In a letter dated May 17, 1935, to a Josephine Johnson, Tom says tactfully that he is almost fully recovered from the illness which "forced" him to quit the shoe factory. He has not touched a typewriter for a month, he says, but is sure that he will soon be back writing his head off. After he returned to St. Louis, he entered Washington University to continue his college education. When he heard good reports about Dr. E. C. Mabie's playwriting course at Iowa State, however, he moved on to do his final year there and graduated in the spring of 1938.

After graduation Tom left home to travel, taking odd jobs along the way, and introduced himself to a world far different from his insulated home life. "I came to the French quarter of New Orleans in December of 1938 after my college years were over," he said to TV interviewer Dick Cavett, "and was shocked by the Bohemian way of life I found there. Now it seems my natural ambience." Williams took a small room in a tacky boarding house and did odd jobs to pay his rent. The place was presided over by a paranoid landlady who took to pouring hot water through the cracks in the floor on the photographer who lived below her (an incident which he would use in the film of *A Streetcar Named Desire*). "I was hauled into court as a material witness," Williams recalls, "and had to testify against the landlady. She lost the case and fired me, and so I went to California."

Williams and a friend, James Parrott, a clarient player (whom he identifies as a trumpeter in his *Memoirs*), made the trip in a 1934 Ford. The peregrinations of the impoverished pair were to serve as the inspiration for some of Williams's itinerate heroes, most notably Valentine Xavier in *Orpheus Descending*. They ran out of both gas and cash in El Paso, but a ten dollar bill from Grandmother Dakin, neatly stitched to a letter, helped them to get the rest of the way.

Once in California, Williams received word that the batch of one-act plays and the four full-length plays, which he had submitted to a New York drama contest sponsored by the Group Theater while he was still living in New Orleans, had won the first prize of $100. Because the contestants were supposed to be no more than twenty-five, Williams, who was twenty-eight, listed himself as being the eligible age. ("I felt entitled to those three years," he quips, "to make up for the three years wasted in the shoe factory.") As a result, confusion about his age persists to this day, with some biographical accounts still listing his birth spuriously as 1914 instead of 1911.

Parrott remembers that the Group Theater Prize precipitated Williams's receiving a handful of letters from agents offering to handle his writing. "He took them and went, 'eeny, meeny, miney, mo,' " and mo turned out to be Audrey Wood, who was to serve as William's agent for the next three decades. Ms. Wood started her canny representation of her new client by engineering a one thousand dollar Rockefeller grant which would enable Williams to come to New York to study dramaturgy and to continue work on this fifth long play, *Battle of Angels*.

While Ms. Wood was still working on the grant proposal, Williams lived on the Parrott pigeon ranch outside of Los Angeles and worked at Clark's Bootery in Culver City, within sight of the Metro–Goldwyn–Mayer studios. That was as close to the film industry as Williams got in that summer of 1939. But he would return.

After *Battle of Angels*, his first play to receive professional production, closed out of town prior to a Broadway opening, Williams's next connection with the cinema took the form of being an usher in Manhattan's Strand Theater where he saw classic films of the Forties like *Casablanca* countless times. Because he had been an inveterate moviegoer from childhood, Williams loved working at the Strand. "When I was young I went to the movies all the time," he said to me in Cannes; "so I am quite certain that they influenced my style as a playwright."

Williams's weekly salary suddenly jumped from $17 a week to $250 a week when the intrepid Audrey Wood got him a six month contract at MGM in 1943, which represented Williams's first official association with the movie industry. He soon learned that movies in the heyday of the studio system were more of an industry than an art form. His first assignment was to adapt a novel called *The Sun is My Undoing* for the screen. The project proved to be his undoing as well, as he got nowhere on the adaptation. He was switched to working on a script for a Lana Turner vehicle called *Marriage is a Private Affair*, but his script was rejected after weeks of work because his dialogue was thought to be too high-toned for Ms. Turner, even though, Williams says wryly, he tried to stick to monosyllables which she could grasp. The young screen writer felt that Ms. Turner, known in press releases as the "Sweater Girl," could not act her way out of one of her own form-fitting cashmeres; so he dubbed the movie *The Celluloid Brassiere*. When he later saw the film he could recognize only two lines of dialogue as having come from his draft of the script.

Then he was put to writing a film for child star Margaret O'Brien and this time he simply refused to accept the assignment, explaining quite frankly that "child stars make me vomit," and that Ms. O'Brien in particular was merely "a smaller and more loathsome edition of Shirley Temple." At this point Williams and the studio parted company, and he was told to sit out the remaining three months of his contract. He did so by writing a screenplay called *The Gentleman Caller* on the beach near his modest Santa Monica apartment. He thought of calling the story *Not So Beautiful Pople* or *The Human Tragedy*, he quipped to a friend at the time, because the situation was taking on the atmosphere of his own family's apartment in St. Louis.

A conscientious author, Williams thought that he should at least submit an outline of the script to MGM since he was writing it on company time. He attached an enthusiastic note to the synopsis which predicted that the projected movie would run three times as long as *Gone With the Wind*. The studio executives assumed that his sanguine proclamation referred to the length of the proposed film rather than to the number of weeks it would play in the theaters, and immediately turned thumbs down on *The Gentleman Caller*, saying that they were not interested in making another *Gone With the Wind* so soon. Ironically, once Williams had turned his screenplay into his first Broadway smash, *The Glass Menagerie*, MGM was among the studios competing for the film rights of the story that Williams had originally offered them for the price of his salary, and for which Warner Brothers eventually paid him $500,000.

Williams rented a cottage at Malibu where he transmuted his screenplay called *The Gentleman Caller* into his stage play *The Glass Menagerie*. He was not particularly enthusiastic about the play when he had finished it because, as he confided to a friend, "it lacks the violence that excites me." Nonetheless he sent it off to Audrey Wood, and prepared to leave Hollywood which he had found to be peopled with liars and degenerates who cared for screen credits and contracts and little else. He manifestly had no plans ever to return.

Meanwhile Audrey Wood had submitted *Menagerie* to Eddie Dowling, who decided not only to produce the play but to enact the leading role of young Tom Wingfield, although he was well into middle age. Dowling had trouble finding backers for this fragile play which even its author did not find very exciting. Some prospective backers suggested that Williams provide a happy ending in which the pathologically shy heroine would really fall in love with a gentleman caller, but this the young playwright absolutely refused to do.

Herbert Machiz, who has known Williams for a quarter of a century and has directed several of his plays in the theater, recalls the trouble Dowling had getting backing for *Menagerie* "until he persuaded a business man named Louis J. Singer to put up the money, a man who had never backed a play before and never backed a play again." Singer, the owner of a chain of second-string hotels, put up $75,000 to finance the show, and when he got around to attending a rehearsal during the out-of-town tryout in Chicago he was sure that he had backed a loser. Williams was no more optimistic than Singer was, and felt that the actors' pseudo-Southern drawls made the show sound like "the Aunt Jemima Pancake Hour."

On stage was the fifty-three year old male lead and director bickering with the star, Laurette Taylor, an aging has-been actress whose drinking problems had made her unemployable for years. Ms. Taylor had the key role of Amanda

Wingfield, the overbearing mother of Laura (Julie Haydon); but she apparently had no interest in learning her lines or paying any attention to Dowling's direction. He got even by referring to Ms. Taylor condescendingly as "a poor old thing with a wet brain," and she responded in kind by deprecating his suitability for the role of young Tom. In the midst of these temperamental outbursts Williams muttered, " 'The Menagerie' is no lie about this company—and neither is glass!" He pictures himself in his memoirs sitting glumly in the back of the rehearsal hall "wondering what menial occupation was next in store for me" after the play folded, since he had up to this point in his career done everything from handing out trays in an Iowa state mental institution to running the elevator in a fleabag hotel in New York City.

It was not until opening night in Chicago, December 26, 1944, that Williams and everyone else really understood that during all those weeks of rehearsals the frail Ms. Taylor had actually been saving herself for opening night, on which she made theater history with her incandescent performance as Amanda Wingfield. She repeated this triumph throughout the New York run, which began on March 31, 1945, until a few months before her death in December, 1946.

"Despite her vehement denial in her autobiography, *Remember Me to Tom*, Amanda Wingfield is the spitting image of my mother Edwina Williams," writes Dakin Williams in *My Brother's Keeper*. When Ms. Williams accompanied Tennessee backstage after the Chicago premier of *Menagerie*, Laurette Taylor asked her in the Southern drawl which she had perfected for her role, "How did you like yourself, Miz Williams?" Both mother and son shared an awkward moment, and then "Miz Williams" recovered herself—just as Amanda would—by adroitly changing the subject and saying, "You were magnificent, Laurette."

Menagerie did not do a brisk business at the box office during its first days in Chicago, despite excellent reviews from the Chicago critics; and Singer considered closing the show at the end of the first week. "Claudia Cassidy of *The Chicago Tribune* went to the play several times and mentioned it in her column each time," says Herbert Machiz. "She said it was tragic that no one realized that this play marked the beginning of a meteoric major career. She was greatly responsible in sparking enough interest in the show to bring it to New York." "Too many theatrical bubbles burst in the blowing," wrote Ms. Cassidy in one of her encomiums, "but *The Glass Menagerie* holds in its shadowed fragility the stamina of success."

It is ironic that Williams was pronounced an overnight success as a result of the critical and popular reception of his first Broadway play. Not only had the thirty-five year old playwright toiled over at least five other full-length plays that never saw the lights of New York, but he had also labored during those early years on innumerable one act plays and short stories. *The Glass Menagerie*, in fact, began its artistic life as a short story called "Portrait of a Girl in Glass," and can still be read in the Williams collection of stories entitled *One Arm and Other Stories*. The family situation in the story is the same as that which Williams draws in the play, and Williams has even incorporated some of the story's narration into the speeches in the play in which Tom acts as narrator for the audience, giving expository background material and providing a bridge from one scene to the next.

But a single reading of the story is sufficient to indicate Williams's growth as an artist by the time *Menagerie* took to the boards. For the story remains a sketchy presentation of characters which—except for Laura—are not created with any real clarity. It remained for Williams the playwright to delineate fully the complex personality of Amanda Wingfield which eluded Williams the fiction writer.

When Williams was suffering from nervous collapse in 1969, he fired this devastating question at his mother the first time she visited him in the mental ward at Barnes Hospital in St. Louis: "Why do women bring children into the world and then destroy them?" He comments in his memoirs that he still thinks this a thought-provoking question, as he must have when he wrote *Menagerie*, for the paradox of how a mother can hurt her children by loving them too much is at the core of the play.

"My devotion has made me a witch and so I make myself hateful to my children," laments Amanda in the play, and that line is really the key to Williams's depiction of her. She is a dedicated woman who loves and wants to protect her children; but she does so to the point of smothering them; and therein lies her tragic flaw and the reason why we, like Tom, love and hate her at the same time. As Williams writes in his introductory notes on the characters in the play, there is much to love, pity, and admire in this little woman clinging frantically to her romantic memories of the past, for she has endurance and tenderness; but there is no doubt that her foolish and unrealistic determination to relive her youth in the Old South in her daughter makes her unwittingly cruel at times. The maternal love which she all too generously lavishes on her children has a selfish tinge which motivates her to bind them ever more tightly to herself by the deepest emotional ties possible.

Laura's situation, he continues, is even graver than her mother's, for her extreme timidity, which is the outgrowth of the crippled condition which causes her to limp, has drawn her into a world of fantasy in which she has become like a piece of glass in her own collection, too exquisitely fragile to move from the shelf without breaking. Because Laura's physical disability is but a symbol of her more serious crippling of the spirit, Williams wisely suggests in profiling her character that this defect need not be more than suggested by the actress who plays the role.

"I don't think it is right for an actress playing Laura to emphasize that she is physically crippled," says Herbert Machiz, who directed the first revival of

Menagerie after its New York run. "An accident that you had yesterday is painful in a purely physical way. But a defect that you have borne with since childhood, as is the case with Laura, sinks into the psyche where it remains a serious psychological disability that is painful in a deeper way, after the physical pain has long since been forgotten. An actress does not get this particular psychic dimension of Laura's personality across merely by affecting a noticeable limp. Someone with a physical defect usually tries to de-emphasize it, not accentuate it as actresses who play Laura are sometimes tempted to do."

Tom, to whom the playwright lends his own given name, sees himself permanently caught between his attachment to these two female members of his family just as Jim O'Connor, the Gentleman Caller, finds himself temporarily caught between them in a somewhat similar fashion—but only for one evening. As the Gentleman Caller, Jim takes on great symbolic significance, not just as the emissary of the world of reality that Amanda and Laura in varying degrees shun, but more universally as what Tom calls "the long delayed but always expected something that we live for." All of us know the experience of building up our expectations of something which we look forward to so much that we are inevitably doomed to disappointment if and when it comes to pass, and it is not surprising that the story was once called *The Gentleman Caller*.

But the central image of the play, of course, is the one which came to be enshrined in the final title of the play. This image dates back to Williams's childhood in Mississippi when he used to accompany his Grandfather Dakin on his parish rounds. There was one lady named Laura Young whom they would visit that little Tom liked very much. In an arch between two rooms in her home there hung some multi-colored glass pendants. "That's a prism," she explained to the youngster, and she would often lift him up so that he could shake them and hear the delicate music which they made. Williams paid tribute to that lovely lady of his childhood memories by lending her name to the delicate girl of his play, for he was often reminded of Laura Young when, after he and his family had moved to their dim and stifling St. Louis flat, his sister Rose began collection glass ornaments to make her little room a private sanctuary for herself and her brother. "They were mostly little glass animals," says Williams, and they came to represent "all the small and tender things that relieve the austere pattern of life and make it endurable to the sensitive."

As he grew older and looked back on his St. Louis days, Williams found that by poetic association they had come to stand in his memory for "all the softest emotions that belong to recollection of things past." It is no wonder, therefore, that Williams calls *Menagerie* "a memory play." We see the events as they enfold as Tom the narrator remembers them. Perhaps the Wingfield tenement flat was not as murkily lit as Tom recalls it to be; but as a reflection of the bleak lives of the inmates of the apartment, the dim atmosphere is perfectly appropriate to the setting. Even the candles which Amanda lights to entertain the Gentleman Caller are not sufficient to dispel the shadows from the living room, especially once the electric lights are extinguished by the power company because Tom neglected to pay the electric bill.

Williams was not striving in this play for minute naturalistic detail. He was, rather, trying to present the predicament of each of the Wingfields with symbolic truth. The straight realistic play, he remarks in his production notes, with its genuine refrigerator and authentic ice-cubes, is closer to a photograph of reality than he cares his play to be. His drama is more akin to a painting than to a photograph, for the artist has interpreted the reality which he presents in *Menagerie,* not just captured it with documentary authenticity.

Thus Edwina Williams is correct to some extent in contending that the play is not an authentic rendering of the Williams family's life in St. Louis. The author has selected, heightened, and added to the details of his homelife as he remembers it in order to produce not a mere autobiographical record of his youth but a work of art in which he has refashioned his own deeply felt personal experiences in a way that can yield universal implications for his audience.

On the one hand, some of the elements of the play are painfully close to the way things were when Williams was still living at home with his mother and sister. Fellow writer Clark Mills, who knew Williams in those days, recalls being pressed into service by his friend Tom at the behest of Edwina Williams to serve as a Gentleman Caller on one occasion: "Williams's poor sister was dressed in an old fashioned Southern costume and she was lovely. She never talked at all but her mother never stopped talking—empty verbage about their status in the South. The mother didn't give her a chance."

On the other hand Williams admits in his production notes to having taken poetic license in creating his memory play, for memory takes a lot of poetic license: it omits some details and exaggerates others "according to the emotional value of the articles it touches." One realistic item in the milieu surrounding the Williams apartment in St. Louis which the dramatist used in his short story "Portrait of a Girl in Glass" but omitted from the play concerns the numerous neighborhood alley cats that were constantly fighting like savage dogs beneath Rose's window. The gorey alley became so repulsive to her delicate sensibilities that Rose kept the shade in her room drawn, leaving her in a perpetual twilight.

"Something had to be done to relieve this gloom," Williams writes in the program notes for the play. "So my sister and I painted all her furniture white; she put white curtains at the window," and on the shelves around the room she placed her glass menagerie, which gave the room as a whole a light and delicate appearance, despite the lack of illumination from outside. "It became the only room in the house that I found pleasant to enter." The alleyway where the cats tore each other to pieces provided a sharp contrast to his sister's room with its white curtains and tiny menagerie of glass. "Somewhere between them was the world that we lived in."

In the play Williams has replaced the alley cats' domain of the story with another, less turgid symbol of the outside world from which Laura feels alienated; it fits much better with the generally softer imagery of the play and yet still provides a contrast between Laura's insulated cell and and the world at large, so that Tom in the play can still say that somewhere between these two very different milieus "was the world that we lived in." This locale in the play is the Paradise Dance Hall, whose music insinuates itself into the Wingfield apartment, suggesting a romantic dimension to life which is totally foreign to the Wingfield family.

When Jim O'Connor comes to spend the evening at Tom's invitation and finds himself cast for the evening in the role of Gentleman Caller on Tom's bashful sister, he listens to the music wafting its way into the living room and then insists that Laura dance with him. In effect he is bringing to Laura the dance hall which she is too shy to visit on her own. Jim clumsily dances her into the table on which stands Laura's prize figurine, a glass unicorn, and knocks it to the floor. He discovers that he has broken off the little horn that made it different from all of the glass horses in the collection, but Laura does not seem to mind. She is happy that the horn has been removed so that the unicorn can now feel less of a freak. This is her delicate way of telling Jim how much she appreciates his willingness to treat her like an ordinary girl and not as someone freakishly shy. Jim's good-natured attempt to help Laura rise above her inferiority complex backfires, however, when he senses that the predatory Amanda wants to forge a permanent relationship between him and her daughter.

Slowly he begins to reveal that he is engaged to a girl who has been out of town for the past few days, and that this is the reason why he was available to come to dinner with the Wingfields on this particular evening. He adds that his fiancée is coming home on the evening train and that he must leave immediately to pick her up at the depot. I have always wondered if Jim really was engaged, a factor which all of the critiques of the play take for granted. For me it is intriguing to speculate about whether or not Jim is not manufacturing the whole engagement story step by step in order to beat a hasty retreat from the Wingfield household, down to the last urgent detail that his girl is even now expecting him at the station. Jim in all likelihood probably does have a steady girl; but once he senses Amanda closing in on him, it becomes evident to him that nothing short of his imminent marriage will extricate him from Amanda's clutches. Some support is given to my theory by Amanda's pointing out to Tom after Jim is gone that it is curious that Tom knew nothing of his own best friend's wedding plans.

The spectacular quarrel which ensues after Jim's departure confirms Tom in his resolution to join the Merchant Marine and thus leave home for good, even though he knows that this means that he is following in his father's footsteps in deserting the two women of the family. Earlier, when he first mentioned his resolve to leave home to Laura, he apologized in advance for the pain that this would cause her and her mother by describing a magician's trick of liberating himself from a sealed coffin without removing a single nail. It does not require any intelligence to get oneself nailed into a coffin, he explained to Laura; but to get out without removing a single nail, as the magician did, calls for an expertise which he does not possess. (The "coffin trick" may be a private reference by the playwright to his own father's leaving home, for Cornelius Coffin Williams also did not possess the magician's ability to escape from home without leaving some hurt behind.) Nonetheless the play ends with Tom starting out on his own and then confessing to the audience in his role of narrator how much he misses his family, his sister Laura in particular.

The Glass Menagerie ran a year and a half in New York, won the New York Critics Award for Williams as playwright (on the first ballot) and for Laurette Taylor as best actress. So it was inevitable that Hollywood would buy the movie rights, though Williams was wary of what Warners might try to do to his play in order to make it more commercial. Even as a youth Williams had been cynical about Hollywood, for he wrote a satirical play while attending the University of Iowa about "an ignorant producer revising a great classic for the movies."

The prospects of a good movie adaptation of *Menagerie* brightened when Katharine Hepburn and director George Cukor, who had both been associated with excellent screen adaptations of Philip Barry's plays *Holiday* and *The Philadelphia Story,* inquired about the possibility of shooting the film in New York City with Laurette Taylor as Amanda, Ms. Hepburn as Laura, and Spencer Tracy as the Gentleman Caller. But they discovered that producer Charles K. Feldman, who had already acquired the film rights for Warner Brothers, had his own director and cast in mind. (In point of fact Katharine Hepburn was to wait for almost three decades to appear in *Menagerie,* and then as Amanda in the 1973 teleplay which I will take up at the end of this chapter.)

Feldman had initially considered Ethel Barrymore for the role of Amanda, but finally settled on Gertrude Lawrence. He was even willing to wait two years for Ms. Lawrence to become available to do the movie; so the film was not finished until early 1950, at which time she declared that she was pleased with the picture and that she felt that it did justice to the play since Tennessee Williams had himself worked on the screenplay (with Peter Berneis). Williams was not so sure.

The play had seemed in some ways to be a promising screen property from the outset because Williams had designed the play in a succession of short scenes not unlike the progression of a movie script, a format which he had retained from the earlier version of the story which he had written as a screenplay entitled *The Gentleman Caller.* The plot of the play progresses as a sequence of episodes, told in flashback, which flow one into the other, with Tom as narrator serving as the linking device; and this construction is very cinematic indeed. This is particularly true of the finale of the play in which Amanda and Laura are seen for the last time in a pantomime sequence which is accompanied by Tom's final commentary. As the image of the two women slowly dissolves into darkness, the effect is that of the kind of slow fade-out often used at the end of a motion picture.

Why, then, did a play that started out as a screenplay in the first place and which even on the stage owed so much to the approximation of cinematic techniques not turn out to be a better movie? Williams, who has dubbed the film the first and worst screen adaptation ever done of his work, feels that, despite "the enormous advantage of the participation of Gertrude Lawrence, unfortunately the poetic quality of the play was not present in the direction of the film." The director in question was Irving Rapper (although Roger Manvell's *New Cinema in the U.S.A.* lists Elia Kazan!), who had impressive screen adaptations of such plays as *The Corn is Green* and *The Voice of the Turtle* to his credit before being assigned to direct *Menagerie*. Since Rapper has said that he always followed the script which he was given to direct "to the letter," some of the weaknesses of the film must stem from the screenplay, which in effect tosses the ball back into Williams's court.

Feldman and Jerry Wald, his co-producer, very much wanted Williams to work with Peter Berneis on the script and they dispatched Rapper to Rome to entice the playwright to come to Hollywood to collaborate on the script. Perhaps because of his unpleasant memories of his previous stint in the movie capital and because of his shyness, Williams was diffident about going to the studio. "He hated Hollywood and hated movie studios," Rapper has said to interviewer Mike Steen; and Williams was consequently too eager to entrust the making of the film to the people at the studio who had been assigned to the project. "But we finally persuaded Tennessee to come to Warner Brothers."

Williams's retiring manner was typified by his first meeting with Jack Warner, in the course of which the studio chief at first mistook Williams's secretary-companion Frank Merlo for the author who happened to be standing shyly behind his friend.

While he was in Hollywood Williams did write some extra scenes for the film, but the script was revised during shooting by the producers and other interested parties. The playwright's presence would have been invaluable during this period, especially since a considerable amount of disagreement developed about the nature and extent of the contemplated revisions in the scenario. But, as Rapper insists, "it would be far from Tennessee's make-up" to participate in such wrangling, even though his word would have undoubtedly carried some weight.

Jane Wyman and Kirk Douglas on the set of *The Glass Menagerie*.

The compromises which were made in bringing *Menagerie* to the screen began with the casting of the leads and ended with the studio-imposed happy ending. As for the casting, Rapper was told that superstars would be needed to merchandise the film in the far-flung areas of these United States unfamiliar with Broadway and Williams's play. Hence, even if she had still been alive at the time of filming, Laurette Taylor would never have been considered to repeat her stage triumph in the film of *Menagerie* since she was not well known beyond the borders of Broadway theater circles. Rapper preferred Tallulah Bankhead, whom he says did a superb screen test for the part of Amanda. She was Southern-born and also knew and admired Williams and his work. But Ms. Bankhead not only lacked sufficient box office draw but she was also drinking heavily at this stage of her life; and so Jack Warner vetoed her selection, telling

Rapper that one Errol Flynn around Warner Brothers was quite enough.

Gertrude Lawrence was the compromise candidate—a curious compromise since Ms. Lawrence had no more of a screen reputation than Laurette Taylor or Tallulah Bankhead. She felt that she was too young to play a frowzy mother, as did other actresses who considered the role, such as Bette Davis. Feldman finally mollified her on this score by promising to include a flashback in the film of the young Amanda, and Ms. Lawrence finally agreed to play the role with this understanding. "Otherwise," she said at the time, "the part of Amanda would have been only a character study of a middle-aged woman, and I don't want to get mother roles, and unglamorous ones at that. I'd be afraid that if I succeeded I'd never do anything else."

Yet when the film was finished she demurred to a *New York Times* reporter that she had harbored any such motivation in doing the flashback scene at all. She said that if this sequence illustrating Amanda's youth as a Southern belle did not add to the total effect of the film she hoped it would be deleted from the final print. "I would hate to have anyone think that it was inserted just to give Lawrence a chance to look glamorous,"—which is precisely why it was included in the first place!

Still, Ms. Lawrence gave a fine performance in the movie, as did her co-stars, Jane Wyman (who had just won an Oscar for *Johnny Belinda*) as Laura, and Kirk Douglas as Jim. The studio wanted another star to play Tom, but Rapper prevailed in getting Warner to accept Arthur Kennedy, who was not well known in pictures at the time. Rapper's choice was vindicated when Kennedy, alone among the principals, received an Academy Award nomination.

After the film premiered, Hugh MacMullan, dialogue director of the movie, wrote an article called "Translating *The Glass Menagerie* to Film" for *Hollywood* (now *Film*) *Quarterly* in which he said that the completed picture demonstrates that Williams's play was not, in its own right, suitable for filming without considerable overhauling. (He was obviously unaware that the play had been conceived first as a screenplay.) MacMullan believed that the play's confinement to a single set, its use of what he considered to be the artifical theatrical device of a narrator, and its single plot line about Laura snagging a suitable beau all conspired to make the play unpromising material for a motion picture. I would disagree with all three points.

For a start, the play's confinement to a single basic setting is one of its virtues, since the apartment represents the stifling little world in which the Wingfields are locked, and too much opening out of the action into the world at large would simply dissipate the tension that this suffocating atmosphere creates among the characters. Secondly, Tom's narration would be uncinematic only if he delivered it to the camera lens, as if he were standing at the edge of the footlights; but the bulk of his spoken commentary employs the time honored movie technique of being delivered voice-over on the sound track, once he has been introduced reminiscing about his family on the deck of a ship. Finally, the dramatic line of the plot is not as simple as MacMullan assumes, since Laura's acquisition of a Gentleman Caller is only one aspect, although a very important aspect, of the entire plot.

In actual fact, the screenplay's reshuffling of the play's continuity is responsible for making it appear that the plot is concerned almost exclusively with finding Laura a marriageable male. The script places the scene in which Amanda asks Tom to bring home an eligible bachelor for Laura closer to the beginning of the film in order to establish from the start that Amanda's resolve to save Laura from spinsterhood is the governing force of the story. This scene corresponds to the latter half of the fourth scene in the play. Coming as it now does so near to the opening of the film, it involves some awkward lapses in continuity that are confusing to the filmgoer. The most glaring lapse centers around Tom's apologizing to his mother for a quarrel that clearly does not take place until much later in the movie, at the conclusion of which she explicitly demands the apology which Tom now gives much earlier in the movie.

More importantly, however, the positioning of the scene so near the beginning of the movie obscures and oversimplifies the development of Amanda's plans for Laura's future. Amanda's overruling concern is to see Laura established in life, not necessarily to have her get married. The first stage in Amanda's campaign involves training Laura for a career in business; and it is only when this maneuver fails that Amanda's thoughts turn to the second stage, finding Laura a suitable beau with a view to marriage. The introduction of Amanda's desparate decision to secure a suitor for Laura at the opening of the film, therefore, is premature, and not in keeping with her character, for a shrewd woman like Amanda manifestly understands that it would be an easier task to groom Laura to find an employer than to find a mate. It is a pity, consequently, that Williams was not on hand to advise against this reordering of the film's scenes with its attendant rupture in the continuity of the story.

As is evident from the prologue of this book, I would also take issue with MacMullan's assumption that the more a play is opened out for the screen the more successful the movie will be. Judicious opening out of a play can broaden the action by introducing more of the wider world in which the characters exist, it is true. But this opening out must be done cautiously, as William Wyler attests in the prologue when he warns that "you can alter a play for the cinema to the point of obliterating the qualities that made it a good property in the first place. Just because the film director has the facilities to carry the action outside the relatively few sets where the play took place, it doesn't follow that he should automatically exercise that freedom. The playwright had to discipline himself to concentrate his action in a circumscribed area, and this often serves to tighten the play's construction."

Wyler might almost have had *The Glass Menagerie* in mind in what he says, for his remarks apply perfectly to the adaptation of that play to film. The play's action is very concentrated and should fundamentally remain so in the film. In general, however, much of the opening out of *Menagerie* for the screen is tastefully done, and often the new locales introduced into the movie were already suggested by references in the dialogue.

The key settings outside the Wingfield apartment which are interpolated into the film are the shoe factory where Tom works and the business college where Laura gives up her hopeless efforts to prepare for a secretarial career. We are introduced to these new playing areas early in the picture in a series of brief scenes which directly depict exposition which had to be worked into the dialogue of the play.

In the factory sequence Tom is catching packages of shoes as they slide down a conveyor belt toward him, and his boss tells him to rush the order. Tom comments to a fellow worker, "Why rush when the shoes will only sit in the store windows and get sunburned—which is what I would like to be doing right now on a beach in Miami!" Tom begins to wheel a load of boxes away for shipping and the scene ends. As originally shot this scene was to continue with Tom wheeling the boxes up to the place where Jim is chatting with some of his co-workers. But co-producer Jerry Wald decided to hold off the introduction of Jim until later in the film-even though the factory scene had already been filmed as a unit. This alteration of the film's continuity proved to be more felicitous than the one mentioned above, because the balance of the factory scene, which consists of a conversation between Tom and Jim, leads up to the climactic dinner scene in the Wingfield flat.

Introducing the Gentleman Caller too early in the story, as previously planned, would have been a serious mistake since the dramatic development of the story calls for him to remain the anonymous embodiment of Amanda's expectations for Laura until he finally appears upon the scene in the concluding portions of the action. Although the material of the factory scene was shot as a single sequence, as finally edited, there is a natural break in the action of the sequence between the introduction of Tom in his factory milieu and the introduction of Jim; and hence the latter half of the sequence easily fits into the later section of the movie where it was ultimately placed.

Extending the action of the film to show Tom in the shoe factory and Laura in the business school does not dissipate the constricted atmosphere of the play as filmed, because Tom and Laura feel just as hemmed in by their respective places of work as they do at home. The film presents two scenes in the business school, both of which are elaborated from dialogue references in the play. The first shows Laura collapsing under the pressure of trying to take a speed drill in typing as the thundering sound of the other typewriters pounds in her ears; in the second Amanda discovers on a visit to the business school that Laura has ceased attending classes.

Arthur Kennedy and Kirk Douglas in the factory scene added to the film of *Glass Menagerie*.

Originally these two scenes were placed almost back to back in an early part of the movie, but Wald decided to separate them further in his revisions of the film's continuity. This made way for the insertion of a montage of shots depicting Laura spending her days in the public library, the art museum, the park, and the zoo, while her mother assumes that she is busily pursuing her career education at the business college. This succession of pictorially pleasant images takes on a grim undertone from the context of the story: all the while one watches Laura wandering through "all those places where the lonely spend their time," as Tom comments on the sound track, one ruefully wonders how long it will be until Amanda discovers Laura's deception.

Thus, the delaying of Amanda's inevitable visit to the business school and her subsequent confrontation with Laura, like the delaying of the first appearance of the Gentleman Caller, turned out to be a fortuitous way of maintaining audience expectancy by not telling them too much too soon.

As I mentioned above, extending the action of the movie to encompass the places where Tom and Laura spend their days does not slacken the dramatic tension of the film. But MacMullen mentions other scenes that were concocted to free the film from the restrictions of time and space imposed by the play, and even he is prepared to admit that they diluted the total impact of the film when they were inserted into its continuity. This type of error can easily occur, he says, "since one is always eager to take advantage of the new medium." Such scenes, which eventually wound up on the cutting room floor, included one of Tom walking along the river front longing to go to sea, and one of Laura stopping on her way home from the grocery to gaze in awe at the gaudy interior of the Paradise Dance Hall.

One misguided attempt to enlarge the scope of the movie which unfortunately did not wind up on the cutting room floor was the flashback to Amanda's youth as a Southern belle, which was inserted into the film primarily to counteract Ms. Lawrence's misgivings about playing the role of a woman several years her senior. This flashback is based on Amanda's monologue in the play in which she describes how she received seventeen Gentleman Callers in one day and had to quell their quarrels over her.

The monologue scene was shot first just as it had been played on the stage, with Amanda recounting in loving and exaggerated detail those bygone times. Then it was reshot in a manner calculated not only to show off Ms. Lawrence's beauty to better advantage but also to make fuller use of the movie medium. Amanda begins her recollections while looking at a photograph of herself on the mantelpiece in which she is decked out in a lacey ball gown. This shot dissolves to one of Amanda sweeping down the grand staircase of a Southern mansion and choosing her first dancing partner of the evening from among the group of masculine admirers anxiously awaiting her at the foot of the stairs. The sequence, which continues with Amanda dancing first with one young man and then another, caused Williams to comment that such a scene belonged in an epic of the Old South like *Gone with the Wind,* not in a small and intimate film like *The Glass Menagerie*. It ends with Amanda expressing her regret, voice-over, that she married the man she did when she could have chosen any one of these eligible bachelors, as the camera comes to rest on still another photograph on the mantelpiece, this time of the husband who abandoned her (in reality a picture of Arthur Kennedy in World War I battle dress).

To depict Amanda's girlhood memories of herself in flashback was a serious mistake for several reasons. First of all, this elaborate sequence, as Williams indicated in his reference to *Gone with the Wind,* is completely out of keeping with the austere tone of the film as a whole. Secondly, there is a touching tinge to

The flashback to the youth of Amanda (Gertrude Lawrence) as a Southern belle, added to *Glass Menagerie*.

the scene when it is played as Williams wrote it, for we are able to see the pathetic gap between the shabby elderly lady who is recounting these tired memories and the elegant and youthful content of these recollections as she narrates them, and this quality is forfeited by the intrusion of the flashback. Thirdly, actually seeing a radiant and youthful Amanda with her seventeen Gentlemen Callers lends an authenticity to Amanda's memories which they manifestly do not possess in the play, since Amanda exaggerates her own past in inverse proportion to Laura's failure to live up to her mother's expectations of her. Finally, and most importantly, it is Tom's memories and not Amanda's that we are sharing in the story; and, as MacMullan concedes, "Amanda's flights of fancy are valid only as he remembers them, not as she does."

On the credit side, there is a fine montage sequence which neatly draws together the various strands of the story and leads into Jim's first appearance. We see Amanda peddling magazine subscriptions from door to door as her way of helping support the family until Laura is settled in life and wistfully staring at a bridal gown in a shop window; and finally the introduction of Jim as the Gentleman Caller in what is really the remainder of the factory sequence that was transferred to this point in the action from its earlier place in the film.

Jim, as Kirk Douglas plays him in this scene written especially for the movie, has been called a bumptuous know-it-all who does not correspond to the wonderful, sincere Gentleman Caller of the later scenes taken more directly from the play. When the boss interrupts Jim's discussion of football with some of his fellow factory hands, Jim quickly recovers by countering that he was using football as a metaphor for teamwork on the job; and his employer is duly impressed. As I mentioned in discussing the play, Jim has always impressed me as something of a smoothie who can glibly talk his way out of any situation; and for my money his handling of the boss here presages the way he talks his way out of the Wingfield apartment later. That Laura is completely captivated by him and that Tom admires him so much says more about their naiveté than it does about Jim's genuine strength of character. This factory scene, therefore, seems to me to be making more explicit than the playwright did in the play the implication that Jim is a little too slick and superficial to have ever lived up to the Wingfield's individual and collective expectations of him.

Jim literally sweeps Laura off her feet in the dinner sequence by dancing with her to the music that intrudes into the Wingfield living room from the Paradise Dance Hall across the alley, and his attempt to bring into her life a little of the glamour of the outside world which the Paradise represents is nicely done in the film—until the point is needlessly underlined by Jim's taking Laura over to the dance casino to continue dancing there. This extra bit of opening out the action of the play, moreover, blunts the implication in the play that whatever experiences of the outside world Laura shares will have to be brought to her because she is too insecure and timid to make her way in the world at large.

This pattern in her character, painstakingly and painfully established by her retreat from the business college, makes her accepting Jim's invitation to go with him to the Paradise extremely improbable. It is very likely intended, however, to pave the way for the film's happy ending by showing Laura already responding positively to a sympathetic person. As she tells her mother after Jim is gone, "I've had a lovely evening. I danced for the first time. I'm so glad I met Jim."

Kirk Douglas as the Gentleman Caller meets Amanda (Gertrude Lawrence) and her daughter (Jane Wyman) in *The Glass Menagerie*.

Laura expresses no such positive sentiments in the play, where it is evident that Jim has left Laura to retreat into her world of glass once more. As Benjamin Nelson writes in his book on Williams, "Her brief joy is snuffed out and her loneliness is only intensified. It is obvious that she will never allow a Jim O'Connor to happen to her again." In the film, however, Richard, a new Gentleman Caller, comes down the alley toward Laura and Amanda on their fire escape "terrace." Laura introduces Richard to her mother and Tom, voice-over, calls him "the long delayed but always expected something we lived for." When Williams uses this expression in the play, he means just the opposite of what the line is made to mean here: that most of us have a cherished desire which we know in our more realistic moments will never be fulfilled, "a long delayed but always expected something" which never comes. Yet, like Amanda, we go on hoping against our better judgment because all of us need something to look forward to.

This happy ending in the movie, in which Laura finds her eligible bachelor,

Jane Wyman with her glass menagerie.

was conceived by the studio front office in deference to the Hollywood taboo that stated that downbeat endings were box office poison. The logic of the film is designed to lead to the same inevitable, sad conclusion with which the play ended—until the unconvincing moment when Jim is able to coax Laura to accompany him to the Paradise Dance Hall. But even this eleventh hour detour in the action is not sufficient to make the happy resolution of the picture ring true. Yet MacMullan shrugs that this contrived happy ending "brings to a suitable resolution all the problems raised by the plot's premises and their development—if on a sentimental level."

This complete reversal of the intent of his play infuriated Williams then, and still does when one raises the issue: "The worst film ever made of any of my plays was that made of *The Glass Menagerie*, where a happy ending was provided by bringing in another, and eligible, Gentleman Caller." He continues, "Imagine how I feel when someone mentions to me this most dishonest of all film adaptations of my work and says, 'Oh, it's so beautiful when that poor crippled girl has a new, promising beau at the end of the film. I was afraid, for a while, that the picture was going to have a depressing, more realistic ending.' Gertrude Lawrence deserved better, as did the play."

Dakin Williams tells me that the ending of the film was a compromise between the legitimate ending which his brother had written and still another, even more preposterous possibility that had been devised by the studio: "Tennessee threatened to sue Warner Brothers when they were planning to have Laura marry Jim to the tune of Mendelssohn's 'Wedding March' at the finale. Personally I don't think the upbeat ending of the movie version was too bad. But no really definitive rendition of *The Glass Menagerie* has yet been done on the screen or on TV, nothing to compare with Laurette Taylor's smash."

Tennessee Williams is, of course, more pleased with the Katharine Hepburn television production, which was aired for the first time in December, 1973, than he was with the film. He was particularly glad that some of Tom's narrative passages were deleted from the teleplay (as they were from the movie): "There were too many of them and the play itself holds up without much narration." Herbert Machiz, who has directed *Menagerie* on the stage, thought that Ms. Hepburn was a trifle miscast as Amanda. "She is an elegant, aristocratic lady," he points out, "and has little in common with Amanda Wingfield; but then the same can be said, I'm afraid, of Gertrude Lawrence in the original film of the play." It was difficult for both of these imposing ladies of stage and screen to look the part of the faded, frumpy Amanda in the way that the petite Laurette Taylor did, which is why Ms. Lawrence need not have worried about being relegated exclusively to playing elderly females after she enacted Amanda on the screen anyway. But both Ms. Lawrence and Ms. Hepburn acted the role quite genuinely, though the author thought Katharine Hepburn's performance was "a touch too New England."

Ms. Hepburn was enthralled with the play from the first time she saw Laurette Taylor in the original production, and had herself hoped to play Laura in the film. "It's a great play," she said in an interview at the time of her TV appearance as Amanda; "it says more about what the lack of money can do to human being than any play I know. Tennessee put all of his early suffering and

Katharine Hepburn and Sam Waterston in the teleplay of *The Glass Menagerie*.

frustration into it. Amanda is the most tenderly observed, the most accessible woman he ever created."

Ms. Hepburn's interpretation of Amanda was a trifle too energetic, possibly because she was trying too hard to communicate Amanda's desperation. Pauline Kael, however, was unfair when she criticized Ms. Hepburn for cribbing gestures and mannerisms from her earlier movie roles that did not fit the older woman she was playing, and when she decrees that Ms. Hepburn's performance thus amounted to a desecration of her earlier screen work. On the contrary, Amanda was the sort of middle-aged woman who might well fall into the fluttery, girlish gestures of her youth when trying to charm someone. So Ms. Hepburn was on target in imitating herself as a younger woman in these moments, since that is just what Amanda subconsciously would have done.

Tennessee Williams is given sole script credit for the teleplay. This means that the production, which was filmed in England under the direction of Anthony Harvey, stuck closely to the original play, with the exception of some minor deletions, such as those in the narrative passages which Williams himself favored. At the same time Harvey sought to exploit this visual medium's potential by moving his camera adroitly among the actors to bring the viewer

Joanna Miles and Katharine Hepburn in the teleplay of *The Glass Menagerie*.

more into the action. The cast, which included Sam Waterston as Tom, Joanna Miles as Laura, and Michael Moriarity as Jim, rehearsed for two weeks and then the story was shot in sequence in order for them to build their performances methodically throughout the teleplay.

Of course the teleplay excluded the opulent flashback to Amanda's youth which was so intrusive in the earlier film. The only visual touch of elegance in the teleplay is supplied by Ms. Hepburn's wearing the wedding gown, which she had worn in the stage version of *The Philadelphia Story* more than three decades before, in the scene in which Amanda dresses up to entertain the Gentleman Caller and says to Laura, "I led the cotillion in this dress." The teleplay also resists the temptation, to which the motion picture succumbed, of having a scene set in the Paradise Dance Hall in order to retain the claustrophobic atmosphere of the play. The Paradise remains a subtle presence throughout the dinner scene, however, with its faintly heard music and flashing neon sign extending an invitation to romance which Laura is too withdrawn and shy to accept beyond dancing with Jim to its distant music in her own living room.

When Jim takes his final leave of Laura toward the end of the teleplay, he is framed in the open door through which the bright lights of the Paradise can be seen behind him, beckoning to a world in which the extrovert Jim will always feel at home but which will always be alien to the introvert Laura. There is no open door for Laura, but there is for Jim and there is for Tom. After Tom's departure there is no manufactured Hollywood ending for the teleplay, and hence Amanda's heartbreaking line, "Things have a way of turning out so badly," is very appropriate; for we know that there will be no new Gentleman Caller named Richard waiting in the wings to replace Jim in Laura's life.

The telecast, which received an excellent Neilsen rating, was repeated in June of 1975; and it is now circulated in 16mm to the educational market by Cinema 5, a distinction which few made-for-TV movies ever achieve. It seems that Williams's wish, expressed at the beginning of this chapter, that some of the films of his plays could be remade with the authentic endings restored, may be fulfilled by distinguished TV productions such as that which *The Glass Menagerie*, which represents an enormous improvement over the original film. I shall deal with this possibility again in the course of this book as other teleplays of Williams's work are mentioned, but especially in the epilogue.

Irving Rapper, the director of the 1950 film of *Menagerie*, has said that the studio looked upon the project as a "prestige piece" and apparently did not mind when it did not do well at the box office (even with a happy ending). As far as the producer, Charles Feldman was concerned, one of the best things that came out of the *Menagerie* screen venture was that it brought Williams to Hollywood long enough for Feldman to purchase the screen rights to the playwright's second Broadway hit, *A Streetcar Named Desire*, for $350,000. Surely a film of such a hot stage property could be turned into an equally successful movie if the censor's objections to the play's sensational story line could be met. But meeting those objections would not be easy.

Elia Kazan:
A Streetcar Named Desire and *Baby Doll*

"IN *The Glass Menagerie* I said all the nice things I have to say about people," Tennessee Williams said after the successful launching of his first Broadway play. "The future things will be harsher." He fulfilled that prophecy with *A Streetcar Named Desire*, thought by many commentators of his work, including myself, to be his masterpiece. "In *The Glass Menagerie*," Claudia Cassidy once wrote, "the outer dusk is a jungle. In *Streetcar* the beasts have moved indoors and the jungle is the heart."

Although *Streetcar* is a harsh, even a violent work in some respects, it also has a wistful, fragile quality. This is because the personality of Blanche DuBois, its harried heroine, is really made up of equal parts of both Amanda and of Laura Wingfield from *The Glass Menagerie*. Blanche is a determined, strong-willed woman like Amanda; but she has her soft and sensitive side like Laura. Which is to say in effect that Blanche is really an amalgam of Williams's mother and sister, since Amanda and Laura were based in turn on Edwina and Rose Williams respectively.

But the strongest overall prototype for Blanche was Williams's Aunt Belle, his father's sister. "She was a Sunday school teacher in the South," he recently recalled in *The New York Times*. "But I have based Blanche on her personality, not on her life. She talked like Blanche: hysterically, with great eloquence." Elsewhere he adds that she was afflicted with obsessive religiosity and "was always ascending to some high spiritual level and writing people about it," a trait which reminds one of the endless round of peaks and valleys which Blanche experiences in her emotional life. Aunt Belle was childless, having married

65

someone much older than herself, and died prematurely at the age of twenty-eight of an infected wisdom tooth.

During her brief lifetime Aunt Belle encouraged her nephew's interest in writing, believing that he had inherited his literary gifts from her ancestor, the poet Sidney Lanier, after whom Thomas Lanier Williams was named. One can almost hear the high-minded Blanche DuBois verbalizing these words from one of Aunt Belle's letters to the aspiring young writer: "Never let anyone discourage you by attempting to measure your success by the money you make. This poor world has sordid ways of counting things—but take the high way, Tom, and never mind the world." Edwina Williams comments, after quoting this letter in her autobiography, "Perhaps Tom stood a little in awe of her. She was very intelligent and beautiful but also very rigid, insisting everything be done her way." This reflection demonstrates that, like Blanche, Aunt Belle had her tough side, as well as the tender side indicated in the letter itself.

Streetcar began taking shape in the playwright's mind while *Menagerie* was still in rehearsal. Williams devised a scene in which he saw Blanche sitting alone in a shaft of moonlight waiting for a Gentleman Caller who was long since overdue. He attached the tentative title of *Blanche's Chair in the Moon* to this fragment and set it aside for the time being.

Elements that Williams would later integrate into the finished play appear in two of his one-act plays, *The Lady of Larkspur Lotion* and *Portrait of a Madonna*. In the former a sympathetic writer defends an erstwhile Southern belle's right to cherish delusions of grandeur very much like Blanche's: "Is she to be blamed because it is necessary for her to compensate for the cruel deficiencies of reality by the exercise of a little—what shall I say?—God-given imagination?" *Madonna* ends with an even more dessicated Southern spinster being led away to an asylum by a doctor who treats her with the gentlemanly courtesy to which she would like to believe she has always been accustomed. This scene is, of course, a forecast of the way Blanche exits from *Streetcar*. It was in fact her appearance in the title role of *Madonna* that won the part of Blanche for Jessica Tandy in the original production of *Streetcar*.

Marlon Brando was selected to play Stanley Kowalski, Blanche's he-man brother-in-law after John Garfield decided that Blanche's role would over-shadow Stanley's. Brando had to journey to Cape Cod, where Williams was vacationing, to read the part for him. Williams was occupying a rather ramshackle house at the time and the bashful Brando repaired the plumbing and replaced a blown fuse before he summoned the courage to face the audition which assured him the role of Stanley and with it superstardom on both stage and screen.

Streetcar marked the first creative association of Williams and director Elia Kazan, who went on to direct several Williams works on stage and screen. Rehearsals for *Streetcar* were held in the theater on the Amsterdam Roof, with

Williams in attendance. Kazan's method of directing has always been to let the actors shape their own conception of the part they are playing before he makes any suggestions of his own. Brando proved to be a remote, even rude enigma to his fellow actors as he struggled, apparently with more trouble than they, to define for himself the character of Stanley. Gradually he developed Stanley's coarse voice and swaggering walk, and the characterization began to come to life. Later Brando looked back on his playing of this role and allowed that he had missed at least one important element in Stanley's personality: his gaiety. "Nothing reaches him, other people's pain, their needs, nothing. The only way I could zero in was to say, 'This guy is a big, lusty animal with no sensitivity.'"

During the tryout period in New Haven, Boston, and Philadelphia, the local notices got better and better, so that there was no doubt that when the play reached Broadway on December 3, 1947, it would be an even bigger smash than *Glass* had been. In fact *Streetcar* became the first American play ever to win all three major drama prizes: the Pulitzer Prize, the New York Critics Circle Award (his second), and the Donaldson Award.

Williams also managed to capture the public's imagination with one of the most legendary figures of Twentieth Century popular culture, Blanche DuBois. Blanche, battered suitcase in hand, walked straight into theatrical history with her very first line in the play, "They told me to take a streetcar named Desire, and then transfer to one called Cemeteries, and ride six blocks and get off at Elysian Fields." ("Desire really is a section of New Orleans," Williams explains; "I didn't make it up.")

This evocation of the old streetcar system in New Orleans, where the play is set, comes from Williams's youthful days there. He lived near Royal Street, and it was down this main thoroughfare of the French Quarter that two streetcars, one named Desire and the other named Cemetery, used to run. "Their undiscouraged progress up and down Royal Street struck me as having some symbolic bearing" not only on life in the Quarter, "but everywhere else for that matter." (One of the original streetcars named Desire stands on display near the French Market in downtown New Orleans today, now that the line has long since ceased to run.)

Williams admits to having availed himself of poetic license in Blanche's opening speech since if one were to follow the instructions given Blanche to find the Kowalski household in the Quarter in those days, one would have quickly discovered that the streetcar line did not run as far as Elysian Fields. "And even if it did, you wouldn't be in the Quarter any more. I used it because I liked the name Elysian Fields."

Williams chose the names of the three streetcar stops which Blanche mentions because together they coalesce into a symbolic cluster of meaning that epitomizes Blanche's desparate situation. She has come to seek refuge with her sister Stella, who is married to Stanley, because (we later learn) she has been ordered out of the town of Laurel, Mississippi, where she had taught high school English, because of her scandalous private life. She has become a slave of desire, "the name of that rattle-trap streetcar that bangs through the Quarter, up one old narrow street and down another," as she says later in the play to Stella. "It brought me here." Desire did indeed bring her to her sister's tenement flat in the sense that her sordid past has closed every other door to her; and she is aware from the moment of her arrival that this is her last stop, for she has no place else to go.

The opposite of desire, Blanche contends, is death. In her loneliness she fears that without companionship she will die; and she has, therefore, taken to settling for any kind of companionship that she can find, usually with strangers. Cemeteries is the appropriate name for her intermediate streetcar stop on the way to her sister's apartment, then, because she has been dogged by death for some time: from the demise of her parents and other aged relatives to the untimely death of her young husband. So, by way of desire and death, Blanche has arrived at Elysian Fields, the paradise beyond death of classical lore. But Elysian Fields proves to be a paradise for her sister Stella, who has adjusted to life with her virile but crude husband, not for Blanche, who cannot long live in a slum with a brutish brother-in-law.

Blanche's grasp on reality grows more and more tenuous as the play progresses and she takes refuse more and more in a fantasy world of her own devising because, like her prototype in *The Lady of Larkspur Lotion,* she cannot face the grim realities of her own past and present, which combine to leave her with little hope for the future. In the end she finds her Elysian Fields in a paradise which exists totally in her fevered imagination, a paradise where she will always be the youthful and beautiful Southern belle with a Gentlemen Caller ever ready to please and protect her.

"To find protection," Elia Kazan recorded in his director's notebook during rehearsals, is Blanche's basic motivation. The tradition of the Old South dictates that this protection must come through a gallant male admirer who will ultimately commit himself to her in marriage, making her the fair lady of the domains of which he is lord. The old Southern aristocrats, Kazan continues, made the Southern belle feel her special worth, her unique place in the elitist society to which they all belonged. That society is now gone with the wind, but Blanche believes that in trying to preserve in herself the refinements of the old Southern culture she is helping to preserve the last vestiges of all that is noble and civilized in the American character. It makes her sticking by Belle Reve, the DuBois homestead, until it finally goes into receivership, what Kazan calls "an act of heroism rather than of absurd romanticism." When Blanche loses Belle Reve (Beautiful Dream) to her creditors, the whole structure of the old Southern society to which she had clung so desperately, collapses as far as she is concerned; and she is left bereft and alienated from society at large.

Her solitary efforts to uphold the archaic traditions of the past isolate her further from the contemporary world, and she seeks solace first in drink and then in human contact, which she finds not on her own terms, but on the terms of those who offer it to her: travelling salesmen, soldiers, and others. Since she cannot reconcile the demoralized state into which she has sunk with her idealistic conception of herself as the last of the Southern belles, Kazan concludes, she rejects her present status in favor of living in a dream world that makes her a misfit in the eyes of everyone else.

Blanche is adrift in an alien world which she deems inferior to the one that she cherishes in her memory and imagination. Hence she treats the very people to whom she looks for protection and affection with a condescension that in turn alientates them from her. She turns first to Stella and Stanley and tries unsuccessfully to come between them in order to win back Stella's devotion to herself and her dated attitudes. When she fails on this front she looks to Mitch, a friend of Stanley's, and for a time it appears that he will provide her with the safe harbor which she seeks, until Stanley informs Mitch of Blanche's past.

It becomes increasingly clear that the only refuge which she will ever find that corresponds perfectly to her preconceived specifications is in a fantasy world of her own design. Her thoughts return to Shep Huntleigh, a wealthy former suitor. Despite the fact that Shep married someone else, Blanche becomes convinced that Shep is going to arrive at any moment and elope with her.

We watch Blanche systematically withdraw into her own insulated, private world as the play progresses. She decorates her little cubicle in the Kowalski flat to look like a miniature, though pathetically shabby, replica of Belle Reve, decorated with whatever scraps of finery she still has left. Even though only a wispy curtain separates her little domain from the rest of the slovenly Kowalski flat and the harsh world beyond it, she is proud that she has managed to make it look "almost dainty." The plantation estate of Belle Reve has thus shrunk to this little square of space which Blanche has appropriated for herself.

Within the boarders of her little realm Blanche is able to create a soft, exotic atmosphere which veils the unpleasant realities of life which she does not care to confront, one of which is the ravishments which time and her past indulgences have left upon her once beautiful face. To this end she covers the naked light bulb in her cubicle with a colored paper lantern which subdues the light. Her efforts to cover up her past are reflected in this attempt to keep anyone from getting a good look at her. She defends her right to idealize herself and her life to others by exclaiming, "I don't want realism. I want magic! . . . I don't tell the truth, I tell what ought to be true. And if that is sinful, then let me be damned for it!"

How fitting it is, therefore, that her favorite song is "Paper Moon," for her cardboard world takes on substance only insofar as she can get others to believe in it too, which is just what the song implies. By the same token, her addiction to

Vivien Leigh as Blanche Dubois and Wright King as the newsboy, *A Streetcar Named Desire.*

spending hours in a hot tub indicate her compulsive efforts to cleanse away her sinful past as well as to place her in a serene, insulated atmosphere in the present.

The other side of the coin from Blanche's looking for protection in an unsympathetic world is her desire to be a protector of those whom she views as even more vulnerable than she. Her penchant to be overprotective is rooted in her childhood relationship with her "baby sister," and Stella obviously resents any efforts which Blanche makes to resuscitate that dependent relationship of their Belle Reve days.

This protective strain in Blanche was also manifested in her marrying a sensitive young man named Allan Grey. He presumably was looking for a mother more than a wife, for she soon discovered after their marriage that he was homosexual, and her cruel rejection of him drove him to suicide. The blinding exposure of that revelation was like a searchlight being snapped on momentarily and then just as quickly snapped off again. From that time on, Blanche's world has been lit with the dimmest illumination possible.

Blanche has subconsciously sought to make expiation for her husband's death by attempting to revive their sad, sweet relationship in a succession of other young men. She wishes to give these lads the understanding which she denied her husband. First there were the young recruits in the army camp near Belle Reve; then the seventeen year old student in one of her classes; and, in the course of the play, the newsboy whom Blanche kisses maternally; and finally Mitch, the overgrown mama's boy in whom she once more finds a reflection of Allan Grey. (Mitch has been called a Tom Wingfield who never left home.)

Although Mitch is a naive boy at heart, he is also a physically strong man and a responsible adult wage earner. He therefore represents the one individual who can satisfy Blanche's two-fold longing to protect and to be protected. Blanche's expectations are doubly smashed, consequently, when Stanley crushes Mitch's illusions about Blanche's character. With the defection of Mitch, Blanche's sole remaining hope for a fresh start in life can only be Shep Huntleigh, whom she still insists wants to marry her; and it is for him that she is waiting when she is taken away to the asylum, still clutching the paper lampshade as a last relic of her romantic dream world. (Hence Stanley's rape of Stella shortly before she is committed is not the exclusive reason for her lapse into madness, because her mind and spirit have already been broken by then.)

Blanche takes the proferred arm of the doctor from the state hospital who has come for her, saying, "Whoever you are, I have always depended on the kindness of strangers"—which only goes to show, Williams remarks dryly in his autobiography, "what sometimes happens to ladies who always depend on the kindness of strangers." Blanche's last Gentleman Caller has finally arrived, only to escort her to a mental institution. The matron who is with the doctor notes Blanche's long nails will have to be trimmed, for Blanche will no longer need talons to defend herself in the hostile jungle of existence from which she is now retiring, a milieu in which she was too delicate to survive.

That Stella allows Stanley to have her sister committed to an asylum does not necessarily mean that she has callously sacrificed Blanche in order to mollify her husband and save her marriage. By this point in the play Blanche herself has once and for all opted to retreat into the kindlier haven of her illusions. And so she finds the protection and shelter and care that she has long sought for within the confines of a mental ward in which she can shut out the world in a way that she never could in her cubicle in the Kowalski apartment.

Stella is really a more pivotal character in the play than many critics have realized. She is the only person who understands and sympathizes with both her sister and her husband. She defends Blanche to Stanley by explaining that

The finale of A *Streetcar Named Desire*, with Vivien Leigh as Blanche and Richard Garrick as the psychiatrist.

Blanche was once tender and trusting, "but people like you abused her and forced her to change." But she is also aware that Blanche thinks Stanley a brute who has cheapened her "baby sister" and that Blanche would like to see them part. (Although the name Stella means star, she is not the celestial being her name implies—any more than Blanche, whose name means white, is the unsullied creature her name suggests, although she has discarded her married name Grey, to make believe that she is.)

Blanche endeavors to force Stella to judge Stanley by the standards of gentility of the old South, and by that norm Stanley is severely wanting. She is a tigress fighting for her declining world with any means at her disposal, and Stanley is right in resenting his sister-in-law as an intrusive interloper who threatens to disrupt his home life. As Jessica Tandy once pointed out, "The

Vivien Leigh as Blanche, Kim Hunter as her sister Stella in *Streetcar*.

extent of Stanley's brutality is the measure of his insecurity and ignorance."
Kazan sums up the situation in his notes this way: "Stanley, whom she's
antagonized by her destructiveness aimed at his home, but especially by her
need to be superior, uses her past, which he digs up, to destroy her." When he
finally assaults her in the play's climax, moreover, it is the action of a desparate
man equipped with more brawn than brains to cope with a calculating creature
who declared war on him when she first stepped across his threshold.

I do not mean to justify Stanley's rape of his sister-in-law but to explain it.
Even Stella's image of Stanley has been tarnished by his treatment of Blanche.
Taking his cue from the way that Stella nestles her new baby in her arms after
Blanche has departed for the asylum, Kazan comments in his notebook, "Like
so many women, she will begin to live more and more for her children," for her

relationship with Stanley will never be quite the same again.

The critical question arises, then, as to whose side Williams wants the audience to take in this tug of war between Stanley and Blanche, since there are things that can be said pro and con for both characters. Williams really tries to be fair to both adversaries in this deadly domestic feud so that the audience can make its own choice between them. Ultimately, however, I think that the scales tip in Blanche's favor, and Williams's own summing up of the play bears out my hunch: "Our illusions are all we have, any of us. That's what *Streetcar* is about. Some people, maybe most people, can only live by illusion, and the cruellest thing in the world is to deprive them of those illusions, which is what Stanley does to Blanche." And to an interviewer who opined that he thought Blanche was a sordid character, Williams replied, "I don't think troubled people are sordid. I think Blanche was rather noble."

Nonetheless there were some who saw the play who thought it sensational and sordid and consequently care would have to be exercised if a film version was to steer successfully through the narrow straights of the Production Code and reach the screen with its artistic integrity intact. Williams was engaged to do the script with the help of Oscar Saul, and the screenplay kept very close to the original text of the play. Kazan was signed to direct; Vivien Leigh, the star of the London production, was set to play Blanche; and most of the Broadway cast were brought out to Hollywood to repeat their roles in the film, including Marlon Brando, Karl Malden (Mitch) and Kim Stanley (Stella). This combination of talents, all of whom had been associated with *Streetcar* on the stage, was assembled to ensure that the film would be as close to the genuine article as possible; and so, for the most part, did it turn out.

Screenwriter Budd Schulberg once said that Elia Kazan is one of the very few film directors who treats a screenplay with the same respect that he would give a work for the stage, and this remark is certainly borne out in his direction of *Streetcar* on the screen. The only significant alterations made in the original play were dictated by censorship demands, as we shall soon see. If one places the movie script next to the text of the play and compares the two page by page, it is immediately apparent that the screenplay follows the stage play scene for scene and almost line for line.

"I filmed the play as it was," Kazan told me, "because there was nothing to change. I have no general theory about opening out a play for the screen; it depends on the subject matter. *Streetcar* is a perfect play. I did try to open it up initially, but not successfully, so I decided to go back to the original script. It was a polished script that had played in the theater for a year and a half."

With the exception of a few excisions and transpositions, most of the play's dialogue was preserved in the screenplay. Given Williams's propensity for writing long speeches of highly charged poetic language, his stage idiom transfers to the screen with surprising smoothness. Even the few lines of dialogue added to the original text take on that same poetic flavor. For example, when Mitch berates Blanche for hiding her past, he says accusingly, "I thought you were straight." She answers, "What's straight? A line can be straight or a street. But the heart of a human being?"

Referring to the fact that Williams's theatrical dialogue works on the screen, Kazan says, "In the case of *Streetcar* the whole play was put on the screen as a piece of heightened realism. It doesn't pretend to be literal realism, much less a gutter-type of realism; it is a heightened realism and it was so directed and so played. I think the heightened speech fits into this context very well. If the film had been directed and acted in a different fashion, the dialogue might have seemed somewhat artificial; but since that wasn't the case, in my opinion the dialogue works."

This adherence to Williams's original play did not mean that the film of *Streetcar* was at any time in danger of becoming a mere photographed stage play. For a start, the play does not have the customary dramatic structure of two or three acts which are perhaps divided in turn into two or three scenes. The play is made up, like *Glass Menagerie*, of a series of scenes, "eleven slabs of action," as George Brandt calls them in his essay on the cinematic structure of Williams's work: "Since the pattern of the drama is not the conventional act structure but something close to the sequence of a film, it is not surprising that the play translated exceptionally well to the screen."

Williams has said that he feels that the freedom and mobility of form of his plays is one of the things that attracted Kazan to his work in the first place, both as a stage and a screen director. In striving for a continual flow of action in his plays, Williams has tried to bring the techniques of the screen into play on the stage and in so doing has made his plays more easily adaptable for the movies.

Kazan scrapped his initial notion of opening out the play when he found that it would serve no useful purpose. He had thought of beginning the film in Blanche's hometown and dramatizing the events that precipitated her leaving home and moving on to other places, and then finally arriving in New Orleans like a refugee at her sister's front door. After such a version of the script was worked out, he put it away for a while, then re-read it a week or so later and found it "a total loss. I realized that the compression in *Streetcar* is its strength. And so I decided to photograph the play almost as Williams had composed it for the stage."

Nevertheless the screenplay does open out the play in a few carefully selected scenes by taking the action to places that are only referred to in the play. But this is always done for a dramatically valid reason. Thus the opening scene of the movie is a short location sequence showing Blanche arriving at the New Orleans train depot. After a wedding party runs by in a happy flurry, an engine emits a blast of steam from which Blanche emerges like an apparition materializing from a cloud of mist.

Vivien Leigh as Blanche getting off the Streetcar named Desire.

She boards the streetcar named Desire and arrives at Elysian Fields. Told that Stella is with Stanley at the neighborhood bowling alley, she sets out to meet her sister there instead of waiting for her at the tenement as she does in the play. Amid the noise and sweat of the bowling alley Blanche still seems like a vaporous apparition from another planet as she stands next to the garish juke box in her frilly white frock. In contrast, Stanley and Stella are clearly in their element, and Blanche already senses that she is going to be painfully out of place in their alien world.

In another instance of opening out, Blanche tells Mitch about the death of her husband while they talk on the pier fronting a dance casino, rather than after he takes her home as in the play. This new setting for the scene is appropriate because Allan Grey killed himself at a dance casino very much like the one where Blanche recalls his suicide. Furthermore the fog swirls around the pier as she talks, providing a spectral atmosphere for Blanche's tale of regret and death.

Another brief location scene dramatizes a scene not portrayed directly in the play in which we see Mitch express shock and disbelief at Stanley's revelations about Blanche's shady past as they take time out at their factory jobs. The grating clash of the machinery expresses the jolt that Mitch has just received.

The only addition to the original play which I find superfluous is the material added to the end of the play's ninth scene, just after Blanche becomes hysterical when Mitch walks out on her. A crowd collects around the porch of the tenement and a policeman knocks at the door of the Kowalski flat to investigate. Blanche assures him from inside that everything is fine and he disperses the crowd. This interlue serves only to slow down the tempo of the action temporarily and adds nothing to the audience's understanding of Blanche or her situation, since her increasing withdrawal from the threatening, inquisitive outside world has been thoroughly documented by this point in the film. The other extensions of the play's action, however, from the train depot and the bowling alley to the dance casino and the factory, are nicely and neatly done.

Any further attempts to have the camera roam beyond the principal setting of the squalid tenement building would have been extremely ill-advised because the atmosphere of the story is one of confinement, of people locked together and in conflict at close quarters. Kazan employed tight close-ups and deep shadows to help create this sense of constriction, betokening Blanche's imprisonment of both body and soul. The cluttered Kowalski apartment has a claustrophobic air which seems to suggest that the very walls are closing in on the trapped Blanche. In fact the walls really were closing in as the film was being shot. "What I actually did," Kazan explains, "was to make the set smaller. As the story progressed I took out little flats and the set got smaller and smaller."

Foster Hirsch praises the brooding texture of the film, which set the tone for later Williams movies like *Baby Doll*, *The Rose Tattoo*, and *The Fugitive Kind*. All of them have what he terms a look of "steamy Southern Gothic." These densely atmospheric settings take on a life of their own, he contends, and moving the action away from these inherently pictorial settings any more than is necessary would only dilute the total impact on the film: "The plays don't need much rearranging for the movies. Those that stay the closest to the original structure, to Williams's original visual design, are usually the most successful."

Although Kazan's camera is confined for the most part to the tenement setting, he adroitly keeps moving it round the set so that the film does not become static or stagey. In effect he was using the same method of making *Streetcar* into a *moving* picture which William Wyler described in the prologue of this book while filming another play, *Detective Story*, made the same year as *Streetcar*: "My approach to filming a play has been to retain the basic construction of the original, while at the same time lending the story the illusion of more movement than took place on the stage." Wyler extended the action of *Detective Story*, which on the stage took place in a couple of rooms in a police station, by playing it throughout the entire two story building, from roof to basement. "The constant movement back and forth among the various playing areas kept the film from becoming static while retaining the tight construction of the play," Wyler concludes.

This is exactly what Kazan did in filming *Streetcar* and with equal success. He moved the action fluidly throughout the whole tenement building without, at the same time, sacrificing the stifling feeling of restriction that is so endemic to the play, since Blanche sees the entire tenement, not just the Kowalski flat, as a jungle in which she has become trapped. Kazan's use of different areas of the tenement is exemplified in the poker scene, in which the director cuts back and forth between the occupant of the flat above Stanley's and Stanley's apartment where the game is being held. She prepares to pour scalding water through the floor boards on the poker players as an incentive for them to break up their raucous game (an episode suggested by an incident that took place when Williams was a young writer living in a New Orleans tenement). In a hilarious bit of comic relief, the players move their table away from the target area just before the irate lady can flood them, and continue playing.

In the movie, as in the play, Blanche's curtained-off cubicle is established as her preserve, the territory where she feels untainted by the vulgar slum in which she has been forced to live. She likes to think of it as her citadel of enchantment, but the barred shadows that fall across her face at times when she shuts herself into her room imply that she is locked into a suffocating world of illusion. Another example of Kazan's skilled use of lighting occurs in the scene in which Mitch ruthlessly tears the fancy paper lantern off the light bulb in her cubicle to see her as she really is. He holds the now naked bulb next to her cheek, and its merciless glare exposes a face marred with lines of age and dissipation which even heavy cosmetics can no longer conceal.

The cinema audience was able to see Blanche's tortured face at this moment in a way that was impossible for any theater audience, and this is one reason why Vivien Leigh, who played Blanche on both stage and screen, felt that the movie was superior to any of the stage productions: "The camera, in bringing the characters so close to the audience, was able to highlight nuances in expressions on the actors' faces and to reveal subtleties of feeling that were lost in their passage over the footlights."

Vivien Leigh was the only star in the film, since Brando's one previous film had not as yet been released. There was a rightness about her playing Blanche, not only because she had essayed the role on the London stage, but because Blanche was just the kind of used-up Southern belle that Scarlett O'Hara, whom Ms. Leigh had played in *Gone with the Wind* in 1939, probably would have become after she lost Rhett Bulter; and the actress won Academy Awards for

Karl Malden as Mitch exposing Blanche to the naked light bulb in *Streetcar*.

playing both ladies. At first the rest of the cast, many of whom had played *Streetcar* for more than a year on the stage with Jessica Tandy, resented Vivien Leigh as an interloper into their ensemble. But she quickly won them over by working closely with them in an atmosphere of informality and mutual respect.

Kazan had a mockup of the apartment set built in a corner of the sound stage, and while the technicians were setting up a shot he would rehearse his players for the following day's shooting. Since the actors brought with them the experience of playing their parts on the stage, the shooting went along very smoothly. "The only person who had any difficulty in re-thinking the play for the screen was myself," Kazan remembers. "It was difficult to get involved in it again, to generate the same kind of excitment which I had had for it the first time around. The actors were fine—but for me it was like marrying the same woman

Vivien Leigh, Tennessee Williams, and director Elia Kazan on the set of *Streetcar*.

twice; you know that there won't be any surprises this time.

"Vivien Leigh had done *Streetcar* in London under Laurence Olivier's direction. I never saw that production, so I don't know how his approach to the play may have differed from mine; I just did my own. After the first week of shooting she seemed quite agreeable to going down a somewhat different path." When, during the first week or so of production, Ms. Leigh would begin a rehearsal with, "When Larry and I did it in London . . ." Kazan would politely intervene and say, "But you're not doing it with Larry now; you're doing it with me." After this happened a few times she began to follow Kazan's lead.

According to Ms. Leigh, in an interview which she gave at the time that the film opened, Olivier (her husband at the time) wanted to emphasize that Blanche was "a soft and gentle creature" yearning for love, while Kazan concentrated more on Blanche's stronger qualities, delineating her as a person "whose tongue was the weapon of a frustrated woman." All of these elements are in Blanche, as Kazan indicates in his notes on directing the play; and he was able to bring out both sides of Blanche's personality in Ms. Leigh's performance in the film. Underneath her surface toughness Blanche comes through in the film as a fragile creature longing for love and security, and finding neither; and Kazan made sure that Ms. Leigh's performance did not allow the latter facet of Blanche's character to overshadow the former.

Williams's compassionate play had a somewhat notorious reputation in the public mind when Kazan turned to making the movie, despite its reputation as a distinguished Pulitzer Prize winner in more sophisticated cultural circles. The industry censor, Joseph Breen, was worried that a play that was quite acceptable on the stage would not be an appropriate film project. As the official administrator of the Code of the Motion Picture Association of America (MPAA), he wrote to Irene Mayer Selznick, who had produced the play on the stage and was considering the possibility of a movie version, that the provisions of the Production Code presumed that "motion pictures, unlike stage plays, appeal to mass audiences, the mature and the immature." In fact the Production Code contained a section declaring that "everything possible in a play is not possible in a film" because motion pictures command a mass audience, and "the larger the audience, the lower the moral resistence to suggestion." In explaining the practical implications of this concept to Ms. Selznick, Breen continued, "Material which may be perfectly valid for dramatization and treatment on the stage may be . . . completely unacceptable when presented in a motion picture."

What the Code was saying in essence was that movies are a family medium and hence only pictures suitable for the entire family should be produced. It followed that *Streetcar* was not a family play and it could not be retooled into a family movie without refining to some degree its mature content. Accordingly Kazan began the delicate task of satisfying the Breen office while making as few concessions as possible in altering the play for the screen in order to preserve its serious intent and artistic integrity. Breen's demands were twofold: reference to the homosexuality of Blanche's late husband Allan Grey must be obscured if not obliterated, and Stanley's rape of Blanche must be entirely eliminated from the screenplay.

Williams agreed to rewrite Blanche's monologue about her husband's suicide with no little regret that "we couldn't mention homosexuality as a human problem." Kazan feels that the implications about the nature of Allan's problem come through on the screen in Williams's revised treatment of that scene as well as they came through on the stage. Essentially Williams reworked the speech by substituting for Blanche's recollection of discovering Allan in bed with another man the suggestion that Allan was impotent with his new bride: "At night I pretended to sleep and I heard him crying." Finally, when she guesses the reason for his failure in the marital bed, she tells him just as she does in the play that he is weak and that she "has lost all respect for him."

These hints, along with Blanche's description of Allan as unusually sensitive and tender, are enough to telegraph to a mature moviegoer that Allan is homosexual, even without the play's explicit reference to his having a male lover. That Blanche seems unable in this scene in the film to bring herself to mention explicitly what Oscar Wilde called "the love that dare not speak its name" is easily understood in the context to mean that the incident is still too painful a memory for her to talk about directly. Therefore, Vivien Leigh felt that Williams rewrote the speech in question for the film so cleverly that not only was the suggestion of Allan's homosexuality left intact "but the due effect that the experience had had upon Blanche was clarified and heightened."

Williams absolutely refused to yield to Breen on the question of deleting Stanley's rape of Blanche from the picture, however. Although the playwright proved to be somewhat shy around the industry moguls when he visited Hollywood when *Glass* was in preparation, this time he was determined not to allow his work to be compromised by either front office or censor. He wrote Breen a strong letter in which he maintained that "*Streetcar* is an extremely and peculiarly moral play, in the deepest and truest sense of the term. . . . The rape of Blanche by Stanley is a pivotal, integral truth in the play, without which the play loses its meaning, which is the ravishment of the tender, the sensitive, the delicate, by the savage and brutal forces of modern society. It is a poetic plea for comprehension."

He reminded Breen that he had come out to Hollywood in the midst of preparations for his new play, *The Rose Tattoo*, to deal with the demands of the censor's office and that everyone associated with the film had shown similar cooperation, even deference to the Code Commission. "But now we are fighting for what we think is the heart of the play, and when we have our backs against the wall—if we are forced into that position—none of us is going to throw in the towel! We will use every legitimate means that any of us has at his or her disposal to protect the things in this film which we think cannot be sacrificed, since we feel that it contains some very important truths about the world we live in."

Two years before *Streetcar* went into production in the summer of 1950, *Johnny Belinda*, a film in which Jane Wyman won an Oscar as a deaf mute who becomes the victim of a rapist, had established that this previously taboo topic could be treated tastefully in a Hollywood movie. So Breen finally consented to allow the rape to remain in the movie of *Streetcar*, provided that Stanley was appropriately punished for his transgression.

In directing the film Kazan was able to deal with a psychological dimension of the rape that did not come out as clearly on the stage: to what extent does Blanche share some of the guilt for her rape? Because the camera brings the

Marlon Brando as Stanley Kowalski in *Streetcar*.

audience closer to the action than was possible in the theater, moviegoers sense that to some extent at least Blanche subtly encourages Stanley's sexual interest in her throughout the film. Her coquettish glances and gestures in his direction bring out the fact that Blanche is as drawn to Stanley's animal charm as much as she is revolted by his brutish vulgarity. As René Jordan notes in his book on Brando, all along Blanche has envied Stella's sexual fulfillment, and now that

Blanche is left alone with her drunken brother-in-law while her sister is in the maternity ward having his baby, Blanche, likewise drunk, seems subconsciously to be toying coyly with Stanley. When one recalls Blanche furtively peeking at Stanley's biceps when he changes his shirt the first time she meets him, it is difficult to see her delicate request that he close the curtains before he changes his clothes in this later scene as genuinely sincere.

When Stanley, like a teased animal, finally grasps Blanche, Kazan depicts the ensuing rape as subtly as he portrayed Blanche's subconscious goading of Stanley to the deed without diluting its dramatic power. Blanche smashes a whiskey bottle, ineffectually aimed at Stanley, into an ornately framed mirror and passes out. We see her limp form lying in Stanley's arms as it is reflected in the cracked glass, symbolizing how Stanley is finally shattering Blanche's illusions about her own refinement and moral character. (In the last scene, as Blanche goes off to the asylum, there is a new mirror hanging on the wall, for by then Blanche has repaired her illusions about herself and sees herself once more, when she passes the mirror, as an immaculate Southern belle.)

Kazan cuts from the image of Stanley holding Blanche's body framed in the smashed mirror to a street cleaner's hose in the gutter outside just as a blast of water gushes forth and dwindles to a trickle. "Some of the symbolic cutting in the film, such as cutting from the rape to the street cleaner's hose, seems to me in retrospect to be a little too obvious," Kazan says today, "though I thought it was good at the time. In any event it was certainly a forceful cut, and enabled me to underline the rape implicitly, because in those days we had to be very indirect in depicting material of that kind."

The director had prepared the audience for this symbolic suggestion of Stanley's violation of Blanche by the use of similar phallic imagery midway through the movie when Stella makes Blanche a highball and the soda overflows the glass, spilling foam on Blanche's dress. Blanche is upset until she is reassured that the lathery liquid has left no stain on her white frock. In the rape scene itself Stanley, the jubilant father-to-be, uncaps a bottle of beer and sends foam squirting up to the ceiling, a spectacular symbol of his potent virility. The visual impact of these two phallic images prior to the rape, then, combine with the third immediately following it to suggest with artistic indirection the climactic rape itself, which is in fact not seen on the screen at all.

But Breen was still not satisfied. Stanley had to be punished for his lust, even though there is a strong possibility that Blanche was at least subconsciously responsible for encouraging him to seduce her. The ending of the film was revised, therefore, to give the impression that Stella was leaving Stanley by having her say to her newborn infant, "We're not going back in there. Not this time. We're never going back." This was a shrewdly ambiguous way to end the movie, since the unsophisticated could believe that Stella would make good her resolution. The more mature viewer, however, would realize that Stella had left

Stanley earlier in the film in the wake of a domestic brawl, and returned to him when he begged her forgiveness; and there is ample reason to believe that she will do so again.

Still Williams tells me that he has never been satisfied with this compromise ending: "*A Streetcar Named Desire* was a brilliant film until the very end, when the distortion of the censorial influences made it appear that Stella would no longer live with Stanley because of what had happened to Blanche at his hands. I am sure that Kazan was as reluctant as I was to accede to this moralistic demand."

Kazan does feel that the film suffered somewhat from censorship, though it was not marred in any substantial way. "Every little bit is important to the integrity of the work as a whole. For example, the censorship took away some of the ambivalence from the character of Stella: the fact that she was both angry at Stanley and attracted to him at the same time." This latter eventuality was the result not just of the changes made in the script while the film was in production, but of some minor cuts made in the finished film by the studio before its release in order to get a favorable moral rating from the Legion of Decency.

Once the movie had been granted the seal of the Code Commission, Kazan and Williams assumed that there would be no further negotiations over the picture's moral content; and both went on to other projects while awaiting the picture's release in the fall of 1951. Kazan began to hear rumors that the film's editor, David Weisbart (who had also edited *Glass*) had been summoned to the executive offices of Warner Brothers in New York for further editing of the film. Since Kazan could get no straight answers from the studio in Hollywood as to the nature of these cuts, he flew to New York to investigate. He learned that the Legion of Decency, which rated the moral suitability of films for their Catholic subscribers, had advised Warners that *Streetcar* was going to receive a "C" (condemned) rating, meaning that Catholics would be discouraged from seeing it.

Since the MPAA did not develop a rating system of its own as a guide for parents until 1968, many non-Catholics followed the Legion ratings and hence Warners feared heavy losses at the box office if the Legion condemned the picture. "I was told that the 'C' rating was an invitation for every local censor board in the country to snipe at a picture," Kazan wrote in *The New York Times* when the movie was released. Consequently, although the Legion had not requested cuts in the film but simply pronounced its verdict on their rating of it, Warners invited a prominent Catholic layman to suggest to the studio how the film might be altered in order to gain a more favorable rating from the Legion.

In all, twelve cuts were made in the movie at his behest, amounting to about four minutes of screen time. Although none of these cuts were fatal to the film, Kazan nonetheless felt that they left their mark on the movie's artistic merits. The material that was excised represented for him "small but necessary bits that built mood or motivation as I needed them," as he explained in *The Times*. "Their rough excision leaves small holes or unprepared climaxes that make my work appear cruder than it was. I see it as lost fragments of a subtly told story, whose omission leaves the characters less fully explained than the author intended and than the actors, before, had conveyed."

The cuts range from the last three words of Blanche's remark to the newsboy, "I would like to kiss you softly and sweetly on the mouth," to the re-editing of the scene in which Stella slowly descends a flight of stairs to accept the embrace of her weeping and repentant husband. In the latter instance a long shot was substituted for a series of close and medium shots that were judged by the Catholic adviser to be "too carnal." In reality they simply conveyed Stella's anger melting gradually into forgiveness, and her succession of emotions is not apparent when viewed from the distance imposed by a long shot. This explains Kazan's feeling that the censorship cuts robbed Stella's character of some of its ambivalence.

Some of the complex motivational forces at work in the rape scene, which I discussed above, were also obscured by yet another cut. Stanley's line, "You know, you might not be bad to interfere with," uttered shortly before his attack of Blanche, indicates that he is acting impulsively and had not considered raping her until her coquettish behavior stimulated him to consider the possibility. The removal of this line makes his action seem premeditated and therefore more coarse and brutal that it probably was. "How it serves the cause of morality is obscure to me," Kazan commented, "though I have given it much thought."

One of the overall elements of the film which bothered both the Breen office and the Legion of Decency was the fact that it was difficult to determine who were the "good guys" and the "bad guys" in the movie. Making Stanley seem more cruel in the rape scene and Stella less "carnal" in the reconciliation scene presumably were adjustments geared to stress the meanness of Stanley and the goodness of Stella in order that a clear distinction between the villainous and the admirable characters could be established in the Hollywood tradition of family films. But this approach to the movie involves precisely the kind of oversimplification of character which Williams had avoided in his design of the play/film. "You're not in there rooting for someone," Kazan said at the time. "There is no hero, no heroine; the people are people, some dross, some gold," possessing the kind of complex personalities that are not easily understood and assessed.

Looking back on the controversy over *Streetcar*, Kazan later said to an interviewer that Warners wanted the MPAA seal of approval to ensure that the movie was a family film that would keep no one away. At the same time they wanted it to have a notorious reputation that would pull more people in to see it. "The whole business," he concluded, "was rather an outrage."

But no tampering with the film could make *Streetcar* family fare in the old

Hollywood sense of that term. It was an adult film in the very best sense of the phrase and its box office success proved to the industry as a whole that films designed with mature audiences in mind could be just as profitable as movies aimed at the whole family. As Breen's successor, Geoffrey Shurlock, put it, *Streetcar* marked the first time that the censor's office was confronted with a Hollywood film that was definitely not family entertainment. "*Streetcar* broke the barrier," he said, because Williams's fine play and Kazan's skillful direction proved that any subject could be proper material for the screen if treated with the kind of discretion and artistry that this movie exhibited.

If *Streetcar* in retrospect seemed a landmark film, it was looked upon at the time in industry circles not as a trend setter at all but as an interesting exception to the rule that Hollywood films should cater to family patronage. Williams and Kazan learned this fact when they had to wage the same controversy over their second film together, *Baby Doll* (1956), an original screenplay by Williams.

By this time in his career, Williams had written two other original screenplays, *The Gentleman Caller*, which he reshaped into *The Glass Menagerie*, and the unfilmed *Pink Bedroom*. The latter was a script which he showed to Greta Garbo shortly after the opening of *Streetcar* in December of 1947, hoping that it would provide her with a vehicle for her comeback to the screen, from which she had retired six years earlier. Garbo seemed entranced as Williams read her the scenario in her suite in the Ritz Towers; but when he had finished she sighed, "It's wonderful, but not for me."

The only other screenplay on which Williams worked which was not an adaptation of one of his existing full-length plays, before he turned to write *Baby Doll*, was *Senso*, a 1954 Italian film. He collaborated on this movie, which starred Valli and Farley Grainger, because of his admiration for its director, Luchino Visconti, who directed the Italian company of *Streetcar*. When he later saw the picture he found that little was left of his contribution to the script except one scene in which a couple are awakening in the morning and one says, "There's always a sound in a room when you wake." Visconti explained the line by having a fly buzzing round the bedroom; but Williams says that what he really meant was that some people belch upon awaking in the morning to clear away what he calls "the poisons of the night before." Yet for his pains Williams was listed in the credits of the film as a co-author of the English language version, presumably because the Italian producers thought that his name might help the box office of the film in the United States.

Summing up his experiences in movieland, Williams says, "I've never had any success writing for the screen unless it's a film script of one of my own plays." *Baby Doll* was in fact based on two of his one act plays, *Twenty-Seven Wagons Full of Cotton* and *The Unsatisfactory Supper*, which he set about at Kazan's request to meld into a single, coherent, story for the screen while he was spending the summer of 1955 in Rome.

Williams and Kazan had been discussing this project intermittently since 1952, when the working title of the proposed screenplay was *Hide and Seek*. Originally he and Kazan had considered doing an omnibus film of four separate one-act plays, possibly suggested by the success a few years earlier of two such anthology films which centered on the stories of Somerset Maugham, *Quartet* (1949) and *Trio* (1950). The four plays under consideration for the Williams movie were the two plays that eventually were used as the basis of *Baby Doll*, plus *This Property is Condemned* and *The Last of My Solid Gold Watches*. When this conception proved too ambitious and unwieldy, they finally settled upon only two of the plays and decided to weld them into a unified whole. (*This Property is Condemned* was subsequently used as the source of the film of that name and will be treated in the next chapter.)

In Rome, Williams wrote additional dialogue in order to fill out the characterizations and to aid in cementing the script into a single story. He would send batches of material on to Kazan in New York and Kazan would fit it in to the overall structure of the burgeoning screenplay. Then Kazan got Warners, which had made *Glass* and *Streetcar*, to finance the project which would be made by Kazan's own production company, Newtown Productions.

The impetus for making *Twenty-Seven Wagons Full of Cotton* the principal ingredient of *Baby Doll* was provided by the favorable reception which the play received when it was produced on Broadway in the spring of 1955 as one segment of a three-part package which also included Leonard Bernstein's opera *Trouble in Tahiti* and a program of dance. The Williams one-acter is subtitled *A Mississippi Delta Comedy*, but it is the blackest kind of comedy. Flora Meighan is the voluptuously overweight wife of Jake Meighan, a seedy cotton gin owner many years her senior. Jake burns down the cotton gin owned by Silva Vacarro, the Sicilian superintendent of the plantation syndicate, in order to force Vacarro to use his facilities instead.

While Jake is busy ginning Vacarro's twenty-seven wagons full of cotton, Vacarro is busy using his ever-present whip to frighten Flora into admitting Jake's guilt as an arsonist. When she does so, he cruelly rapes and beats her as his way of taking revenge on Jake, who witlessly agrees to let Flora "entertain" Vacarro every time he brings a load of cotton over for Jake to process.

A melodramatic plot to be sure, and when *Twenty-Seven* was revived on Broadway in early 1976, Walter Kerr congratulated Williams on the deftness with which he can employ melodrama to propel a play vigorously forward toward emotionally revealing scenes in a way that is neither florid nor forced. Walter Kerr is right when he writes that Williams has always been more interested in character development than in plot contrivances; but to get to the portraiture in depth, says Kerr, Williams has to have an occasion, "a first pressure." In this little play that pressure is supplied by the arson that Jake commits against Vacarro, which is the basis of the clash of character that follows, and which is also the driving force of *Baby Doll*'s plot.

The other one-act play which was integrated into the *Baby Doll* screenplay was *The Unsatisfactory Supper* (also called *The Long Stay Cut Short*), a much less substantial character sketch of an elderly spinster, Aunt Rose Comfort, who has worn out her welcome with her niece Baby Doll and the latter's husband Archie Lee (the counterparts of Flora and Jake in *Twenty-Seven*). The last straw is Aunt Rose's failing to light the stove under the greens which she is preparing for the evening meal, which makes for a very unsatisfactory supper indeed. Archie Lee takes this opportunity to order Aunt Rose out of the house; and she leaves in the midst of a storm. She is literally blown away by the wind, a symbol of the way she has been shunted about from relative to relative throughout her declining years.

The plight of Aunt Rose was suggested to Williams by his beloved grandmother who, he tells us in the autobiographical sketch called "Grand" in *The Knightly Quest,* always feared having to live out her days in the cold care of in-laws. It is the fate against which Amanda Wingfield warns Laura in *The Glass Menagerie*. Laura, she fears, will one day be one of those "little bird-like women without any nest," stuck away in a mousetrap of a room, living on the grudging patronage of relatives who constantly encourage their unwanted house guest to move on and visit somewhere else, with the county poorhouse looming as the last stop on her pitiful journey. Such a pathetic creature is Aunt Rose, who has spent her life extending devotion like "an armful of roses that no one had ever offered a vase to receive." Her situation is also reminiscent of that of Blanche DuBois, another itinerate relative unwanted by her kin.

It is amazing how well the two originally unrelated plays meshed into a single screenplay. The characters of Flora and Jake Meighan from *Twenty-Seven Wagons Full of Cotton* were easily fused with those of Baby Doll and Archie Lee, respectively, of *The Unsatisfactory Supper* to become Baby Doll and Archie Lee Meighan: while Vacarro was brought over from the first play and Aunt Rose from the second to form the quartet of principals in the finished screenplay. In the course of composition the working title of the screenplay changed from *Hide and Seek* to the more lurid *The Whip Hand* and *Mississippi Woman,* and finally was fixed as *Baby Doll*.

Just how firmly the two one-acters solidified into one unified work of art is evidenced by the substantial amount of dialogue which Williams was able to retain from the two previously separate plays. The second scene of *Twenty-Seven,* for example, in which Vacarro coaxes the truth about Archie Lee's arson from Baby Doll, is incorporated almost verbatim into the movie script. But Williams has also contributed some additional dialogue to the screenplay which is as good as anything in either of the two short plays, and which elides perfectly with the original lines.

When Archie Lee turns on Aunt Rose and tells her to pack up and leave (in a scene similar to the one in *Streetcar* in which Stanley gives Blanche a bus ticket for a birthday present), Aunt Rose responds with a heartbreakingly beautiful speech: "I've helped out my relatives, my folks whenever they needed me to! I was always invited, sometimes begged to come! When babies were expected or when somebody was sick, they called for Aunt Rose and Aunt Rose was always ready. Nobody ever had to put me out!"

Vacarro says in her behalf, "When a man is feeling uncomfortable over something, it often happens that he takes out his annoyance on some completely innocent person just because he has to make somebody suffer." Here we have Vacarro, a character from one play, coming to the defense of Aunt Rose, a character from the other play, and creating one of the most touching scenes in all of Williams.

There is one completely new element in the screenplay, however, which is not implied in either of the source plays. That is the agreement which Archie Lee made with Baby Doll's father before the marriage that he would not exact his marital priveleges from his nubile bride until the girl's twentieth birthday. To this stipulation Baby Doll added one of her own: that Archie Lee must provide her with a fully furnished home by the same twentieth birthday or he would forfeit his right to her as a wife. The film opens shortly before Baby Doll turns twenty, with the finance company threatening to repossess the furniture before Archie Lee can possess Baby Doll. It is under these additional pressures in the film that Archie Lee, at his wit's end, sets fire to Vacarro's cotton gin in order to have Vacarro patronize his gin and enable him to obtain the money to meet the furniture payments on which the consummation of his marriage depends!

This new motivation for Archie in the movie makes him appear less venal and mercenary, if not really sympathetic, when he commits his act of arson, than he does in *Twenty-Seven*. It also serves better to explain his distracted, frenzied manner throughout the film. He is no mere comic grotesque but a harried human being about to crack under the strain of an impossible situation.

The script of the movie also humanizes Baby Doll and Vacarro as well as Archie Lee by explaining their motives a bit more fully than was called for in either of the two short plays from which they sprang. Baby Doll is attracted to Vacarro in the film because he treats her less and less like a child, which is Archie Lee's approach to her, and more and more like the young woman she really is. She responds to Vacarro's treatment of her by behaving with more maturity as the movie progresses, moreover, and acting less like a spoiled brat, which has always been her response to Archie Lee.

But it is Vacarro's character that is most changed for the better in the transfer from stage to screen, for in *Twenty-Seven* he was nothing more than a hardboiled and sadistic ruffian taking his revenge out on the wife of the man who had wronged him. In the movie, on the other hand, Vacarro is primarily interested in getting Baby Doll to provide him with testimony which he can use against Archie Lee is a court of law, and not in seducing her—although he enjoys teasing Archie Lee into suspecting that he has been cuckolded. (This conception of Vacarro is more in keeping with the personality which Williams created for him

Karl Malden, Carroll Baker, and Eli Wallach in *Baby Doll*.

in an early draft of the story that was to become *Twenty-Seven Wagons Full of Cotton:* a wiry young man flicking a whip playfully at a girl with whom is trying to engratiate himself.) The film also makes Vacarro more sympathetic, relatively speaking, than he was in the play by emphasizing the hostility of which he is the target because he is a foreigner in a remote country area where all outsiders are looked upon with suspicion and coldness. Such a person easily becomes a cool and calculating opportunist in retaliation for this sort of community rejection; yet Vacarro's sympathies are awakened by the plight of Aunt Rose whom he views as another outsider like himself, and he accordingly treats her with a consideration and kindness that shames Archie Lee and the rest of her in-laws.

Given the softening of the characters of Archie Lee, Baby Doll, and Vacarro in the transition from play script to screenplay, it is logical that the ending of the movie is more promising, even benign, than was that of either one-acter. *Twenty-Seven Wagons Full of Cotton* concludes with the prospect of the heroine having to continue to submit to Vacarro's sadistic sexual inclinations; and *The*

Unsatisfactory Supper ends with Aunt Rose simply abandoned to the elements, literally gone with the wind, along with the genteel society of which she was a last worn-out relic.

In the film's finale Archie Lee becomes hysterical when Vacarro informs him that he has wheedled evidence of the arson from Baby Doll and suggests that he has coaxed other favors from her as well. Archie Lee runs around the property drunkenly firing off his shotgun wildly and indiscriminately, and is finally hauled off by the sheriff to spend the night in jail. Vacarro gallantly offers to take Aunt Rose in as his housekeeper and Baby Doll decides to leave Archie Lee for Vacarro. (Since her May–December marriage to Archie Lee was never consummated, it will not be difficult for her to obtain an annulment.)

"We only shot one ending, though we worked out several on paper," Kazan recalls. While Williams was on the set he had tried to find a strong curtain line for the film but could come up with nothing really compelling. After he had left town, however, he sent Kazan the last bit of dialogue by mail. "He came up with that wonderful last line which Baby Doll speaks to the old lady and we had the perfect ending for the picture." When Aunt Rose asks Baby Doll if she thinks that Vacarro will make good his promise to return to them both in the morning, she answers, "We've got nothing to do but wait for tomorrow to see if we're remembered or forgotten."

Granted that the ending of the film is purposely ambiguous, since the audience never learns whether Vacarro comes back for the two women or not, the conclusion does reflect a note of hope and optimism that is nowhere in sight in either of the two more somber source plays. Baby Doll's encounter with Vacarro has in any event given her a new lease on life. Her brush with the tough adult world which he represents (as opposed to the childish existence which she has led with Archie Lee, an overgrown boy like Mitch in *Streetcar*) has been a sobering experience for her which will enable her to cope better than she otherwise would have with whatever the future has in store for her and Aunt Rose—even if the future takes the form of their both staying on with a very much chastened Archie Lee.

Kazan and Williams's tinkering with the ending of *Baby Doll* right up to the moment that it was shot points up the difference between the script for *Baby Doll* and that of *Streetcar*. The latter was a polished piece of work which was shot very closely to the way that it had been played in the theater, whereas the screenplay of *Baby Doll* was an amalgam of two separate short plays which was in a much less finished state when it went before the cameras. "*Baby Doll* was somewhat made up as we went along and it needed all the color that location shooting could bring to it," says Kazan. "We didn't have the same kind of firm script for *Baby Doll* that we had for *Streetcar*. I like *Baby Doll* very much, but it needed the kind of environmental support that came from location work; *Streetcar* didn't."

Kazan had learned a lesson in making *Pinky* in 1949 that not even a resourceful director could make the studio back lot look like an authentic Southern backwoods setting. So he took his cast and crew to Benoit, Mississippi, to shoot the bulk of the picture in a location that would lend the film the genuine sense of place which he thought it required. "The amount of location work that I did on *Baby Doll* was not extraordinary for the time that it was made," he told me. "I had done several pictures on location by then. I did, however, make an extra effort on that film to use local people of the town in the picture. I liked them; I found them charming. I even gave some speaking parts, such as that of the sheriff, to townspeople. The extensive location work on *Baby Doll* gave a social context to the film that *Streetcar* didn't have, because the environment is much more stressed, much more particularized."

Kazan feels, therefore, that *Baby Doll* is the film in which he has best portrayed Black characters. He hired members of the Black community of the town to play the old Black retainers on the delapidated Meighan plantation who laugh indulgently at Archie Lee's shenanigans to save his property from the finance company and his wife from Vacarro.

The crumbling mansion which Baby Doll inhabits with Archie Lee recalls Blanche DuBois's Belle Reve, and its disheveled state reflects the decay of the archaic Old South with its irrational resistance to modern industrial innovations, represented in the film by Vacarro and his plantation syndicate. Archie Lee's destruction of one corporation-owned cotton gin will not halt the industrial revolution engulfing small time landowners like himself any more than it will save his own fortunes; but it is a measure of his die-hard allegiance to the outdated agrarian society of the ante-bellum South that he thinks that somehow it will. Kazan is right, consequently, in saying that the plot of *Baby Doll* has a strong social frame of reference in which the more personal story of the principals is told, and that this social framework was enhanced by shooting the film in Mississippi.

The director with his cast and crew of sixty arrived in Benoit in November, 1955, and swelled the population of the town to an even five hundred. "At first we were received warily," he remarked in *The New York Times* when he returned to the East. "They were on their guard. But you know a lot of human differences are solved when people are thrown together. People really basically want to be liked." The director and the actors, Karl Malden (Archie Lee), Carroll Baker (Baby Doll), and Mildred Dunnock (Aunt Rose), went around getting acquainted by having dinner in the homes of local residences and attending weddings and other celebrations. "Mildred Dunnock could have been elected mayor; they adored her. We got more open-heartedness, more genuine hospitality there than in any location I've worked at." One day Kazan called for a mule for use in a scene and one of the locals appeared a few minutes later with not one but three animals so that the director could take his pick. On the chilly night when Kazan filmed the burning down of the barn housing Vacarro's cotton gin, the whole town turned out to root for the actors and crew.

"Kazan knows how to use a location," says Boris Kaufman, who photographed the picture. "I never saw a conventional or uninspired staging. Once you had his confidence you felt free. He welcomed and appreciated my visual conception and the climate I tried to convey by lighting and composition." One day when they were shooting an exterior, the sky was a baby blue which would have photographed as too cheerful a background for the shot. To avoid this Kaufman used a filter which gave the sky a more heavy, menacing feeling. "I told Kazan that it involved the risk of a retake, coming back to the same location if it didn't work. He accepted the risk without hesitation. Fortunately it worked and the filter blended perfectly, leaving a sliver of white along the horizon."

After ten weeks of location work in and around Benoit, Kazan and company returned to New York with eighty percent of the movie in the can. They completed the balance of the picture with three weeks of shooting interiors at the old Warner Brothers Vitagraph Studio in Flatbush in February, 1956. In the late afternoon of the last day of shooting, everyone assembled on the set for a group picture. "You feel so wedded to a crew," Kazan was heard to say. "It's one of the strongest bonds I know."

His actors and technicians felt the same way about working with him. Boris Kaufman remembers that Kazan had the habit of using the same kind of "telegraphic code of semi-orders" in dealing with both cast and crew in order to challenge the artist in question to do the best that he can on his own before the director makes comments and suggestions. Eli Wallach, who worked for Kazan on the stage in Williams's *Camino Real* as well as in *Baby Doll*, which was his first film, bears out Kaufman's observation: "Kazan is magical in imbuing the actor with a great sense of self discovery. He plants the directorial seed in the actor's mind and then reaps the harvest of a good performance." Wallach recalls Kazan telling him before the cameras rolled on the scene in which Vacarro was making lemonade in the plantation kitchen for Baby Doll, "Make the lemonade interestingly or I'll cut away from you." Comments Wallach, "All my creative resources were then called into play. Never has lemonade been made better!"

Kazan never seems to be at a loss for ways of eliciting the right reaction from a player. When Carroll Baker was called upon to break into tears in one scene and was unconvincing, Kazan recalls, "I was just on the verge of giving up. Then I thought of one last desperate effort to jog her into something, and furthermore she wanted to be jogged. So I said to her, 'Look, I just don't think you're able to do it.' And she burst into tears and never stopped. From then on I got all the takes I needed."

Karl Malden and Mildred Dunnock have both said that Kazan—and Williams, too, when he was on the set—encouraged a climate in which the actors could improvise a bit in the course of rehearsing a scene, but always in the framework of Williams's dialogue. Ms. Dunnock says that when she was discussing Aunt Rose's character with the author one day on the set he finally said, "Honey, I'm so sick of that old woman! You know her better than I do anyhow, so do anything you want to do with her."

While the technicians were lighting a scene Kazan would block out an upcoming scene with the actors, a practice which he had used while making *Streetcar*. While the company was working in the South, it was frequently warm enough to rehearse the scene in the backyard of the mansion which they were using for the film while the crew was preparing for a shot inside the house. Karl Malden has given interviewer Mike Steen an illustration of how the improvisational interplay of actors with director would work out in practice. During the shooting of the supper scene, just before Archie Lee explodes at Aunt Rose, Kazan set up a shot in which the huge old chandelier, a painful reminder of the house's bygone splendor and Archie Lee's lost affluence, would be visible in the frame. When Malden saw the composition of the shot, he suggested that he begin the scene by grabbing the little crystal ball at the base of the chandelier and having it come off in his hand as a visual indication of Archie Lee's precarious position at this point in the story: everything that he touches comes apart in his hands.

Some of the comic touches in the movie do not appear in the published script and were improvised on the spot. Many of them center around Archie Lee's efforts to hide his not-so-secret tippling from his young wife. Just as he is sneaking a drink from the bottle of whiskey which he keeps hidden in the bathroom medicine chest, Baby Doll happens in and he quickly begins to gargle with the liquor. Later, when the finance company is repossessing the furniture, Archie Lee reaches into the drawer of a bureau as two moving men carry it past him and pulls out a bottle of whiskey before they load the dresser onto their truck.

Asked to sum up his approach to directing *Baby Doll*, Kazan replied, "*Baby Doll* was directed and acted with the same kind of stylized realism that characterized *Streetcar*, and which, as I said before, seems to fit Williams's work so well. If you go down South you really won't find anyone acting quite the way that Williams's characters act. Heightened realism seems to go with the way that his lines are written."

This heightened realism was also visible in the setting and decor of the film, just as it was in the scenic design of *Streetcar*. The shabby old house which is the principal set of the movie is suitably squalid, and Kazan plays out the scenes there against the background of peeling wallpaper, falling plaster, battered furniture, and broken chandeliers, all of which visually symbolize how Archie Lee's life is falling to pieces around him.

There are some other fine visual metaphors in the film, such as the shot of Baby Doll seen through the bannister bars on the staircase as she clutches the railing. When I suggested to the director that this image was a reminder of the

Elia Kazan (right) directing Carroll Baker and Karl Malden in a scene set in the squalid mansion in *Baby Doll*.

crib in which the immature girl still sleeps, he replied that "photographing Baby Doll through the bannister implied to me that she was holding on to something all the time. It never occurred to me at the time that this was a symbolic image of her in a crib, but it seems plausible."

Other images recall that Archie Lee is really too old for Baby Doll, most notably when he is taken away by the sheriff at the end, a beaten man. He is looking plaintively out of the sheriff's car window at the camera and then hangs his head in despair, exposing the bald spot on his pate which Baby Doll had always enjoyed taunting him about.

What is Kazan's own assessment of the movie? "I like *Baby Doll* very much and Tennessee Williams has said at one time or another that he does too. But making films is not a horse race—it's for critics to say this film is better than that one, not for the people who made them. I think of *Baby Doll* as a quiet little black comedy and I have never been able to understand what all the fuss was about at the time of its release."

Seeing the movie today, it is hard to believe that it stirred up a controversy, next to which the one that surrounded the release of *Streetcar* pales in comparison. Neither Kazan nor Williams anticipated any serious objections to the picture, especially when it was passed by the MPAA Code Commission, now headed by Joseph Breen's successor, Geoffrey Shurlock, who had called *Streetcar* a landmark film. Shurlock promulgated a more flexible Production Code in December of 1956, and *Baby Doll* had been granted a seal of approval in the fall of that year under the provisions of the old Code of 1930. (Hence *Baby Doll* remains one of Williams's favorite films because, as he says, it escaped being tampered with by the censors and was released without cuts or alterations of any kind, exactly as he had written it and Kazan had directed it.)

Both writer and director were amazed, therefore, when the Legion of Decency condemned the movie on November 28, 1956, just prior to its December opening in New York, as "morally repellant in both theme and treatment." Kazan replied to the Legion decision, "I made *Baby Doll* as I saw it. I did the best I could to get on film what I felt in the South. Not the way things should be, not the way they will be some day, but the way they appeared to me there and then. I wasn't trying to be moral or immoral, only truthful."

Because Kazan had formed his own independent production company to make the movie and was only using Warner Brothers's distribution facilities to release the film, he was in a better bargaining position with Warners on *Baby Doll* than he had been in the case of *Streetcar* and could insist that the studio not offer to make cuts in the movie to seek a more benign rating from the Legion of Decency. Besides, the intransigent tone of the published Legion statement did not seem to leave any room for bargaining anyhow.

But the matter did not end just with this stalemate. In an unprecedented action Francis Cardinal Spellman, Archbishop of New York, mounted the pulpit of St. Patrick's Cathedral in Manhattan on Sunday, December 16, 1956, to denounce the motion picture as a corruptive influence on American society. His action was unprecedented because the Cardinal rarely preached at Sunday Mass and when he did it was usually to comment on something of national or international importance such as the jailing of Josef Cardinal Mindszenty by the Communist government of Hungary a few years earlier. The release of *Baby Doll* hardly seemed to be in the same league with the kind of crises to which the Cardinal usually addressed himself in his infrequent appearances in the pulpit of St. Patrick's Cathedral.

Therefore, the very fact that Cardinal Spellman chose the film as a topic of one of his rare sermons led a large segment of the Catholic population to assume

Mildred Dunnock as Aunt Rose in *Baby Doll*.

that the film posed a threat to American life of truly epic proportions. Following Cardinal Spellman's lead, other bishops in the country advised their flocks not only to stay away from *Baby Doll* but to threaten exhibitors with a six-month boycott of any theater which showed the film. The American Civil Liberties took this occasion to protest that such a boycott could "threaten a theater's existence and may deny to other groups within the community a chance to see films of their choice."

"When Cardinal Spellman denounced the film, I couldn't imagine what he was going on about," says Kazan today. "I gave a newspaper interview in which I suggested that he hadn't seen the film, and I had him dead to rights because he had to admit that he had not. He was simply quoting some assistant of his who had." Kazan responded to Cardinal Spellman that he believed that in this country people make judgments on matters of thought and taste for themselves: "That's the way it should be. It's our tradition and our practice. In the court of public opinion I'll take my chances." Bishop James Pike, dean of the Episcopal Cathedral of St. John the Divine in New York, expressed himself in a similar vein when he referred to the film in his sermon on December 23.

When he was asked for a response to the Cardinal, Tennessee Williams answered by saying that, while he did not wish to reply aggressively, "I would like to say that as I wrote *Baby Doll* I was not conscious of writing anything that corresponded to the terms he has used against it. I don't think that it has any corrupting influence on audiences." He continued, "I cannot believe that an ancient and august branch of the Christian faith is not larger in heart and mind than those who set themselves up as censors of a medium of expression that reaches all sections and parts of our country and extends the world over."

Once Cardinal Spellman had denounced the picture, the British press was interested in seeing what the Catholic Film Institute, at that time the English counterpart to the American Legion of Decency, would say about *Baby Doll*. Father John Burke, the amiable Irishman who was head of the CFI in those days, recalls that "several journalists mentioned in their columns that they had all sat next to me at the press screening, which of course was impossible. They claimed to have talked to me personally about the film and most of them hadn't. As a matter of fact I found the movie a serious psychological study of the lives of some poor whites in the backwoods of the American South, and not a prurient picture at all."

Father Burke deemed that he was merely expressing his personal opinion about the movie and did not consider himself as directly taking issue with Cardinal Spellman. Yet newspapers carried headlines like, "Is *Baby Doll* immoral? Cardinal Spellman says 'Yes' and Father Burke says 'No!' " "What I had actually said was that I considered *Baby Doll* a powerful denunciation of social and racial intolerance, and as such was something that thoughtful people should see."

But not many thoughtful people did go and see *Baby Doll*, at least in this country, where *Variety* reported that the movie received only four thousand domestic bookings, about one quarter of the potential playdates of a Hollywood movie in the United States, though it did better in some countries abroad. *Baby Doll* has never been shown on national television in America, and a legend even grew up in the Sixties that there were no longer any prints of the movie in existence. Not only is there a print officially stored in the Film Archive of the Library of Congress in Washington, which I have screened, but the movie is actually available for rental in 16mm from Charlon Productions in New York City.

"If you see *Baby Doll* today, now that the controversy has long since died down," says Kazan, "you can see that it is a charming black comedy, poetic and funny, and that is all that it ever was." In comparing *Streetcar* and *Baby Doll* he adds, "Neither is a sentimental film. The issues are not oversimplified and you're not rooting for somebody; there is no hero or heroine. The people are people, with both faults and virtues. Therefore for a while you are muddled about them, the way you would be in life."

It is probably because the characters presented in *Baby Doll* are portrayed as complex human beings rather than as clearly defined good people or bad people that the movie, like *Streetcar*, unsettled those who tried to analyze its moral stance according to any preconceived standards. As I mentioned in treating *Streetcar*, Hollywood in the Fifties was not willing to recognize as a permanent policy governing the making and merchanidising of motion pictures the distinction between adult and family film fare, and to accept the fact that a film that was not suitable for children could provide mature entertainment for what Fr. Burke called the thoughtful moviegoer.

Although Hollywood did not come up with a viable system of film classification until 1968, Williams had said more than a decade earlier that he believed that a film like *Baby Doll* could have avoided all the fuss that was made over it if it had been "forbidden to adolescents—to anyone under the age of sixteen." Said the author of *Baby Doll*, "I like the idea of limiting films to certain age groups. It's practiced in England." Although *Baby Doll* was shown in a cut version in some locations in America with an "Adults Only" label tacked on by Warner Brothers, the film never received the benefit of a uniform and official system of classification in its distribution in the United States. To that extent it was too far ahead of its time.

Even in 1956 some reviewers recognized the artistic worth of the movie. Drama critic Henry Hewes recorded in *The Saturday Review* that he saw the picture as a thought provoking work typical of Williams's stage pieces. "He abhors phony resolutions; he believes that we all go to our graves wondering. He has no answers; he refuses to sit in judgment on people."

Film critic Arthur Knight, writing in the same issue of *The Saturday Review*, pointed out the very same ambiguities of character and theme in the movie which Hewes found challenging to the viewer. "Williams's Southerners are presented frankly for what they are: simple, lustful, and crude. The script makes no effort to reward the good and punish the wicked. . . . *Baby Doll* is presented as another chapter in the human comedy, sketched with considerable amusement, some sympathy, and a tremendous gusto for authentic detail." Knight found that Kazan had exhibited the same detached attitude toward his material in directing the movie as Williams had in writing it. "If he has any strong personal conviction about these people, any private resentment or objection to their way of life, it is kept well hidden." In effect, both writer and director leave the audience to draw their own conclusions about the characters portrayed in the picture. As Kazan put it, "I wasn't trying to be moral or immoral, only truthful."

What, then, were the aspects of the movie that were the target for moral criticism when the picture was released? Fundamentally there was only one scene in the film that was usually singled out by those who reacted negatively to the movie: that in which Vacarro teases Baby Doll into admitting that Archie Lee burned down his barn and cotton gin. But this scene in which Vacarro toys with Baby Doll's affections throughout a long and languid afternoon is ultimately a comic interlude in the movie. It is true that Baby Doll is flattered by the attentions of this handsome, suave foreigner; but it is also true that Vacarro's principal interest in the girl is to engratiate himself with her to the point where she will sign the affadavit that will empower him to have Archie Lee indicted for arson.

They engage in a game of cat-and-mouse that takes them from the yard into the house and up to the attic where Vacarro finally corners Baby Doll and forces her to sign the paper. She does so, not because he has titillated her sexually, as Jack Vizzard contends in his book on censorship, *See No Evil,* but because Vacarro has trapped her in the attic where the rotten floor boards are beginning to give way beneath the weight of her body while he watches safely from the doorway. Trembling, she scrawls her signature on the paper which he has extended to her on a plank, and when he retreives it he kisses the document warmly. Baby Doll is keenly disappointed that there is no kiss for her and asks, "Is that *all* you wanted?" "You're a child, Mrs. Meighan," he answers. "That's why we played hide-and-seek, a game for children."

Exhausted by the exertions of the afternoon, Vacarro takes a nap in Baby Doll's crib, which is one of the few pieces of furniture that has not yet been carted off by the finance company. Baby Doll tucks Vacarro in and he falls asleep, and some moviegoers assumed that Vacarro seduced Baby Doll in the crib after the fade-out—a most implausible inference when one considers the dimensions of the crib! In discussing this scene with Michel Ciment, Kazan said that he never thought that anything did happen between Baby Doll and Vacarro while Vacarro was lying in the crib because "I think he was more interested actually in business, in getting revenge on her husband, than in having anything to do with her." Vacarro does admit to Archie Lee later, however, an incipient attraction for Baby Doll, now that he no longer thinks of her solely in terms of his legal action against her husband; "but nothing has been rushed."

Kazan uses visual images in *Baby Doll* in the same manner that he employed them in *Streetcar:* to telegraph sexual implications to the alert and sophisticated viewer; but this kind of artistic indirection was not as readily accepted as appropriate in the later film as it was in the first, though it is equally valid in both movies.

The director employs visual symbols to suggest Baby Doll's gradual sexual awakening as she takes her first steps toward maturity in the company of a man who treats her increasingly like a young lady and not like a little girl as Archie Lee continues to do. The gap between Vacarro's virility and that of the older Archie Lee is illustrated when the sultry Italian vigorously pumps water for Baby Doll from the pump in the yard which is never as obliging to Archie Lee. The same point is made when one juxtaposes the shot of Vacarro playfully astride Baby Doll's rocking horse in one scene with Archie Lee's rusty old rifle collapsing in his hands in another. "Caught in cold print the symbolism comes over as obvious," comments George Brandt. "But it is visual and not conceptual, and it is intended to be funny."

Furthermore, some of the images in the movie were taken to have a sexual intent when they did not. Baby Doll's sucking her thumb and licking an ice cream cone were not meant to depict the young girl's subconscious longing for fellatio, as some critics maintained, but to show, as Kazan himself says, that "she's still a baby. She's not grown up. That's all I had in mind: arrested development." In the course of the movie, under Vacarro's influence, she begins to move from her state of arrested adolescence and grope toward growing up. Surely this is a legitimate theme for a motion picture.

My own judgment on the furor over *Baby Doll* is that much of the controversy over the movie would have been seen to be largely irrelevant if censors, critics, and public alike would have recognized that the picture is more of a comedy than a drama. In that event, they would not have taken the whole movie so seriously. "*Baby Doll* was just a comedy," Williams has said more than once. The script has "a wanton hilarity to it, in my opinion." As I shall have occasion to note with other Williams works like *Period of Adjustment* and *The Seven Descents of Myrtle*, the humorous dimension of his plays is not readily recognized because of the serious subtratum that always underlies his writings. This is certainly the case with *Baby Doll*, in which Williams injects the delicate question of a young woman's emotional growth and the pathetic problems of an old woman into an otherwise knockabout farce. And it is certainly true of *The Rose Tattoo*, to which we turn in the next chapter. Perhpas the term which Williams devised to characterize two of his one-act plays when they were produced on Broadway in 1966 could be extended to describe works like *Baby Doll* and *Rose Tattoo*: slapstick tragedies.

The creative association of Williams and Kazan was to continue in the theater, but they have never again collaborated on a film. This is a great pity since two of the very best movies on which either of them have worked are the two which they made together. They continue to nurture a mutual respect and friendship, however. When I inquired of Kazan how he felt about working with Williams, he answered, "When you are working with a fine playwright you use what he gives you and don't juggle his material. You're his servant. Nor do you do it when you are filming the work of an author whom you esteem. And of course I certainly esteem the work of Tennessee Williams."

Asked how he felt about Kazan, Williams replied without hesitation, "I had the great good fortune to work with Kazan when he had just reached the height of his directorial powers. He is still a first-rate director. He exercises a phenomenal rapport with actors and with the most difficult of playwrights. He has never felt any envy of the writer's role, certainly not to the extent that he has ever tried to impose his own interpretation on the work which he is directing. In the days when we made our two films together we were all the victims of censorship. He suffered as much as I did from the pressures of the censors because he respected the integrity of my work. I hope to work with Kazan again."

One can only hope that he will.

3
James Wong Howe:
The Rose Tattoo and *This Property is Condemned*

"*THE ROSE TATTOO* is a play that was so accurate and beautiful an exposition of the Italian temperament," Dakin Williams writes in his book about his brother Tennessee, "that even Sicilians who attended the play were speechless in their admiration. 'How could an American write such a truly Sicilian play?' they asked. The answer lay in my brother's deepest and truest friend and companion for many years until his death from lung cancer in 1963, Frank Merlo." A Sicilian by birth, Frank Merlo gave Tennessee Williams most of the inspiration that he needed to write the play, says Dakin Williams, by helping the playwright to understand the Italian people among whom they travelled in the winter of 1949. The play is aptly dedicated, therefore, "To Frank, in return for Sicily."

In it Williams tried to capture "the vital humanity and love of life expressed by the Italian people." The Italians, he found, "showed a different side of human nature than any I had ever known. I think Italians are like Southerners without their inhibitions. They're poetic, but they don't have any Protestant repressions. Or if they do have any, their vitality is so strong, it crashes through them. They live from the heat."

Williams settled down in Rome and worked on a play about a colony of Sicilian immigrants in the American South and also on a novella about an American expatriate actress living in Rome. The play would become *The Rose Tattoo* and the novella, which I will treat later, would evolve into *The Roman Spring of Mrs. Stone*. The setting of the play is a mythical village on the Gulf Coast between New Orleans and Mobile, and he wrote four drafts of the material before he was satisfied with it, while the working title went from *The Eclipse of*

May 29, 1919 through *Eclipse of the Sun* to *The Rose Tattoo*.

"What I am getting at in this play," he explained upon completing it, "is the warmth and sweetness of the Italian people" as he experienced it while living in their country. "If this is a warmer and happier play than anything I've written, it is because of that experience. I would not have missed putting these feelings into a play for anything in the world." Williams playfully warned that "if anyone mentions 'neurotic' in connection with this play, I'll reach for a gun"; but the fact remains that the lusty Italian matron who is the play's heroine does grow increasingly neurotic after the death of her husband and sinks into a prolonged period of despondency that reaches operatic proportions.

Like *Baby Doll* and other Williams works that possess a decidedly comic strain, *Rose* is not so much a comedy as a tragicomedy, a genre developed and practiced by Shakespeare late in his career with such plays as *Winter's Tale*. A tragicomedy in the Shakespearean sense is a play in which the playwright has concocted a situation which could easily lead to irreversible unhappiness for the principal characters if the action were to continue to develop according to the pattern that the author had set for it at the beginning. But the plot takes an unexpected turn for the better near the finale and works out happily, or at least hopefully, rather than tragically. As I suggested in dealing with *Baby Doll* in the preceding chapter, perhaps Williams's own term, slapstick tragedy, best describes plays like *Rose Tattoo* and *Period of Adjustment*, which mingle the stuff of potential tragedy with undeniably farcical material. In essence Williams asks us to laugh at a ridiculous situation while at the same time we recognize the characters' agonized involvement in the situation.

No critic would claim tragic stature for Serafina Delle Rose, the heroine of *Rose Tattoo*, as they might for Blanche DuBois, because Serafina's sorrowful situation is placed in a boisterously bawdy context for which Williams has written some of his funniest dialogue ever, and because her story ends on a decidedly positive note. Yet we do take Serafina and her plight seriously and care about her deeply.

Williams seemed to be aware that some theatergoers would say that this hapless widow's problems are simply not worth all of the histrionic fuss which he allows the lady to make over them, for he wrote a piece in *The New York Times* prior to the play's Broadway opening implicitly defending his new play in advance against such a charge. In it he reminds the potential playgoer that a work of art seeks to isolate critical moments in a character's life in order that universally valid human values may be extracted from the characters' particularized and personal circumstances. A person whose problems might seem trivial to us if we encountered them in the rat race of everyday living takes on greater significance when we take the time in the course of watching a play above them to examine how their plight reflects the human condition. Williams sees human beings as haunted by a truly awful sense of the impermanence of human existence; but "the timeless world of a play" is removed from the atmosphere of impermanence "which makes people *little* and their emotions fairly inconsequential."

What happens when the private world of a widow in a small fishing village is on the brink of being shattered to bits may not seem to have cosmic importance. Yet, the author continues, because that little world is all that she has, she becomes worthy of all of the compassion and concern with which the playwright can treat her. Other playwrights, Arthur Miller among them, have expressed similar views about the heroes and heroines of their plays, explaining that the lives of rather ordinary people can take on tragic importance when portrayed in a dramatic fashion which emphasizes the universal human significance implicit in their stories.

George Jean Nathan quite unfairly damned Williams's *Times* essay as pretentious rhetoric when it appeared, but he might have criticized Williams's subsequent explication of *Rose Tattoo* in *Vogue* more justly as being pretentious. In this piece Williams likens Serafina's deceased husband, Rosario Delle Rose, whose ashes Serafina keeps in an urn, to Dionysus, the Greek god of love and fecundity, who is in turn akin to Bacchus, the Roman god of wine and revelry. Williams makes clear in the play, as he does not in this article, the ludicrous gap between Rosario the man—who died in a scuffle with the police over the bootleg whiskey which he was illegally transporting in his banana truck, and who two-timed his wife for more than a year before his death—and Rosario the god, whom his widow has virtually deified since his death.

Yet in his *Vogue* essay the author almost seems to want the reader to accept Serafina's idealized view of Rosario, a view that is thoroughly discredited, even for her, by play's end. Williams writes that Rosario Delle Rose, like a god, is never seen in the play, but known indirectly through what others say about him. "He cannot be confined to memory nor an urn," says the author, and the true memorial to Rosario is his daughter Rosa, who has inherited his hot Latin blood. The play is therefore "the homely light of a kitchen candle burned in praise of a god. I prefer a play not to be a noose but a net with fairly wide meshes. So many of its instants of revelation are wayward flashes, not part of the plan of an author but struck accidentally off, and perhaps these are closest to being a true celebration of the inebriate god."

In spite of the Monday morning quarterbacking of which Williams is guilty in the *Vogue* article, the true theme of the play remains that which he announced when he wrote it. *The Rose Tattoo* is a tribute, not to any gods of classical mythology, but to the warmth, vitality, and especially the resilience of the Italian temperament as embodied particularly in Serafina. When she is crushed by learning about her husband's infidelity, she is rejuvenated by still another Sicilian truck driver, Alvaro Mangiacavallo (whose last name literally means "Eat a horse" and suggests his stallion-like virility), a happy-go-lucky if not terribly intelligent young man who offers Serafina "love and affection in a world that is lonely and cold." Alvaro helps to restore Serafina's native warmth and affection after her world had grown lonely and cold in the wake of her husband's demise and her subsequent disillusionment about him. ("Everybody is nothing until you love them," says Rosa in the play, a line which applies as much to Serafina as it does to Alvaro, and which is "the topic sentence of the play," as Philip Kolin points out in the critical anthology *Tennessee Williams: A Tribute*.)

Parallel to this main plot is the subplot involving Serafina's daughter Rose and her boyfriend, a young sailor named Jack Hunter. The interlacing of these two plot strands has been carefully worked out by Williams so that the outcome of the main plot largely determines the outcome of the subplot. Once Alvaro has softened Serafina's nature once more with his loving devotion, she is able to see that her daughter's love for Jack is genuine and to give the youngsters her blessing. There is little doubt about the mutual commitment of Rosa and Jack at the finale, but one wonders if Serafina will ever be able to love another man totally after her cruel disappointment in Rosario.

In any event, Serafina's love for Alvaro will necessarily be of a different kind than that which she nurtured for Rosario simply because the two men are entirely different in character. Rosario, though descended from Italian nobility, was a selfish, devious man; while Alvaro, though descended from a village idiot, is a generous, guileless person. The implication of the union of Serafina and Alvaro is that the immature younger man will doubtlessly allow the strong-willed older woman to dominate him in the way that she had dominated Rosa.

Some of Williams's strongest portraits of woman have been of mothers or mother figures whose maternal grip often brings anguish to all concerned, a gallery of ladies that ranges from Amanda Wingfield in *The Glass Menagerie* to Violet Venable in *Suddenly Last Summer*. T. E. Kalem, in reviewing Williams's *Memoirs* in *Time*, states that all of these indomitable females have their archetypal model in the playwright's mother Edwina Williams: "Self-willed and prone to fits of delusive grandeur, Ms. Edwina is the greatest single influence on Williams's life and work." Williams himself says that in one way or another she is in all of his plays, not just *The Glass Menagerie*, in which the parallel of Amanda and Edwina is most manifest. "She had the gift of gab," he said in discussing his *Memoirs* in *The Times*. "I must say she contributed a lot to my writing—her forms of expression, for example. I still find her totally mystifying—and frightening. It's best we stay away from our mothers." Williams, of course, never has.

Williams believes that his work has two limitations: structural weaknesses and overwriting. About the second point he has said, "I overdo symbols; they're the natural language of drama, but I use them excessively." But he also believes that "if things are powerfully directed and acted the purple writing becomes true."

If *The Rose Tattoo* has a strong enough structure in its two interwoven plot lines to escape one of his two prevailing faults, several commentators on *The Rose Tattoo* agree that he did succumb to the other, because the rose symbolism in the play is really belabored to a fault. Drama critic John Mason Brown said that in this play Williams had tried too hard to "say it with flowers," and went on to enumerate the incidence of rose symbols that permeate the play. When the curtain rises, Serafina is married to a man named Rosario Delle Rose, and has a daughter named Rosa. There is a bowl of roses on the table, rose-tinted paper on the walls, and Serafina is awaiting her husband's return from what turns out to be his last bootlegging run attired in a pale rose dress. She is wearing a rose in her hair and is carrying a fan with a rose painted on it. So much for the first scene.

As the play progresses we learn that Rosario had a rose tattooed on his chest and that the night on which Serafina conceived Rosa a burning rose appeared mystically on her own breast for a moment. Furthermore, Rosario's mistress, Estelle Hohengarten, has had a rose tattooed on her breast to please Rosario; and later Alvaro does the same thing to ingratiate himself with Serafina. At the final curtain Serafina again experiences the burning presence of the *rosa mystica* on her breast as a sign that she has once more conceived new life within her body.

Not since the War of Roses, concludes John Mason Brown, have roses been employed so incessantly as a symbol: "To Mr. Williams roses are mystical signs, proofs of passion, symbols of devotion, and buds no less than thorns in the flesh." Gilbert Maxwell suggests in his biography of Williams that the proliferation of roses everywhere in the play represents Williams's preoccupation, not to say obsession, with the tragedy of his sister's mental illness. In the play Rose's namesake, Rosa, finds a suitable Gentleman Caller to take her away from her domineering mother, something which never happened to Rose Williams in real life. Be that as it may, Williams is right in saying that "the purple writing" works if the play is powerfully staged and performed, because both the stage and screen versions of the play were blessed with strong casts.

Williams had exploited the extended metaphor of the rose in the play with painstaking care and consistency even if the symbolism surfaces too often in the work. The transference, as it were, of the rose from the dead Rosario's breast to Alvaro's implies the latter's attempt to identify with Serafina's deceased mate in order to replace him in her life. This reasoning is not lost on Serafina who is upset by Alvaro's premature attempt to fill the void left by the idolized Rosario in her heart. In addition, when Alvaro first comes courting her, he clumsily drops a contraceptive on the floor which infuriates Serafina even more. The night of Rosario's death she suffered a miscarriage, symbolizing that her union with the philandering Rosario had long since ceased to be fruitful. Hence Alvaro's contraceptive signals that her union with him will be sterile as well, and she rejects his intensions out of hand. By the final curtain, however, Serafina has passed on to Alvaro a rose-colored shirt which she made for Rosario and which he never lived to wear, indicating that she is at last ready to give to Alvaro the place once exclusively occupied in her heart by her deceased spouse. Also she feels new life stirring in her body, betokened by her sensing the mystical rose once more burning on her breast; and thus the carefully calculated rose symbolism of the play has come full circle.

There are some thematic metaphors in the play which are not quite as elaborately plotted but which are just as effective as the rose symbolism. Serafina keeps her husband's ashes in an urn as a tribute to his memory; but this also foreshadows how her worship of Rosario will turn to ashes when she discovers his infidelity. Serafina later smashes the urn as a gesture that she has liberated her affections, which have been bottled up in the vessel of ashes, and is now able to be receptive to Alvaro.

The other symbol that pervades the play is that of the statue of the Madonna before which stands a vigil light whose flickering flame implies Serafina's wavering religious faith. When she asks the Madonna for a sign to reaffirm her husband's fidelity to her and then finds the contrary to be true, she blows out the little fire, saying, "I don't believe in you, lady! You're just a poor little doll with the paint peeling off, and now I blow out the light and I forget you the way you forget Serafina." Later, however, after she comes to accept Alvaro as the answer to her prayers, she sets the vigil light before the statue burning again, and with that implies the rekindling of her faith.

So the play ends happily, confirming its status as a comedy, though one that has many tragic ingredients in it. Williams's taste for slapstick tragedy is most in evidence in the scene in which Flora and Bessie, two female clowns reminiscent of Laurel and Hardy, stop by Serafina's on their way to an American Legion convention to pick up a blouse which Serafina has made for one of them. (Their discussion of their prospects of meeting some eligible males at the convention amounts to a comic turn, and Williams later lifted these lines and expanded the situation into a one-act play entitled *A Perfect Analysis Given by a Parrot*.) Williams mingles tragedy with slapstick in this scene by having these two gossipy females, whom one at first dismisses as inconsequential characters, sow the first seeds of doubt in Serafina's mind about Rosario's deception. It is sometimes as hard in a Williams play, as it is in life itself, to separate elements of the serious and the comic, as this scene proves.

Ultimately this play is Williams's toast to the indestructability of the human spirit as concretized in general in the Italian temperament and in particular in Serafina. Williams had written the role for Italian actress Anna Magnani, but she declined to play it on the stage because she feared her English was not good enough to sustain her playing a long and difficult role; but she promised to play the part in the subsequent screen adaptation of the play.

Serafina was consequently created on Broadway by Maureen Stapleton, though at first Williams feared that she might be too young for the role. Ms. Stapleton went on to act in many Williams plays and movies, and has become one of Williams's favorite interpreters of his work. Eli Wallach, who played Alvaro, also became associated with Williams's work on stage and screen, most especially as Vacarro in *Baby Doll*.

The play had a respectable run of more than three hundred performances and producer Hal Wallis purchased the screen rights. He had first seen the play during its Chicago tryout in February, 1951, and went backstage at that time to open negotiations for making a film of the work, and asked Williams to collaborate on the screenplay. Williams agreed to do so, and he and screenwriter Hal Kanter worked on the adaptation of his Tony Award winning play for the movies. The dramatist had several script conferences with Wallis and the latter found his suggestions and revisions to be "invaluable in working out the final shooting script."

Then Williams went to Italy to bring Anna Magnani back to star in the film opposite Burt Lancaster as Alvaro. Williams and Frank Merlo coached Ms. Magnani in mastering her role in English as they sailed aboard the Andrea Doria back to the States. They used a special script which had been prepared for her, with the English version on one page and a literal Italian translation of it on the facing page. When the ship docked in New York, Ms. Magnani was word perfect in her role and went on to win an Academy Award as best actress of the year in this, her first English language film.

The film was made largely on location in Key West, Florida, which was sunnier than the Gulf Coast between New Orleans and Mobile where the story is officially set. The movie was directed by Daniel Mann, who had also directed the play in the theater, and photographed by the late James Wong Howe, one of the foremost cinematographers of all time, who also won an Oscar for his work on the picture.

Howe's Oscar for *Rose Tattoo* brings into relief the fact that his recognized skill as a veteran cinematographer was a stronger creative influence on some of the films which he photographed than that of the directors with whom he worked, and I would hazard that this is the case with both *The Rose Tattoo* and the other movie treated in this chapter, *This Property is Condemned*. The men who directed these two films were both relatively new to the film medium at the time that the two pictures were made, and neither had the experience of Howe or could match the imposing accomplishments of Howe's track record for movie making, which dated back to 1922. That is why I shall emphasize Howe's creative contribution to these two films more than that of the two directors involved.

By carefully lighting the sets and choosing appropriate camera angles, the cinematographer makes a major contribution to the creating of the proper "look" for a film. Howe's basic orientation was always toward giving the films which he photographed an authentically realistic look. He accomplished this by, among other things, natural source lighting; that is, by having the light in a given scene seem to be coming from whatever source would normally produce it in real life: a window in a daylight interior scene, a lamp at night. For Howe, who died in 1976 only a year after completing his last film, no detail was too trivial to be considered when setting up a shot. Everything in a shot, he always maintained, either adds to or detracts from the total atmosphere which the cameraman is striving to build up in the picture. In *The Rose Tattoo* Howe's limpid black-and-white photography transcended the physical detail of the small town locale and of Serafina's home to embody in compelling images the feeling of inner loneliness and longing which she feels after the loss of her revered husband. In effect he went beyond the surface of the story to its very soul.

And this is also true of the way that the sharp eye of Howe's camera encompasses all the details of Serafina's unkempt appearance in order to suggest the disordered frame of mind in which she has existed since her husband's death and her discovery of his infidelity. As Ertem Asral writes in her unpublished thesis on the stage and screen versions of Williams's plays, "Since she is brought closer to the audience by the camera, Serafina's slovenliness during her self-sentenced exile becomes more shocking in the movie than it was on the stage. A close-up reveals her sweat-stained dress, which is too tight for her ungirdled body and unbuttoned in the back so that her damp, crumpled slip is exposed. Part of her hair is pinned up; the rest hangs loose. After her first encounter with the truth, the truth that she vehemently rejects, the camera photographs her grief, her panicky movements and her hysterical prayers. She appears distracted to the point of madness. Great shadows have appeared beneath her eyes; her face and throat gleam with sweat."

But Howe was never a devotee of realism to the point of rejecting symbolic images in his work when they were called for by the script. An important visual metaphor which he developed in his lighting of *The Rose Tattoo* centered around the conflict between light and darkness in the story. The bright sunlight of the exteriors, which represents the warm, exuberant vitality of the Sicilian villagers, is contrasted with the murky shadows of the interiors in Serafina's home, which represent the deathly cold, melancholy turn which her temperament has taken in her excessively prolonged mourning over the loss of Rosario.

"The dark, shadowy atmosphere of the house was achieved by low-key lighting, which gives a scene a kind of dusky illumination," Howe explained to me. "I have used low-key lighting so often that I became known in the industry as 'Low-Key' Howe. In the scenes between Serafina and her daughter I would let the light fall directly on Rosa so that she would look fresh and young; but I lighted her mother more indirectly so that she had a darker, more shadowy look since she was older and had seen more of life." The sequence in which Rosa brings Jack Hunter to meet Serafina for the first time bears out this lighting

Anna Magnani and Burt Lancaster in the courting scene of *The Rose Tattoo*.

pattern. Rosa opens the drawn drapes to let in the sunlight, but it is shed only on the two youngsters, while the self-pitying Serafina remains steadfastly sitting in the shadows, ignoring their attempts to cheer her up.

This light–darkness motif is maintained when Alvaro, who is several years younger than Serafina, comes courting. The first time he visits her home he throws the shutters open to brighten the room, an early indication that he will be a source of sunlight and warmth in her life.

Serafina's withdrawal from the world outside her little cottage and her resistance of any attempts on the part of others to make her rejoin the human race demand that the film take place largely within the confines of her self-imposed prison as it did in the play. Therefore any efforts to open out the play with location scenes are kept to a minimum and generally involve characters other than Serafina. For example, the movie depicts the exciting episode in which Rosario drives his truck through the police barricade which has been set up to capture him while he is in possession of his illegal cargo. The police pursue him and open fire, sending his truck careening off the road and into a ditch where it bursts into flame.

Howe photographs the crash and explosion of the truck from the foot of the embankment, and he holds the shot while the police survey the wreckage of the truck, along with the cases of bootleg whiskey and the decoy boxes of bananas that are strewn about and are still visible in the flickering light of the flames—a perfect employment by Howe of natural-source lighting.

In other location scenes Rosa and Jack are pictured as meeting at a school dance and later spending the day at the beach, both of which scenes are referred to in the play's spoken exposition. The function of this location material is not just to remind the audience that they are watching a movie and not a play, but to show the whole expanse of youthful experience that Serafina would selfishly deny her daughter by keeping her cooped up in the house with her and the bottle of Rosario's ashes that Serafina has morbidly set up as a sort of shrine to her deceased husband.

As Billy Wilder points out in the introduction of this book, sometimes a playwright himself might have opened up a play for the screen had he not been straightjacketed by the format imposed by the theater's procenium arch. Thus in *Rose Tattoo* Serafina leaves her retreat on two occasions in the course of the film, in circumstances in which Williams would have very likely had her do so in the play as well, were he not committed to using only her home and its immediate environs for his stage setting.

In the first instance she attends a church bazaar in the hope of cornering her parish priest and extorting from him whether or not Rosario had ever confided in him about his extra-marital affairs. Serafina becomes hysterical when the priest refuses kindly but firmly to devulge information about matters pertaining to the Confessional, and Alvaro intervenes and takes her home to calm her down. This way of handling Alvaro's first chance meeting with Serafina is infinitely more credible than the awkward device that Williams was forced to employ in the play, whereby Alvaro has a traffic accident near Serafina's house and follows the other participant, a traveling salesman, to her front porch after the salesman leaves the scene of the accident.

The other time when Serafina leaves the house in the film is to go to a seedy gambling casino where Estelle Hohengarten, Rosario's mistress, is a blackjack dealer, in order extract the truth about her relationship with the dead Rosario

Ben Cooper and Marisa Pavan in *The Rose Tattoo*.

from her. This confrontation is accomplished by telephone in the play and hence does not strike nearly as many dramatic sparks as does the casino scene in the film. The earthy Estelle (who is no more the ethereal being that her name implies than the similarly named Stella was in *Streetcar*) opens her blouse to reveal the rose which she had tattooed on her breast to celebrate her devotion to Rosario. Needless to say, Serafina (who is not the celestial being that her name, which refers to one of the angelic choirs, implies), has to be restrained from throttling Estelle.

These and other revisions of the play came out of Williams's script conferences with Hal Wallis, and both men had reason to be pleased with the results on the screen. Wallis remembers having very few of the usual "producer-author" differences of opinion with the playwright.

There are some revisions of the play reflected in the finished film which do not involve opening out the play with additional location work, but rather opening up the play with richer visual imagery in order to enhance the thematic meaning of the story. At the beginning of the film there is a scene in which Serafina begs the silent Rosario not to go out on his run that evening but to stay at home with her because she has just learned that she is pregnant. Rosario lies languidly in the shadows where his face is never visible, though the rose tattoo can be seen gleaming on his chest. It is important that the audience never see what Rosario really looks like if they are to accept Serafina's image of him as an exotic and godlike figure in the earlier stages of the film. He must remain wrapped in the misty aura of enchantment which Serafina has evoked for him until she—and we—find out otherwise. Thanks to Howe's low-key lighting, that is just how Rosario appears in this scene.

Closely associated with Rosario in the film is the player piano in Serafina's living room, which bursts into a joyous rendition of "The Shiek of Araby" at the least provocation. This lighthearted song recalls the gaiety of Serafina's bygone days when she cherished her relationship with Rosario. When Alvaro tries to liven up their first date by switching on the piano, therefore, Serafina quickly shuts it off to keep it from intruding on the atmosphere of mourning which she has maintained since her husband's death. Besides, the song points up that Alvaro is no "Shiek of Araby" à la Rudolph Valentino, as Serafina has always fancied Rosario to be; and she does not want to be reminded that Alvaro in her mind represents quite a comedown from Rosario.

At the close of the picture, however, she equivalently accepts Alvaro as the replacement of Rosario in her home and heart by not only giving him Rosario's rose colored shirt but also by turning on the piano to play the tune in Alvaro's honor. They laugh boisterously together while the spirited music plays and she invites him to stay a while "to go on with our conversation." This is her way of saying that they have at last learned to communicate with one another. In accepting Alvaro as he is, she is implicitly admitting that if the boyish and clumsy Alvaro is no Latin lover such as the song praises, neither was the tawdry and deceptive Rosario.

The implication of the film's conclusion, like that of the play's ending, suggests that, now that Rosa has gone off with Jack with Serafina's blessing, Serafina will probably turn to mothering Alvaro in Rosa's stead. But since Alvaro is really an adolescent at heart, he is probably searching for a mother figure as much as for a wife anyhow. In a sense, then, the pair deserve each other.

In adapting *Rose Tattoo* to the screen, Williams found that he had to concede to making only minor adjustments to mollify the censors, even though the screenplay follows the bawdy dialogue of the original play very closely. Even the *double entendres* about both Rosario and Alvaro's principal cargo being king-sized bananas are left intact. One noticeable change in the story line which was necessitated by the Production Code was the removal of the suggestion that

10207-87

Burt Lancaster sporting a rose-colored shirt and a rose tattoo.

Serafina and Alvaro sleep together after Serafina is convinced of Rosario's unfaithfulness to her. The film elides over this possibility by having Alvaro get drunk and pass out on Serafina's living room rug instead of accompanying her to her bedroom.

Two other changes in the script were made to forestall the possibility of difficulties with the Legion of Decency. The first involved shortening Serafina's statement of disappointment in the Virgin, which I have already quoted from the play, to this terse remark which still retains the flavor of her original feelings: "I

Anna Magnani approving of her daughter's new-found love (Marisa Pavan and Ben Cooper). *Rose Tattoo*.

wanted help but who helped me! Alright, I blow out the candle!" The film makers probably need not have worried about the original line of dialogue, since it is as clear in the movie as it is in the play that Serafina's faith in the Blessed Mother is reconfirmed when she ultimately accepts Alvara Mangiacavallo as the answer to her prayers.

The other change in the play script that was incorporated into the film with a view of heading off objections from the Legion might also have caused difficulties with the Code because it involved the unsympathetic treatment of the priest in the original story; and the Code has this to say on that subject: "The reason why ministers of religion may not be portrayed as comic characters or as villains so as to cast disrespect on religion is simply because the attitude taken toward them may easily become the attitude taken toward religion in general. Religion is lowered in the minds of the audience because of the lowering of the audience's respect for a minister."

The specific case in point is the cold and narrow-minded attitude of Serafina's parish priest, Father De Leo, toward having Rosario's remains cremated and kept in an urn. It is not the priest's insistence that Serafina's plan is against Church law (although in point of fact it no longer is) that might have bothered the Code Commission and the Legion, but the totally high-handed and unsympathetic way in which Father De Leo confronts Serafina on the subject. Serafina's family doctor entreats the priest in the play to be more understanding: "Father De Leo, you love your people but you don't understand them. They find God in each other. And when they lose each other, they lose God and they're lost. And it's hard to help them."

As Asral notes, there is no need for the doctor's speech in the movie and it is accordingly eliminated—simply because Father De Leo in the film, while not changing his position on cremation, nonetheless states it with a compassion and consideration for Serafina which he completely lacks in the stage version. And the same can be said of his later gentle refusal, which is no less firm, to discuss Rosario's confessions to him with Rosario's widow. In any event, Williams was very likely closer to the truth in the play in portraying the local parish priest of a small village to be paternalistic as well as paternal, but such a genuinely realistic portrait of a clergyman in similar circumstances would not appear on the screen until Trevor Howard's brilliant portrayal of the village priest in David Lean's *Ryan's Daughter* almost a decade later.

When the film was released, movie critics were as unsettled by Williams's mixture of slapstick and tragedy as theater critics had been. Andrew Sarris was typical of this point of view and when he declared that only the imcomparable Anna Magnani was capable of maintaining the integrity of her performance as she tore a dramatic scene to tatters one instant and turned on a brilliant comic style the next. "The line between drama and farce is always very thin in a Williams play," Sarris wrote in *Film Culture*. "Williams has them separated in his mind, no doubt, but unless he has a director like Kazan to keep the line rigid, his scripts degenerate in the playing. Daniel Mann is still relatively new in the film medium, and although his direction shows some promise, he is still weak in developing a unified conception for his actors."

Still, to me Burt Lancaster is not far behind Magnani in giving a colorful performance that deftly leaps by turns from pathos to farce so that the on-screen performances of the co-stars mesh very well. Hal Wallis recalled for interviewer Mike Steen that the two co-stars got on very well off-screen too; but Williams wrote to his grandfather from Hollywood, where some of the interiors were being shot, that Magnani and Lancaster did clash on the set: "Anna Magnani and Burt Lancaster had their first fight on the set yesterday, as she was directing the scene and he didn't like it." According to Williams, Lancaster walked off the sound stage, and shooting resumed only after heated consultations. Williams expressed the wish that he could stay on as referee until the shooting was wrapped up, but he had to fly to New York to help Kazan cast the stage production of *Cat on a Hot Tin Roof*, which we will take up in the next chapter. "I shall just have to hope and pray that Danny Mann, the director, can keep peace between them long enough to finish the picture."

The Chamber of Commerce of Key West helped the film company choose location sites during their sojourn there, and the toughest thing to find was a sufficiently weather-beaten house to serve as Serafina's home. Wallis spotted the perfect place but there was a fence too close to it. When he inquired if the owner of the house next door would mind having his fence removed for the duration of shooting there, he was told that he could ask the owner himself, who happened to be Tennessee Williams. The author was, of course, delighted to have the film shot practically in his own backyard; and he would visit the set every afternoon, after working all morning on the final revisions of *Cat*, to kibitz.

On the day that the beach scene between Rosa (Marisa Pavan) and Jack (Ben Cooper) was shot, Williams was on hand. He inadvertently made his presence felt by slipping on the gangplank leading to a boat that the film crew was using and falling into the water. Newspaper accounts reported that for a time he was wedged precariously between pilings and the boat, which was surging with swells; but he was rescued without injury. Location shooting, he learned, can be much more hazardous than filming in the studio. It can also be uncomfortable and boring. While the gambling casino scene was being shot in Key West, Wallis and Williams decided to appear as extras, standing by the bar as they witnessed Serafina's brawl with Estelle. They did it as a lark but got more than they bargained for. The pair stood around all day long with the other extras while the temperature hovered around one hundred degrees, and the perfectionist Howe conferred with the director and shot take after take from various angles.

James Wong Howe has often attested that shooting outside the controlled conditions of a sound stage always increases the technical problems of film making. In the case of *Rose Tattoo*, all the scenes shot in the house which was rented for the film had to be designed and staged to fit the dimensions of the rooms of the structure that was being used. Howe carefully designated in each room where he wanted his light source to be and then proceeded to work out the lighting arrangements accordingly. "The rooms in a house are usually smaller than the ones that would be built in the studio," he explained. "Because the lights are much closer to the actors in a small room than on a large set, it is difficult to keep the shadows from becoming large and exaggerated; therefore the lights must be so placed that most of the shadows are kept in perspective or directed toward the floor where they will not be noticed."

The care that he lavished on photographing the film was rewarded by the intensity and beauty of the images that he created for the picture, and by the Academy Award which he won for his work on the film. The mood of the movie called for black-and-white photography, and so did the tone of *This Property is Condemned,* which he photographed in 1966 from another Tennessee Williams work. But by then color television was firmly enough established on the American scene that the studio insisted that the film be made in color because black-and-white films are more difficult to sell for use in prime time. Howe got around that difficulty by making the color in *The Property* look as much like black and white as possible by using subdued tints and hues whenever possible, for, as the title indicates, the story deals with the shabby side of life.

The film, which runs 110 minutes, was based on a one-act play of Williams' that can be played on the stage in about twenty minutes. An enormous amount of expansion was imposed on the play's slender plot to bloat it into nearly two hours of screen time, and this is fairly evident when one views the movie. It has been said that inside every fat man there is a thin man struggling to get out, and in the movie *This Property* one senses the original playlet likewise struggling to come across as it did on the stage.

The play simply presents a thirteen year old girl named Willie who was given a boy's name because her mother and father had hoped for a boy when she was born. In this sense, then, Willie was rejected by her parents from birth, a foreshadowing of the desertion first of her mother and then of her father. But her sister Alva stayed with her until her untimely death from lung cancer, and so it is Alva that she idolizes and wants to imitate in her own life. Unfortunately, since Alva was a prostitute in her mother's boarding house for railroad men (which was also a brothel), Willie naïvely but firmly believes that the kind of life which her older sister led is the only truly glamorous and happy existence for any young lady. Willie strengthens her identity with Alva by proudly wearing Alva's faded finery and dime store jewelry, and by imagining that she will soon inherit all of her deceased sister's admirers as well.

Willie stands awkwardly between the world of childhood, represented by the tattered doll which she hugs to her breast, and the adult world into which she has been prematurely initiated, represented by her sister's ill-fitting clothes and tarnished accessories. Williams dramatizes her precarious emotional and psychological position by depicting her as teetering on the rail of a railroad track and then losing her balance and falling to the ground along side the track. She then meets Tom, a lad slightly older than she, who has heard that she is willing to conduct "experiments" in sex. She brushes aside the diffident overtures which he makes to her by explaining that she only indulged in that sort of thing with mere youngsters when she was lonely. She assures him that she is no longer lonesome because of her imminent prospects of taking over Alva's clientele when they come by looking for her older sister. They had deserted Alva when she became ill with lung cancer, but Willie is certain that this string of Gentlemen Callers is only waiting for her to blossom fully into the girl that Alva was to reappear on the scene, which presumably will be almost any day now.

Considering his disappointment with Willie's rejection of his timid solicitation, the boy Tom somewhat surprisingly treats her with gentle kindness, only hinting tentatively now and again that Willie's grand plans for luxury and happiness are a pathetic tissue of fantasies meant to insulate her from her drab existence, living as she does in a condemned house by the side of a railroad track and hiding from the social workers who come looking for her. Perhaps this older lad is still young enough to be intimidated by Willie's haughty self-confidence in spite of his better judgment.

But Williams makes it abundantly evident that Willie is already condemned to a sordid way of life just as the abandoned house in which she hides out is condemned to deteriorate further. She, too, has been abandoned, for there is no relative or friend of her family who cares enough for her personally to see that she will turn out any differently than Alva did. Soon the perfunctory investigations of the welfare workers will stop and Willie will be left alone to be exploited by any tramps and youngsters who happen by at the times when she is prepared to admit that she is still lonesome. Her life is firmly established on the wrong track, and so she once again climbs onto the railroad tressle and weaves her way down the rail out of sight, looking in the distance very much like the delapidated doll to which she still clings.

Willie in the course of the playlet often refers to the milky white winter sky as a clean piece of paper on which she can draw whatever images she imagines. But Willie is not yet so much the victim of her fantasies that she does not realize that there is a gap between the way things are and the way that she would like them to be. In the course of her musings with the boy, she contrasts Alva's death with that of Greta Garbo in *Camille*. Both Alva and Camille died young, but Camille's death on the silver screen was accompanied by weeping violins and the return of her lover; whereas for Alva's deathbed scene there were no violins and no lovers, the latter having deserted Alva, in Willie's unvarnished phrase, "like rats from a sinking ship." Alva's death, says Willie, was not at all like death in the movies, and she is even willing to concede that her own death will probably not be either. But she will be content to die as Alva did, decked out on her deathbed with the same pearl earrings and gold beads which Alva had acquired in Memphis, because whatever was good enough for Alma will be good enough for Willie.

When one critic suggested that Willie was plainly damned to a dreadful existence, Williams replied, "I don't think of my little people as damned—not as long as they keep courage and gallantry. These are very important Southern qualities, bred in the bones of the people I write about, such as Amanda Wingfield and even the little girl on the railroad tracks."

Philip Weissman, in his essay on Williams's heroines in *Focus on A Streetcar Named Desire*, compares Willie not to Amanda but to Blanche DuBois. Like Blanche, Willie seeks solace in reconstructing her unhappy existence into the ideal of an attractive Southern belle with many prospects for an enviable life with any number of handsome, well-to-do Gentleman Callers. Also like Blanche, Willie is bereft of family and friends, and clings to the image of a family homestead which recalls better days: in Blanche's case it is Belle Reve, in Willie's case it is the family boarding house. Both look for rescue by some prosperous male admirer: for Blanche it is Shep Huntleigh, her old beau from college days; for Willie it is Mr. Johnson, the railroad superintendent whom she is convinced will unquestionably transfer his once strong attachment for Alva to her. With only a minimal stretching of the imagination, Weissman concludes, "it is possible to see the thirteen-year-old Willie grown into the thirty-year-old Blanche." At least Alva, from what Willie tells us of her, never deluded herself about who she was or what she was.

Nor does she in the film, in which she displaces Willie as the central character of the story. Throughout the movie she fights a losing battle to avoid the kind of life that her mother has mapped out for her, though Willie, as in the play, views her sister's life as a star-studded success story ("She was the main attraction," Willie boasts of Alva after she has died).

As early as 1943 actor Hume Cronyn, who has always had a predilection for Williams's short plays, tried to interest Metro Goldwyn Mayer in filming *This Property*, which was just about the time when Williams himself was employed briefly at the studio as a script writer. Cronyn sent the script to Judy Garland's agent on the hunch that she could be perfectly cast as Willie in a movie adaptation that would retain Willie as the central character. Nothing ever came of Cronyn's suggestion in 1943, though such a screenplay might well have met with Williams's approval.

But the authors of the 1966 film version elaborated Williams's slender little tale so far beyond his original conception that he asked that his name be taken off the film's credits. A compromise was reached whereby his screen credit would read, "Suggested by Tennessee Williams's one-act play," instead of "Based on Tennessee Williams's one-act play." To the uninitiated the difference in the opposing screen credits might seem minimal; but there is a distinction between using his play as the springboard of a movie, which is what happened with *This Property*, and sticking close to the original in developing it further in a film script; and Williams's final screen credit is grounded in this distinction. The screen story for *This Property* was padded out first by three principal writers—Fred Coe, Edith Smith, and Francis Ford Coppola—but an additional dozen script doctors tinkered with the screenplay before it was completed. And the meandering continuity of the film reflects that too many cooks well nigh spoiled the broth.

This Property is Condemned was one of the two one-acters that were discarded as a source for *Baby Doll,* as I mentioned in chapter two; but it was given a television production, along with two of Williams's other short plays, *The Last of My Solid Gold Watches* and *Moony's Kid Don't Cry,* on April 19, 1958, on the Kraft Television Theater. The three plays together fitted neatly into program's one-hour format. They had all been written before 1944, in the days when Williams was living in furnished rooms and enduring the long period of poverty and failure that preceded his first major success, *The Glass Menagerie.* "The dominating idea in each of the plays is, I suppose, loneliness," he said at the time of the broadcast; it was a theme that reflected his frame of mind when he had written the plays, although loneliness has not ceased to be a preoccupation in his work since then.

The Kraft Television Theater production of Williams three one-acters was directed by Sidney Lumet, who was to do two Williams films, *Orpheus Descending* and *The Last of the Mobile Hotshots,* which will be taken up in chapter six. Williams was quite satisfied that *This Property,* as well as the other two plays, was done on TV in a way that approximated his original intent. But the film adaptation of *This Property* eight years later was something else again. Still, one can sympathize with the formidable task which had been set before the movie writers. Williams had combined two one-act plays in order to have enough material for *Baby Doll;* but in the present instance the studio had only purchased the rights to a single one-act play, and the script writers had to invent enough additional material to make a full length movie.

The basic format which the screen writers hit upon was to make Williams's play the framing device for the picture. Accordingly they broke the one-acter roughly in half, presenting the first portion as a prologue to the film and the remaining segment as an epilogue. In this way they utilized almost all of the play's original dialogue in their screenplay.

In the prologue of the film Willie describes her family and present situation for the boy Tom, and in the epilogue she wraps things up by telling Tom what happened to each of them. The scriptwriters then had to devise a full-blown story told in flashback to fit between the prologue and the epilogue.

Since the problem of turning a one-act play into a much longer motion picture involves a considerable amount of expansion, it is interesting to investigate precisely how the script writers went about lengthening this poignant character sketch into a feature-length film. There are some interesting visual tie-ins between the framing material and the film proper. The tattered evening gown which Willie wears as she talks to Tom is the same dress worn by Alva the first time we see her, though of course it is fresh and fine while Alva is sporting it. Also the ruined doll which Willie hugs in the prologue and epilogue is seen throughout the film as beautiful and new when Willie carries it about. Both the dress and the doll, then, stand out in the framing sequences as battered relics of Willie's long lost happy days with her sister.

As might be expected, several of the characters in the picture are derived from people to whom Willie refers in the play. Alva Starr (Natalie Wood) is very much like her younger sister (Mary Badham) describes her in the play; and the same can be said of Sidney (Robert Blake) and Mr. Johnson, two of the Starr boarders who pursue Alva. Some of the other characters in the film are scarcely mentioned in the one-act play, and the fleshing out of their personalities seems to have been dictated by counterparts to them which exist in other Williams plays. Hazel Starr, the girls' mother (Kate Reid), is cut from the same cloth as many of Williams's other strong-willed mothers are, such as Amanda Wingfield and Serafina Delle Rose, although Hazel is willfully mean-spirited in a way that most of the others are not.

Willie says in the play that her mother deserted her before her father did, but in the movie it is the father who has already taken off for parts unknown while her mother is still around. The father of the Starr family, who never appears in the film at all, seems to be the reincarnation of the father of the Wingfield family in *The Glass Menagerie*, for Alva describes him in terms similar to those employed by Tom Wingfield in *Menagerie:* he is a man who is revered by his offspring as an intrepid adventurer despite the fact that he deserted them.

The one character who seems to be cut from whole cloth in the movie and who has no discernible counterpart in the one-act play (or any other play of Williams's) is Owen Legate (Robert Redford). He is a railroad inspector who stays long enough with the Starrs to make Alva dissatisfied with her dead end existence there and to beckon her to a cleaner life in New Orleans as his wife. His offer of regenerative love is nowhere implied in the play; but it provides the major source of conflict in the body of the movie, since the mercenary Hazel prefers that Alva have a liason with the married, middle aged Mr. Johnson, who has a more lucrative position with the railroad than Legate does.

That Legate is fundamentally a man whose character places him above the other people around the Starr boarding house is visualized in the movie when Howe photographs Owen looking down from his second floor window on Alva and one of her "suitors" on the porch below. Moreover, Owen occupies her father's room in the boarding house, and this signifies that he will take her father's place in her affections and help Alva to grow from being "daddy's little girl," which she still fancies herself, into a mature woman.

The one legacy that Mr. Starr bequeathed to his daughter Alva is a penchant for daydreaming, a habit that Alva has in turn passed on to Willie. There are several symbols in the movie of Alva's penchant for taking refuge in unreality: a

Robert Redford as Owen Legate, one of the several characters added to the screenplay of *This Property is Condemned*.

glass ball filled with snow that reminds her of the vast world beyond the small Southern town of Dodson where she grew up, and a retired railway carriage with her name painted on the side, which her father decorated for her so that she could sit inside and make believe that she was being transported away from Dodson. In addition, Alva dreamily refers to the sky as being a white piece of paper on which she can sketch out her fantasies, a phrase which Willie uses in the framing scenes and which, therefore, we are to infer that Willie picked up from her older sister.

Sitting with her one day in the immobile carriage, i.e., in the very midst of her

Robert Redford and Natalie Wood with the toy snowman in *This Property is Condemned*.

private fantasy world, Owen desperately tries to force Alva to face reality and to make her mind up to come with him to New Orleans. "The sky is not white, it's blue," he says emphatically. "This railway car is not sprinkled with talcum, it is old and dusty. It has been sitting here for years and is not ever going anywhere." But Alva airily turns away from him and the facts which he is trying to impress on her mind and tenaciously refuses to come to a decision about going away with him or not. Like Blanche DuBois, whose attitudes Alva evokes in the movie even more than Willie does in the original play, she replies, "I don't want to think about your leaving. It's easier to pretend that you are not."

On another occasion Owen attempts to make Alva admit the harsher realities of life which she prefers to ignore when they are leaving a movie theater where the main feature has been *One-Way Passage*, a 1932 film in which the fatally ill

Kay Francis has a tragic shipboard romance with William Powell. To Alva's comment that she likes to see a sad movie twice in the hope that it will turn out happily the second time round, Owen responds, "No matter how many times you see it, she always dies in the end." Besides manifesting how deeply entrenched in her fantasy world Alva really is, the conversation about *One-Way Passage* serves as a foreshadowing of her own death, and grew out of Willie's references to *Camille* in the play.

The poetic imagery associated with Alva's daydreaming is brought to a climax when Owen announces his decision that he is leaving for New Orleans without her. "That railway carriage and the snow storm in the glass ball," he says in exasperation, "are enough for a fake like you." After Owen's departure, Alva impulsively and drunkenly marries J.J., one of Hazel's lovers (Charles Bronson), in a frenzied effort to escape her mother's clutches. The morning after the impromptu wedding, however, she burns the marriage license and flees to New Orleans and Owen Legate, whose last name signifies that he is the emissary of a better and higher kind of life for Alva than she has ever known.

In New Orleans Owen and Alva share a brief period of idyllic happiness together. But just as Owen is about to make an honest woman of Alva, Hazel shows up one stormy night accompanied by enough thunder and lightning to herald the most wicked of witches. She spitefully reveals to Owen that Alva is still married to J.J.; and Alva responds by running hysterically out into the darkness, never to be seen again. The film then closes with the epilogue in which Willie recounts Alva's death from lung cancer and Hazel's running away with Mr. Johnson, leaving her to cope with life alone.

Between Alva's flight and the epilogue, there was a scene which was cut from the final release version of the movie. It depicted Alva returning to her life as the town trollop in Dodson. As director Sydney Pollack described it in *Film Comment,* she looked very much like Willie does in the framing scenes, "with a straw hat and ripped stockings. Although she's still talking about the white sky, you see her picking up a travelling salesman. But the producer complained about too many endings, so he insisted that I cut that one."

The deletion of Alva's final scene in the film as superfluous to the story brings into relief the basic problem with the screenplay as a whole. One does have to admire the script writers for their ingenuity in inventing a whole plot line to fill out Williams's brief play. Nevertheless, it seems that they did their job not wisely but too well, making the movie over-long and top-heavy with plot. Complicating Alva's life with the secret marriage to J.J., when she is doomed to lose Owen all too soon by her premature death anyway, seems quite unnecessary. In addition, there is a whole subplot about Owen's laying off several railroad employees because of the Depression that is so extraneous to Williams's original story that I have not even bothered to detail it here.

In short, the story has been stretched to feature length by piling incident upon incident in a way that does not really help the viewer to get to know the central characters much better, but serves only to delay the inevitable outcome of the story for too long. *This Property is Condemned* is a good movie that could have been better if the ending had been placed a little closer to the beginning.

Reviews of the film often singled out James Wong Howe's cinematography as one of the picture's definite pluses. Although director Sydney Pollack was later to make such imposing movies as *They Shoot Horses, Don't They?*, *This Property* was only his second feature motion picture. It was Howe's 119th, and inevitably the experienced cinematographer found it tough to take orders from a director who had not begun to know the picture business as he did; and so there were disagreements between them. "Howe knows his business," Pollack conceded to Rex Reed, who visited the set while the company was shooting in New Orleans. "He's one of the world's greatest cameramen, a member of the old school, used to calling the shots himself. We've had a few blowups, . . . but I think he's pleased with the results."

When I asked Howe how he handled the situation when friction developed between himself and his director on a picture, he replied, "When I differ with a director on how a scene should be shot, I usually suggest that we shoot the scene twice, once his way and once mine. Then he is free to choose either for the final version of the film. Once a director realizes that I am trying to be helpful and not trying to take over his job, we get along."

One thing that director and photographer agreed on was their preference for location work. "New Orleans, this crazy, broken-down city, you could never duplicate it in Hollywood," said Pollack. "Everywhere you look you see history." Unfortunately, rain fell steadily for two weeks while the cast and crew were filming in the French Quarter of the city, and this delayed the shooting of all but the two scenes that were supposed to take place in a cloudburst. Ironically, despite the generous supply of rain provided by the heavens, Howe had Natalie Wood sprayed with an additional 300,000 gallons of water from a hose attached to a moving truck as she made her way along the sidewalk. Howe used the extra water source because he had learned from experience that real falling rain is almost invisible on the screen unless it is properly back-lighted—something that was impossible to do in the streets of New Orleans at 7:00 a.m. when the day's shooting began.

Pollack asked Howe to change the style of the photography for the New Orleans scenes from that which he had used in the boarding house scenes shot in Bay St. Louis, Mississippi. The Mississippi scenes have a gritty, naturalistic look which suits the tacky environment of the Starr boarding house-cum-brothel. But in New Orleans, where Alva's dream of being reunited with Owen comes true, a softer, more romantic ambience was in order. When Owen and Alva find each other in a New Orleans park, Howe photographs the couple beside a bubbling fountain which shimmers in the dazzling sunlight, to imply

Natalie Wood in the idyllic New Orleans sequence of *This Property is Condemned*.

their joy. Then he shows their insubstantial images reflected in the water of the pool at the base of the fountain to foreshadow that their happiness together will soon evanesce like their fragile reflections in the park pond.

Howe always had a predilection for helicopter shots to provide panoramic views of the action at key moments, and in this Pollack also concurred. The most spectacular aerial shot in the movie occurs when Alva is riding the train from Dodson to New Orleans, from her old life to what she hopes will be a fresh start for her with Owen. The camera starts close to the train, focusing on her tear-stained face framed in the train window, and then pulls back to show the whole train crossing a bridge over a lake. To make this complicated shot, a helicopter carrying the camera crew had to fly so close to the train for the shot of Alva's face at the window that its blades were spinning over the top of the railway car in which she was riding and just barely missed scraping the roof of the railway carriage. Then the copter flew high above the moving train and turned on its side so that the camera could shoot straight down at the train crossing the bridge, which figuratively spans the distance between Alva's old life and her new. (If the copter had not rolled over on its side for the camera operator to make this high shot of the train, the copter's landing skids would have been visible in the shot.)

The helicopter shot at the end of the film was just as difficult to execute. Willie continues her trek down the railroad tracks singing "Wish Me a Rainbow," the popular song composed for the picture which has since become a standard pop tune. As the camera pulls away from her, Willie becomes a tiny figure lost in the general desolation surrounding the railroad tracks, the grubby milieu in which she has elected to stay in a misguided devotion to the memory of her dead sister, despite the fact that all of the railroad employees whom Owen had to fire have long since moved on to look for work elsewhere. And the movie ends.

Howe had used a similar aerial shot to conclude *Picnic* a decade earlier, so he was willing to try it again because in the earlier instance the final pull-away shot, he said, "turned out to be the most interesting shot in the film and an excellent way to end the picture." Still, both Howe and Pollack agreed that it was risky because it involved a helicopter taking off from a flatcar parked on the tracks. As the copter rose above the flatcar, with the camera operator photographing the scene all the while, the flatcar had to be pushed quickly down the track in the opposite direction from which Willie was walking so that it would not appear in the shot along with Willie's retreating figure, which was supposed to be the sole object visible on the tracks. This shot turned out just as well as its predecessor in *Picnic* ten years earlier.

Considering Howe's arduous efforts to make *This Property is Condemned* a visually interesting movie, it is sad that all of his creative energy did not yield a more impressive picture, though it is a film that is always worth watching. Donald Reed, in his book on Robert Redford, speaks somewhat benignly of the movie, naming it Redford's first film of consequence (though it does not rank high in the canons of Redford, Williams, Pollack, or Howe when placed alongside their other achievements).

Williams understandably declines to discuss this film much beyond pointing out the wording of his screen credit, which I mentioned earlier. One can only guess, therefore, what elements disturbed him most about the manner in which his one-act play was expanded for the screen, for his only other comment on the movie (to which he refers in his autobiography erroneously as *Period of Adjustment*) is that it was "a vastly expanded and hardly related film with the title taken from a very delicate one-act play. The film was hardly deserving of the talents of Robert Redford and Natalie Wood." Or, one might add, the talents of James Wong Howe; Sydney Pollack; or of scriptwriter Francis Ford Coppola, who later co-scripted and directed such pictures as the two *Godfather* films.

I suspect that it is the Redford character which most nettled the playwright because Owen seems to be a Prince Charming out of a book of fairy tales more than a character out of any story connected with the name of Tennessee Williams. Owen is ready to accept Alva's past without a whimper, provided that her future will be devoted to him; he is even ready to absorb the revelation of her secret marriage to J.J. without so much as batting his golden eye lashes, although Alva runs away in shame anyway. Owen, in sum, is simply too good to be true. Granted his willingness to forgive Alva's past indiscretions, a true-to-life Williams character would have had to endure some inner struggle before he could take Alva for what she is, or promises to be, rather than for what she has been. In the movie as it stands all of the emotional conflict seems to be on Alva's part as she strives to meet Owen's expectations of her. Owen remains a one-dimensional character who never raises his voice, even when he— rarely—blows his cool.

But Redford makes the part as credible as can be. "The screenplay hinges on Owen's ennobling love of Alva—its power to purify and transport a slightly tarnished coquette into glowing, mature womanhood," Donald Reed writes. "Owen's character was conceived as an almost impossibly sterling and romantic character. To his credit, Redford makes what could have emerged as a dullish, pompous rendition of every maiden's prayer into an engaging, credible, and *human* young man."

Redford and Pollack were to continue working together on such films as *Jeremiah Johnson, The Way We Were,* and *Three Days of the Condor,* but never again on a Tennessee Williams picture. Natalie Wood, however, later starred in the TV version of *Cat on a Hot Tin Roof,* which I shall deal with in the next chapter; and Howe joined forces with director Sidney Lumet to make his third Williams film, *The Last of the Mobile Hot Shots,* which I shall take up later in connection with Lumet's other Williams film, *The Fugitive Kind.* Looking back on Howe's work on the two films covered in this chapter, one sees that they are marked by an intelligent cinematic style which is ever concentrated on bringing the screenplay to life with greater force and clarity. As an artist he never used a technical effect for its own sake, as a mere gimmick to show off his technical expertise, but only as a way of heightening the dramatic or thematic impact of a scene.

"As you grow older and become more experienced in cinematography," he told me late in his career, "your work becomes simpler and more unobtrusive, and you avoid technique for technique's sake. Still sometimes you have to break a few rules in order to get the effect that you want. You can't play it safe all of the time and still make progress in your work." The kind of craftsmanship which results from such an approach to film making implies that Tennessee Williams was well served by James Wong Howe in the trio of films which Howe photographed. Though the overall quality of the films ranges from first-rate in the case of *The Rose-Tattoo* to second-rate in the case of *This Property is*

Cinematographer James Wong Howe.

Condemned, all of the films are marked indelibly by his camerawork. All three of his Williams films are vivid recreations of the world of Tennessee Williams as embodied in the steamy, strongly atmospheric settings which Howe captured with his camera.

In terms of cinematography at least, all of the Williams films on which Howe worked travel first class.

4
Richard Brooks:
Cat on a Hot Tin Roof and Sweet Bird of Youth

IF WILLIAMS'S MOTHER Edwina and his sister Rose were the inspiration of Amanda and Laura Wingfield in *The Glass Menagerie*, his father C.C. Williams and (to a lesser extent) his brother Dakin seem to underlie the characters of Big Daddy and his son Gooper in *Cat on a Hot Tin Roof*. In fact, C.C. Williams seems to be the source of no less than three equally domineering males in Williams's plays, at least two of which are presented with a certain amount of sympathy. This is not surprising since, as I pointed out in the first chapter, Williams came to regard his father in a more and more favorable light in retrospect, especially after C.C.'s death. "My father loved my mother, but I don't think she ever reciprocated to the same degree," he once said. "If only once she had said to him, 'Come on, let's have a sherry before dinner,' things might have been a lot different." But that invitation was never forthcoming, and so C.C. Williams did his drinking alone or, like Charlie Cotton in Williams's short play called *The Last of My Solid Gold Watches*, while he was on the road representing the St. Louis shoe manufacturer for which he worked.

Charlie Cotton, "the last of the Delta drummers," appears to the the first sketch of Big Daddy Pollitt in *Cat*. Like Big Daddy he is a corpulent, imposing man who knows that his time is growing short as age, drink, and ill health all begin to exact their toll of him. "It ain't even late in the day any more," he exclaims as the curtain descends, "it's *night!*" And, like Big Daddy, there is something admirable about this grand old man who prefers to wear out rather than to rusy away. Even though Charlie has won several solid gold watches for his salesmanship (as did C.C.), he goes on working.

But there is another, less sympathetic side of Charlie's character, the side which seeks to dominate those around him. Charlie talks down to a younger salesman whom he feels does not show him proper respect, just as Big Daddy dominates his whole family in *Cat*. This latter trait is equally manifest in the aptly nicknamed Boss Finley in *Sweet Bird of Youth*, the third father figure to be fashioned from Williams's memories of his own father. But, unlike Charlie Cotton and Big Daddy, he has no compensating good points. He is a cantankerous, crooked Huey Long-type political demagogue who tyrannizes over his family and his staff alike. While Boss Finley's tantrums are no doubt modeled on Williams's memories of his father's rages, Boss Finley embodies only one side of C.C. Williams's personality, whereas Big Daddy gives a much more complex picture of Williams's father. This is because Boss Finley, as the villain of *Sweet Bird*, is really more of a plot device than a fully realized character like Big Daddy in *Cat*.

Although Big Daddy Pollitt dominates both his family and the play, he does not appear at all in the short story which was Williams's dry run for the play, which is entitled *Three Players of a Summer Game*. The story details the marriage of Brick Pollitt, a weak-willed drunk, and his wife Margaret who systematically manipulates her husband into doing her bidding. Williams symbolizes Brick's status as a circumstance that she is always in the driver's seat when they drive through town because Brick has lost his driver's license after repeated drunk driving convictions.

The overbearing Margaret of *Three Players* was refashioned into the much more engaging Maggie the Cat of *Cat on a Hot Tin Roof*, who wants to support and encourage, rather than overpower, Brick. But the Brick Pollitt of *Three Players* is very much the Brick Pollitt of *Cat*. The Brick of the story is a ruined man whose "self disgust came upon him with the abruptness and violence of a crash on a highway. But what had Brick crashed into? . . . What reason was there for dropping his life and taking hold of a glass which he never let go of for more than one waking hour?" This question, left unanswered in the short story, becomes one of the moving forces of the play. It seems almost as if Williams wrote *Cat* to answer just that question. The answer is at least hinted at in the story, however, when Williams writes, "The acrobatics and sports of his youth seemed to haunt him." He will develop this facet of Brick's psychology brilliantly in the play.

There is little doubt, after reading Williams's autobiography and his many interviews, that the love–hate relationship of Brick and Big Daddy in the play is a working out in dramatic terms of a similar relationship between Williams and his father (to whom the writer sometimes refers as "Big Daddy" in his memoirs). Williams was only able to begin to resolve this conflict after he had gained the perspective that followed his leaving home for good, and the fruit of his reflections is in the play.

While he was doing his stint at MGM in 1943, his father came to Los Angeles on business and Williams went to visit him at his hotel where the elder Williams was meeting with some of his subordinates who worked for his company. In a letter to a close friend Williams commented that he had found his father a pathetic, drunken old man who genuinely elicited his compassion. "Now and then it occurs to me that the time has about come to shut the windows and turn on the gas," wrote Williams, whose career had not really gotten started as yet; "but that old man in the hotel room, fawned upon and feared by his salesmen and regarded with horror by his family, has probably experienced more bitterness than I could dream of. The loneliness and hunger for affection!"

Shortly after C.C. died in 1957, Williams paid tribute to his deceased parent in *The New York Post* and focused on C.C.'s detestation of mendacity, one of the hallmarks of Big Daddy's character in *Cat:* "My father was a totally honest man; he was never known to tell a lie in his life or to take unfair advantage of anybody in business. He had a strong character and a sense of honor. He lived on his own terms, which were hard terms for his family; but he should not be judged as long as he remains the mystery that he was to us who lived in his shadow. Maybe I hated him once, but I certainly don't anymore."

Williams's creation of Gooper, Brick's brother, appears to represent some aspects of his own younger brother Dakin, though to a lesser degree than Big Daddy represents his father. Dakin Williams does not share Gooper's venal and selfish nature, but there was a sibling rivalry between the two Williams boys for their father's attention and affection just as there is between the two Pollitt boys. The elements that Dakin and Gooper have in common include their both being lawyers who have made it in the professional world of business while their respective brothers have led far less conventional lives.

Gooper is a subordinate character in the play, while Big Daddy, Brick, and Maggie represent the trio of major characters, any one of whom at first glance might be the chief character on whom the plot centers: Brick suspects that his relationship with Skipper, his fellow athlete, was latently homosexual and is drowning his fears and his marriage to Maggie in alcohol. He blames Maggie for forcing Skipper to admit that he was homosexual, and that his relationship with Brick had strong homosexual undertones at least for Skipper. She had invited Skipper to her bed to prove the contrary, and, after failing ignominiously to do so, he killed himself. Skipper's death has therefore occasioned Brick's estrangement from his wife, despite her determined efforts to win back his affections. Brick's incipient alcoholism and refusal to be reconciled with his wife trigger Big Daddy's fears that his favorite son Brick will produce no heir to inherit the Pollitt plantation and carry on the family name, and that by default everything will pass to Gooper's offspring. Moreover, Big Daddy's concerns increase when he learns that he is in the mortal grip of cancer.

Which of these three important characters is the chief figure in the drama? After a close study of the text, especially in the light of Williams's revisions of the third act of the play before it opened on Broadway, it seems that Big Daddy is the central character in the drama, since all of the other characters, major and minor, are drawn largely in terms of their relationship to him. Big Daddy strives to make his immature son Brick face himself and his responsibilities, and looks upon his daughter-in-law Maggie as his ally in carrying out his resolution. He sees his other son Gooper's obsequious fawning on him as motivated by Gooper's intention to gain the Pollitt estate for his descendants rather than for Brick's, and means to thwart Gooper's plans. In brief, Big Daddy's drive to straighten out his family affairs, both on the personal and the business levels, before death overtakes him becomes the motivating force that presses the action of the play forward to the denoument.

After William Faulkner saw the play, he commented that he thought that Williams might have done well to strengthen further Big Daddy's position of eminence in the story's structure. "The problems of children are not worth three acts," he commented. "The story was the old man, I thought, the father." Initially Big Daddy only appeared in the second act, but even so he still dominated entirely this central section of the action, which encompasses his monumental confrontation with Brick about Brick's failing marriage and possible homosexuality, and learns of the lethal nature of his own cancer.

Homosexuality was all but a forbidden topic in the Broadway theater at the time when Williams wrote *Cat* and it had to be introduced into the play gingerly. When Big Daddy finally broaches the subject to his son, Brick's hysterical disavowal that no such feelings between him and Skipper ever existed makes one suspect that he is protesting too much. Even though this does not mean that there was any overt expression of homosexual sentiment between the two athletes, any recognition on the part of Brick that such feelings existed in him would tarnish his carefully constructed self-image as a super-masculine god of the playing field.

The price which he forces others to pay so that he can maintain his own delusions of grandeur of himself as superhuman and untemptable is a dear one. After Skipper's failure in Maggie's bed, he phones Brick and confesses his feelings for him, but Brick cruelly hangs up on him. This total rejection by the one person to whom Skipper looked for understanding and compassion precipitates Skipper's suicidal descent into alcohol and drugs. Yet Brick blames Maggie for Skipper's death and refuses to accept her as his wife from then on. Surely her frantic method of trying to keep Skipper from coming between her and her husband was ill-advised, but no more so than Brick's calloused refusal to admit his own greater responsibility for Skipper's death.

Although Big Daddy is no psychologist, he is wise enough to infer that one deep root of Brick's emotional relationship with Skipper was basically an adolescent fellow feeling that was symptomatic of the fact that the immature Brick has never grown up. Refusing to face the responsibilities of marriage and a business career, Brick hovered in a state of prolonged adolescence in which he made believe that he and Skipper were still carefree school boys playing for the home team, even after they had long since left school and were reaching the age when they were both getting too old even for pro football. His father forces Brick to admit that he depended on Skipper to help him keep alive that adolescent world in which they would both be ageless athletes and would never have to grow up and face the unromantic facts of adult life.

Brick's refusal to confront reality is borne out by his constantly contrasting his present real relationship with Maggie unfavorably with his idealized past relationship with Skipper, since the real always suffers by comparison with the ideal. Maggie tells Brick precisely this when she says that his relationship with Skipper was so noble and incorruptible that it had to be kept on ice, "and death was the only icebox where you could keep it!" Brick's guilt-ridden affection for Skipper recalls Blanche DuBois's equally guilt-ridden love for Allan Grey, who also committed suicide when he was rejected by Blanche upon her discovery of his homosexuality. Brick is really suffering from his own self-disgust with the self-deception in which he is indulging, and not, as he contends, from his disillusionment with the mendacity rampant in the world around him.

Big Daddy accordingly tries to get Brick to understand in the course of their long quarrel scene that Brick's emotional involvement with Skipper has branded him not so much as a latent homosexual as an immature and irresponsible thirty year old who still refuses to relinquish the adolescent world which he and Skipper co-created for themselves in order to stave off growing up. Yet because homosexuality was such a sensational subject when *Cat* was first produced in 1954, it was thought to be the central issue of the play. "The subject of Brick's sexual confusion is no longer the sensation it was," says Williams today, "so that the real theme of the play—the general mendacity of our society—is more clearly seen."

Besides Brick's self-deception, mentioned above, there are numerous other instances of mendacity throughout the play: the family at first lies to Big Daddy about the lethal quality of his illness; Gooper and his wife May try to deceive him into thinking that their concern for him is genuinely unselfish; and the play ends with Maggie's lie to the family assembled around Big Daddy that she and Brick have been reconciled and that she has within her the new life that Big Daddy had hoped for. But this last lie is the only one uttered in the play that has some chance of coming true, and the determined Maggie means to see that it does.

There are still some unresolved questions when the curtain descends; but as Williams notes in his commentary in the published play, a playwright must steer away from pat conclusions "which make a play just a play, not a snare for the truth of human experience." Similarly, though the playwright must probe the personalities of his characters as clearly and as deeply as he can, "some mystery should be left in the revelation of character in a play, just as a great deal of mystery is always left in the revelation of character in life, even in one's own character to himself."

Still, when Elia Kazan read the typescript of *Cat,* he had some misgivings about the structure and development of the play which he thought Williams should consider before they put *Cat* into production. Kazan's reservations were three in numer: he was worried that such a crucial character as Big Daddy should disappear at the end of the second act, even though his lingering presence is felt through his abiding influence on the other characters right up to the end; he also felt that there should be some evidence of Brick's taking a new lease on life as a result of the self-knowledge which he has gained from his painfully frank talk with his father; and finally Kazan believed that Maggie should be more clearly sympathetic to the audience.

Williams quickly acceded to the third point because he had grown to like Maggie more and more as he delineated her character in the play more fully than he had in *Three Players of a Summer Game*. As far as Brick was concerned, Williams hesitated to make his change of heart seem too sudden because he did not believe that one revelatory conversation could effect an immediate change in the outlook of a person in Brick's state of spiritual disrepair. The author also did not want Big Daddy to reappear on stage after the second act because he feared that Big Daddy would unduly overshadow Brick in the play as a whole. But Williams conceded to all three of Kazan's suggestions and revised the third act of the play accordingly.

Nevertheless, in most editions of the play Williams prints both his original third act and the revised version which he introduces with a preface detailing how the revised third act came into being. He states frankly that, while Kazan did not deliver his suggestions as an ultimatum, he was afraid of losing Kazan's participation in the project if he did not re-examine the play from the director's point of view. Williams also concedes that there is no living playwright who could not learn something of value from "a director so keenly perceptive as Elia Kazan," and points to the enormous critical and financial success of the revised Broadway version of the play as proof of this: *Cat* not only became Williams's longest running play but also won for him his second Pulitzer Prize and his third New York Critics Prize.

His reason for printing both versions of the third act of the play is to allow the reader to draw his own conclusions about which one suits the play as a whole better. Here are mine:

First of all, it seems right that Maggie should appear more sympathetic because it is her concern for Brick and for Big Daddy too, and not just greed for the Pollitt fortune, that motivates her to help effect a reconciliation between the dying man and his estranged and errant son.

Secondly, there is no doubt that not bringing back Big Daddy in the third act created a serious structural flaw in the play. In fact the chief reason that veteran producer Cheryl Crawford, who produced *The Rose Tattoo*, turned down the chance to produce *Cat* was Big Daddy's premature disappearance from the play. "I have only one important criticism," she wrote to Williams after reading the play in the fall of 1954, "but I think it is important for your success. Boldly put, we have no one to root for. All the people seem monstrous except Big Daddy," who was not in the last act. "I don't think the audience can take such an unrelieved attack. In *Streetcar* they had their catharsis in good Greek fashion through Blanche."

Big Daddy holds the family together by being the hub around which the rest of the Pollitts revolve, and he also holds the play together for the same reason. Consequently, without his active participation in the final stages of the action, the play loses focus to some extent and becomes just a mad scramble for the old man's money while he is drawing his last painful breath somewhere in the wings. But in the revised "Broadway" version of the third act Big Daddy returns and arranges that Brick, with Maggie's help, will be his successor in running the Pollitt plantation.

This does not mean that Brick has suddenly grown to emotional maturity, as it were, in the intermission between the second and third acts of the play; rather Brick has now at least gained a new perspective on his past relationship with Skipper and can begin to move toward a solid reconciliation with Maggie, and thereby grow into a responsible human being capable of overseeing the Pollitt estate. Big Daddy has not solved Brick's problems; but he has brought them out into the open, and that in itself is a step forward.

In complying with Kazan's three points Williams has indicated more explicitly than in his earlier draft that Brick is on the road to rehabilitation at the final curtain, but there is still no doubt that the road will be a long one. The play was definitely improved by Williams' heeding Kazan's suggestions, therefore; but this does not make the revised version any less his for all that. Although the revisions were prompted by the director, it was the playwright who worked them out and then integrated them into the text of his play.

"Both of those third acts are mine," Williams reminds us; "I wrote them both." He furthermore has often insisted with interviewers (myself included) that any rewriting he did at Kazan's instigation was done willingly: "Kazan simply tried to interpret, honestly, what I have to say. He helped me reach my audience, which is my aim in life—the bigger the audience the better."

As theater critic Henry Hewes has written of the Williams–Kazan relationship, "Kazan works on the theory that it is part of the director's function to produce a play in such a way as to make the playwright's attitudes and personality come over the footlights with greater intensity than is explicit in the script." Ultimately all of Kazan's suggested revisions were calculated to explicitate elements that were already present in the script implicitly. The Broadway version of the third act strengthens the unity of the play, therefore, by showing with greater clarity than the previous versions that the dying Big Daddy's interest in Brick and Maggie is rooted in his governing preoccupation with securing himself a successor and an heir; he wants Brick, with Maggie's help, to be for the former, and the two of them together to provide him with the latter. When things begin to look like they are beginning to shape up this way, Big Daddy in turn is able to face the prospect of his imminent death with mellowness and composure. And one is left with the impression that in the future Brick will be more influenced by the memory of his dead father than by the memory of his dead buddy; and with that appropriately bittersweet reflection the play ends.

Looking back on the revisions which he made in *Cat*, Williams admits that the Broadway version of the third act was an improvement over his earlier draft. Because he worked on it longer, it is textually the better written of the two. "Kazan's the only one I would do it for, though," Williams explained to Jim Gaines of *The Saturday Review*. "He is a man of great vitality and great directorial talent. . . . It was thrilling to work with him. He wanted me vitally involved in every rehearsal. He was always pleased to see me there. He would say, 'Tennessee, come up here. Show us how you would do this.' "

If there was ever any real suspicion that Williams resented Kazan's advice on *Cat* as an intrusion of a director into the writer's domain, it was disspelled two years later when Williams welcomed Kazan's cooperation in structuring the two one-act plays which comprise the substance of the screenplay of *Baby Doll* into a coherent movie script. As I mentioned in the second chapter, Williams would air mail material to Kazan from Rome with a note attached that read, "Insert this somewhere." Perhaps the greatest tribute which Williams has paid Kazan is the one with which I have ended chapter two, in which he says that Kazan always respected the integrity of his work and never tried to impose his own point of view on it.

In addition, Williams has consecrated the Broadway version of the third act of *Cat* once and for all by retaining the bulk of it both in his definitive 1974 version of the play as presented by the American Shakespeare Festival Company on Broadway and in the 1976 television version (probably because his original version was acted on the London stage and was not nearly so well received as the Broadway version).

When I asked Kazan to comment on the adjustments which he asked Williams to work out in *Cat*, he answered simply, "Regarding Williams's preface to the published version of *Cat* I have no comment. I'm not going to contest his point—I like him too much for that. I am still pleased with the third act as he finally worked it out for the original production. He constantly reworks his plays and this is admirable as I see it. You can do that in the theater: he just keeps mounting productions until he gets the play right."

Catharine Hughes in the preface of this book cites the 1974 American Shakespeare Festival production of *Cat*, which was transferred to Broadway, as an instance in which a Williams play benefited from his subsequent reworkings of the text. For one thing, she notes, the mendacity theme emerges with greater effect in this last version of the play. Williams explained to Gaines that once a play has gone through several drafts he can finally go back and incorporate the best improvements into the final version, and *Cat* is a case in point. The 1974 version, as I mentioned above, sticks very close to the Broadway version of the play, including most of the revised third act; but it also includes some minor improvements which cropped up after the original mounting of the play.

Williams wrote an anecdote about an elephant in heat for Big Daddy to tell in the Broadway version of the third act, but it was deleted from the show two weeks after the premier to avoid difficulties with the New York Department of Licenses, which advised the producers that they might otherwise consider revoking the license to present the show in the city. The dramatist later substituted several lines of dialogue about mendacity for Big Daddy's ribald story when the acting edition for non-professionals was published. And when the American Shakespeare Festival production was in preparation he not only reinstated Big Daddy's elephant joke but retained the additional passage about mendacity as well—which accounts for the mendacity theme emerging some-what more clearly in the 1974 production of the play than it did in the original production two decades earlier; although it was always a strong thematic preoccupation of the play from the beginning.

When *Cat* was ready to go into production in the fall of 1954, Williams was in Hollywood for the shooting of some of the interiors of *The Rose Tattoo*. He wrote to his grandfather Dakin before leaving for New York to advise on the casting of the play, "The fact that I have Kazan on the play is reassuring and takes a lot of the anxiety off me." His confidence was well placed, and the play racked up almost seven hundred preformances in New York alone before being sold to Hollywood for a million dollars, the highest figure which Williams has ever received for one of his works from a film studio.

Cat on a Hot Tin Roof remains Williams's favorite among all of the plays because he believes that in the kingly Big Daddy he reached beyond himself "to a kind of crude eloquence of expression" which he has never managed to give any other character he has created. He also favors the play because for the first time he accomplished the *tour de force* of having the action of the play co-exstensive with its playing time: the entire action of the play is acted out in the course of a birthday celebration for Big Daddy on a single evening. This element in the play's construction was made even more obvious on the screen than it was on the stage because the movie had no intermissions to interrupt the flow of the action.

It is, of course, the Broadway version of the play that was adapted to the screen by scenarist-director Richard Brooks. MGM had purchased the film rights of the play as a starring vehicle for Grace Kelly who decided instead to marry the Prince of Monaco and terminated her movie career; so the part went to Elizabeth Taylor. Paul Newman was chosen as her co-star, with Judith Anderson as Big Mama, Jack Carson as Gooper, and, repeating their original stage roles, Burl Ives as Big Daddy and Madeleine Sherwood as Mae, Gooper's wife.

Before Brooks signed on to write and direct the picture, MGM had commissioned another screenwriter, James Poe, to do a preliminary treatment that would indicate the direction which the adaptation of Williams's play should take. Since the Poe outline of the action differs considerably from Brooks's eventual script, it is worth examining briefly before going on to Brooks's adaptation.

Poe's approach was to open up the play as much as possible by dramatizing directly all of the incidents referred to in the play's dialogue, including several flashbacks which were to portray the events leading up to Skipper's suicide. The only hints in the screenplay of Skipper's homosexuality were to be embedded in these flashbacks. One such flashback was to be a drinking bout between Skipper and Brick:

"Skipper comes in with a bottle and two glasses, want to talk about his troubles. . . . He's never been much of a man with girls—for all his pretense of virility. *And that frightens him!*" Poe notes at this point that Skipper's sexual inadequacy with the opposite sex is an important point in the play, "the one we are trying to get over without being too overboard." When Skipper in another flashback phones Brick to confess his sexual encounter with Maggie, he first threatens to kill himself and then makes good his threat while Brick helplessly pleads with him over the long distance wire. Poe thus makes Skipper's death something totally beyond Brick's control, whereas in the play Brick finally admits to Big Daddy in their confrontation scene that he feels partially responsible for Skipper's death because he slammed down the telephone receiver in revulsion when Skipper told him why he had been impotent with Maggie.

Removing totally Brick's complicity in Skipper's death likewise removes a good part of the explanation of Brick's slide into dipsomania, and this substantial change in Brick's behavior and motivation illustrates the tendency of the Poe treatment to retool Brick into a conventional movie hero. Poe also provides the story with a much more upbeat ending than Williams had in mind. The camera pulls away in the final shot to reveal Big Daddy and Big Mama standing in the mansion's belvedere overlooking the plantation after a storm, implying that they are finally reconciled after years of virtual estrangement. Below them on the balcony are Brick and Maggie, equally reconciled and anticipating the birth of their child.

If Poe's treatment seems to exude too much sweetness and light, it is only fair to point out that he was faced with the task of coming up with an adaptation of Williams's play that would not run aground on the shoals of censorship and pressure group opposition in the way *Baby Doll* had a year or two earlier. Richard Brooks was also very much aware of the problems involved in handling the potentially explosive material of the play in a way that the public would accept. But he was also concerned with being as faithful as possible to Williams's work. So he all but jettisoned Poe's treatment and started to work on his own blocking out of an adaptation that did not resort to several flashbacks to etch in the exposition.

"The biggest problem was to find a substitute for the homosexual implications of the play," Brooks said to me in conversation. "At the time the movie was made, even the word *homosexual* was strictly against the Motion Picture Code regulations—and all American movies had to have a Production Code Seal. It also was studio policy to avoid having their pictures condemned by the Legion of Decency," as *Baby Doll* had been.

Brooks had run up against the taboo against treating homosexuality in the popular arts when he almost was court-martialed from the Marines for writing a novel about it many years earlier. "While I was still in the Marine Corps I wrote a novel, *The Brick Foxhole* (1945). In the novel one of the principal characters was a homosexual. He was written out of the story when the book was filmed as *Crossfire* (1947). In the novel the homosexual was murdered because he was a homosexual, murdered by marines who preyed on them during World War II. I was summoned for court-martial when the book was published because I had not submitted the manuscript for perusal by Marine Corps officials. I felt that since I was not revealing confidential or secret data, there was no need to have the novel censored. The Marine Corps officials did not see it that way.

"On my behalf Edward Aswell, my editor at Harper's, ·called on Sinclair Lewis (who had lavishly reviewed the book for *Esquire* magazine); Richard Wright, author of *Native Son*; Bill Mauldin, celebrated artist for *Stars and Stripes* (the Armed Forces newspaper); and Morris Ernst, the attorney who broke the "Boston ban" on James Joyce's *Ulysses*. Aswell notified the Marine Corps that the men he had assembled were ready to appear as witnesses for me. The court-martial proceedings were dropped, but my typewriter was taken away and I was sent to Camp Pendleton. There, a few months later, at war's end, I was honorably discharged.

"While at Camp Pendleton I got a call from Clifford Odets, the playwright. He wanted to do a dramatization for the stage of *The Brick Foxhole*. Elia Kazan was to direct it. Ultimately Odets could not find the time to write the play and Kazan went on to another project. However, Odets introduced me to a movie producer, Adrian Scott. He wanted to film *The Brick Foxhole*. Scott said the movie script could not possibly include the homosexual element in the story. (The same reason I couldn't use it in *Cat* several years later: for the screen, the subject was taboo.) In place of homosexuality RKO Studios substituted anti-Semitism, a minor theme in the novel."

Now, almost a decade later, Brooks was confronted with the problem of finding a substitute for the homosexual component in the plot *Cat on a Hot Tin Roof*. "My job was to find something to replace the unexpressed, latent homosexuality of Brick, something that would fit in with Brick's close relationship with Skipper, something that could possibly explain why Skipper had leaped to his death from a hotel window." The death of Skipper is one of the "deep secrets of the past" which often surface in a Williams play, Brooks explains, "the kind of secret that boils up at a crucial moment when it must be confronted by the characters."

An additional problem which Brooks had to solve in his film script was caused by the screen images of the two superstars in the film. "On the screen," he continues, "it would be difficult for an audience to accept Brick's rejection of Maggie, played by the beautiful, sensual Elizabeth Taylor. What audience would believe that Brick would refuse to go to bed with Maggie, would refuse her advances? Not many men in the movie audience would reject Elizabeth Taylor. Not many women in the audience would understand why Brick turns her down.

"We tried to overcome this problem with an intimate image: There is a moment when Maggie pursues Brick in their bedroom, and he threatens to hit her with his crutch. He escapes her arms by hobbling into the bathroom. Hanging on the bathroom side of the door is Maggie's nightgown. As Brick slams the door shut and locks it, he inadvertently touches the perfumed nightgown. He buries his face in her nightgown, which is symbolic of Maggie herself. He hereby expresses his desire for her but does it privately. It's clear, however, that Brick, despite his verbal protests, has a deep need and feeling for Maggie. It was acceptable to the movie audience; they felt he must be rejecting Maggie for reasons other than loss of manhood."

The solution that Brooks came up with to explain Brick's rejection of Maggie in the movie was to emphasize Brick's basic immaturity, his refusal to grow up and meet the responsibilities of adult life, which was also at the root of his emotional attachment to Skipper, who supported him in his desire to remain a boyish athlete-hero well beyond his alloted time. Once Brick persuades himself that Maggie was responsible for Skipper's suicide, therefore, he punishes her for the death of his comrade by rejecting her as his wife, for the loss of Skipper means the loss of the adolescent world in which they existed together.

As I have pointed out already, emotional immaturity was present in his character in the play, but Brooks had to bring it much more into relief in the film in order that it could adequately explain Brick's emotional deterioration quite apart from the fear of latent homosexuality which also dogs him throughout the play. Although the veiled allegation of Brick's latent homosexuality is still present in the movie, it is thus ruled out as a decisive motivating factor in

Paul Newman and Elizabeth Taylor in *Cat on a Hot Tin Roof*.

Brick's relationship with Skipper and in his alienation from Maggie.

"We tried to show in the movie that Brick refuses to face the reality of the present. He wants to live in the past. He tries to hold onto the past by exaggerating the importance of sports. Once a young athlete, he is now a sports announcer for the radio." Brick projects onto Maggie his own guilt about

Skipper's death, "not being there when Skipper *needed* him," because he is still a selfish, spoiled boy.

Instead of exonerating Brick of any guilt for Skipper's death as Poe's treatment did, Brooks sticks closer to the play: in the film Maggie tries to come between Skipper and Brick because she feels that Skipper had monopolized too much of her husband's life. Skipper retaliates by phoning Brick and drunkenly confessing his abject emotional dependence on his buddy and his inability to live up to Brick's unrealistic expectations of him both as athlete and friend. Brick is revolted by Skipper's attempt to leap from the pedestal on which Brick's adolescent hero-worship of Skipper has placed him. So he ruthlessly hangs up on Skipper, and Skipper in drunken despair leaps from his hotel window.

While in no way a "substitute" for the homosexual theme, Brick's arrested emotional development, his prolonged adolescene, was used, says Brooks, to motivate his rejection of manhood, "manhood as understood by Big Daddy, by a sensual wife, by most of middleclass America." In their confrontation scene "Big Daddy hammers at Brick to grow up. Unwilling to listen, incapable at this moment of facing reality, Brick hobbles out of the house on crutches into a rainstrom and gets into his car, hoping to escape his father's pursuit and continuing harangue. But Big Daddy won't let him drive off." A close-up of the wheels of Brick's car spinning in the mud underscores the impasse that he and his father have reached at this moment.

"Big Daddy matches the elements with a torrent of words accusing his son of being a man still playing a kid's games. He rages that *living* is more than having your picture in the paper; it's more than the excitement of a two-hour football game; more than crowds cheering; *living* is something you have to do twenty-four hours a day, every day, for the rest of your life." As Brooks envisions him, part of Brick's failure to grow up and become a mature man and husband is his own fault; but part of the failure is also Big Daddy's fault, for Brick's dependence on Skipper is in part at least explained by Big Daddy's failure to provide the kind of paternal strength and love that Brick needed when he was growing up. Brick makes this point in a scene that Brooks devised in the basement of the mansion, "where all of Brick's athletic trophies and citations are gathering dust and cobwebs" (and a poster featuring a real photo of the young Newman throwing a football is on display).

"Brick's rage equals his father's," Brooks says in describing the scene. "He accuses Big Daddy of having aspirations for him that he can never meet. In a somewhat parallel case, Big Daddy reveals the love he had for his own father. The basement sequence is one in which father and son finally confront one another at a gut level," and Brick expresses his anger and frustration by smashing some of the antiques piled up in the cellar, a symbol of the affluence of the Pollitts which belies their spiritual and emotional poverty. "At the conclusion of the sequence, they mount the stairway out of the basement, out of

Paul Newman and Burl Ives in the cellar confrontation in *Cat on a Hot Tin Roof*.

the lower depths, out of the past with its cobwebbed trophies. They help each other up the staircase: Brick, with his injured ankle, Big Daddy with his terrible spasm of pain caused by cancer of the stomach."

"Aside from writing the homosexuality out of Brick's character," Brooks says in summarizing his approach to the screenplay, "few basic changes were made in the play." Veteran director George Cukor had turned down the chance to direct the film because he felt that "the screenplay wouldn't hold up without that component of the plot." He was pleasantly surprised to see how well the movie turned out anyhow, and remarked after he saw it, "The story is so persuasive that the lack of this strong motivational element of the plot wasn't even missed on the screen."

As I said above, Brooks decided against opening out the play for the screen with a variety of location scenes and flashbacks as Poe had opted to do in his

Paul Newman venting his rage in the cellar sequence of *Cat*.

treatment, but he did strive to move the action around the plantation mansion to keep the pace of the film from lagging. He follows the action from Maggie and Brick's bed-sitting room upstairs down to the cellar where Brick and Big Daddy plumb the depths of their relationship. Just as we found to be the case with such Williams films as *Streetcar* and *Rose Tattoo*, the director was right to keep the action close to the central setting of the home of the principals because this was a wise way of symbolizing the manner in which the members of the family are equivalently locked together in their continuing struggle for love and security.

Brooks did, however, add one important location sequence to the story. The picture opens with a scene which explains how Brick broke his ankle and came to be using the crutch which is so symbolic of his crippled emotional state. In the play the audience learns of this incident via the dialogue; but, as Brooks reminds us, the very nature of a movie allows for action to replace dialogue:

"Brick is seen in an empty stadium at night. He is drunkenly trying to recapture his 'dreams of glory' as an athlete. He 'hears' the cheers of the crowd as he tries the high hurdles, but he fails to clear one of the hurdles. He falls and breaks his leg. The cheers fade away. He looks to the thousands of seats—his cheering audience—all empty seats: there is no one in the stadium. This prologue was intended to establish the problem underlying Brick's character at the start of the story: a grown man with an adolescent's dream of acceptance on a mass scale—the crowd. Thus, in *Cat*, there was no need for a later flashback to *show* how Brick was injured. At the same time, it eliminated the need for lengthy dialogue."

Brooks was careful throughout his screenplay to save significant passages of William's dialogue, while at the same time he whittled down some of the play's longer speeches which, while completely acceptable on the stage, would seem tedious in a film simply because movies are meant to move. As the writer-director himself puts it, "Film is a visual medium and the theater is an auditory one." He ensures that the moviegoer's attention will not flag during the protracted scene between Big Daddy and Brick, which comprises nearly the whole of the second act of the play, by moving them about the house as they talk and by introducing Maggie into the sequence in order to break up their long duologue. Maggie's admission that she tried to break up Skipper's relationship with Brick takes place in the first act of the play; but Brooks inserts it here to make the scene as a whole take on the nature of an investigation at which Big Daddy presides, now hearing Brick, now hearing Maggie, as he attempts to piece together what really is at the root of Brick's estrangement from his wife. This structuring of the material further reinforces Big Daddy's central position in the working out of the story and how he is, therefore, clearly its unifying factor.

Because he began his career in films as a screen writer, Brooks has always been convinced of the necessity of a strong script. He says in *Directors at Work*, "Your film can be no better than the script. If the story is bad, the actors can be sublime, the music magnificent, the color breathtaking; but your film in the end will be a failure." He even sees directing as an extension of writing in that "the director is really writing with film. You have nothing to direct until you have a story, and then you take that story and put it on film."

In filming *Cat*, Brooks was working with a host of what he calls "sublime actors," but he had to fight to get MGM to agree to some of the casting, particularly of Paul Newman. The studio had several other contract players in mind for Brick's role; but Brooks wanted Newman, who was also under contract to Metro. Brooks finally convinced his producer to use Newman because the part of the passive Brick requires an actor who can react as much as act. "You've got to have a young man here who, when everybody else is talking, is playing a drama for us right on his face," he explained. The director thought Newman had that quality and he was vindicated by the actor's skillful performance. Brick hardly says anything in the first half of the movie while he is listening to Maggie and others talk at him; and yet Newman is a dynamic screen presence throughout these early scenes of the film. Both Newman and Elizabeth Taylor gave performances in *Cat* that are among the best they have ever done, with the possible exception of the other Williams films which they also made, as we shall see.

Brooks recalled in a recent TV interview with Peter Lawford that Ms. Taylor went through a great personal crisis while shooting *Cat*; and the way that she came through it demonstrated her status as a consummate professional, not just a superstar. It began when her husband Mike Todd asked Brooks if she could fly with him to New York over a weekend in his private plane to be present when he received the showman of the year award for producing the film *Around the World in Eighty Days*. Brooks tactfully put Todd off by pointing out that trouble might result with the front office over the insurance risk involved were Ms. Taylor to make the trip. He also gracefully turned down Todd's offer to take him along, pleading the necessity to make some script revisions over the weekend.

The next day Brooks heard the shattering news that Todd's plane had crashed, and he drove up to the canyon home of the Todds where he found his star in a state of total collapse. She screamed at him, "You came here just to find out when I'm coming back to work!" Brooks replied, "Elizabeth, this movie doesn't mean a damned thing in comparison with what you are facing now. Don't come back until you're ready." When she did return to the set, Ms. Taylor looked worn out from her ordeal and frail from not eating. So Brooks decided to shoot Big Daddy's birthday party immediately as a subtle way to coax her into eating once more. "We brought in ice cream and cake and sandwiches, and we kept doing extra takes as long as she was eating," Brooks remembers. "I would say to her, 'It's not you, Elizabeth; it's the crew. Let's do that shot again.' "

When they arrived at the scene where Maggie accuses Brick of being inadequate as a husband, Brooks explained to her that because the possibility of Brick's latent homosexuality had virtually been eliminated from the screenplay, she had to bring across to the audience the first intimations that it is Brick's emotional immaturity which has caused him to be excessively involved in sports and in his friendship with Skipper in a way that has hurt their marriage. "Maggie is the spine of this scene," he said in coaching the actress. "All that Paul is

Elizabeth Taylor in the title role of *Cat on a Hot Tin Roof*.

doing is listening to you; you have to give the scene whatever strength it has because what you are saying is the thing that causes a change of direction in the story at this point." She listened carefully, and then played the scene exactly as Brooks had hoped.

Since it was impossible for Ms. Taylor to take her mind completely off her personal tragedy during the shooting of *Cat*, Brooks believes that she actually transferred some of her feelings about the death of her husband in real life to the context of Big Daddy's imminent death in the film while filming was underway. "Here was something that had happened to her in real life at the time and she was pro enough to realize that this was something that she could use honorably to help her give the best she could to her work. From that time on she would always dig into her experience and background to enable her to encompass the demands of the role she was playing."

Both Paul Newman and Elizabeth Taylor were nominated for Academy Awards for their work in *Cat,* as were Brooks and cinematographer William Daniels. The picture was also nominated as best film of the year. Curiously, Burl Ives won an Oscar as best supporting actor, not for his role in *Cat* but for his part in *The Big Country*. It seems to me, however, that Ives's award was in some sense really for his performances in both films. There is, after all, nothing in his portrayal of the patriarchal rancher in *The Big Country* that is not matched by his portrayal of the patriarchal plantation owner in *Cat on a Hot Tin Roof*. Indeed, his performance in the latter film at certain moments surpasses any acting that Ives has ever done in any movie. There is nothing anywhere else in Ives's career to match his thundering at Brick this crucial line in *Cat,* "I've got the guts to die! Have you got the guts to live?" The ways of the Motion Picture Academy of Arts and Sciences who vote the Oscars have always been inscrutable, but never more so than when Ives won an award for *The Big Country* instead of for *Cat*.

In spite of the great critical and box office success of *Cat on a Hot Tin Roof,* Williams has never been much enamored of the film. "I don't think the movie had the purity of the play," he has said. "It was jazzed up, hoked up a bit." Perhaps one reason for his disappointment with the movie stems from the final scene, in which Brick seems more enthusiastic about joining Maggie in the bedroom to produce the heir which Big Daddy so desparately desires than was the case in either version of the play's third act. Williams has always felt that the reconciliation of Brick and Maggie should always be presented as tentative at best at the point the story ends.

In any event Brooks did a conscientious job of adapting *Cat* to the screen, given the pressures and taboos which existed in the film industry at the time the film was made. After all, the movie received six Oscar nominations and grossed ten million dollars domestically. Williams nonetheless looked forward to the 1976 television production to see if it would be an improvement on the earlier motion picture. Lord Laurence Olivier had signed with London's Granada Television Network and with NBC-TV to direct and star as Big Daddy in the teleplay. His co-stars were Natalie Wood (Maggie) and her husband Robert Wagner (Brick), along with Maureen Stapleton (Big Mama).

The text of the play which served as the source of the TV version, first telecast December 6, 1976, was the 1974 version which, as I have noted above, incorporates some minor but felicitous improvements that Williams developed

Judith Anderson and Burl Ives in *Cat*.

after the original Broadway run, but still adheres substantially to the Broadway version. The two-hour telecast divided the original three acts of the play into six shorter segments, but otherwise followed the text of the play very closely, even to the point of retaining all of the homosexual implications that had to be phased out of the film in 1958.

Hence the dispeptic comments of TV critic John O'Connor in *The New York*

Times seemed particularly overheated when he criticized the six act format of the teleplay as fatally disrupting the rhythm of the original play and amounting to a mere "series of set acting pieces." Effort was made to break the action at natural pauses in the dialogue and the play therefore unfolded in a fairly smooth fashion. O'Connor also faulted Olivier's performance as Big Daddy, insisting that the actor's Southern drawl had a manufactured quality that could not be elided into Lord Olivier's normally clipped British accent. For myself, I prefer to agree with *Time* reviewer T. E. Kalem, who terms Olivier's "flawless Southern accent" a testimony to his "lifelong perfection of craft."

Olivier played Big Daddy as a Southern feudal lord, emphasizing his self-proclaimed stature as the master of "28,000 acres of the richest land this side of the Valley Nile." But he is also the gruff and imposing patriarch that Williams created; and his performance, far from being the "little cameo" that Olivier called it, rightly dominates the teleplay in the same way that Burl Ives's portrayal of Big Daddy dominated the original Broadway production and the motion picture. In fact Judith Crist in *TV Guide* asserted that Olivier, as creative and artistic producer of the teleplay, influenced the entire production. "Unlike the great stars whose glitter dims all that surrounds them, Olivier enhances and elevates both the play and the players by his own artistry."

Even though the television version, which was directed by Robert Moore, was franker than the Richard Brooks movie, the latter is still superior to the former since the trio of performances given by Paul Newman, Elizabeth Taylor, and Burl Ives remain the definitive interpretations of their respective roles, against which all others will continue to be measured. Moore's direction of the TV production simply did not serve to probe the complex relationships of the characters as delicately as Brooks did in his sensitive handling of the 1958 movie.

After doing *Cat* on the screen, Brooks went on to adapt and direct the film of *Sweet Bird of Youth* three years later, and in so doing reconfirmed his status, with Kazan, as one of Williams's foremost screen interpreters. There are several parallels between *Bird* and *Cat*, and so it is not surprising that Brooks was drawn to filming the one as much as to the other. Once again there is an aging adolescent hero played by Paul Newman—this time on stage as well as screen; and the domineering father figure again inspired (with important modifications mentioned at the beginning of this chapter) by the author's father, C. C. Williams.

As early as 1953 Williams was working on a short play tentatively titled *The Enemy Time*, about a young man who loses his girl, Heavenly, after he gives her venereal disease. He expanded this play, though still keeping it to one act, by adding another plot line, about the young man, Chance Wayne, becoming the male companion of Alexandra del Lago, whom Chance calls the Princess. She is an aging actress who abandons him when her floundering career gets a fresh start. In this form the play was presented under the new title of *Sweet Bird of Youth* at the Stuiod M Theater in Miami, Florida, in the summer of 1956. Finally Williams developed the play into a full length work.

Very likely because *Bird* represented the stitching together of two separate plots into a single three-act play, the full length version seems rather disjointed. "I said at the time that I was directing the original Broadway production of *Sweet Bird of Youth* that it seemed to be two one-act plays, one about the Princess and one about Chance Wayne and his girl," says Elia Kazan; "but that is not a very preceptive remark since the Princess is hardly in the second act at all. I thought that this created something of a structural problem, but Williams carried it off with his virtuosity."

Williams is the first to admit that his greatest weakness as a dramatist is structural, as I have had occasion to point out before. But it is also true, as in this case, that what Kazan calls Williams's virtuosity, his talent for creating vivid characterizations and dialogue, and his overall strong sense of the theatrical, often carry his plays over the rough spots.

In Alexandra del Lago, the has-been actress who seeks to drown her past in pills and liquor, Williams has created another one of his unforgettable female characters. She was undoubtedly inspired by a woman whom Williams had met in the early Forties when he was a destitute would-be writer living a hand-to-mouth existence in Greenwich Village. Williams had taken a job as a waiter in a Village nightclub, but lost it after a disagreement with his employer over tips. He was able to keep the wolf from the door temporarily, however, when he was befriended by a group of alcoholics whom he had first met at the club. Williams would accompany them each evening to the home of a retired actress called the Baronness. If he stayed long enough, someone always got around to ordering chicken sandwiches. For days at a time he subsisted on sandwiches and mixed drinks. The actress's cupboard was always bare because she simiply never bothered to eat. Whenever she felt near physical collapse, she would check herself into a hospital for a series of blood transfusions, and would soon be back drinking with her friends as usual.

Geraldine Page, who played Alexandra on both stage and screen, suspects that another model for her character was Tallulah Bankhead. Williams had always felt that Ms. Bankhead was an actress of great ability and was saddened by the way she systematically destroyed herself and her talent with drugs and drink. Her career was already on the wane when she undertook to play Blanche DuBois in the New York City Center revival of *Streetcar* in the winter of 1956, while Williams was working on the first draft of *Sweet Bird* for production in Florida. Working with her on *Streetcar* at the very same time that he was in the midst of composing *Sweet Bird* no doubt strengthened the association already present in his mind between Tallulah and Alexandra.

The other person who served as a source for Alexandra, I believe, is Williams himself. This may not seem farfetched when one considers Williams's own remark in the preface to the published edition of the play that when he attacks human behavior in his plays he includes himself, as a member of the human race, in the attack. He continues, "In fact, I can't expose a human weakness on the stage unless I know it through having it myself." Alexandra is a hypochondriac who carries a portable tank of oxygen with her wherever she travels for fear that she should suddenly cease breathing. Ever since he was seriously ill as a child, Williams too has worried inordinately about his health. One early interviewer found him to be conscious of "the pulsations of his heart, the act of respiration, and the flow of blood in his arterial system," and Williams himself has confessed to a deep-seated fear of suffocation. (In actual fact Williams was undergoing psychoanalysis to rid himself of these psychosomatic symptoms at the very time that he was writing *Sweet Bird*.)

Williams, too, admits sharing Alexandra's fear of failure. The immediate reason that the Princess is fleeing across the country with Chance as her companion is that she wrongly assumes that her comeback film has been a fiasco, just as Williams was certain on opening night that *Cat on a Hot Tin Roof* was a disaster until the reviews appeared and proved him completely wrong.

A third affinity with Alexandra is one which Williams candidly admits in his autobiography: his bout with alcohol and drugs, which became more pronounced when he experienced a writing block after launching *Cat*. Living in the shadow of *Cat's* extraordinary success, he was convinced that he would never be able to write competently for the theater again, and turned to artifical stimulants to activate his creative juices. Although his own addictive problem was to get worse in the late Sixties before it got better, by the late Fifties the playwright was sufficiently on top of the problem to treat it frankly in *Sweet Bird*. In sum, Williams has himself said that there is a fairly close parallel between the play and his own life experiences before and during the period in which he wrote *Sweet Bird*. Now to the play itself.

As the curtain rises, Alexandra is just emerging from the twilight world of oblivion in which she has sought temporary escape from the black despair of her assumed movie debacle. As she comes to, Alexandra fights off consciousness as one would an enemy, her arms flailing about to avoid waking up to the unkind glare of the morning sun. Finally she peeks ever so furtively out from beneath her black satin sleeping mask at the world surrounding her rumpled bed and wakes up in spite of herself. She breathlessly calls for oxygen, and replaces one mask with another. Surely this is one of the most brilliant "entrances" in the modern theater, a fine indication of what I referred to a moment ago as Williams's unsurpassed intuition for what makes good theater.

As she breathes in artificial air from the oxygen tank, one sees this as a symbolic manifestation of the insulated, stifling, self-centered existence which she lives. She then picks up her glasses, only to find that one lens is cracked,

Geraldine Page in *Sweet Bird of Youth*.

another indication that she views the world subjectively through a distorting lens in line with her neurotic preoccupations.

Yet, if Alexandra is a monster, Chance is correct in calling her "a nice monster." There is a spark of humanity left in her underneath her tough exterior, a façade that she has fashioned because, unlike Blanche DuBois, she has learned not to depend upon the kindness of the brand of male strangers who prey on lonely women. She consequently has no delusions about her relationship with Chance, and is not even surprised when he tries to blackmail her about her drug habits in order to force her to arrange for Heavenly and himself to get into pictures. "When a monster meets a monster," she jeers, "one monster has to give way; and it will never be me."

Though she believes that she has "a disease of the heart" that is eating away at her vitals, she still has enough heart left to be moved when Chance recalls for her (and the audience) his checkered past: Boss Finley, the local demagogue in

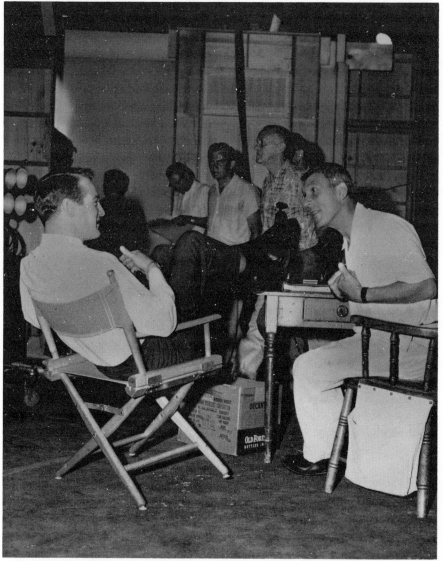

Paul Newman listens to writer-director Richard Brooks on the set of *Sweet Bird*.

St. Cloud, the little Southern town where he and Alexandra have taken up temporary residence, would not let him marry his daughter Heavenly until he had established himself in a career; when the right doors did not open for him, he went in the wrong ones and wound up in his present occupation, the only career for which he now seems qualified.

When Chance says that he is determined not to leave St. Cloud this time without Heavenly, Alexandra knows that it is too late for him to recapture the lost innocence which he once shared with Heavenly. The sweet bird of youth has flown away and is as irretrievable for him as it is for her. She kisses him almost maternally and calls him a lost little boy whom she would like to help find himself. Alexandra is amazed at her unselfish response to Chance's story: "That means my heart's still alive, at least some part of it is, not all of my heart is dead yet."

Near the end of the play, when she decides to leave town, she tries to get Chance to give up his illusions of winning back Heavenly and to come with her. She even nurses a hope that he can help her stop being the monster that she has become, and that she in turn can help him to reverse the process of his own deterioration as a human being. She has by this point discovered that she is back on top, but even as she packs to return to Hollywood she knows that her successful comeback is but a temporary reprise of her past glamor and glory. Hence she still thinks of herself and Chance as two orphans in a storm who should huddle together to share whatever warmth each of them has left to give to the other.

But Chance refuses to travel on with Alexandra, no longer because he thinks that he can make his dreams for Heavenly and himself come true, but because he knows that all of his chances have waned and that he might as well stay to face the consequences of his wasted and corrupt life. A change has come over Chance in the course of the play. He now realizes that the dissolute life which he led away from St. Cloud, and which he tried to keep separate from his relationship with Heavenly, has tainted that relationship beyond purification. Even if Boss Finley had not had Heavenly sterilized in the wake of her having contracted gonorrhea from Chance, their union could never have been a fruitful one. All that Chance possesses to impart to Heavenly is corruption and disease, symbolic of his own sickness of soul as well as of body. Chance is shaken by the realization that he has not only squandered his own youth but Heavenly's as well, since he is indirectly responsible for rendering her a childless old woman.

It is this recognition that motivates Chance not to escape with the Princess but to await Boss Finley's henchmen to deprive him of what is left of his youth by the emasculation that will leave him a childless old man. "The age of some people can only be calculated by the level of rot in them; and by that measure I'm ancient," he muses without self-pity. "Time—who could ever defeat it? Maybe some saints and heroes, but not Chance Wayne." Turning to the audience he concludes, "I don't ask for your pity, but just for your understanding—not even that—no. Just for your recognition of me in you, and the enemy, time, in us all."

When Oscar Hammerstein II, co-author of such sunny musicals as *The Sound of Music*, was quoted in *The New York Times* as resenting Chance Wayne's invitation to the theater audience to identify with him, Williams replied, "People are humble and frightened and guilty at heart, all of us, no matter how desparately we try to appear otherwise. We have very little conviction of our essential dignity nor even of our essential decency, and consequently we are more interested in characters on the stage who share our hidden shames and fears, and we want the plays about us to say, 'I understand you. You and I are brothers, the deal is rugged but let's face and fight it together.' "

All of us have things in our past which call for regret and expiation, Williams suggests in Chance's brief monologue at the end of *Sweet Bird*, and when our past at last catches up with us, we all need some of Chance's courage to come to terms with it, though neither he nor we would style him a saint or hero just because he is willing to take what is coming to him. There is a religious element in the play, however, which has usually been overlooked, and which is in harmony with Chance's self-sacrifice at the end of the play. *Sweet Bird* takes place on Easter Sunday and begins with Chance sharing the living death of the Princess's hotel suite, where they employ sex, liquor, and hashish in their mutual search for a spurious nirvana; the play concludes with Chances' groping, according to his lights, for redemption through expiatory suffering, in the hope that he can transcend his sordid past and come to life once more.

In the course of the play a heckler, who has only contempt for Boss Finley's posturings as a God-appointed savior of the people, remarks that the silence of God has yet to be broken to any man who has lived on earth, and that there have been no exceptions, "least of all Boss Finley." By the final curtain, however, it would seem that God has spoken to Chance, at least to the extent that Chance is inspired to confer some meaning on his life by paying for his past. Perhaps maturity has come to rest on Chance now that the sweet bird of youth has flown away for good.

Since *Sweet Bird* is a thought-provoking play, it is a pity that Williams was never able to mesh the material which he had drawn from his two plot lines into a completely coherent three-act play. He admitted after the play opened in New York, "The truth is, the second act of that play is just not well written. I was already tired when I came to rehearsals and I was in no condition to do all the rewriting I had to do. I couldn't function, except just on a craftsmanship level. Kazan wanted a great second act, and I couldn't give it to him."

The episodic second act shifts the focus of the play from the Princess to Chance's efforts to win Heavenly away from Boss Finley, who demands that she appear on the platform with him that night at a political rally to squelch the rumors about her secret hysterectomy. The rally erupts into a riot when the heckler shouts out the truth about Chance and Heavenly, and Chance loses contact with Heavenly in the ensuing chaos. Then the third act returns to the Princess, who all but disappeared from the story until she reappears in the final act.

Williams was able to meld two one-act plays into one continuous story in *Baby Doll* because in *Baby Doll* he subordinated the plot of one story to the other. The structural problem in *Sweet Bird* is that the play really has two main plots which run along side by side; and only rarely do the parallel lines intersect. Technically Alexandra del Lago is a subordinate character in the play, but Williams has drawn her so powerfully that she usurps center stage whenever she appears and finally overwhelms the whole play. It would have been better, in retrospect, if Williams had made her the focal point of the action in all three acts, as Blanche is in *Streetcar*, rather than to allow her to take over on her own.

Williams revised the play for the acting edition available to non-professionals by merely building up Heavenly's character in the second act and reducing Boss Finley's role to a walk-on; but he still failed to solve the essential structural problem of the play, which involves the Princess's place in the play as a whole, not that of Heavenly or the Boss. Williams now recognizes this fact and says that if he ever revises the play again he will rewrite the second act so that the action remains at the hotel with Chance and the Princess, in order that she can dominate the play more completely.

The first actress to play Alexandra del Lago in the full-length version of the play was Geraldine Page, though her first reaction was to turn down the part. "In the theater there are Alexandra del Lagos and Chance Waynes by the gross," she told Kazan when he discussed it with her; and she wanted no part of a play about the degenerate lives of a has-been actress and a would-be actor. She also feared that if she missed capturing the essence of such a flamboyant character her performance could turn out to be atrociously overdone. But Kazan finally persuaded her to accept the role in which she would make both theater and movie history.

When she was working out her characterization, Kazan gave her a sheaf of photographs of several silent film stars and asked her to choose the one that she thought most resembled the Princess. She selected the shot of Norma Talmadge, whom she had never even seen on the screen, because she felt that Ms. Talmadge's expression projected a vulnerability which had been hardened by the shocks and hurts which are part of the acting profession. It is with that frame of mind that she played Alexandra del Lago.

The play reached Broadway with an advance ticket sale of almost $400,000, and the film rights went to Metro for a like sum. Paul Newman and Geraldine Page were signed to repeat their stage roles in the film, as were Madeleine Sherwood in the role of Lucy, the Boss's mistress, and Mildred Dunnock in the role of Aunt Nonnie, the Boss's spinster sister. Shirley Knight later won an Oscar nomination for her portrayal of Heavenly in the film and Ed Begley received an Academy Award for his performance as Boss Finley.

Richard Brooks was again at the helm as writer-director of the movie, and he quickly discovered that adapting *Sweet Bird* for cinema posed many more problems than *Cat on a Hot Tin Roof* had. "*Cat* was more adaptable to the screen

Shirley Knight and Paul Newman in *Sweet Bird*.

than *Sweet Bird* in terms of having less material that was censorable," Brooks told me. In *Cat* homosexuality was the only taboo that posed a serious problem for screen treatment, whereas "there were several inherent subjects in *Sweet Bird* that could not be dramatized in the movie—or rather, they were not allowable": Heavenly's contracting venereal disease from Chance, her subsequent hysterectomy, and the resulting downbeat ending with its implication that Chance is to be emasculated by Boss Finley's son Tom and his goons. Brooks had to alter all of these components of Williams's play to render his screenplay acceptable to the Motion Picture Code.

"Since in the play Chance had infected his sweetheart with gonorrhea," says Brooks, a substitute was required to motivate Boss Finley's vengeance on Chance. "So Heavenly's pregnancy replaced gonorrhea; and her pregnancy also motivated her intense dislike for her father in the movie, because it was her father who insisted that she abort the child, with Chance waiting willingly to be castrated in order to vindicate his commitment to Heavenly as the love of his youth whose life he has ruined.

"In the play, at the final curtain, Chance Wayne delivers a monologue to the effect that there is a little of him in all of us," Brooks continues. "As he concludes, the lights begin to dim. The shadows of Heavenly's revenge-seeking brother Tom and his cronies move toward Chance; their intention to deprive him of his manhood is quite clear." But castration was no more acceptable to the Code than homosexuality had been in *Cat*. "The only acceptable substitution for castration: to have Tom Finley smash the beauty of Chance Wayne's face—a face that had been his meal ticket for the past few years. Mr. Williams's play is built on a pyramid of incidents dealing with Chance Wayne's youth and beauty. Chance manipulated those assets to ingratiate himself as a male stud for middle-aged female movie stars. In payment for his youth, beauty, and virility, he expected to be made a movie star in Hollywood. When his face was smashed and broken, what was destroyed was his most valuable asset, his only 'currency': his beauty and youth."

To Brooks the ending of the picture just described would be an adequate substitute for Williams's finale; but Brooks also thought of an alternate ending which would be closer still to the spirit of the play, and he took this proposal to the front office:

"MGM had promised (verbally) to let me shoot two separate, different endings for the movie. In the first ending just referred to, Chance goes to Heavenly's house and, despite threats to his personal safety, calls for her to go away with him—away from her father—wherever it might lead. Her brother arrives in a car with his cronies. They gang up on Chance and batter his face. Heavenly comes out of the house. She still loves him, and they stumble off into the darkness together.

"The second ending was an outgrowth of a scene exposed early in the play. Boss Finley insists that Heavenly never see Chance Wayne again. In the movie the scene is staged on the beach near their mansion. Boss Finley's threat is graphic. He points to the Gulf, where the lights of garbage scows are seen as they make their way toward the open sea. He threatens that if she ever sees him, even once, Chance Wayne will end up on one of those scows like the garbage and scum he is.

"The alternate ending was meant to play back on this scene between Boss Finley and Heavenly. Chance Wayne calls for Heavenly to run away with him. Her brother and his companions arrive, as in the first ending; they batter his beauty into a pulp. At that point, the scene shifts to a ferry boat. It is the same boat on which, at the movie's beginning, the Princess and Chance Wayne crossed the bay into Boss Finley's territory. Now, the Princess is leaving town on the same ferry boat; her companion this time is Boss Finley's ex-mistress, whom he had brutally discarded. The two women leave the Princess's car, walk to the prow of the ferry boat. Several garbage scows are sea bound to dump their refuse. On one of the scows—atop the piled garbage—lies Chance Wayne. That was to be the alternate ending to the movie.

"Our plan was to finish shooting the 'first ending' and then, with a minimum crew and one night's work, go out to the ferry boat and film the 'second ending.' In my opinion, the second ending (with Chance Wayne on the garbage scow) was more in keeping with the intention of Mr. Williams's play. However, despite their verbal promise to allow the shooting of the alternate ending, the studio closed down our company as soon as the first ending was completed. 'They'—the omnipresent 'they'—wanted the so-called happy ending: Chance Wayne and his girl going off together. That's what's on the screen. Promises, promises!"

Film reviewers like Bosley Crowther and Dwight Macdonald, unaware of Brooks's efforts to provide a more suitable finale for the film, pilloried him for the movie's upbeat ending, saying that it contradicted the cold logic of the preceding two hours, turning Chance's defeat into victory. At least one reviewer thought that even the ending of the film as released retained implications of Williams's play, however. In removing Chance's castration from the film, *Variety* commented, Brooks accomplished this revision "as if winking his creative eye at the 'in' audience, saying, 'Yes, we have compromised, but you get the general idea.' The 'general idea' is that the menace, or grisly potential, can be equally as frightening as the act."

In fairness to Brooks I must confess that I prefer the movie's actual ending to the one that Williams wrote for the acting edition of the play referred to above, in which he substitutes Chance's non-violent, psychological castration for the physical one of the original play by having him leave town still employed as the Princess's giggolo. Since the foregoing action remains clearly geared toward the original ending, the replacement of the real emasculation with a symbolic one in this revised version of the play comes across as a cop-out. Brooks, on the other hand, has substituted one kind of violence (the brutal slashing of Chance's face) for another (castration), which is not a cop-out at all, but rather retains the harrowing quality of the original ending of the play.

And, Crowther and Macdonald notwithstanding, the logic of the total film is not compromised by the ending as shot, because all of the changes which Brooks had to make in order to satisfy the censors coalesce into a logical consistency of their own at this point. In the play Heavenly's sterilization and Chance's corresponding castration underscore the hopelessness of their situation in indicating that Chance has sold his sexuality to the highest bidder for too long, and it is now too late for him ever to be able to give it freely in marriage and parenthood. But in the film Chance has given Heavenly not gonorrhea but made her pregnant, symbolizing that in the movie it is not yet too late for them to cultivate a fruitful and lasting relationship. For although the Boss makes Heavenly have an abortion, she is not sterilized; and although Chance is disfigured, he is not emasculated. Hence, both are still capable of giving and receiving love physically and can still look forward to a permanent union.

Brooks prepares the audience for Chance's regeneration at film's end by staging a scene in the local church during Easter morning services in which Chance and Heavenly see each other for the first time since his return. The religious symbolism of resurrection and renewal associated with Easter Sunday (which is more implicit in the play) provides a significant context for this meeting since Heavenly by her first name and outlook continues to be the inspiration of whatever rejuvenation is possible for Chance to experience. In the play, however, Chance brings Heavenly down to his level more than she elevates him to hers.

I do not wish to imply that I prefer the dry cleaning which Brooks had to administer to the play so that it could receive a seal from the MPAA to Williams's original work. But I do want to say that, granted the adjustments which Brooks made in the play in composing his screenplay, the upbeat ending of the film does grow out of the foregoing two hours with logic comparable to that with which the downbeat ending of the play develops out of the its foregoing two hours. The film's relatively happy ending is not simply tacked on to the plot of the play, but really emerges with inner consistency from the movie's revised story line.

Nevertheless the positive ending of the picture suggests a more optimistic theme than Williams had conceived to be at the basis of the play as he wrote it. "*Sweet Bird of Youth* was a brilliant film till the end," he says; "the happy reconciliation between Chance and Heavenly destroyed the whole theme of the work." For me the theme of the inevitable loss of youth and the futility of trying to prolong it still comes through in the film. But I do agree with the playwright that the happy ending of the movie undercuts the power with which this theme is brought home to the viewer of the picture. As critic Robert Haller has written, in the film the main characters are forced to see the truth themselves, to recognize their frailties for what they are; but then they are allowed to go free to build their lives on this new, dearly bought, self-knowledge. Williams's point in the play, on the other hand, was that unfortunately in life people too often gain self-knowledge too late for it to be of any practical use to them in reshaping their lives.

It is this latter situation which Williams wanted his audience to face in the play, which ends with Chance bereft of Heavenly and happiness, and the Princess returning to a success that can be at best a short-lived reprieve from later failure and despair. Instead the movie concludes with Chance going off with Heavenly and with the Princess going back to Hollywood, each secure in the knowledge that happiness and personal worth do not depend on good looks and youth. This conclusion, though thought-provoking, is admittedly must less sobering and much more promising than anything which Williams had intended.

Although Williams was disappointed in the ultimate thematic implications of the movie, he freely concedes that Brooks's screenplay is better constructed than his play ever was. "It was awfully hard for me to write the second act, which was largely about the social background of the story," he says. "Sometimes I wish I had made it a shorter play and not tried to deal with so much."

Brooks realized this when he set to work on the film script, and the first thing he did to achieve more unity in the story was to drop the subplot about Boss Finley's machinations to make political capital out of the segregationist sentiments of his white constituents. In a play already overloaded with episodes, this was one aspect of the Boss's villainy that could easily be thrown overboard to keep the film as a whole from listing. He then went on to tackle the problem of bringing into closer allignment the two plot lines of the play, so that Alexandra would not all but disappear from the whole middle portion of the movie as she did in the play.

Brooks obviously agreed with Kazan that the play was more or less divided into two segments, with the princess dominating one and Chance the other. Because, as Brooks notes, there are no "curtains" dividing a movie into "acts" in the way that a play is divided, a movie usually flows along without a break "or pause for refreshment" from start to finish. It was, therefore, even more crucial in the film than in the play to have the Princess's story and Chance's story develop in a unified fashion; otherwise the shift of focus from the Princess's despair over her career to Chance's despair over losing Heavenly would seem more jarring on the screen than it did on the stage, where it took place, as it were, between acts.

"It was necessary, therefore, to delay the Princess's story, to prevent it from reaching its climax too soon, to integrate it more with the development of Chance Wayne's story," says Brooks. "This would allow the Princess to remain prominent throughout the movie. It would keep alive Chance Wayne's hope for Hollywood success and it would also keep alive the Princess's need for Chance when her career is reestablished."

Paul Newman and Geraldine Page in *Sweet Bird*.

At the point where Alexandra learns by long distance phone that Hollywood wants her back, she plays one of the most poignant scenes in the movie. In the play Alexandra offered to take Chance with her to Hollywood as her lover, with the possibility of some kind of genuine love growing up between them. But at the corresponding moment in the film she goes much further and promises to make good her original offer to get him into pictures now that her own stardom is reconfirmed.

As Brooks explains this scene in the movie, "Earlier, when she wasn't high on vodka or hash, when she could evaluate herself and the stud who was sponging off her, she would laugh at Chance Wayne's aspirations to stardom; she would taunt him with being a hired boy. Now, with news of her success, she pleads for Chance Wayne to come back to Hollywood with her. She fears if he returns to Heavenly, he will be brutalized. If only he will come away with her *now* she will help him, use her success to advance his career. It is one of those rare moments of compassion and tenderness in a story of laceration, self-loathing, and hopeless dreams.

"If Chance goes off with the Princess, he surely will get the opportunity he has paid for. Her plea is earnest, tempting. But, when he turns down her offer, at this point in the story, it is clear that his real commitment is to his love for Heavenly. By playing this sequence late in the story, by giving Chance this choice so near the end," a choice which is more generous than the one which she offers him at the corresponding moment in the play, "the choice can be followed immediately by the action." Brooks so worked out this sequence that it would have dovetailed perfectly with his alternate ending to the movie. The studio-preferred ending, he feels, "was as ill-fated as the tinsel dreams of Chance Wayne," and he likes it no better than Williams.

Since Brooks rejected the use of flashbacks in *Cat on a Hot Tin Roof*, I wondered why he used them so liberally in *Sweet Bird of Youth*. In both cases the action is compressed into a short period of time—a single evening in *Cat*, a single day in *Sweet Bird*—and Williams was constrained to cram no little exposition about past events into the dialogue. But the background material in *Cat* was relatively simple and centered around virtually the same topic, Brick's involvement with Skipper. *Sweet Bird*, on the other hand, is burdened with an enormous amount of exposition about the intersecting past personal histories of several characters with widely diverse and separate backgrounds. To expound all of this material exclusively through dialogue, Brooks reasoned, would have proved tedious for the moviegoer. In his own words:

"While *Cat* did not require the flashback technique, *Sweet Bird*, I felt, would be enhanced by carefully designed 'moments of the past' juxtaposed to advance the story. Chance's youthful exuberance, his beauty, his relationship with Heavenly, his secret meetings with her at the lighthouse, his dreams of glory and success—all these and more were *shown* in the film rather than *talked about*.

"Logically, there was no one with whom Chance could reveal his past through dialogue because the 'remember when' method of playing plot is not particularly suitable to movies. He could, of course, have played a few of the scenes with the Princess; but he never would have felt free enough to discuss either his deeper personal feelings about Heavenly, the details of his youthful romance, or his dreams of glory. Then, too, I felt a flashback could better depict how Heavenly felt about Chance. Dialogue is rarely remembered in a movie; images are not easily forgotten.

"The use of flashbacks had to be triggered, of course, by moments in the present. One example comes to mind. Chance and his old friends meet in the hotel bar. The pianist plays a tune from Chance Wayne's younger days, 'It's a Great, Big Wonderful World.' And we see Chance as he was several years ago doing a swan dive at the swimming pool. The scene was shot in slow motion. Chance truly looked like a bird in flight." The image of Chance's beautiful body floating across the screen for a few seconds and then slowly gliding downward into the water provides the perfect visual symbol of the elusive, ephemeral sweet bird of youth as embodied in Chance, soaring for a moment into the incandescent blue sky and then disappearing, never to be recaptured.

Brooks also uses flashbacks to depict directly in the film Alexandra's memories of the making of her comeback movie from her own distorted point of view. We see the camera bearing down on her for a close-up like a cruel one-eyed monster bent on exposing her once youthful face to be now unmistakably marked with traces of dissipation and age. This flashback is followed by another portraying her hysterical exit from the premier of the film, certain that her fans see her only as a faded glamour queen rather than as the mature actress she has shown herself to be in her new film.

Flashbacks, of course, are only one way of opening out a play spatially for the screen, and Brooks took advantage of the motion picture medium's freedom to carry the action of *Sweet Bird* to multiple locations. This was in keeping with the spirit of Williams's play because, as Foster Hirsch has written, the dramatist "for once was hampered by the physical confinements of the proscenium, and he had trouble . . . getting all of his characters into the hotel in which the action is set" during most of the play.

Brooks remedied this drawback of the play easily in the film. He has the sympathetic Aunt Nonnie meet Chance outside the church before Easter Sunday services to warn him about the reprisals which Boss Finley plans to take on Chance. In the play Williams was forced to have this delicate Southern lady seek out Chance in the hotel bar, a place to which it is hardly likely she would ever go. Another inventive device for expanding the scope of the action of the play, which at the same time proved a deft way of sketching out Boss Finely's background and character in shorthand for the viewer, occurs earlier in the film. The Boss and his staff view a documentary about his career as a politican which is reminiscent of the newsreel that surveys Charles Foster Kane's life at the beginning of *Citizen Kane*. In quick succession the filmgoer is given a capsule distillation of the events that led to Boss Finley's rise to power in the state which infuriates the Boss but informs the audience of the kind of man which Chance is up against.

Furthermore Brooks is able to stage the climactic political rally-cum-riot on the screen in a much more spectacular way than was possible on the stage. The rally sequence illustrates that, unlike *Cat*, which by contrast is an intimate family drama which would have profited little by much opening out for the screen, *Sweet Bird* was conceived by its author on a much broader scale; and its panoramic sweep calls for the kind of epic staging that Brooks has given it in color and wide screen.

Ed Begley in the climactic political rally scene of *Sweet Bird*.

Brooks had never worked with wide screen before and he expected that it might prove cumbersome for intimate scenes. He solved this problem by darkening the area around the players and shortening the camera's depth of field to meet the requirements of such scenes.

Roger Manvell in *New Cinema in the U.S.A.* recounts how the director also considered various ways of making the color scheme of the film contribute to the total texture of the movie. Brooks decided to use stunningly beautiful color compositions as an ironic contrast to the wretchedness of the characters' lives; "I thought, here's this harsh picture which had to do with hashish, bastardy, vicious politics, and I don't know what. It's a very harsh picture, and I didn't see why the photography had to be as harsh as the content, so I wanted everything to be soft and beautifully colored." Brooks also believed that this color scheme would reflect Alexandra's outlook on life: "She may be realistic in her business life, but she is very unrealistic in her personal life. This figure sees everything as soft and wants it to be that way." Chance, of course, shares her views for most of the film, and so the lush colors in which much of the movie is photographed reflect the phony dream world of instant success and glamorous romance in which Chance, the Princess, and other characters as well have sought to take refuge. Only toward the end of the picture, when Chance's immature and unrealistic aspirations for easy success are shattered by the departure of the Princess and his disfigurement by Tom Finley and his gang, does Brooks shift the color pattern of the movie to darker, more somber hues which betoken Chance's more sober approach to the harsh realities which he must finally face.

Paul Newman brought to his portrayal of Chance Wayne in the movie the experience of playing the role on the stage for several months and as a result gave one of the best performances of his career. Newman had returned to the stage to stake out a Tennessee Williams role that would be his alone, so that when he did the film version he would be in no one's shadow but his own; and also because he feared that his superstar status in Hollywood was making him too complacent. "There's always that terrible fear that one day your fraud will be discovered and you'll be back in the dog kennel business," Newman explained during the run of the play in New York. "You know you'll get the hell knocked out of you once in a while here, but if you don't, you'll fall back on a lot of successful mannerisms." As a token of his conscientiousness as an actor, Newman never missed a single performance during the forty-two weeks in which he appeared in the show, and his portrayal in the movie reflected the care with which he had created the role of Chance and played it for 336 performances on Broadway.

Like Newman, Geraldine Page garnered fresh accolades for repeating her stage role on screen and also earned an Oscar nomination for her part in the film. She had worked hard during shooting to tone down her bravura stage performance for the camera; and Ms. Page was particularly grateful to Brooks for allowing her to take her time in rehearsing crucial scenes such as the now famous telephone sequence, in which a call from Walter Winchell informs her of the success of her comeback film. Usually a director would give an actress a couple of shots at a monologue scene of this sort and then move on to the next scene. Not so Brooks. She remembers lying across the bed on the set in a state of depression because she had not as yet mastered the scene to her satisfaction after a couple of tries. The soft-spoken Brooks whispered quietly in her ear,

"There's no rush; take it easy." His encouragement had a calming effect on her that made her sense the momentum which she needed for the scene gathering inside her. She signalled that she was ready and immediately did the take that was used in the finished film. (Brooks's tactful handling of his star recalls his equal adroitness in dealing with Elizabeth Taylor on *Cat*, described earlier in this chapter.)

Brooks in fact was careful and painstaking throughout the whole period of adapting and directing *Sweet Bird* because he wanted the movie to be worthy of its source. "I have a tremendous respect for Tennessee Williams," he said to me in summary. "I wanted to be faithful to his work, to the intention of the play. Unfortunately, I have never met Mr. Williams. We conversed several times during the preparation on *Cat* via long distance phone. He was in Key West, I believe. Perhaps some day we'll meet. I'd like to thank him for the pleasure his plays have given me. Mr. Williams and his work are an important slice of my life."

Despite the tinkering done to the original plays at the behest of the censors, Brooks himself is essentially pleased with *Cat* and *Sweet Bird*, and he has reason to be. For, all things being considered, the pair of Williams works which Brooks wrote and directed hold up under repeated viewings, as the Williams films by other first-class directors such as John Huston, Elia Kazan, and Joseph Mankiewicz also do. Let us next look at the Williams films by one of these men, Mankiewicz's *Suddenly Last Summer*.

5
Joseph Mankiewicz:
Suddenly Last Summer

IN THE SUMMER of 1957 Tennessee Williams entered psychoanalysis for a period of several months with Dr. Lawrence Kubie in New York City. The psychosomatic symptoms with which he had been afflicted since youth had become more acute as the pressures of writing for the boom-or-bust conditions of the commercial Broadway theater took an increasing toll on his psychic and physical energies. A born pessimist, Williams took little consolation from successful ventures like *Cat on a Hot Tin Roof* which for him were always dimmed by failures like *Camino Real*. His abiding anxiety that he was written out increased after each successive play; and so he was afraid to take a vacation from writing because, as he said, "I'm afraid if I quit I'd never be able to start again."

Finally, when *Orpheus Descending,* a play which he had been revising for more than fifteen years, received disappointing notices and closed abruptly in the spring of 1957, Williams decided to seek psychiatric help for the gloom that had engulfed him. "*Orpheus* brought all my problems to a head," he said in *The New York Herald Tribune* after some months of therapy. "I knew I must find help or crack up, so I went to an analyst and poured out all my troubles. I felt the most enormous relief."

One of the unresolved psychological conflicts which surfaced in analysis was Williams's continuing pain about the prefrontal lobotomy which his beloved sister Rose had undergone twenty years earlier, an irreversible psychosurgical procedure that would keep her confined to a mental institution for the rest of her days. This happened shortly after Williams had left St. Louis to finish his final year of college at Iowa State in 1937. Rose withdrew more and more into a paranoid fantasy world, and her father C.C. Williams decided to commit her to an asylum. She was first taken to the Catholic sanatorium on the outskirts of St. Louis where her condition was diagnosed as *dementia praecox*, now usually called schizophrenia, and was then removed to the state asylum at Farmington, Missouri. At the state hospital three psychiatrists advised a lobotomy which they said was a newly discovered way of dealing with incurable psychosis, a delicate operation on the brain which enabled the patient to live free of torturing fantasies by destroying the chain of memory.

C.C. Williams was convinced that the operation would help Rose and when he learned that a noted surgeon was going to try the new procedure on thirty selected patients free of charge, he insisted that Rose be one of them. Edwina Williams says in her memoirs that her husband and the doctors told her that if she did not approve the operation Rose might become a raging maniac, and so she too gave her permission for the lobotomy. She later regretted doing so, however, since the operation did not restore Rose to sanity as her parents had hoped, but instead effected a permenent change in her personality that left her passive and remote and unable to function without supervision. C.C. Williams never visited his daughter in the institution after the operation because he believed that Rose Williams no longer existed.

As for her devoted brother Tom, he always felt guilty for not being on hand to intervene when the decision for the lobotomy was made. As I recorded in the first chapter, Rose was her brother's closest companion throughout childhood and early adolescence, and he felt that he had to some degree lost that deep relationship with her as she advanced toward womanhood. But after the lobotomy he realized that he had lost her in a more decisive, final way. "Tom's sense of loss and loneliness must have been devastating," writes Edwina Williams, "as he saw his beautiful, imaginative sister, whom he had always idolized, partially destroyed."

Williams bears out his mother's remarks in his own autobiography where he speaks of his sister as having been tragically becalmed by her psychosurgery. He is certain that without such surgical intervention Rose could have eventually recovered and returned to normal life in ordinary society, which, "despite its assaults on a vulnerable nature, is still preferable to an institutional existence." Although Williams has always seen to it that Rose has had the best care that a private sanatorium can provide, he has always cherished the hope of bringing Rose and a companion to live near him in Key West; and he expresses this fond wish once more at the close of his memoirs. In the meantime he visits her regularly at Stony Lodge in Ossining, New York, where she now lives.

While he was working through the emotional conflicts occasioned by his family relationships with Dr. Kubie, a play prompted by Rose's prefrontal lobotomy began to take shape in his imagination. Williams had never shied away from drawing on even very painful personal experiences in his work, and *Suddenly Last Summer* would be no exception in this regard. "Some people accuse me of being too personal in my writing," he said when he had written the play. "The truth of the matter is, I don't think you can escape being personal in your writing. . . . What this means simply is that the dynamics of the characters in the play, their tensions correspond to something that you are personally going through." Williams in fact counts himself lucky that he has had his writing as an outlet for his reaction to his personal experiences. "Otherwise I would have really gone off my trolley." A writer's work, he says, "is his escape from his life—at least mine is."

Of course Williams only used the circumstances of Rose's lobotomy as the starting point for an imaginative work of art. Nonetheless, he has given to Catherine Holly, the heroine of *Suddenly Last Summer,* some experiences that recall Rose's girlhood in addition to the prime parallel of being faced as Rose was with psychosurgery. For example, Catherine is a lonely young lady whose debut was not a success, which was also the case with Rose when she "came out" as a debutante. After Rose returned from Knoxville, where her father's sister had sponsored her coming out party, she confided to her brother that she was just not charming enough to be popular. With that, she began to withdraw still further from any active social life.

Rose's journey toward mental breakdown was a gradual one, but in the play Catherine suffers an experience so traumatic that she is thrown into a state of shock that makes her appear insane. This one-act play takes place during the period when Catherine is undergoing observation prior to her family's making their final decision whether or not to approve her having a lobotomy. The surgery is being urged by her Aunt Violet Venable to excise from the girl's memory the scurrilous story of her son Sebastian's death.

Sebastian died mysteriously in Cabeza de Lobo (Wolf's Head) while on a Caribbean cruise accompanied by Catherine as his travelling companion. He was a poet who composed a single poem each summer about his annual trip to some exotic part of the world, and was, until this particular summer, always accompanied by Violet. He wrote no poem on his final excursion because, Catherine maintains, her cousin was cannibalized by a group of rapacious native boys whom he had used sexually and then tried to discard.

As a young poet who died an early death, Sebastian was based on Hart Crane, whose poetry Williams has always greatly admired. In one of his later lyrics Crane expressed his fear that the flame of his poetic inspiration was guttering out. Since composing poetry was the ruling passion of his life, he became progressively depressed as his work consistently failed to live up to his high aspirations. He sank into alcoholism and drowned himself in the Caribbean while travelling back to America from Mexico. Williams says that Crane was eventually burned alive by his own unquenchable poetic fire and that through the self-immolation of his work he offered the entire truth about himself to the sensitive reader.

There are several parallels between Hart Crane and Sebastian Venable.

Sebastian too was a homosexual, a devotee of Melville, and a poet who committed suicide when he felt that his artistic gift was atrophying—though Sebastian's self-immolation was of a very peculiar and bizarre nature, as we shall see. Another real life counterpart for Sebastian as the rich homosexual writer flinging coins at a bevy of street arabs to make them stop following him is none other than Oscar Wilde, who comported himself in this way on a visit to North Africa, as Herman Weinberg notes in *Saint Cinema*—though Wilde was ultimately to suffer imprisonment for consorting with young men rather than death, which was Sebastian's fate. Thus did Williams draw on both of these real life authors to create the character of Sebastian according to the demands of the plot which he was constructing.

The requirements of the story also dictated that Sebastian be so physically attractive on the surface that Williams wisely never allowed him to appear on stage, since no human actor could embody the stunning image which the author conjures up in the descriptions of Sebastian's personal charm throughout the play. Beneath that surface lies a deeply troubled psyche. Sebastian's adoring mother explains in the first scene of the play (without realizing the dark implications of what she is saying) that Sebastian made his yearly quest to some far-flung corner of the globe not only to find inspiration for his annual poem, but also to search out the place where he could experience God as directly as it is possible to do so on this planet.

According to Violet, Sebastian felt that he had finally experienced a clear image of God at least once in their summer travels. They had journeyed to the Galpagos Islands, which are called the Ecantadas, the Enchanted Isles, of which Melville wrote, "In no world but a fallen one could such islands exist." But they witnessed something there which Melville had not written about. As their schooner lay off shore, they watched the hatching of thousands of sea turtles on the beach. When the newly hatched baby turtles began to crawl toward the sea, the sky was darkened by savage birds that swooped down and devoured the soft underflesh of their helpless prey before most of the turtles could reach the safety of the sea. Sebastian commented to his mother, "Well, now I've seen Him," and he meant God. "He meant that God shows a savage face to people and shouts some fierce things at them," Violet concludes. "It's all we see or hear of Him."

Violet narrates this incident to Dr. Cukrowicz (Polish for sugar), who must decide whether Catherine's allegations about Sebastian's horrible death signify that she is telling a truth that Violet Venable refuses to accept or rather that she is mad enough to be lobotomized. The doctor is revolted by Violet's narrative about the sea turtles and retorts that the massacre which Sebastian viewed can be equated with some aspects of the human condition, but not with God. Man's inhumanity to man, he suggests, is of his own selfish devising, and should not be blamed on God.

Montgomery Clift and Katharine Hepburn in the garden sequence of *Suddenly Last Summer*.

It is from this interchange between Violet and the doctor that the theme of the play begins to emerge, that of human greed, and the lengths to which selfish human beings will go in manipulating others in order to get what they want. As Catherine says later in the play, "We all use each other and that's what we think of as love; and not being able to use each other is hate." Metaphors for the victimizer and the victimized, the predator and the preyed upon, are everywhere in the play as Williams assembles images from every level of existence to picture a world where charity and generosity are in short supply—the kind of world in which unscrupulous people like Violet and Sebastian Venable can thrive.

On the level of plant life, there is Sebastian's tropical garden which is attached to the Venable mansion, and which Violet continues to cultivate in order to keep his memory alive. On closer inspection it is really a prehistoric jungle where she nurtures such exotic plants as the carnivorous Venus flytrap, "aptly named after the goddess of love," says Violet. On the animal level there is the ravaging of the sea turtles by the scavenger birds which Sebastian and Violet saw in the Encantadas. On the human level the savagery is superficially more sophisticated and less obvious, but just as genuine.

Violet Venable's incestuous devotion to her son has caused him to grow up homosexual. She has fed on him emotionally and he in turn learns to manipulate this devotion for his own aggrandisement, for it is through her attractive wit and charm that he was able to make contacts for his sexual partners on their yearly travels. (It was only when his mother began to show her age that he took Catherine along in Violet's stead as last summer's decoy.)

Given the fact that Violet trained Sebastian to see the world as an arena of savage exploitation at every level of existence, his distorted image of God as the most cruel and selfish being of all is but a magnified version of the universe as he views it. He accordingly assumes that God is a pagan deity who will exact the most savage kind of expiation imaginable from him for his profligate life. Sebastian must have envisioned the devouring of the sea turtles as a premonition of his own destruction since he seems to arrange subconsciously a situation in which his own death will be a grotesque parallel to it: the boys who eat him alive being the counterparts of the predatory birds who ate the sea turtles alive.

Without his mother to convince him that they are both ageless, Sebastian becomes aware that he, too, is growing older. "Suddenly, last summer, Sebastian wasn't young any more," says Catherine in recounting the events surrounding his death. As he becomes obsessed with the notion that his lascivious life has cost him his poetic gift, like Hart Crane he no longer sees any point in living. He begins to look and feel his forty years; and for one, like Oscar Wilde's Dorian Gray, to whom youthful charm and beauty are everything, not to be young any more is to be already dead. He gives up looking for the perfect mate just as he has given up trying to write the perfect poem. No longer

Elizabeth Taylor in *Suddenly Last Summer*.

bothering to conceal his own predatory forays after sexual perversity under a cloak of respectability, he openly solicits the starving native boys on the public beaches to be his companions for a price, and thereby unleashes a storm of pagan passions in them which he will not long be able to control.

When he finally tires of them they nevertheless take to following him through the streets demanding further payment for their past favors. At this point Sebastian senses masochistically that he is to be sacrificed to the terrible God of his imagination as atonement for his depraved life and wasted literary talent by submitting to their cannibalistic instincts. As Williams has written in his short story "Desire and the Black Masseur," there is a kind of masochistic individual who believes that the principal of expiation dictates "the surrender of self to violent treatment by others with the idea of thereby clearing one's self of his guilt." Sebastian appears to be one such person.

He offers token resistence to what he sees as his fate by tossing coins at his potential attackers and fleeing when they continue to stalk him. But he stubbornly goes in the wrong direction, running uphill toward a dead end instead of downhill toward the open beach. As the band of naked native boys easily overtakes him, they descend upon him just like the scavenger birds swooped down on the hapless sea turtles on the shores of the Encantadas. The boys tear away his flesh and devour it, leaving his corpse stripped to the bone, crushed, and bleeding. As a self-styled human sacrifice to the vengeful God whom he had created in his own image, Sebastian's misguided self-immolation is a grotesque parody of the martyrdom of the early Christian St. Sebastian, after whom Williams has ironically named him.

Philip M. Armato, in his article in *Tennessee Williams: A Tribute,* points up the aptness with which Williams draws the ironic parallel between Sebastian Venable and St. Sebastian. The saint's death at the hands of the anti-Christian Roman emperor Diocletian's archers symbolized his total devotion to God and his fellow Christians, while Sebastian Venable becomes totally demoralized by his perverted view of God and man alike. "His death is an expression of masochistic self-contempt. Truly, Williams's ironic pun on Sebastian's last name reveals his character. Venable is not venerable; unlike St. Sebastian, he deserves pity, not veneration."

The cannibalism of the primitive savages who destroy Sebastian is shocking; but, Williams suggests, it is nothing compared to the coldly calculated cannibalism of the civilized and cultured human beings in the play, as exemplified in Violet Venable: she seeks to bribe Dr. Cukrowicz with a huge endowment for his research, and Catherine's mother and brother with a large portion of Sebastian's inheritance, if they will all agree to the carving of Catherine's brain in order to keep Catherine from sullying the spurious reputation of her dead son. In other words, Catherine is to be sacrificed to Sebastian just as Sebastian was sacrificed to the pagan god of his own peculiar subjective vision. Violet Venable is thus bent on devouring Catherine Holly as surely as the Venus flytrap devours insects, the predatory birds devour the sea turtles, and the voracious boys devour Sebastian. Significantly, the hospital where the lobotomy is to be performed is called Lion's View; Violet Venable indeed has a lion's view of the world as a kingdom which she holds in her sway and whose subjects are at her disposal.

Williams seems to be speaking through Catherine when she says relative to Sebastian's death, "I know it's a hideous story but it's a true story of our time and the world we live in." Some critics took umbrage at the implication that we live in a world as vicious as the one which the author has depicted in this play, just as some rejected Chance Wayne's invitation to see a little of him in each of us. "Life is cannibalistic," Williams said in response. "Truly. Egos eat egos, personalities eat personalities. Someone is always eating at someone else for position, gain, triumph, whatever. The human individual is a cannibal in the worst way. In *Suddenly Last Summer* it was more symbolic than actual, but many persons felt I meant it actually."

The dramatist is not suggesting that we are all potential Sebastians or Violets, but that all of us have within us the seed of self-centered selfishness which grew to such hideous proportions in the Venables. He balances his view of human nature, moreover, by contrasting Violet and Sebastian with Dr. Cukrowicz, one of the most generous and dedicated characters that he has ever conceived. At the final curtain the doctor insists that Catherine's story must be investigated and substantiated, even though it means the loss of Violet's endowment for his research. "Williams's point," says Herbert Machiz, who directed the original production of *Suddenly*, "is that there are still some people who really are incorruptible."

Someone once said that man is the missing link between the primitive apes and civilized human beings; and *Suddenly Last Summer* could be said to be based on that assumption, since the play implies that man must strive for mutual cooperation and understanding with his fellow man if he is ever to become more than semi-civilized, regardless of the degree of cultural veneer which he may have acquired. "I think that hate is a feeling that can only exist where there is no understanding," Williams reflected at the time the play opened. "Significantly, good physicians never have it," because they always come to understand their patients. In Williams's vision, then, men like Dr. Cukrowicz represent a step in the right direction toward the realization of this goal of a more humane humanity.

Suddenly Last Summer is one of the playwright's most perfectly structured plays. "What other playwright today could hold audiences spellbound with no more than soliloquies," said the late Diana Barrymore while she was playing Catherine in the Chicago Company opposite Cathleen Nesbitt as Violet. "For me that's what the play is primarily—two soliloquies by Cathleen and me. Tennessee Williams is the modern Shakespeare." The first scene is given over mostly to Violet's long monologue about Sebastian's noble character, a speech which she has designed to discredit in advance the gory tale of his death, which Catherine in turn delivers in the fourth scene. The two short intervening scenes establish Catherine's credibility over Violet's by detailing the latter's efforts to bribe the doctor and Catherine's family. The play moves without a wasted word swiftly and implacably to its stunning climax, the revelation of Sebastian for what he really was, leaving his corrupt character as exposed to view as his naked corpse was on that sunbaked hilltop in Cabeza de Lobo.

Because of its brevity, Williams decided to precede the play with a curtain raiser called *Something Unspoken*, which was also set in the Garden District of New Orleans, and he therefore called the joint presentation of the two one-acters by the overall title of *Garden District*. The failure of *Orpheus Descending* on Broadway earlier the same year led Williams to launch *Garden District*

Off Broadway at the York Playhouse, which was about half the size of the standard Broadway theater. Williams told a TV interviewer that anyone connected with the theater has good reason to feel insecure about facing a Broadway opening: "Nobody is as good as publicity makes them appear, and if he's reasonably objective about himself, he knows that's true; and it gives him an awfully shaky feeling which increases with each production. As his reputation grows he becomes more conscious of the discrepancy between his reputation and his actual self."

Williams's abiding consciousness of his imperfection as an artist makes him quite willing to revise a play as much as need be, and *Suddenly Last Summer* was no exception to this rule, as Herbert Machiz, its director, well remembers. It was Machiz who read Williams's very first draft of the play and suggested that it might be expanded further: "*Suddenly Last Summer* developed from a monologue—the final speech which the girl recites when she is under sedation. When Tenn first handed the script to me while I was vacationing in Southampton, it was called *And Tell Sad Stories of the Deaths of Queens*. I read it and said, 'Surely that boy Sebastian had a mother.' Williams then developed the idea by writing the whole play that led up to that final speech."

"No playwright understands the meaning and necessity of rewriting as much as he does," Machiz continues. "You have to beg some playwrights to change a word or a sentence; but Tennessee Williams will write a whole scene for you if you ask him to and if he feels it is essential to the thematic structure of the work." The rewriting certainly paid off, for the play arrived in New York as a smash hit. Williams own assessment of the play is that it contains passages that are as well written as anything he has ever done; but he was overwhelmed with surprise by the general praise heaped upon the work, considering its violent elements. "When it was done Off Broadway I thought I would be critically tarred and feathered and ridden on a fence rail out of the New York theater," he said after the opening.

Williams went on to say that he beleived that the violence of a play like *Suddenly* is a true reflection of the world in which we live and that he has the right to express the tortured condition of the world as he sees it. "I was brought up puritanically and I try to outrage that puritanism. I have an instinct to shock, but I think it's a constructive one," and he appeals to Aristotle to support this contention. "If there is any truth in the Aristotelian idea that violence is purged by its poetic representation on a stage, then it may be that my cycle of violent plays have had a moral justification after all. I know that I have felt it." Elsewhere he adds that if some of his plays seem excessively melodramatic it is because "a play must concentrate the events of a lifetime in the short span of a three-act play. Of necessity these events must be more violent than life."

"I dare to suggest," he wrote in *The New York Times* when the premiere productions of both *Suddenly Last Summer* and of *Sweet Bird of Youth* were still fresh in playgoers' minds, "that the theater has made in our time its greatest artistic advance through the unlocking and lighting up and ventilation of the closets, attics, and basements of human behavior and experience." Going a step further, he noted, "I think that there has been not a very sick but a very healthy extension of the frontiers of theme and subject matter acceptable to our dramatic art, to the stage, the screen, and even television. . . . No significant area of human experience, and behavior reaction to it, should be held inaccessible, provided that it is presented with honest intention and taste, to the screen, play, and TV writers of our desperate time."

When Hollywood turned to considering a screen version of *Suddenly*, potential producers were challenged by the prospects of filming a play that dealt with several areas of human experience that had previously been all but inaccessible to the film maker, such as cannibalism and most especially homosexuality. As I demonstrated in discussing *Cat on a Hot Tin Roof*, homosexuality was, until comparatively recently, a very sensitive subject which had to be treated on stage and even moreso on screen with extreme caution. "Homosexuality used to be the sensational gimmick in a play," says Mart Crowley, author of the play and screenplay of *The Boys in the Band*. "The big revelation in the last act was the the guy was homosexual and then he was expected to commit suicide offstage"—just as Allan Grey did in *Streetcar* and Skipper did in *Cat*!

Other Williams plays had also incorporated homosexuality into the fabric of their plots, but it was always of secondary import. "I have never found the subject of homosexuality a satisfactory theme for a full-length play," Williams explains, "despite the fact that it appears as frequently as it does in my short fiction." But in *Suddenly Last Summer* homosexuality is more crucial to the plot than the subject had ever been in any of Williams's longer dramatic works, and it would therefore be difficult for a movie adaptation of this relatively short play to sidestep the issue in the usual Hollywood manner employed in the adaptations of full length plays like *Streetcar* and *Cat*.

We have already seen how Blanche's discovery of her husband's homosexuality was veiled when *Streetcar* was brought to the screen in 1951, and how Brick's relationship with Skipper was clouded over in a similar way in the film of *Cat*. If Sebastian Venable's homosexuality was soft pedaled in this manner in the movie of *Suddenly*, the plot would have to be changed beyond recognition. But it was high time for a breakthrough film that dealt with homosexuality with integrity, and *Suddenly* might as well be it. This was the attitude toward the project of veteran Hollywood producer Sam Spiegel when he phoned Williams long distance about buying the screen rights to the play. Williams was vacationing in Miami after the play opened when he received Spiegel's call, and for the first time in his career he made a movie deal himself. After discussing Spiegel's approach to the screen adaptation of his successful play, Williams said, "How about fifty grand plus twenty per cent of the profits." Spiegel agreed that the wheels were set in motion for the production.

Spiegel hired Williams's fellow writer and friend Gore Vidal to write the screenplay. Being a respecter of words, Vidal was careful to preserve the texture of Williams's writing in his script. This has not always been the case, says Herbert Machiz. "Movies, which usually operate on a superfical level, often eliminate the subtleties of Williams's writing. Being a poet as well as a dramatist, Tenn is very concerned about language and the meaning of words, and this richness in his writing is not always carried over into the screenplay. In editing a Williams play for the screen you have to be careful about cutting lines that may not seem important to the plot but can be very important to the inner meaning of the story. When Sebastian's mother says to the doctor, 'This is Sebastian's garden,' it seems like a casual line. Yet if you cut it out of the script you would be cutting out the heart of the play, excising the richness and density of imagery, the real poetry of the play, all that the garden symbolizes.

"It is true that films can sometimes telegraph meaning by an instant image which can take the place of several lines of dialogue in a play. On the other hand, Williams uses language to give his plays texture and depth. You could cut out many of Shakespeare's lines and still keep the plot, but you wouldn't have the play, the true quality of his writing. It's like reading a synopsis of a play: it gives you the plot but you miss the essence of what the playwright originally wrote. Hence the films of Williams's plays have sometimes sacrificed too much of what is really essential in the original."

Williams received official screen credit as co-author óf the script of the film, but Vidal says that his colleague did not actually collaborate with him on the scenario. "It was based on his play," says Vidal, "and his name was good for box office." Vidal on his own expanded the material of Williams's seventy minute play into a 114 minute movie by elaborating further what was already contained implicitly in the play—as opposed to the way that *This Property is Condemned,* the only other Williams one-acter to be made into a motion picture, had a story line which had been woven virtually out of whole cloth imposed upon it by the time it reached the screen.

According to Bernard Dick's book on Vidal, *The Apostate Angel,* Vidal divides his screenplays into two classes: "Those that *are* all mine and those that *were* all mine." Among the former he includes *Suddenly,* his favorite among all of his movie scripts. As Vidal set about rethinking the play in cinematic terms, he found the play's single set, the house and garden of the Venable estate, had "reduced motivation to exposition," as Dick succinctly puts it. As I noted in the previous chapter, Williams had trouble getting all of his characters into the principal hotel setting of *Sweet Bird of Youth* and the movie remedied the situation by increasing the number of locations in which the action of the story took place. So too, when Williams had opted to limit himself to one set in

Suddenly, certain incongruities arose in bringing all of the characters together into one location, and Vidal was able to eliminate them in composing the screenplay.

For instance, in the play Dr. Cukrowicz has his initial consultation with Catherine in Violet Venable's home rather than in his private consulting room at the asylum, where he could interview her away from the watchful eye of the very woman who is trying to have Catherine lobotomized. Vidal decided to move the first encounter of the doctor (Montgomery Clift) with Catherine (Elizabeth Taylor) to the asylum, where it appropriately belonged, and then proceeded to set other scenes there too, in order to work the exposition less intrusively into the dialogue of the film than Williams did at times in the play. On the stage Williams has Catherine refer to Sebastian's growing preference for blondes when she recalls how he became "fed up with the dark ones and famished for the light ones: that's how he talked about people, as if they were items on a menu." Vidal retains these lines in the movie, but instead of having Catherine mutter them almost absentmindedly in the living room of Violet Venable (Katharine Hepburn), a place where Catherine would have been on her guard about referring to Sebastians's sexual proclivities, Vidal transfers these lines to a hospital scene in which Catherine utters them just after she has been given a sedative by a male attendant who just happens to be a blonde.

The hospital sequences also allow for the creditable addition of more characters to the story. The most important of these is Dr. Lawrence J. Hockstader (Albert Dekker), the superintendent of Lion's View Hospital, who serves as a foil character for Dr. Cukrowicz: in contrast with Cukrowicz, Hockstader makes no bones about his willingness to offer Catherine to Sebastian's mother as a human sacrifice in exchange for the endowment that will build a new wing onto the hospital as a memorial to Sebastian's memory. The presence of Dr. Hockstader creates additional suspense in the film since Dr. Cukrowicz has his superior as well as Violet pressuring him to declare Catherine as a suitable subject for a lobotomy. That Cukrowicz is finally able to withstand the pressures to which he is subjected and to treat Catherine's case fairly and honestly is the index of an integrity which was not so explicitly spelled out in the play, where he was a less impressive character.

As Bernard Dick comments, Dr. Cukrowicz's function in the play seemed to be to feed cues to Violet and Catherine, and as such he was too nebulous a figure to be the only genuinely noble figure in th entire two-hour film. To dramatize his sense of commitment, therefore, Vidal began the picture with a sequence in the operating room at Lion's View in which Cukrowicz performs a lobotomy under deplorable conditions, and he complains about this situation to Hockstader afterwards. Hockstader counterattacks by telling Cukrowicz that Violet Venable's endowment money can change all that. This line of argumentation would surely give a less heroic man pause in his resolve not to be swayed by financial

Elizabeth Taylor being sedated in one of the mental hospital scenes from *Suddenly Last Summer*.

considerations in making his decision about Catherine.

At another point Hockstader, with Cukrowicz at his side, surveys the vacant lot where the Sebastian Venable Memorial Neurosurgical Wing of Lion's View is to be erected. Hockstader is again touching Cukrowicz at the point where he is most vulnerable, his cherished desire to push back the frontiers of knowledge about psychosurgery. Setting these and other scenes from the play at the hospital also enables the director, Joseph Mankiewicz, to make palpable to the audience the danger to Catherine's psychic life which the lobotomy presents by showing some lobotomized patients, and hence to indicate the motivation that is holding Cukrowicz from acceding to Hockstader and Violet's importuning.

The film, like the play, is set in the mid-Thirties, the time when Rose Williams underwent such an operation, and the risks involved were many, and often unpredictable. Mankiewicz has been criticized for employing cheap B-movie effects in using close-ups of demented mental patients in the movie.

But I, for one, believe he was taking his cue from the script in jolting the viewer into realizing that Catherine may wind up among these wretched creatures if the operation fails—which is why lobotomy even in those primitive days of psychosurgical experimentation was administered only to genuinely hopeless cases on whom every other means of treatment had failed. This realization makes all the more patent the heinousness of Violet Venable's determination, with Dr. Hochstader's connivance, to have Catherine lobotomized, since Catherine is surely not insane, however traumatized she may be by her experiences of last summer.

In summary, by alternating the setting of the movie between the steamy, hothouse ambience of the Venable estate and the even more claustrophobic atmosphere of the locked wards of the asylum, Vidal opened up the play spatially for the cinema without at the same time decimating the stifling intensity of the one-act play. Yet he also avoids fashioning a scenario that is too talky by movie standards by distributing much of the expository material throughout different scenes, rather than having it in more concentrated helpings as Williams did in the play.

There was no question, however, that Catherine's revelatory monologue, which she delivers under the influence of a truth serum, would have to be dished up to the audience in a single serving as the grand finale of the film. Vidal tells me that he was all for having Catherine speak her climactic monologue without the use of flashbacks, but that Mankiewicz wanted to portray Sebastian's melodramatic destruction on screen. "Joe Mankiewicz was generally good until the liberal rendering of the ending," says Vidal," which was a huge error."

Gordon Gow writes in *Hollywood in the Fifties* rather unkindly that possibly the director feared that Elizabeth Taylor at this point in her career was not as skilled a cinema actress as Katherine Hepburn, and could not therefore hold the attention of the viewer during the course of her long speech about Cabeza de Lobo in the way that Ms. Hepburn clearly was capable of doing in giving her long account of the trip to the Encantadas at the beginning of the movie. In any event, Mankiewicz finally decided on a kind of compromise somewhere between having Catherine give her speech to the camera without flashbacks and shooting the events in flashback without showing Catherine narrating the story.

That compromise consists in an inset of Catherine in close-up appearing at the upper right-hand corner of the frame as she narrates the gruelling events leading up to Sebastian's death while those very events occupy the rest of the screen. This format enables the viewer to see the painful experience which reliving this harrowing episode is for Catherine, while at the same time empowering the viewer to share these events with her, starting with Sebastian's using Catherine on the beach as bait to lure attractive youths to him.

In his book on homosexuality in the movies, *Screening the Sexes*, Parker Tyler gleefully attacks this element of the plot as preposterous because he says

Elizabeth Taylor with the actor playing her cousin Sebastian, whose face is never seen in the film, *Suddenly Last Summer*.

that he has been told "on reliable authority" that in the tropics there is no need to lure native boys into sexual liasons by such indirect methods. All that someone like Sebastian would have to do is "to step outdoors alone to have boys drop from the sky and roll under his feet." They look up at the prospective buyer, "flutter their lovely black eyelashes, and the deal is made."

Actually what Tyler's wrong-headed remarks really prove is that he did not follow the plot line of the story very closely. Catherine's narration makes it quite clear that the combination of Sebastian's money and his female companion's charm was needed to lure the kind of high-class males to whom the fastidious Sebastian was attracted into his seductive web. It is a measure of Sebastian's rapid disintegration that he ceases using Catherine as a decoy and, abandoning all caution, goes after the destitute and desparate "rough trade" readily available in the manner which Tyler describes.

Since Sebastian never appears in the play at all, Mankiewicz follows Williams's lead in the film by never showing Sebastian's face in this extended flashback, allowing him to remain what he is in the play, the superficially attractive embodiment of evil, tainting all that he touches, and of man's gruesome capacity for self-destruction which is crystallized in the death wish that rules his life and dictates his tortured demise.

Williams was, nonetheless, severely disappointed by the direct depiction on the screen of Sebastian's last days because for him this approach to the sequence emphasized the realistic portrayal of Catherine's narrative at the expense of the symbolic and thematic meaning of the passage, and as such represented an unfortunate concession to the realism that Hollywood is too often loath to discard. And so, he said after seeing the film, his short morality play composed in a lyrical style "was turned into a sensationally successful film that the public thinks was a literal study of such things as cannabalism, madness, and sexual deviation." As the author said in describing the play, the cannibalism portrayed in *Suddenly Last Summer* "was more symbolic than actual, but many persons felt I meant it actually."

Williams believed that if some theatergoers missed this point that he was using cannibalism as a metaphor for man's selfish inhumanity to man, many more moviegoers, overwhelmed by the vivid visualization on screen of the grisly happenings that happened off-stage in the play, certainly missed the thematic implications of the movie. That theme, it may be recalled, is that the ruthless behavior of cultured and civilized human beings like Violet and Sebastian is infinitely more cruel and hideous than the savagery of primitive pagans or predatory birds. Williams's words articulating this theme are worth recalling: "The human individual is a cannibal in the worst way" when he preys on another for position, gain, triumph, or some other greedy motive.

In *Suddenly,* consequently, Williams was not as concerned with the cannibalism of the native boys of Cabeza de Lobo as he was with the self-aggrandizing cannibalism of people using others in the most cruel and calculating ways which is epitomized in Violet's incestuous love of her son and willingness to destroy Catherine on his account, and in Sebastian's manipulating his mother and cousin Catherine to obtain for him the young men he prefers to seduce; but it is also reflected in the behavior of Catherine's mother and brother (and in the film in Dr. Hockstader, too) who are willing to authorize Catherine's operation for monetary considerations.

Williams felt in effect that these deeper meanings of his story were mislaid in passage from stage to screen because of Mankiewicz's earthy and heavy-handed style. Here I must disagree with the playwright in favor of the film maker. Had Mankiewicz ignored Williams's verbal narration altogether and simply

The native boys pursue Sebastian in *Suddenly Last Summer*'s climactic flashback.

portrayed its content on the screen, Williams's objection would be valid. But the director was careful not only to preserve Catherine's monologue with all of its symbolic implications on the sound track, but also actually to show her on the screen simultaneously delivering her long speech so that the audience cannot overlook the thematic significance of what she is saying at the same time they watch the events themselves unfold before them.

Foster Hirsch in his book on Elizabeth Taylor praises Mankiewicz for the way that Catherine's words are complemented by his pictures, as the briskly edited images keep pace with Elizabeth Taylor's urgent recitation of Williams's brilliantly evocative prose. Hirsch calls this monologue Ms. Taylor's finest moment in the movies. Elsewhere he adds that this set speech lends itself to visualization in a way that most of Williams's similar prose arias do not. Violet's recollection of the carnage of the sea turtles by a skyful of birds, for example, was conceived by the dramatist primarily as a projection of Sebastian's peculiarly subjective conception of God as a savage pagan deity, and any documentary-like depiction of this episode in the movie as it really happened would not enable the filmgoer to view it as it was assmilated by the fevered imagination of Sebastian.

Conversely, the viewer is able to relive Sebastian's last days with Catherine in the flashback to Cabeza de Lobo just as it appeared to her. In fact, her presence on the screen in an inset as narrator (in addition to her figuring in the action as a participant in the events she is narrating) reminds the audience that they are seeing everything that happened just as she saw it. Hence when Catherine averts her eyes from the spectacle of the boys engulfing Sebastian as she stands helplessly by, the camera logically turns away as well. Although Mankiewicz never shows Sebastian's ravaged corpse on the screen, he suggests the horrible results of the boys' savagery by artistic indirection. In the foreground of the shot in which the boys catch up with Sebastian on the hillside the director has placed a grotesque statue of a skeleton clothed only in a cloak which reveals the bones of its torso. As Sebastian disappears beneath the crowd of young cannibals crawling all over his body, the sparsely clad skeleton in the foreground implies that his clothes are being ripped from his body and the flesh torn from his bones. This suggestion of the atrocity which is being committed is quite enough to enable the viewer to grasp the horror of the scene, and marks Mankiewicz's handling of the scene as more discreet than the director's critics are prepared to concede.

It seems to me that the sophistication with which Mankiewicz has employed artistic indirection throughout the film to imply more than he actually portrays accounts for the fact that *Suddenly Last Summer* encountered no serious difficulties with the MPAA Code Commission or the Legion of Decency. The film came to grips with the problem of presenting the officially taboo subject of sexual perversion on the screen in a way that none of the previous Williams movies had done—although it just may be that the censors looked upon the hideous death of Sebastian as sufficient "justification" for the motion picture's dealing with homosexuality in the first place.

In any event, after the box office success of *Suddenly Last Summer*, the Production Code moved away from the stance it had taken in the Code provisions promulgated in December, 1956, which forbade any reference to sexual perversion. In 1961 a qualifying emendation was made to this statement in the Code which recognized such subject matter admissible when treated "with care, discretion, and restraint," a description of which Mankiewicz's film is unquestionably worthy. (Producer Spiegel stated in *The New York Times* at the time of the movie's release that the film had been granted a Code seal after only two minor deletions: "a scene of two youngsters in the Spanish town and one mention of the word *procuring*.")

As for the Legion of Decency, *Variety* expressed pleasant surprise in its issue of December 30, 1959, that the Catholic group had not taken the film to task as it had other Williams films such as *Streetcar* and *Baby Doll*. A Legion spokesman (probably Rev. Patrick J. Sullivan, S.J., under whose influence the Legion was becoming more circumspect and enlightened in its approach to serious and artistic motion pictures) defined the theme of *Suddenly Last Summer* for a *Variety* reporter as a story about "a man who uses others and their love to his own ends and is finally devoured by the very corruption which he has sown." The film, as the Legion saw it, "does anything but make homosexuality appear attractive or emotionally profitable. It is a stark and horrifying lesson."

The Legion spokesman furthermore stated that the Legion policy was to encourage genuine and sincere artists like Tennessee Williams to raise questions that touch upon man's fundamental relationship with the world and with God, and concluded that Williams was in the vanguard of such creative writers. In the wake of the controversy which the Legion had precipitated over *Baby Doll* in particular, these remarks were welcomed by the playwright who never expected an endorsement of this kind from that quarter.

The only real flaw in the film is the attempt to refashion Dr. Cukrowicz into a conventional romantic movie hero by having him fall in love with Catherine. As Herbert Machiz points out, "There is no romantic interest in the play between the doctor and Catherine because in the play he is already engaged to another girl. That is not, therefore, why he fights to save her from being lobotomized. It cheapens his image as a dedicated humanitarian who can't be bought, established earlier in the film, to imply that his concern for Catherine has its ultimate roots in a romantic attachment for her." Indeed, Vidal must have realized that this romantic attachment rendered Cukrowicz a less reliable judge of Catherine's veracity than he was in the play because the screen writer entrusts Cukrowicz's last line in the play to Dr. Hockstader in the movie: "I think we ought to consider the possibility that the girl's story could be true."

The movie ends with the two lovers, arms linked, walking through Sebastian's garden, which presumably no longer symbolizes the prehistoric jungle that it has been all through the picture but is now supposedly a benign Eden for Catherine and Cukrowicz. This ending to the movie seems roughly equivalent to the old-fashioned Hollywood fade-out of a couple galloping off into the sunset, and as such is deplorably out of keeping with the unvarnished realism of the rest of the film.

But there are many more pluses than minuses to be chalked up for this movie. Although Vidal added more than half an hour to the play's running time, his additional material is for the most part very well integrated into the original story. His expansions of Williams's play are mostly to be found, as one would suspect, in the scenes that take place at Lion's View, where no scene in the play is set. This new material includes Catherine's two inadvertant forays into the wards where hopeless patients exist with only custodial care, as well as the scenes in which Dr. Hockstader, the one new major character in the movie, does his part to try to wear down Cukrowicz's resistance to Violet Venable's blandishments to force him to perform the lobotomy.

Another plus for the movie is that it was shot in austere black-and-white, which is so much more appropriate to a spare, Gothic tale than color photography would have been. The interiors were shot in a London studio where the overhead was lower than it would have been in Hollywood. Oliver Messel designed an exotic tropical garden adjacent to the Venable mansion that gave no indication that it was housed on a studio sound stage. Its jungle atmosphere, however, also proved to be the proper setting for the abudant misunderstandings and quarrels which beset the film unit during shooting.

Katherine Hepburn, who had been devoting herself to doing Shakespeare on the stage, had not made a film in two years when she reluctantly accepted the role of Violet Venable. She was not at first sure that she was suited for the part, though her handsome features and graceful bearing made it altogether plausible that such a woman could have been the attractive lady whom Sebastian needed to serve as his procurer. But Ms. Hepburn has always been wary of playing a character with whom she could not identify, and she certainly could not do so with Violet. Her doubts about playing the part made her edgy, as did her concern about Spencer Tracy, her long-time companion, who was suffering from ill health when she left Hollywood for London.

Moreover, tensions began to surface on the set when it became difficult for cast and crew to discern the precise chain of command between producer Sam Spiegel and director Joseph Mankiewicz. Spiegel belonged to the old school of "creative" Hollywood producers who liked to feel that he had more of a hand in the making of a movie than merely overseeing the budget and keeping to the shooting schedule, while Mankiewicz was an adherent of the new school of "independent" directors who saw the director as having exclusive control of all of the creative aspects of a motion picture production. Misunderstandings were inevitable.

As shooting progressed, a more crucial problem took center stage and exacerbated the other tensions which had been brewing all along. Montgomery Clift, playing Dr. Cukrowicz, was in a poor physical and psychological condition. A recent auto accident had left him with a shattered jaw, and he was afraid that he would never again be a romantic lead, much less the matinee idol of his early career. Plagued with insomnia and headaches, and already drinking to excess, Clift resorted to taking one kind of drug to help him sleep at night and another to get him started in the morning. The combination of drugs and alcohol took their cumulative toll on his performance, since he would often arrive on the set dazed and inarticulate and unable to remember his lines. (He would be dead in seven years at the age of forty-six.)

Under the pressure of keeping on schedule and on budget, both producer and director gradually became so exasperated with what they thought to be Clift's lamentably unprofessional behavior that they seriously considered replacing him. At this point Ms. Hepburn went into action, defending Clift and treating him with great compassion while at the same time castigating both producer and director for their apparent lack of patience and understanding for a sick man. "She felt I was being cruel," Mankiewicz recalls, "but we had a real problem making the picture work; Clift was always late—it was horrible." But somehow Clift struggled through, with Ms. Hepburn's moral support, and finished the film.

On her last day of shooting, Ms. Hepburn, who had been simmering about Clift and other matters throughout the production period, decided to wrap up her work on the film in her own way. As Gary Raymond, who played Catherine's brother George in the movie, recalled the incident for Charles Higham, Ms. Hepburn's biographer, "On her very last day on the set she went up to the director in front of the whole cast and crew and said to Mankiewicz, 'I have nothing more to do with you or the film?' He said, 'No.' And then she spat—right in his face!"

Before she left the studio Spiegel called her into his office to inquire about her treatment of Mankiewicz on the set. "I behaved very well while we were making the picture," Ms. Hepburn responded. "This was later. If I behaved badly, it was on my own time, not yours." She then went on to spell out for Spiegel that his behavior had been no better than the director's toward Clift; and she spat again, though this time on the floor. She later explained to a friend that she believed that all of the various tensions which had been building up in her during shooting had to be released before she left the studio or they would remain pent up within her forever. "I wouldn't have done it if I hadn't had to," she explained; "but I had to."

Opinions vary on the caliber of the performances in the movie. Some maintained that Clift did a very competent job in his role while others, like Herbert Machiz who knows the role from having directed the premiere production of *Suddenly,* thought Clift's personal problems in effect came through in his portrayal and marred his performance considerably. "The doctor seems for whatever reason to have emotional problems of his own in the movie. Despite the fact that Montgomery Clift was a magnificent actor, the doctor seemed overly neurotic in the movie when he really should have appeared as firm as the Rock of Gibraltar. As Dr. Cukrowicz is presented in the movie, I wouldn't trust him to put a knife in anyone's brain."

In Gore Vidal's judgment, "Clift and Taylor were dreadful; Hepburn was miscast but interesting." Williams, on the other hand, speaks of the marvelous performances of Katharine Hepburn and Montgomery Clift and says that for him it was Elizabeth Taylor who was miscast. Paying the actress something of a left-handed compliment, he commented after the film had been released that if

Ms. Taylor's performance in *Suddenly Last Summer* proved nothing else it demonstrated her ability to rise above miscasting. "It stretched my credulity to believe that such a 'hip' doll as Liz wouldn't know at once in the film that she was 'being used for something evil,' " as the posters for the film proclaimed. "I think that Liz would have dragged Sebastian home by his ears, and so saved them both from considerable embarrassment that summer." Williams then called Elizabeth Taylor "probably the finest raw talent on the Hollywood screen," and expressed his hope that she would discipline her talent as she matured as an actress.

Foster Hirsch sums up Ms. Taylor's career to 1973 by saying that the two Tennessee Williams films which she made back-to-back, *Cat on a Hot Tin Roof* and *Suddenly Last Summer*, represent the high-water mark of her career, for in these two movies she channelled her energies into film adaptations of genuine literary commodities rather than of slick best sellers. The two films taken together, Hirsch contends, represent the best material that Ms. Taylor ever had to work with—a judgment with which it is easy to agree. Unfortunately, as we shall see, her third Williams film is not in a class with these two movies.

As it happens, both Elizabeth Taylor and Katharine Hepburn got Oscar nominations for their performances in *Suddenly Last Summer*. George Cukor, who has directed Ms. Hepburn in no less than ten films, has said of her acting in *Suddenly*, "I didn't know until then that Kate's range extended to communicating the cruelty of such a woman as Violet Venable, but she proved that it did." Williams paid Ms. Hepburn's performance in *Suddenly* the most glowing tribute possible when he described her as the playwright's dream, a consummate actress whose matchless beauty and clarity of diction make dialogue sound better than it is. "By a fineness of intelligence and sensibility that illuminates every shade of meaning of every line she speaks," she demonstrated in *Suddenly* that she is "an artist born to her art."

Ms. Hepburn proves worthy of the playwright's praise from the very first moment she appears on the screen in the picture, slowly descending to meet Dr. Cukrowicz in an open-grille private elevator. As she gives the entrance speech which Vidal wrote for the occasion, her voice wafts down the elevator shaft from above as if issuing from some inaccessible goddess who has graciously deigned to come down to earth for an audience with some poor mortal: "Well, it seems that the Emperor of Byzantium when he received people in audience had a throne which, during the conversation, would mysteriously rise in the air, to the consternation of the visitors. But, as we are living in a democracy, I reverse the procedure. I don't rise, I come down."

Vidal reverses this procedure at the end of the picture and in so doing makes Ms. Hepburn's exit as riveting as her entrance. After her bejeweled hand closes Sebastian's book of annual summer poems with a flourish of grim finality, she retreats once more into her private elevator and floats upward, out of sight, conversing with Sebastian, the one person to whom she had devoted her life and who alone exists for her now. The grille-work gate which shuts her into the elevator betokens that she is now insulated in her own private little world with him for good. She has—more obviously than in the play—gone completely mad.

Williams has reason, then, to call Vidal's screenplay by and large a brilliantly constructed adaptation of his play and to heap encomiums on Ms. Hepburn's work in the movie. He was so pleased with her, in fact, that he wrote *Night of the Ignana* especially for her with a view to her playing the role of Hannah Jelkes, an itinerant spinster-artist. Ms. Hepburn read the script with anticipation but ultimately decided that it was not for her, and the part went to Margaret Leighton on the stage and Deborah Kerr on the screen.

Suddenly Last Summer was a highly successful film, proving that audiences were now ready for genuinely adult subject matter tastefully presented on the screen. The movie has been called a "triumpth of talk" since rarely has Williams touched off so many dramatic sparks by relying so heavily on dialogue, a considerable amount of which was preserved in the film. The movie respected Williams's superb dialogue to such a great degree probably because the script writer was himself a noted writer and because the director also had several literate scripts to his credit, including *All About Eve* and *A Letter to Three Wives*.

In spite of the troubles on the set, the combined talents of a distinguished playwright, screen writer, director, producer, and cast produced a first class motion picture. As we shall see in the next chapter, Vidal was to join forces with another excellent director, Sidney Lumet, to bring another Williams play to the screen with much less happy results, even though James Wong Howe, who won an Oscar for photographing *The Rose Tattoo*, was the cinematographer. The next chapter will also cover a second Williams film directed by Lumet which united Brando and Magnani, both of whom had done their best work in previous Williams films, but which also was a painful disappointment. Let us analyze, then, how the right combination of artistic talent, which issued in a fine film like *Suddenly Last Summer,* could in the case of two other Williams movies go so woefully wrong.

6
Sidney Lumet:
The Fugitive Kind and *The Last of the Mobile Hot-Shots*

SINCE TENNESSEE WILLIAMS travelled around the country as an itinerant vagabond in the years immediately following his graduation from college, it is not surprising that the hero of *Battle of Angels*, his first full-length play to receive a professional production, should be likewise devoted to travel. But the difference between Williams and Valentine Xavier is that Williams was looking for a place to settle down, whereas Val Xavier keeps moving on in order to avoid putting down roots anywhere because he sees permanent involvement with others as a threat to his own freedom.

On a return visit to St. Louis in the fall of 1939, Williams finished the first draft of *Battle of Angels* (which was ultimately to be revised as *Orpheus Descending*, which in turn was to be filmed as *The Fugitive Kind*). He was summoned to New York to receive a $1,000 grant from the Rockefeller Foundation and a scholarship to study playwrighting at the New School of Social Research in New York, where he would work with drama scholar John Gassner and the Theater Guild's Theresa Helburn on revisions of *Battle of Angels*. On the advice of Gassner, who was a Guild play reader, the Theater Guild optioned the play and Williams took to the road again while awaiting the Guild's decision about producing the play.

Williams writes in his memoirs that the option payments "mysteriously" failed to reach him in his travels, and by the time he arrived in Mexico he assumed that the Guild had decided against producing the play. (Actually there was no mystery about it: Williams had forgotten to leave any forwarding addresses to which the checks could be mailed!) In any event, he was running low on cash and took a bus from Mexico back to the States and to Los Angeles. There he read in *The New York Times* that *Battle of Angels* had been announced as the first production of the Theater Guild 1940-41 season with Laurence Langer producing, Margaret Webster directing, and Miriam Hopkins, hoping to revive her ailing acting career, in the lead. Williams immediately hopped another bus and was on his way east for the rehearsals.

Although *Battle* was the fifth full length play which he had attempted, he still had little sense of how to construct a long dramatic work in an organized and coherent manner. Up to this point in his career the playwright had devoted himself mostly to writing one-act plays. *Battle of Angels* in fact reads like a collation of the material for several one-act plays strung together to form an episodic full length play with too many subordinate characters and too many subplots. As John Gassner later observed, "He did not yet know his way through the maze of plot sustained for an entire evening."

Williams himself, looking back on those days of his apprenticeship, admits that "probably no man has ever written for the theater with less foreknowledge of it." He had not seen more than two or three professional productions up to that point in his life. As a neophyte playwright he needed more guidance in making his revisions than he got from the Guild. Consequently, Gassner said in retrospect, "the play as produced was even inferior to the script that had been accepted." In addition to the complicated plot, Williams further obscured the intent of his play by freighting it with a load of complex religious symbols which even on close scrutiny yield little coherent thematic meaning simply because they were never fully clarified in his own mind.

Valentine Xavier is named for the brother of St. Francis Xavier, an ancestor of the Williams family. Though no playgoer would be expected to catch this private reference to the Williams family tree, the name does suggest the juxtaposition of love (Valentine's Day) and sanctity (St. Francis Xavier). We are supposedly to regard the vagrant guitar playing hero, then, as a great lover according to his first name and a saint of sorts according to his second.

Val sports a snakeskin jacket which he sheds for the cloak of respectability in the form of the white clerk's jacket which he dons to work at the shoe counter of Myra Torrance's dry goods store in a small Southern town (another private reference by the author, this time to his years in a shoe factory). Myra is married to Jabe Torrance, an invalid who is dying by degrees in his room above the store. Since Myra married Jabe on the rebound after being jilted by her fiancé, there has been little love between them, and she inevitably becomes involved emotionally with Val after he turns up in town broke and looking for a job.

Xavier responds to Myra's tentative advances because he pities her and because he is desperately lonely himself. He confesses to Myra that he has tried all of his life to reach out to others in the hope of communion of some kind, but that he has never succeeded in doing so. "Now I know that *nobody* ever gets to *know* anybody," he muses in the play's key line. "We're all locked up tight inside our own bodies. Sentenced, you might say, to solitary confinement inside our own skins."

It is evident to Myra that her relationship with Jabe is sterile and dead, and she sees Val as providing her with what may well be her last chance to form a vital, fruitful relationship. She accordingly encourages him to break the lock on the storeroom door (to which she has lost the key) so that they can consummate their love. The sexual connotations of the key-lock imagery are clearly defined here, as are the sexual symbols elsewhere in the play; but the religious imagery which is meant to balance them is not. The link between the play's sexual and religious symbolism is provided by Vee Talbott, the neurotic wife of the sheriff, who sublimates her own repressed sexual drives toward the young bucks around town like Val by incorporating them as saintly figures into her religious paintings. Her sexual-religious mania reaches its peak when she enshrines Val as Christ on the Cross in her painting of the Crucifixion—and unknowingly foretells Val's death on Good Friday.

There are other attempts on the part of the playwright to make his series of sexual and religious images mesh. Thus the confectionary which Myra plans to open as an addition to the dry goods store on Easter Sunday is decorated like an orchard in full bloom to suggest new life both in the sense of the fertility and fruitfulness of springtime and in the sense of Christ's Resurrection bringing new spiritual life to mankind. Another instance of religio-sexual imagery occurs near the end of the play when Myra announces, after Val tells her he is planning to move on once more, that he has made her pregnant. She contrasts herself to the barren fig tree which Christ cursed for bringing forth no fruit because she has now at long last conceived new life, and looks forward to going to church with Val on Easter morning so that "the Lord will have to forgive us all our sins!"

But Val and Myra's moment of happiness is brief. Almost immediately after Myra proclaims the new life growing within her, the dying Jabe, like an Angel of Death, descends the stairs from his sickroom with a gun and kills Myra. The impotent husband finally penetrates his wife with bullets and in so doing kills the unborn child within her as well. Jabe uses his last breath to denounce Val as the murderer of Myra; and the men of the town, who are madly jealous of the stir which Val unwittingly has created among their wives, gleefully strip him and hang him from the lynching tree which they maintain in the town for such occasions. One of them even saves Val's snakeskin jacket, just as Christ's robe was preserved after the Crucifixion, making the parallel between Val's death and Christ's crucifixion all the more obvious. But Williams steadily confuses Val's symbolic function as a Christ figure unjustly murdered by evil men with other religious metaphors in the play.

The overarching religious metaphor of the play is contained in its title, a reference to an early Williams poem entitled "The Legend," in which the poet remarks that mortals have little chance to find love in a pitiless universe when even the angels in heaven battle above them—sentiments that are repeated in the play. This scriptural reference is to the Apocalypse of the New Testament in which the Bible records that St. Michael the Archangel led the Good Angels in driving into hell Satan and the Evil Angels who refused to adore God any longer. This is precisely the point where Williams fails to weld his religious symbolism into a solid thematic structure.

Jabe, the villain of the piece, apparently is the Satanic figure in the play, for he is referred to as both the Prince of Darkness and the Angel of Death. Logically that makes Val, the hero, the angelic leader of the forces of light and life. But a well-meaning vagrant, who moves from town to town getting involved with the local housewives in spite of his good intentions ot the contrary, hardly measures up to the kind of heroic stature which suggests the noble qualities of an angelic or a Christ-like figure. One feels sorry for Val as a hillbilly Lothario down on his luck but Val never elicits one's admiration as the truly tragic figure Williams envisions him to be; and all of the pseudo-religious significance with which the playwright tries to endow Val cannot alter this assessment of his character.

Hence Williams wisely removed much of this religious symbolism from his substantially revised version of the play, *Orpheus Descending*, when it was produced on Broadway more than fifteen years later. But *Battle of Angels* never made it to the Great White Way.

When Williams arrived in Boston for the tryout of *Battle*, he was aware that as a fledgling playwright he would have to be very accomodating to both director and cast if he were to profit from their much greater experience in the theater. Miriam Hopkins felt uneasy about the overdose of heavy melodramatics at the play's finale, which included the deaths of several of the principals and the burning down of the store for good measure. The young dramatist tried to oblige the star, but he could not come up with another ending that would fit the play's development up to that point.

On the night of the final dress rehearsal a lazy technician failed to ignite the smoke pots backstage sufficiently to suggest a blazing building, and Williams complained about this to the stage manager because the conflagration symbolized in the context of the play's theme the concept of purification by fire.

To make amends, on opening night, December 30, 1940, the stagehand sent black clouds of suffocating smoke billowing into the auditorium. Most of the remaining members of the audience who had not already walked out on the evening's fiasco before this incident occurred, now struggled toward the exits gasping for breath and waving the fumes away from their faces. Williams had been aware of the audience's general displeasure with his play throughout the performance, which had been punctuated with hisses of disapproval and the frequent banging up of a seat. The next morning the critics added their negative reaction to the dismaying mixture of religion and sex to which he had treated them—although Cecil B. DeMille had been serving up a similar concoction in his Biblical films for years. The Boston City Council joined their voices to the chorus of criticism by serving official notice that the play would have to be censored or closed.

The Council banned, among other things, the scene in which Vee Talbott unveils her portrait of Christ and He turns out to have the face of Val Xavier. They found this scene sacrilegious in spite of the fact that the painting is obviously the product of a religious fanatic's overheated imagination and is not intended by the playwright as an attack on genuine religoius piety at all. Williams had expected artistic flaws to be pointed out in his work, but he had never thought that the play would be deemed immoral. For him the theme of his work was the conflict of contrary desires which can possess the human spirit, a theme which he assumed he had declared in the very title of the play.

"Why had I never dreamed that such struggles would strike many people as filthy and seem to them unfit for articulation?" he reflected afterwards. "It seemed to me that if *Battle of Angels* was nothing else, it certainly was clean; it certainly was idealistic." All of the principals in the play guilty of serious moral transgressions pay rather spectacularly for their sins before the final curtain, so Williams could hardly be accused of glorifying evil, as some of his Boston detractors contended. Miriam Hopkins issued a statement on Williams's behalf that said that *Battle of Angels* was not a dirty play and that the salacious implications attributed to it were "in the minds of some of the people who have seen it. They read meanings into it according to their own suppressed feelings."

As Williams and his agent Audrey Wood crossed the Boston Common on the morning after the opening for an autopsy about the previous night's debacle, loud reports like gunfire inexplicabley exploded somewhere on the block; and the pair laughed hysterically when one of them quipped, "My God, they're shooting at us!" Their levity quickly evaporated when they ventured into the hotel suite of the producer who advised the author that his play would have to be revised extensively if it were ever to see Broadway. The frantic young playwright did his utmost to oblige, but a few days later the Theater Guild announced that *Battle of Angels* would close for good at the conclusion of its Boston run.

In an unprecedented gesture of apology to its Boston subscribers, the Guild sent out a letter which stated that "the play was more of a disappointment to us than to you. *Battle of Angels* turned out badly. But who knows whether the next play by the same author may not prove a success?" The Guild then went on to defend the play against its Boston censorship. "In view of the unfortunate publicity caused by the Boston censor's protest about *Battle of Angels*, we feel it only fair to give you the Guild's reasons for producing the play. We chose it because we felt the young author had genuine poetic gifts and an interesting insight into a particular American scene. The treatment of the religious obsession of one of the characters, which sprang from frustration, did not justify, in our opinion, the censor's action. It was, we felt, a sincere and honest attempt to present a true psychological picture."

In 1957 *Battle of Angels* did reach Broadway, but reincarnated as *Orpheus Descending*. Why did Williams stick so stubbornly to his faith in this play, working on it from time to time throughout the intervening seventeen years? "Well, nothing is more precious to anybody than the emotional record of his youth," he explained in *The New York Times* shortly before the New York opening of *Orpheus*. "And you will find the trail of my sleeve-worn heart in this completed play that I now call *Orpheus Descending*." In short, Williams felt that *Angels-Orpheus* had released and sublimated the emotional crises of his adolescence, which perhaps explains why Val, who is ostensibly close to thirty in both versions of the play, acts most of the time like a naïve, overgrown adolescent.

Although the basic plot line of *Orpheus* and the main characters (despite new names in some cases) are essentially the same as in *Battle*, Williams estimated that about seventy-five per cent of the revised version was new writing, designed to sharpen the theme and the emotional conflicts of the story. The very title of the revised work, lifted from a Williams poem of the same name, indicates that the dramatist had all but abandoned the somewhat muddled religious symbolism of *Battle of Angels* (although he retained the Easter symbolism of *Battle*) in favor of symbolism grounded in classical mythology. Val Xavier is now related to Orpheus trying to liberate his beloved Eurydice (Myra, renamed Lady in the rewritten play) from the clutches of Pluto, the ruler of the Kingdom of Death (Jabe), in order that they can have a new life together. And Val fails just as Orpheus failed before him.

Williams's decision to opt for classical mythology as a thematic framework for his rewrite of *Battle* may have sprung from the fact that one of the characters in *Battle*, Cassandra Whiteside, was meant to suggest the Cassandra of classical antiquity who was a genuine prophetess doomed to have her predictions ignored. Thus Cassandra Whiteside warns Val to leave town with her before the community's antipathy toward him erupts into violence, but Val does not take her seriously until it is too late.

As Carol Cutrere in *Orpheus,* the Cassandra Whiteside character brought over from *Battle* serves a similar function in the later play; but she also becomes more of an integral part of the action than she was in *Battle*, where she seemed to be no more than a commentator on the action and not a fully realized character at all. Thus in *Orpheus* it is established that she had known Val earlier in New Orleans and wants to win him away from Lady.

Williams simplified the overarching design of the play by weeding out some of the superfluous characters, most notably the crazed woman from Waco, Texas, who appears at the end of *Battle* to accuse Val of rape and help to precipitate his lynching. By that point in *Battle*, of course, Val has already been accused of murdering Myra, and the incensed vigilantes hardly need an additional reason to string him up, especially since their sexual jealousy of the super-virile Val is sufficient spur to wreak vindictive violence on him at the least provocation.

Some of the religious symbolism of *Battle of Angels* still clings to *Orpheus Descending* in the person of Vee Talbott and her excessive religiosity, but the heavy-handed religious implications of the earlier play are toned down considerably. As Nancy Tischler comments, in *Orpheus* "Val is less a primitive Christ figure than a variant on Chance Wayne in *Sweet Bird of Youth* who has lost his youth and his purity." Significantly, in keeping with this notion of lost innocence, the only Biblical reference in *Orpheus* which is underlined more firmly than it was in *Battle* is the Old Testament notion that man must be purified of his sins in the fires of suffering. Williams takes this concept quite literally in *Orpheus* by having the mob burn Val to death with a blowtorch after they have hung him on the lynching tree.

There is no doubt that *Orpheus*, as the work of a mature writer, is a far better play than *Battle of Angels* on every level. The main characters are more human and true to life and come off less as symbolic abstractions than they did in *Battle*. For instance Val and Jabe are first and foremost two men struggling for the love of the same woman as well as representatives of the primeval conflict of light and life (Val) versus darkness and death (Jabe). Moreover, Jabe's disease-ravaged body epitomizes the cancerous plague of malice and intolerance that has spread throughout the community, so ironically named Glorious Hill, which will not tolerate outsiders like Val, Lady, and Carol who do not conform to the severe conventions of the insulated little town, and who must, therefore, either be driven out or destroyed.

Because Williams emphasizes the position of all three characters as misfits and outsiders in *Orpheus* even more than he did in *Battle*, the theme of human loneliness is more strongly delineated in the later play. Val's remarks in *Battle* about each of us being sentenced to solitary confinement inside our own skins is of course incorporated into *Orpheus*, but it carries more weight because of the strengthening of the loneliness theme in the rewrite. Val also has a long poetic speech about a legless bird that descends to earth only when it dies which reinforces further the loneliness theme, as does the circumstance of Lady's being an Italian immigrant in *Orpheus*, a factor that alienates her still more from the close-knit, inbred community.

Even the confectionary which she is planning to open on Easter Sunday, and which is decorated like an orchard in full bloom, takes on a note of defiance of the townspeople which it did not possess in the original version of the play. We learn from the exposition that Lady's father had in fact been proprietor of a similar establishment in a real orchard on a lake when she was a girl. Because her father served Blacks, the local vigilante group destroyed his premises by fire and he died in the flames. Lady's attempt to resurrect her father's confectionary right in the heart of town is her way of asserting, therefore, that new life and hope can still be reborn in the very midst of this vile and corrupt community. This situation becomes doubly ironic when Jabe reveals to Lady toward the end of the play that he had led the party that destroyed her father and his little business, and then he proceeds to kill her just as he murdered her father.

Yet Williams has made it evident in the play that even if Jabe did not shoot his wife Lady's dreams of reviving her lost youth by opening a replica of her father's store with Val as her partner (in all senses of the word) were doomed never to materialize. The electric moon, silver paper stars, and artificial vines of her pseudo-orchard could never have been any more than a pale approximation of the living, natural orchard that her father had planted by the lake, any more than Lady herself could ever have resuscitated the past and relived it with Val, whose youth was as irretrievable as her own.

In summary, Williams succeeded in *Orpheus Descending* in knitting together the loose ends of the plot of *Battle of Angels*, strengthened the personalities and relationships of the characters, and clarified the theme and symbolism of the play which center upon the loneliness of the outsider in a hostile and uncomprehending universe. He therefore had great expectations that *Orpheus* would be a success when it reached Broadway in the early spring of 1957; but there were disappointments all along the way once the play got into production.

The first disappointment was that Anna Magnani declined to play Lady Torrence, even though Williams had made the character an Italian immigrant in the hope that she would accept the role. She hesitated to do so, however, for the same reason that she had turned down the role of Serafina in the original production of *The Rose Tattoo* on the stage a few years earlier, i.e., that her tenuous hold on the English language would make sustaining a long stage role too great a strain on her over the period of an extended run. So Williams turned to Maureen Stapleton to take the role, just as he had done when Magnani had decided against playing Serafina.

During the tryout run in Philadelphia, Williams became increasingly dissatisfied with the male lead and Cliff Robertson was called in to play Val a scant eight days before the New York premiere. Producer Robert Whitehead whispered in Williams's ear during Robertson's first performance in the part, "Thank God, this is it!" But unfortunately this was not it, at least not as far as critical response to the play was concerned. *Orpheus Descending*, it was true, was an improvement on *Battle of Angels;* but that did not make it a very good play in itself, the critics maintained. The rewrite was still littered with too many corpses and catastrophes, and Williams had been ill-advised to try to pump new blood into a tired old play. As Henry Hewes wrote in *The Saturday Review*, "Every writer feels that he could write his early works better now that he knows so much more about his craft. But the fact is that the writer is no longer the same person. All the experiences that went into the original work have been rearranged and re-evaluated" in the intervening years. As a result the new writing which he imposes on the old does not mesh into a satisfying whole. The play closed after a meager sixty-eight performances.

For his part Williams thought the Broadway production was "over-written" and "under-directed," and still had faith in a play which he had nursed along for a longer period than anything else which he had ever written. Though *Orpheus Descending* is not top-drawer Williams in either of its stage incarnations, it is still an intriguing study of frustration and repression bursting into open violence in a decaying Southern town, and as such was of interest to Hollywood, even though it had twice failed in the theater. Williams was given yet another opportunity to vindicate his belief in the play, therefore, when two former agents turned producers, Martin Jurow and Richard Shephard, bought the screen rights to *Orpheus* and set about arranging to turn it into a film called *The Fugitive Kind*.

Williams cribbed the title of the film version from one of his earliest plays, which had been produced by a local St. Louis Theater group in the late Thirties; but it bears no other resemblance to *Orpheus*, save for one speech in *Orpheus* in which the phrase is used and which was brought over into the film expressly to explain the title: At the end of both the play and the film based on it, Carol becomes the possessor of Val's snakeskin jacket after Val is murdered by the mob. "Wild things leave things behind them," she says as she fondles the garment tenderly; "and these are the tokens passed on from one to another, so that the fugitive kind can always follow their own kind."

An extraordinary cast was assembled for the film, including three Oscar winners; Anna Magnani accepted the role which she had rejected on the stage; Marlon Brando agreed to play Val, and Joanne Woodward signed on as Carol. Maureen Stapleton was selected to play Vee Talbott in the movie and Sidney Lumet was to direct. Williams collaborated on the script with Meade Roberts, who afterwards wrote an article in *Films and Filming* entitled "Williams and Me," expressing his admiration for his collaborator and insisting that everyone associated with the film tried to be as faithful as possible to the playwright's vision as expressed in *Orpheus*.

"To translate the work of a visionary to the screen is, of course, a delicate matter," wrote Roberts, "requiring a rare dedication on the part of the producer, director, and company. Compromise cannot be considered; nor should it be since compromise can only vitiate and reduce that which is unique to the level of that which is mundane. Therefore Tennessee's thoughts and ideas were held uppermost in everyone's minds, from the moment that work began on the project in June, 1958, up till the time when final editing was completed."

Roberts recalled that the first time he met Jurow and Shepard in the summer of 1958, one of them exclaimed to him, "We don't buy a book or a play to *lick,* only to *do!*'" Never once in the intervening months, Roberts comments, did they try to "lick" Williams's play, "only to do it, and to do it strictly on the terms set forth by the playwright. And I was to discover in the following months that this was the same goal of Sidney Lumet . . . and of all the actors involved."

There is no reason to believe that Roberts was not sincere in his efforts to help Williams create a worthy screen adaptation of *Orpheus* which would not compromise the dramatic and thematic values of the original theater piece for the sake of crass commercial preoccupations. Whatever faults are resident in the finished shooting script were already inherent in the play, which in some ways was improved in making its transition to the screen.

The film opens with a pre-credit sequence in New Orleans which is solidly based on references within the play's exposition about how Val's wild existence in New Orleans forced him to leave town. Val is brought into night court on a drunk and disorderly conduct charge. He explains to the judge that he is sick of the life he has been living and plans to get his guitar, which is his "last companion," out of hock and move on.

The credits are then superimposed on Val's journey in his old jalopy along the highway out of New Orleans into the country, where his battered auto breaks down just as he crosses the state line into Mississippi at dawn and he finds himself on the outskirts of the little town of Marigold (not Glorious Hill, as in the play). He meets Vee Talbott, the wife of the local sheriff, who invites him to stay in the jailhouse temporarily until his car can be repaired.

In another series of scenes devised for the screenplay but—again—substantially based on expository material in the play, Carol tells Val that she remembers him from a New Orleans party at which he "provided the entertainment," and coaxes him to go to a roadhouse with her and then on to a cemetery which she likes to visit for curious reasons of her own. The roadhouse is the appropriate atmosphere for Carol's conversation with Val about how she leads a lascivious life in order to defy the hypocritical conventions of her aristocratic Southern family, represented by her domineering brother who attempts, patently without much success, to make her conform to standards of behavior expected of a Cutrere, standards which exclude her civil rights work as well as her loose living.

As she dances around the room taking swigs from a whiskey bottle "concealed" in a paper sack, her brother gets up from a nearby booth, angrily slaps her across her face, and orders her to leave. No such confrontation takes place between Carol and her brother in the play, but this one in the film effectively dramatizes the conflict between Carol and the detested establishment for which her brother stands, in a way that her simply discussing it with Val in the dry goods store does not. This prudent opening out of the play continues in the following sequence in which Val and Carol drive on to the cemetery where Carol invites him to "hear the dead people talk."

R. G. Armstrong as the Sheriff, Marlon Brando as Val Xavier, director Sidney Lumet, and Joanne Woodward as Carol in *The Fugitive Kind*.

Reclining against a tombstone, she says that their sole message of exhortation to the living is to live as much as possible before coming to join them. Then she rises to a kneeling position and seeks to seduce Val in the deathly darkness of the cemetery. Val shakes himself loose and switches on the headlights of her car, flooding her with light. This is his way of telling her that, despite what she says to the contrary, Carol has, in her despair, thrown in her lot with darkness and death, while he is still very much in league with light and life—an excellent visual metaphor developed from the verbal metaphors of the play about the conflict of light versus darkness, life versus death.

Other crucial confrontations which are referred to in the play and presented directly in the film, to the greater dramatic advantage of the latter, include the scene in Jabe's sickroom in which he tears at Lady's fragile silk nightgown while hissing, "You're still my wife, not my widow yet!" She retorts with equal venom,

"You make my skin crawl. You always have." Jabe becomes an abiding malevolent presence in the film because the movie employs occasional shots of him brooding in his room that remind the audience that he is biding his time until the moment is right for him to reap his revenge. When Val and Lady drive off to visit the site of her father's ruined orchard-confectionary, for instance, the camera catches Jabe watching their departure from his remote vantage point high above them like some pagan deity monitoring how the mere mortals below are playing into his hands.

Throughout the screenplay Williams and Roberts have been at pains to replace words with images wherever possible and to rework long monologues, in which the characters in the play ladled out exposition to one another, into dialogues which allow for more dramatic interaction. Conversely, the screenplay retains a couple of long speeches which are essential to the theme of the story, such as Val's reverie about the legless bird which remains aloof from contact with the earth throughout its whole life until it comes to rest when death draws near.

These lines are an important metaphorical justification of Val's itinerant way of life, but as Brando delivers them in the film Lumet distracts the viewer from their content by making the lights in the store slowly dim to the point where only Brando's eyes are illuminated as he speaks. This device smacks of theatrical rather than of cinematic lighting, and demonstrates why Williams was dissatisfied with Lumet's penchant to play several scenes in shadows. The movie was so dark and murky at times, Williams quipped, "that it looked like everyone was drowning in chocolate syrup."

Lumet was chosen to direct the movie in the first place at the behest of Anna Magnani, who had been impressed with his previous film adaptations of plays. Lumet has always styled himself "a great believer in words in films, and I think that the idea of literature being dead so far as cinema is concerned is one of those temporary little fads," as he said after shooting *Fugitive Kind*. French critic George Sadoul has called Lumet "a talented and conscientious technician with a passion for theater," and in his defense adds that literary adaptations can only be as good as the works on which they are based.

Admittedly *Orpheus Descending* is not a great play, and it could never have made anything more than a good movie, even with its high-powered cast, since a faithful film adaptation cannot but inherit at least some of the flaws inherent in its source. And, except for lapses in lighting techniques, Lumet has done a creditable job in filming *Fugitive Kind*. He was aware that merely taking the audience away from the dry goods store into a roadhouse, a cemetery, and a burned out orchard is not the only way in which a film makes a play more cinematic. The other, more subtle way that this is done is by allowing the camera to bring the viewer into the action of the film, so, as he says, they can see nuances of gesture and facial expression "lost on all but the first seven rows of a

Broadway theater audience." He also has striven to add some fine imaginative strokes to the story, especially at the climax of the picture.

Lady has hired a steam calliope to advertise the opening of the new wing of the store; and when she learns that Jabe was involved in her father's death, her anguished scream is intensified by the wailing music of the calliope outside with which it becomes mingled. Shortly afterwards, when she embraces Val, they happen to look upward and see Jabe maniacally staring down at them through a hole in the artificial vines of the fake arbor which Lady has built to simulate her father's devastated orchard. The unsettling implication of this shot is that Jabe has often watched them together in the garden when they thought they were hidden from his prying eyes. Then he sets a match to the tinsel, streamers, and other phony decorations nearest his window and they immediately burst into a blaze. Once Jabe and Lady are dead, the maddened mob forces Val with firehoses back into the burning building to die with her, emphasizing the

Anna Magnani, Marlon Brando in *The Fugitive Kind*.

purification-by-fire theme of the play. In the play Val is blowtorched on the hanging tree; but having him together with Lady in death in the conflagration is more symbolically right because it visualizes in stunning images the precarious edifice which Lady had erected to give substance to their romantic illusions crashing down around them both.

Given a fairly faithful adaptation, a conscientious director, and a prestigious cast, one must ask why *The Fugitive Kind* did not jell better than it did as a motion picture. According to Meade Roberts, the making of the film was a journey that, like most, "proved to be exhilarating, wondrous, sometimes storm-tossed, sometimes maddening." The storms that brewed during shooting largely centered around the two temperamental leads. "Brando and Anna Magnani engaged in a clash of egos never before equalled," Williams remembers, not even by the verbal bouts of Lancaster and Magnani on *The Rose Tattoo*.

Brando had accepted the role of Val not because of his phenomenal success in Williams's *Streetcar* but because he had made some bad financial investments and needed money. When the producers offered him a cool million to play Val, Brando accepted and thereby became the first actor in motion picture history to receive that astronomical salary for making a single movie. He would otherwise not have agreed to take the role, however, since he realized on his first reading of the script that the film, like the play, belonged not to Val but to Lady. Lumet attempted to mollify Brando by suggesting alterations in the script to Williams. But the author, who has characteristically created stronger female protagonists than male protagonists in his plays, could not re-conceive the entire story according to Brando and Lumet's specifications with a few hasty revisions.

Magnani had a different difficulty bothering her. Now past fifty, she began to fret about looking too old to play a romantic role. "She had arrived at a sad place in her life and none of us could help her," Lumet has said. "That great talent had a great problem, and it was vanity. Suddenly she was worried about the way she looked. The whole staging had to be shifted; and there were things Anna literally refused to do. But Marlon was . . . very giving with her—and yet he bore the brunt of the blame."

Williams recalls the situation somewhat differently. He and Ms. Magnani had both cherished the dream that her appearance in *Fugitive Kind,* playing a role that had been written for her, would be her greatest triumph, even topping her Oscar-winning performance in *Rose Tattoo,* particularly because she was teamed with the gifted Marlon Brando. "But Mr. Brando comes at a high price in more ways than one," the dramatist explains, "especially for a foreign co-player still unsure of the language." Brando's offbeat timing and his slurred diction may have been right for the part, but they unsettled his co-star, who would wait for her cue—only to find that when it came it was sometimes not the one written in the script. *"The Fugitive Kind* is a true and beautiful film in my opinion, but mutilated by that uncontrollable demon of competitiveness in an actor too great, if he knew it, to resort to such self-protective devices."

The truth of the matter probably is that Anna Magnani and Marlon Brando share equal parts of the blame for their clashes of temperament, which they both failed to see as detrimental to their respective performances, to the morale of the cast and crew, and hence to the film as a whole. Each thought the other was trying to upstage them, and by all accounts both of them were right. Tension mounted between them during the long, hot summer of 1959 as the unit moved to the tiny town of Milton, New York (population: 750), whose one thoroughfare was revamped to look like the Marigold, Mississippi, of the screenplay. Finally, with only four days of shooting to go, Ms. Magnani interrupted a take to storm at Brando and stalk off the set to her dressing room. Lumet offered to serve as good will ambassador, but Brando countered that it was up to him to pacify his volatile co-star. After half an hour, Lumet joined the frey in time to hear Ms. Magnani berate Brando about an assortment of resentments, including his getting top billing all over the world, even in her native Italy. The two men managed to lure her back to the set and the production ground on to its conclusion three days later.

When post-production work was completed the following winter, the studio held a sneak preview at the 58th Street Theater in Manhattan in early December. Williams, who had been travelling in Europe for four months, went to the preview. Though some of the audience liked the movie, Williams suffered the disconcerting experience of being booed by a group of teenagers who had seen the film as he passed through the lobby to the street. He cavalierly booed them back before getting into a taxi with actress Diana Barrymore, who had accompanied him to the screening. She later reported to a mutual friend that Williams's bravado quickly evaporated and by the end of the evening he was in a state about the incident. He had regained his composure by the time that a *New York Times* reporter phoned him a few days later, however, and he dismissed the episode.

He did confess that he would have liked to have seen the film adhere more closely to the script which he had worked on with Meade Roberts. Though he would not be specific, he might well have had in mind the tampering which Brando had done with his own lines during shooting in an effort to build up his part, something which both Williams and Ms. Magnani had complained about at the time. Speaking more generally, he admitted that a writer gets too involved with his own work to be fair to the movie makers who commit his plays to celluloid. But he nevertheless expressed a wish that the original author of a film property had more control over the film that ultimately emerges on the screen. "Unfortunately, once a movie gets rolling there's not too much the author can do. Too many people are involved. And it't difficult to keep checking up on it."

Anna Magnani, Marlon Brando, and Joanne Woodward in *The Fugitive Kind*.

The film opened in the spring of 1960 to the kind of mixed reception which had been foreshadowed by the December sneak preview. Stanley Kauffman somewhat testily asked his readers, "How long can you and I go on being represented by riffraff?" He castigated Brando for resorting in his playing of Val Xavier to too many of the mannerisms which he had concocted for Stanley Kowalski. (Williams too had sighed, "I wish Brando didn't remember Stanley Kowalski so well.") Kauffmann also scolded Anna Magnani and Joanne Woodward for mimicking their own past performances from other movies.

Esquire could detect no norm of morality implicit in the picture, by which the characters could be judged, and found the action, therefore, to be devoid of any human meaning. Bosley Crowther, on the other hand, defended the film not once but twice in his *New York Times* space. He discerned human values in the movie that others had missed. Crowther found the film in essence to be the "surprisingly decent account of two lonely and sad, but normal, persons, trying hard to get a little out of life against the adversities compounded by the meanness and weakness of man. Their story is that of the fated disaster that comes when dreams clash with hard reality."

It is easy to agree with Crowther that the fugitive kind sketched for us in the picture are not mere unsympathetic riffraff, as Kauffmann and others would have it, but doomed creatures struggling to regain their footing in a hostile world which offers them no support or encouragement to be better than they are. And I would like to think that my analysis of *Battle of Angels, Orpheus Descending,* and *The Fugitive Kind* bears this out.

Williams's final judgement of the film was that it did not emerge as the definitive version of the play which he had unveiled two decades earlier in Boston as *Battle of Angels,* and with which he had tinkered off and on during the ensuing years. He was by now disillusioned with working in films, as he indicated in his *Times* interview after the sneak preview. The dramatist had found that whether he collaborated on a screen adaptation of one of his plays or not he had little influence, either as the original author or as a script writer, on the actual outcome of the motion picture. Williams therefore announced that he would not do any more movie scripts, but rather leave the screen adaptations of his work to other hands. "There comes a time in life when you have got to conserve your energy for what's more important to you. And the theater is what's most important to me."

The author has broken his resolution not to work on a film adaptation of his work only once, when he helped to prepare *The Milk Train Doesn't Stop Here Any More* for the screen as *Boom!* in 1968. His experience with that picture, however, was enough to confirm his earlier resolution; and he declined to collaborate on the scenario for *The Seven Descents of Myrtle* when Sidney Lumet set in motion plans to film that Williams play after the release of *Boom!*, allowing Gore Vidal to write the script in his stead.

The Seven Descents of Myrtle, like *Cat on a Hot Tin Roof* and other Williams plays, began its artistic life as a short story. In the present instance it was a story entitled "Kingdom of Earth," the title of which Williams wanted to retain for the play until producer David Merrick prevailed upon him to change the play's title to *The Seven Descents of Myrtle* for the Broadway production.

The short story, like the eventual play, centers on Chicken, a brawny manual laborer who deeply resents that the old family homestead has passed to his half-brother Lot. Although he is younger than Chicken, Lot is a legitimate descendant of their father while Chicken is not. To Chicken's great chagrin Lot brings home a buxom ex-showgirl and part-time whore named Myrtle as his new wife. Chicken had counted on inheriting the property, which he as elder son always considered to be rightfully his, as soon as his gravely ill half-brother died of tuberculosis; and now it appears that everything will go to the eleventh-hour widow.

Lot's marriage proves to be no obstacle, however, since Myrtle succumbs to Chicken's animal magnetism on the very same night that the frail Lot succumbs to T.B. So Chicken gets Lot's land and his wife too. Having long ago discarded any aspirations for attaining the Kingdom of Heaven, Chicken is willing to settle for inheriting the Kingdom of Earth.

The Seven Descents of Myrtle inherited not only the basic situation of the short story—embellished, of course, with more material to make a longer play—but also much of Chicken's philosophy about contenting one's self with earthly rather than heavenly salvation. But there are some significant differences between the short story and the play. One is that in the fictional form of the plot Chicken is erroneously thought to have been sired by his father and a Black mistress; in the play there is no doubt that this is the case. This provides another reason, besides his bastardy, for his having been rejected as heir to his father's property. Another difference between the story and the stage play is that in the latter Lot is a transvestite homosexual with a deeply rooted Oedipal complex, as well as a consumptive.

These new facets of Lot's personality intensify the already strong contrast between the two half-brothers: Chicken is the lusty, resourceful heterosexual stud and Lot is the impotent, ineffectual homosexual. Chicken, we learn, earned his nickname because once during a flood he subsisted on the roof of the house by biting the heads off chickens and drinking their blood. Lot, on the other hand, is not capable of such survival tactics, and is coughing up what little blood he has left in his disease-ridden body, which in turn symbolizes the weakness of his neurotic psyche as well.

When Myrtle and Lot arrive at the old homestead, just as a flood warning is being issued, even the dull-witted Myrtle quickly surveys the lay of the land and realizes that her new husband married her for the sole purpose of following his dead mother's orders to keep the racially and socially unacceptable Chicken from coming into his own. The whole situation has a Biblical tinge, starting with the concept of the two half-brothers contending like Jacob and Esau over their birthright and continuing on to the Deluge which, in the framework of the Old Testament, will hopefully cleanse this little patch of earth and its inhabitants in a way similar to that of the purifying fire at the close *Orpheus Descending*. When Lot dies clad in his mother's faded finery, it is clear that not the meek, but the strong, will inherit the earth, but in this case justifiably so.

Lot is another one of Williams's pathetic homosexuals, a breed that dates back to Blanche DuBois's husband, Allen Grey: young men who are simply unequipped to cope with a tough and ruthless world. They yearn for a more refined, peaceful existence, and this is usually sought in evoking the elegent pre-bellum South by holding on to decaying remnants of that bygone era such as the delapidated family homestead. The futility of Lot's attempts to live in the past is crystallized in the once-glittering, now dusty chandelier suspended from the ceiling in the parlor. To the dim-witted Myrtle, who is a total stranger to the traditions and conventions of the Old South, the chandelier recalls the glamor of the lobby of a "classy" movie theater in a big city like Memphis. What such relics of past glory and status as the chandelier betoken to Lot is beyond Myrtle's comprehension. She cannot, therefore, understand why her husband manifests no interest whatever in immediately installing the electrical equipment which they received as gifts in exchange for being married on a daytime TV show. He is as alien to the Modern Age as she is to his Old South.

Lot and Myrtle take up residence in his mother's room, and as his life ebbs away he seeks solace in his memories of her by systematically transforming himself into her and untimately relinquishing his own identity entirely. By the time he actually dies, Lot is really already dead, at least in the sense that he as a personality separate from his mother, has ceased to exist. He has doffed his own identity and donned hers, along with her clothes and mannerisms.

This transformation begins subtly with Lot sitting in his mother's rocking chair, "one of those wicker rockers," as Williams describes it in the stage directions, "that they have, or used to have, on verandahs of old-fashioned summer hotels in the South." Lot then takes to using his mother's ivory cigarette holder and wearing her white silk wrapper. By play's end he has completely outfitted himself in one of her summer frocks, and expires beneath the beloved parlor chandelier. Like his mother, Lot has become a prisoner of the past, totally out of tune with the present; for such a one there is nothing left but death.

It is no surprise that in the course of the play Myrtle periodically liberates herself from the suffocating insulation of the elegant bedroom which she shares with her increasingly remote husband (Lot's Kingdom of Heaven), and goes down to the kitchen to talk to the more vital Chicken (Chicken's Kingdom of Earth). Myrtle is the only character who moves freely between the territories that the two half-brothers have staked out for themselves: from the chilly and ultra-refined bedroom with its decorative fringes and ornate brass bed where Lot withdraws more and more into his fantasies of the past, to the warm and homey kitchen where Chicken busies himself with practical exigencies of the present.

Inevitably, Myrtle's attraction to Chicken's vitality and virility and corresponding revulsion to Lot's languor and effeminacy escalate into a sexual interest in her half-brother-in-law. Williams points up the sexual dimension of Myrtle's growing predilection for Chicken by needlessly multiplying phallic references to Chicken's handsome switchblade and guitar. Even a somewhat less-than-alert playgoer can detect quite early on that to Lot, Myrtle can only be a coddling mother, nursing him in his last illness; while to Chicken there is hope that she can be a real wife.

As Jerrold Phillips writes in his brilliant essay on the play in the critical collection of essays called *Tennessee Williams: A Tribute*, "Lot's Kingdom of Heaven was no more than his relationship with his mother whom he attempts to 'resurrect' through his tranvestistic donning of her clothing. This false and sterile Kingdom of Heaven, however, is also the kingdom of death, fully manifested in Lot's demise near the end of the play." Little wonder, then, that Myrtle is drawn more and more to Chicken's Kingdom of Earth.

Chicken sees in the durable Myrtle a survivor like himself, since she has come through several scrapes in the course of her checkered career as one of the four members of a combo called the Mobile Hot-Shots. She is the only one of the girls still alive, the others having become victims of sex crimes, drugs, or suicide. Myrtle has kept her head above water through the vagaries of her sordid experiences, and there is every reason to believe as the curtain descends that with Chicken's help she can continue to do so, not only as they prepare to climb atop the roof of the house to wait out the Deluge, but in the face of whatever catastrophe, personal or public, they may have to face in the future.

Having finished writing this play about survival, Williams now had to face fire and flood in the form of mounting the production for the New York theater. He chose José Quintero, who by then had directed the superb Off Broadway revival of *Summer and Smoke* and the film of Williams's novella, *The Roman Spring of Mrs. Stone*. The cast consisted of Estelle Parsons (Myrtle), Brian Bedford (Lot), and Harry Guardino (Chicken). The road engagements did not go well and Williams was willing as always to do a great deal of revising and rewriting, though he balked at the title change from *Kingdom of Earth* to *The Seven Descents of Myrtle* which David Merrick forced on him. Estelle Parsons agreed with the author, especially when she discovered after the play opened that some theatergoers took to counting the number of times that Myrtle descended from Lot's room to Chicken's, and complained that there were not "seven descents."

In retrospect Williams finds that Quintero was not a wise choice to direct the play because his delicate sense of humor was not suited to the mood of a bawdy comedy. "Estelle Parsons was quite brilliant," he says, "but the poor thing had no help. José Quintero didn't direct her properly, so everything that happened onstage was her own invention." Furthermore Harry Guardino, a hefty Italian type, was totally miscast as the half-breed half-brother. When the play opened on Broadway and most of the critical fraternity thought it a predictable encounter among three superficial characters, it ran for less than a month.

Personally I have always rated *The Seven Descents of Myrtle* a rather delightful minor work of Williams, an unpretentious three-character play conceived on a small scale which works on that level for those who are willing to accept it for what it is and not expect it to be a fully orchestrated large-scale work. It is true that we have seen Williams's shy, neurotic homosexual, his good hearted whore, and his self-assured stud before; but never have they been mingled in such a lighthearted, heady brew—despite the darker corners of the human psyche into which the play at times intrudes. For myself, Myrtle's witless attempt to seduce Chicken into giving up his inheritance claims by donning her gaudy Hot-Shot costume, as if she were some sophisticated *femme fatale* working her wiles on a country bumpkin, is worth the price of admission or a reading of the play.

Time magazine conceded that the opening night performance rippled with laughter, "a renewed credit to Williams's fluent comic sense." Williams too has always thought of the play as fundamentally a comedy, and refers to it as "my funny melodrama." He consequently suspects that many critics and playgoers alike erred in taking the whole thing much too seriously. When Warner Brothers purchased the film rights, he looked to the movie version as a second chance to launch his work and this time to do it properly. The motion picture adaptation seemed particularly promising because several individuals associated with other Williams films were participating in the venture. The director was Sidney Lumet; the screen writer was Gore Vidal, who had written the screenplay for *Suddenly Last Summer*; and the cinematographer was James Wong Howe, who

Lynn Redgrave, James Coburn, and Robert Hooks in *The Last of the Mobile Hotshots*.

photographed *The Rose Tattoo,* for which he won an Academy Award, and *This Property is Condemned.*

Warner Brothers did not ask Estelle Parsons to repeat her stage performance as Myrtle in the movie, though she had just won an Oscar for her acting in Warners' own *Bonnie and Clyde.* Ms. Parsons told interviewer Mike Steen just before the film went into production that she did not mind losing the part to Lynn Redgrave because, when she looked over the photos taken of the stage production, she decided that she had a much too straightforward personality to portray "that poor little pathetic girl. There's nothing very pathetic about me."

A major casting decision was choosing a Black actor, Robert Hooks, to play Chicken in the film, rather than a White, as on the stage. The story concerns the confrontation between a Negro and his poor White trash half-brother, after all, and how the girl gets caught in the middle between them while they are trying to make mutual adjustments that go beyond the color bar.

James Coburn agreed to play Lot (renamed Jeb in the movie), after some initial hesitation about tarnishing his screen image as the masculine hero of several superspy flicks, because he liked Gore Vidal's adaptation. "Gore Vidal has kept all the good things in Tennessee's play and improved on the bad," Coburn baldly stated in *The New York Times.* (Williams did not agree. As he remarked after seeing the film, "Gore Vidal wrote the script, he said, out of friendship for me. Baby, with friends like that . . .") Coburn refused to play Jeb as a transvestite because, he said, he drew the line at playing someone quite so weird: "I'm making him impotent, but not a transvestite. This way he has more significance."

It is difficult, for me at least, to see how Jeb gains more significance by cancelling the transvestite dimension of his personality. Actually the reverse is true. In the play Lot's attachment to the decaying mansion is rooted in his neurotic identification with his mother, an identification that leads him at first to want to preserve what is left of the tattered elegance of the old Southern mansion so dear to her, then to assume her clothing, and with that finally her personality. By removing this Oedipal content from Jeb's character in the movie, his desire to hold onto the plantation becomes much less frantic and pathetic.

Instead of Jeb donning his mother's dress in the movie, he has Myrtle wear one of his mother's Mardi Gras gowns while he puts on a Confederate officer's jacket. But the effect is ludicrous in the film whereas in the play it is sad that Lot is driven to masquerade in his mother's clothing for reasons much darker and deeper than mere nostalgia for an era that is gone with the wind—which seems to be his sole motive in the movie. The Jeb character, as Williams conceived him, is both psychologically and physically weak, a wretched individual whose psyche is being devoured by his obsessions as surely as his body is being eaten away by disease. (One might say that the Jeb character in the play begins by enjoying his fantasies and ends with his fantasies enjoying him.) Jeb is therefore

James Coburn in a Confederate officer's coat in *Mobile Hotshots*.

less complex and less interesting in the film, and has less "significance," to use Coburn's term.

Of course Jeb is still impotent in the movie, as Coburn pointed out in his interview during shooting, and this malady is still indicative of his inability to be productive in any way. Unlike Chicken, Jeb has no interest in cultivating the fruitful farm land attached to the plantation, but is preoccupied with refurbishing the ramshackle house "to look just the way it did in 1840!" As a radically empty human being, he will never be capable of siring a son to inherit the plantation any more than he will be resourceful enough to carry out his plans to restore the delapidated domicile to the former glories of its ante-bellum splendor.

There is some hint in the movie that Jeb cherishes Oedipal feelings toward his dead mother, for there are several fragmented flashbacks shot in slow motion which punctuate the film, depicting his mother in the same ball gown that Jeb had Myrtle try on. At first his mother is pictured as far off, walking through a meadow. Each time the brief flashback is repeated she advances a little closer to the camera. The last time she appears, the shots of her are intercut with those of a Black servant woman suckling a white baby in the kitchen of the mansion; and Jeb's mother is seen to turn her back and walk away in the opposite direction.

What these images portend is anybody's guess, but I suspect the intention of the director (who had used this splintered flashback device more successfully in *The Pawnbroker*) is to imply that Jeb found his mother a remote and domineering woman who turned him over to a servant for the nurturing and maternal care which she should have given him, and in so doing denied him the maternal love for which he still thirsts—and which he now looks to Myrtle as his mother figure to provide for him.

Another set of fragmented flashbacks, also shot in slow motion, and scattered through the film, are designed to portray how Jeb's impotency made him jealous of his half-brother Chicken and precipitated the rift between them that is perpetuated in their rivalry for the family inheritance. Jeb and Chicken are seen as enlisted men frolicking with a variety of camp followers in these flashbacks; in the last one of this series, the camera first shows a garish peroxide blond astride Chicken on a rumpled brothel bed. As she turns round and bursts into derisive laughter, the camera pulls back to show Jeb, standing nearby wrapped in a sheet and painfully, shamefully looking at the pair. His impotency has reduced him to voyeurism and self-hatred, as well as to sexual jealousy of Chicken, one infers. It seems too that according to this set of flashbacks he has married a voluptuous hooker like the ones which he had known in the army with the conscious hope that such a super sex object could stimulate him to producing an heir—though subconsciously, according to the other group of flashbacks, he really chooses Myrtle to mother *him,* not any child that they might have.

These two sets of flashbacks, which are shattered like so many pieces of a broken mirror in the film, are intended to give some hints to the sources of Jeb's unhappy childhood and youth once the viewer has assembled them into some kind of meaningful coherence. But even after doing so, the average moviegoer would not have anything more than murky insinuations about the nature of Jeb's physical and psychological problems. The straightforward presentation of Jeb in the play as a transvestite homosexual, who has never had any sexual interest in the female of the species at all beyond fathering an heir to beat his half-brother out of the family property, is much more satisfactory than the hazy and eliptical delineation of his character in the movie. In short, Coburn should either have consented to playing the Jeb character as it was developed in the play or let someone else play the part.

The other significant alteration in the play's story line that one finds in the film is Chicken's big revelation to Jeb at the end that he is the bastard son, not of their father, but of their mother. During one of the previous floods, it seems, she was sequestered on the roof of the house with the Black handyman, and that situation was the occasion of the genesis of Chicken. She wanted Chicken to have a chance at the family property, which belonged to her and not to her husband, so she stipulated in her will that in the event of Jeb's death everything would pass on to her next of blood kin. Assuming that she was not Chicken's mother, Jeb has further assumed that her next of kin after him would be his offspring; but it is really Chicken. When he discovers that all of his efforts to conquer his impotency long enough to create an heir have been for nothing, Jeb has a final fit of coughing up blood and dies.

I am not sure precisely why this last twist was introduced into an already complicated plot. Since it is perlucid from the beginning of the film that the sickly, impotent Jeb will never be able to rise to the occasion of generating an heir, especially once Myrtle starts consorting with Chicken, this added bit of plot contrivance seems superfluous and confusing.

Yet the film has some definite merits, beginning with the direct presentation and expansion of Myrtle's long expository speech in the play of how she came to marry such an unlikely bridegroom as Jeb; and it is hilarious. During the credit sequence Jeb is seen hitting the sidewalk as he is tossed out of a bar. He reels into the packaged liquor store next door to the bar, and comes out with a six pack of beer which he consumes while wandering aimlessly into the waiting line for a daytime TV show. He is standing just behind Myrtle and becomes her partner in a volleyball game on stage (on a mud court, no less!) which will determine the couples competing for the chance to be married on the air the following week. Jeb and Myrtle win and he agrees to wed her on the show because, as we learn later, he realized that this was his last chance to provide himself with a son and heir.

As the last credits are superimposed on the screen, Myrtle, decked out in a mini-skirted bridal dress, marries Jeb on TV; and the prologue draws to a close. Myrtle is still sporting her incongruous wedding outfit as they partake of their wedding breakfast at a drive-in diner before setting off for Jeb's family home, along with all of the electrical appliances which the TV station gave them as prizes. These gadgets will be as out of place in the backwoods of Alabama as Myrtle herself will be until she becomes acclimated to her new home through the auspices of Chicken more than of her husband.

Once arrived at the plantation, called Waverly in the film, the script settles down to playing out the rivalry between Jeb and Chicken within the confines of the circumscribed setting dictated by the logic of the play. The two men are isolated from the world outside by the remote location of the estate and isolated from each other by occupying their respective turfs within the house, Jeb in his mother's bedroom upstairs and Chicken in the kitchen downstairs, with only Myrtle to mediate between them.

Because the withered plantation house is the key setting for the entire film, most of the movie was shot on location in just such a rotting house near Baton Rouge, Louisiana, which helps immensely to create an authentic atmosphere for the story. This broken-down house proved to be no obstacle to cinematographer James Wong Howe, who had shot both *Rose Tattoo* and *This Property is Condemned* in equally difficult locations where the technical problems of photographing a movie with the same professional quality as that which would be obtainable on a fully equipped Hollywood sound stage are increased tenfold. Lumet is also a devotee of location shooting, despite the logistics involved, as evidenced by his taking over the town of Milton, New York, to shoot *The Fugitive Kind*.

The greatest challenge which director and cinematographer had to face in filming *The Last of the Mobile Hot-Shots* (as the movie came to be called) in the swampland of Louisiana was the final shot of Chicken and Myrtle atop the roof of the house as the flood waters rise round them. This image symbolizes the union of races as the pair face the future together, and was therefore quite important to

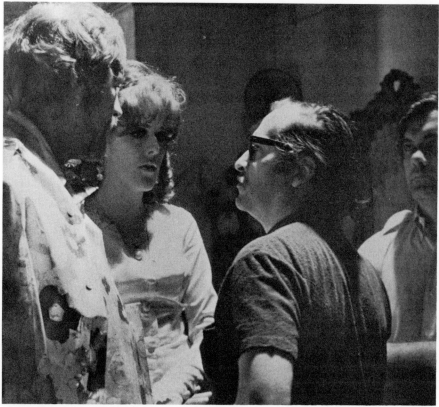

James Coburn, Lynn Redgrave, and Sidney Lumet in the ramshackle mansion used for *Mobile Hotshots*.

the theme and the plot of the movie. Rex Reed, who watched the shooting of this sequence, remembers that it had been raining for several days before the scene was scheduled to be done; but when it came time for the actual shooting of the scene the sun rose with a vengeance and shone brightly all day long.

Lumet decided to delay the scene until evening when it could be done under cover of darkness, so that there would be less chance of filmgoers later detecting that the rain in the scene was supplied totally by fire hoses. The cast and crew went out to the small lake where a rooftop had been constructed and was being kept afloat by waterdrums just beneath the water's surface. By early evening the local fire department had arrived and raised its ladders eighty-five feet into the air. Firemen climbed atop the ladders with enormous fire hoses, awaiting Lumet's signal to spray Robert Hooks and Lynn Redgrave with thirteen hundred gallons of water per minute. Meanwhile James Wong Howe and his camera swung into the air on a crane to record the couple huddling together on their rooftop sanctuary as the waves, stirred by gigantic wind machines off-camera, splashed about them. The camera pulled away from the action, recording the image of the two people clinging to the chimney as the scene receded into the distance; and the shot and the film came to a close.

Among the other merits of the film, besides the opening out of the play for the screen in the prologue sequence and the judicious employment of location settings, I should also point out the visual touches by which the script telegraphs information to the audience without resorting to dialogue. We know, for example, that Myrtle is a frivolous young woman who avoids facing the unpleasant side of reality when during the long ride to Waverly she quickly shuts off the car radio report of flood warnings for the very area to which they are travelling. That Jeb is no more realistic than she is, moreover, is suggested by his wearing tinted glasses as he drives along telling Myrtle about his romantic plans for restoring Waverly. He obviously prefers to see the world from behind rose-colored glasses which soften the harsh realities of the present for him so that he can more easily bask in his reveries of the past.

In contrast to Jeb's rosy picture of Waverly are the realistic shots of the estate which Lumet uses as an ironic comment on what Jeb has been saying. The viewer is introduced to Waverly by a close-up of a weather-beaten sign which looks as if it will collapse at any moment, signalling the disrepair of the house and grounds that Jeb hopes to restore to their appearance in 1840. Later the tarnished chandelier is photographed through a cracked mirror to indicate the gap between the run-down state of Waverly and the way that Jeb prefers to think that things are, or at least can be. The deteriorating mansion, with the help of these images, becomes symbolic of Jeb's own disintegrating life.

The Last of the Mobile Hot-Shots is a finely crafted and well-acted motion picture, and while one does not deny its definite drawbacks, one still can only speculate why it ranks as the most dismal critical and commercial failure of any picture based on a work by Tennessee Williams. Even most movie buffs have never heard of it, much less seen it, despite the credentials of the original author, script writer, director, photographer, and stars, and the fact that it was made by a major studio. Warner Brothers gave the film only token distribution after the poor critical and box office reception of its premiere engagement in New York in 1970. Because the film had an X-rating from the MPAA Code Administration, it was then relegated to the grind circuit to play porno houses and finally be shelved by the studio, which has never sold it to television.

The basis for the X-rating was primarily the scene in which Chicken seduces a very willing Myrtle, which fades out with her kneeling before him. This suggestion of fellatio is just that, something to be inferred by a perceptive adult viewer and is in no way blatantly stated. The consequent X-rating accorded to the movie seems unduly harsh, therefore. In point of fact the industry rating system was relatively new at the time, having been inaugurated in the fall of 1968; and the Code Commission tended to interpret the MPAA Code rather stringently in those early days of industry classification of motion pictures. A film like *Midnight Cowboy*, made the same year as *Hot-Shots*, had a similar scene implying fellatio (though this time between two males), and was also rated X when first released a few months before *Hot-Shots*. But *Cowboy*'s X was later changed to an R-rating, and it would appear that the same sort of appeal could be made for the reducing of *Hot-Shot*'s X to an R-rating in the light of what now has become customarily acceptable in the R-category. But when a film fails commercially in its opening engagement the way that *The Last of the Mobile Hot-Shots* did, the studio is not really interested in either negotiating on its behalf for a more benign MPAA rating or in editing it with a view to a TV sale.

It seems, then, that the combination of poor notices and an X-rating (which misled many moviegoers in those days into assuming that it was a trashy film) conspired to label *Hot-Shots* as box office poison. *Time* did not help matters by calling the film "not so much a version as a perversion" of Williams's play, though the anonymous reviewer was correct in criticizing the cumbersome plot line of the movie as a strain on the average filmgoer's patience, as I have indicated above. Had the movie makers stuck closer to Williams's original story and not tried to make over Jeb according to James Coburn's conception of the role, the film might have percolated. If they feared that audiences of the day would not accept a transvestite as a main figure in a commercial picture, one has only to point to the Norman Bates character played by Anthony Perkins in Hitchcock's *Psycho* a full decade earlier. Norman donned his mother's clothes and mannerisms in *Psycho* just as Lot did in *The Seven Descents of Myrtle;* and *Psycho* just happens to be one of the most commercially successful films Alfred Hitchcock ever made.

"*The Last of the Mobile Hot-Shots* was fine in rehearsal," Gore Vidal has informed me, "but Sidney Lumet hates and misunderstands humor. The camera was always a mile away during key dialogue scenes. Lynn Redgrave was not understandable, but it was not her fault. 'More terror!' he kept saying." Lynn Redgrave's Southern accent was not comprehensible at times, as Vidal notes; it seemed, as one critic put it, to be a mixture of two Birminghams: Alabama's and England's. And Lumet's insistence that she often speak her lines several decibels above what was called for was a further drawback for the English actress. As far as Lumet's attempts to elicit terror from her, which Vidal also mentions, he apparently wanted to give the impression that there is a real possibility of Chicken abandoning her with her dying husband to the flood waters when the levee finally gives way, and that Myrtle and the audience should both find this a real source of terror. But actually it is obvious from the development of Chicken's personality in the course of the story that he is only toying with Myrtle when he playfully threatens her in this manner; and if she takes him seriously the audience should not.

Lumet's too literal interpretation of this facet of the story lends support to Vidal's contention that comedy is not this director's forte. In an interview which Lumet gave after making *Hot-Shots*, the director confessed that he felt unsure of himself in dealing with comedy, and pointed to a film he made the year before *Hot-Shots* called *Bye, Bye, Braverman*, which had the same serio-comic flavor as *Hot-Shots*, as an instance of how he tends to flounder when working with this kind of material. *Bye, Bye, Braverman*, he said, "went off just enough to spoil it. And it was my fault." The same can be said, to a great degree, of *The Last of the Mobile Hot-Shots* as well.

It is highly ironic that Williams sold *Myrtle* to the movies to get a second chance to prove that the play, which he had dubbed his "funny melodrama," really had a substantial comic dimension to it wound up being directed by a film maker who was unable to highlight satisfactorily those very comic aspects of the script which Williams contended had not been fully exploited in the stage production.

Both of the Lumet films treated in this chapter were severe disappointments to all concerned when one recalls the high hopes which both pictures stimulated because of the first-rate talents involved in each of the two movies. But hope springs eternal in an author's heart, and when the summons comes from movieland to submit one of his works for screen treatment, most writers feel that, in addition to the handsome fee which they will receive for the film rights, there is always the chance that this time around maybe the chemistry of the various creative and technical artists involved will coalesce into producing a motion picture of genuine worth. In the case of *Summer and Smoke*, which we take up next, Williams had the assurance of a sympathetic producer (Hal Wallis, who produced *The Rose Tattoo*); a director (Peter Glenville) and a star (Geraldine Page) who had both done the play on the stage (though not the same production); and two screen writers (Meade Roberts and James Poe), each of whom had worked on an earlier Williams film. Perhaps this time things would turn out differently.

7
Peter Glenville:
Summer and Smoke (The Eccentricities of a
Nightengale)

TENNESSEE WILLIAMS was born in the Episcopal rectory of Columbus, Mississippi, where his grandfather Dakin was the Episcopal priest of the town, with whom Williams's family lived before moving to St. Louis. The Dakin family was descended from Quakers, while the Williamses had sprung from early settlers of Tennessee, as I pointed out in the first chapter. "Roughly there was a combination of Puritan and Cavalier strains in my blood," he explains, "which may be accountable for the conflicting impulses I often represent in the people I write about."

One such character is Alma Tutwiler in his short story, "The Yellow Bird," who was to develop into the Alma Winemiller of his play, *Summer and Smoke*. Both Almas were, like their creator, born in an Episcopal rectory, and their fathers (unlike Williams's grandfather) are narrow-minded Puritanical types who have difficulty sympathizing with or understanding their respective daughters. The short story is a humorous fantasy, but its theme is the same as that of the more serious play, that of the conflicting ancestral strains warring within a young woman's personality. On the Puritan side of Alma Tutwiler's background was Goody Tutwiler, who was condemned during the Salem Witch Trials for utilizing a yellow bird named Bobo as her interlocutor in her commerce with the Devil.

The yellow bird represents the urges of the flesh which Goody had failed to repress according to the Puritanical dictates of her husband, and he himself denounces her at her trial. That was the end of Goody, but it was not the end of

Bobo, since the bird continued to exert its nagging influence on Goody's descendants down through the years up to and including Alma Tutwiler. The once shy Alma defies her father by smoking, peroxiding her hair, and finally moving to New Orleans to become a "good time" girl. There she gives birth to a bastard son who, years later, erects a monument to his mother after her death, on which is carved the image of Bobo, the enduring yellow bird.

In "The Yellow Bird" Williams writes in a tongue-in-cheek fashion about the conflict of flesh and spirit which he takes up with deep seriousness in *Summer and Smoke*, in which Alma Winemiller also winds up going off to a "good time" house as if, like Alma Tutwiler before her, she is seeking to negate the Puritan side of her nature and to reaffirm her kinship with the plumed-hatted cavaliers, who are also to be found on her family tree. That she is their descendant too is symbolized by the plumed hat which she acquires in the course of the play. Williams's point is that the flesh cannot be masochistically repressed by the spirit or it will tenaciously rebel in all sorts of unexpected ways: flesh and spirit must exist in an integrated union as mutually complementary to each other— something which neither of the two Almas ever manages to do in a truly fulfilling way.

After the successful opening of *Glass Menagerie* in 1945, Williams worked on the first draft of the new play under the working title of *A Chart of Anatomy*. As the play began to take shape, he showed it to Margo Jones and discussed the possibility of producing it at her new arena theater in Dallas. But the play, now called *Summer and Smoke*, was far from finished and they deferred mounting a Dallas production for the time being. Williams continued polishing the play during the summer of 1946 at his cottage on Nantucket Island where he was joined by his friend and fellow Southern writer, Carson McCullers. Each morning they would sit at opposite ends of the same table and work on their respective projects, Williams on *Summer and Smoke* and Ms. McCullers on the dramatization of her own novel, *A Member of the Wedding*; and each evening they would read to each other what they had accomplished during the day.

Williams recalls in his autobiography that he found *Smoke* a "tough nut to crack." Although Alma Winemiller seemed to come to life with comparative ease "and may very well be the best female portrait I have drawn in a play," Dr. John Buchanan, the young man with whom she is in love, "never seemed real to me but always a cardboard figure." Nonetheless the dramatist doggedly went on with the composition of the play.

One incident which he devised for the plot had its genesis in a very painful incident in his own past life. Back in the mid-Thirties when Williams was still living at home, he took advantage of his parents' temporary absence from home to give a wild weekend party for his friends. His sister Rose, who was at this time becoming more and more of an inhibited recluse, told her parents all about it when they returned and they handed down the edict that young Tom was not to entertain his friends at home ever again. Since this included every friend he had made in St. Louis, Tom was crushed by his parents' proclamation and he turned on his sister and snarled, "I hate the sight of your ugly face!" Rose was severely shaken by her beloved brother's angry attack; and to this day his action stands out in his own mind as the cruelest thing that he has ever done in his life, "one for which I can never properly atone."

This episode found its way into *Summer and Smoke* in the scene in which Alma, madly jealous of John's frolicking with another girl, Rosa Gonzales, phones his father long distance while the latter is out of town to inform him of the wild party which his son is giving for his mistress in the Buchanan home. Just as Williams did in real life, John Buchanan hurls insults at Alma when he discovers what she has done and then regrets his harsh treatment of her later. It is probably Williams's deep affection for his sister Rose, which endured even as she grew more erratic and eccentric, that keeps his portrait of Alma an essentially sympathetic one; for he never portrays her as merely a self-centered, idiosyncratic spinster but as a lonely and sensitive young woman out of touch with those around her.

Williams submitted the completed play to Margo Jones who scheduled it for presentation in Dallas the following summer, where its success prompted the author to arrange for a New York opening in 1948, after *Streetcar* had been launched in late 1947. It is important to note that, although *Summer and Smoke* was produced on Broadway after *A Street Named Desire*, it had its first professional production between the Broadway openings of *The Glass Menagerie* and *Streetcar*, and that therefore in terms of actual composition and initial production, it stands as a transitional work between *Menagerie* and *Streetcar*. This fact is important because Alma Winemiller marks a transition between Laura Wingfield and Blanche DuBois in that she starts out timidly shy of men like Laura and ends up pursuing them aggressively like Blanche. In fact, Blanche's downhill slide from gentitlity to promiscuity and finally to madness may well represent the route of Alma's subsequent life after the conclusion of *Smoke*, at which point she has already followed Blanche's path to the brink of promiscuity.

In "Yellow Bird" Williams remarks that Alma Tutwiler's mother insisted that "every girl who is driven out of her father's house goes right into a good time house. She was unable to conceive of anything in between." One wonders if Williams is capable of conceiving of anything in between for Alma Winemiller, since the substantial change in Alma's behavior that leads her from one to the other is accomplished in the course of only a few months, and appears to be almost too abrupt to be credible. The playwright successfully closes the credibility gap by having Dr. John Buchanan, who has known her since childhood, suggest that in effect a change has been subconsciously taking place beneath the surface of Alma's frigid façade of respectability for some time. This change, he explains to her, has been instigated by her Doppelganger, a secret self which her public self has so far successfully repressed. One infers that some day Alma's other self will get the upper hand, as it did in Alma Tutwiler, and Alma Winemiller, too, will demonstrate that a woman whose emotional life has been starved by a Puritanical upbringing can be capable of great abandon when her desires, too long suppressed, are released. This is exactly what happens to Alma in *Summer and Smoke*. The Alma Winemiller who waits fretfully for a Gentleman Caller to appear early in the play, goes off to a "good time" house with a travelling salesman after she realizes that there is no longer any hope of her marrying John Buchanan, the man of whom she has been enamored since childhood.

John and Alma's failure ever to unite in marriage after years of tentative gropings toward each other is explained by the basic conflict of their respective outlooks, a conflict which they are never able to resolve. Alma, whose name is the Spanish word for soul, is committed to the spiritual side of human nature, while John Buchanan, as a doctor, is preoccupied with the physical side which Alma disdains, and he in turn equivalently disregards the spirit in his profligate personal life.

Obviously both are right—and wrong. Neither Alma nor John is completely human, for each fails to realize that a human being must meld the two elements of his nature into an integrated whole if he is to have a healthy personality. Throughout the play John and Alma are attracted to each other because each implicitly knows that their contrary outlooks are two sides of the same coin and that they really should unite in order to complement each other rather than continue in conflict. Indeed, each strives so hard to respect and understand the attitude of the other that by play's end they have completely reversed their positions: the once hedonistic John becomes a dedicated humanitarian and the once angelic Alma becomes the town prostitute. "The tables have turned with a vengeance," Alma tells John after he gently refuses her proposal of marriage with the news that he is already engaged.

They have traded points of view, Alma continues, like two people simultaneously exchanging a visit to each other, each one finding the other gone out, with the door locked and no one to answer the bell. "I came here to tell you that being a gentleman doesn't seem so important to me any more," she concludes bitterly; "but you're telling me I've got to remain a lady." Each has come to realize within himself the dimension which he had been reaching out for in the other.

Summer and Smoke, perhaps more than any other play by Tennessee Williams, is composed of a cluster of images which are all orchestrated around the theme of the play, in this case the struggle between body and soul, between flesh and spirit, in a fallen world. The dichotomy between these two facets of human nature is concretized in the two basic sets which are both visible on stage all the time: the rectory associated with Alma (soul) and the doctor's office associated with John (body). Each contestant is given "equal time" in the play to articulate their opposing views of human existence. Alma explains her attitude by comparing the human spirit to a cathedral spire which is always aspiring upward toward the heavenly and the divine as something which transcends human limits. For his "day in court" John delivers a lecture on human anatomy to Alma in which he itemizes man's basic needs as centering on the brain (truth), the stomach (food), and the sexual organs (love), and warns Alma that she has yet to satisfy fully all three.

Dominating the no man's land which lies between the rectory and the doctor's office is a fountain topped by a stone Angel which, like Alma's cathedral image, reminds her of the ultimate transcendence of the eternal and the spiritual over the temporal and the physical. John comes to accept this transcendence but Alma ends by repudiating it.

There are several subsidiary symbols in the play which likewise point up one or other side of the body/soul conflict in which John and Alma are engaged. Shortly after her statement about the Angel quoted above, Alma appears in John's office to declare her total capitulation to his view of life. She is wearing a plumed hat, a reference to the plumed-hatted cavaliers of her ancestry to whom she has now switched her allegiance in preference to that of her Puritan forebears. (The third act of *The Eccentricities of a Nightengale*, Williams's rewrite of this play, is entitled "A Cavalier's Plume.")

The earthy Rosa Gonzales, John's mistress, is presented by Williams as being at the opposite end of the spectrum from Alma, and as such is as incomplete a human being in her way as Alma is in hers. The author tries to portray the happy medium between these two extreme types in Nellie Ewell, the young girl whom John elects to marry. The daughter of a prostitute, she is surely aware of the facts of life; yet she has been protected from following her mother's profession by being educated at a distant finishing school. Both Rosa and Nellie fail to come alive on the stage, however, simply because they exist solely to provide John with alternative types of marriage partners and as such to serve as contrasts to Alma.

It is this realization that makes one suspect that Williams has worked out the soul/body framework of the play's theme a little too neatly, i.e., at the expense of creating uniformly credible characters who exist beyond their function within the symbolic scheme of the play. It is a commonplace of dramaturgy that if a character does not engage the playgoer first as a person, he will never stir the playgoer's interest to discover whatever symbolic value he may possess.

Even though Williams was apparently preoccupied with the allegorical qualities of this play more than with plot and character development, even this symbolic dimension gets a bit fuzzy during the final meeting of John and Alma. He lights a match and both stare at the flame flickering in his cupped hand as he explains none-too-clearly that within Alma he sensed a Puritanical ice that was really a glittering flame which he had mistaken for ice. Prior to this moment,

John has more than once categorized Alma as frigid, and the burden of his halting words may be that beneath Alma's cold exterior there burns a fire that will one day succeed in melting her surface chilliness and burst forth into passionate flame. If such is his prediction it certainly comes true in the final scene as Alma picks up her first travelling salesman at the very foot of the statue of the stone Angel and goes off with him to Moon Lake Casino, the gambling-sporting house previously associated with Rosa Gonzales (and which, by the way, figures in *Streetcar* and other Williams plays).

Some of the minor characters, as I have said, seem to be more relevant to the theme of the play rather than to the plot of the play, while others, such as John's father and Rosa's father, were conceived merely as plot devices. The elder Gonzales drunkenly shoots and kills the elder Buchanan when the latter surprises John presiding over an orgy in the Buchanan home to celebrate his engagement to Rosa, and contemptuously orders all of the guests out of the house. It is this unexpected, not to say contrived, turn of events that abruptly brings John to his senses and causes him to dedicate himself to carrying on his father's work.

But these events, melodramatic as they are, admittedly give a spark of life and theatrical excitement to a play that would otherwise sink into a debate between the advocates of flesh and spirit; and Williams was ill-advised to eliminate this material from his later rewrite of this play as *The Eccentricities of a Nightengale*, as I shall indicate later. Yet, whatever the technical problems of the play, Alma Winemiller emerges as a dynamic three-dimensional human being that one can care about, and Williams is correct in calling her one of his finest female creations. Her last desperate effort to win John by abjectly proposing to him is heartbreaking. She attempts to convince him that the proud girl who had turned him down in the past no longer exists: "She died last summer, suffocated in smoke from something on fire inside."

Such an engaging character as Alma should have captured the hearts of Broadway theater audiences, but she did not—at least not in the original New York production in 1948. There are various reasons extraneous to the play's merits that account for this phenomenon. For one thing, although *Summer and Smoke* is a good play, it is no *Streetcar*, and it was inevitably overshadowed by the sensational success of Williams's masterwork, which was still running when *Summer and Smoke* opened. For another, the New York production was housed in a conventional New York theater for which Margo Jones had to redesign her staging of the Dallas theater-in-the-round production. Somehow Williams's fragile play, perfect for the intimate atmosphere of a small arena theater, seemed dwarfed by the cavernous expanses of an enormous Broadway stage.

During the Detroit tryout of the play Williams attended a reception where he was buttonholed by a passel of socialites with blue-rinse hairdos who had attended a Saturday matinee. Their churlish questions about the theme of the play and why the author insisted on writing about frustrated women like Alma telegraphed to the playwright that his work was getting a less-than-sympathetic airing. He replied as best he could that he saw nothing frustrated about Alma's loving "with such white hot intensity" that it alters the whole direction of her life. "The mysterious thing about writing plays about life is that so many people find them so strange and baffling," he commented on this incident afterwards. "That makes you know, with moments of deep satisfaction, that you have really succeeded in writing about it!"

But *Summer and Smoke* turned out to be too baffling for the taste of the critics and the playgoers of the commercial Broadway theater of the day, and it lasted only one hundred performances in its first New York outing. When the notices came out during the opening night party, Williams scanned them dejectedly and went home to bed. The next day his sadness had turned to anger. After two Broadway successes, he thought that critics and audiences alike had already come to expect too much of him each time he went to the starting post. He wrote to the critic of *The Hollywood Reporter* that he resented the way in which he had been forced into competition with himself "by critics who don't stop to consider the playwright's need for a gradual ripening or development," and asked for "a degree of tolerance and patience in his mentors" while he went through the gradual process of evolving new methods and styles. "It would help enormously if there were professional theater centers outside of New York, so that the playwright would not always be at the mercy of a single localized group."

Williams has often repeated these sentiments, and just recently reiterated that the pressures on a playwright working in the commercial theater are detrimental to his talent. "One must be permitted to have failures if they are brave failures, creative adventures," he said. *Summer and Smoke* could undoubtedly be counted one such creative adventure and the author longed for a second chance to demonstrate the worth of the play.

"I'm afraid Margo did a rather mediocre job," he wrote to a friend while the play was still running; "not inspired, not vital as Kazan would have been and as the play so dreadfully needed. . . . I regret that it was not converted into the exciting theater that the best direction could have made it. I always believed it was a play that could live in production (though utterly dead on paper) and what I have seen bears out that conviction. Although what happened did not give it a fair chance."

Four years later *Summer and Smoke* was accorded the second chance for which Williams had hoped when José Quintero revived the play Off Broadway with Geraldine Page as Alma, and Williams's faith in his work was vindicated when the play became the most renowned revival of the entire season. Interestingly enough, the play triumphed again this time in an arena theater format, just as it had in its initial Dallas production prior to Broadway five years before. The audience was thus drawn into a closer participation in the action and into a deeper understanding of Alma's predicament.

Quintero records in his autobiography that Ms. Page at first was intimidated by the demands of the role, but he persuaded her to take the part that would bring her stardom on stage and screen alike. Not the kind of actress who waits till opening night to give a performance, "she plunges into her role at the very first reading," says Quintero. It is almost as if she wanted to forget herself and "utilize everything she owns to become the character that she is playing."

Geraldine Page stayed with the play for a year; and a decade later, when Paramount was planning the film, she immediately came to mind for the role of Alma, although Audrey Hepburn was also considered. Laurence Harvey was selected to play John Buchanan because he had recently made his mark on the international movie scene in the British film *Room at the Top*. The director, Peter Glenville, had directed the London production of *Summer and Smoke*, and so he, like Geraldine Page, was very familiar with the property which they were about to film. In my recent conversation with Glenville he recalled how he had to rethink the story's presentation for the cinema.

"When a director makes a play into a film," Glenville began, "he should strive to be true to the author's intent if the author is a good playwright; and Tennessee Williams is a magnificent one." Still the director must also be aware that the cinema gives him advantages that he would not have had in the theater. "Film enables one to depict so much more of the action of the narrative that can be shown on the stage. In the play, for example, the audience is told that John Buchanan, who has gone away to carry on his dead father's work at the clinic, is a changed character and has become successful. Then he simply appears on the stage and the audience has to take for granted that such is the case. In the film we show this actually happening, which, of course, is a help to credibility."

The film gives us a scene in which John is shown moving among the beds of a hospital ward during an epidemic, mopping one elderly woman's brow, smiling at another, and receiving looks of gratitude and admiration in return. As Glenville notes, the moviegoer is much better prepared to accept John's reformation as a fact when he returns to town than is the playgoer, who only hears about it in a snatch of expository dialogue.

When he was shooting the film back in 1961, the director pointed out to *New York Times* interviewer Murray Schumach that in preparing *Summer and Smoke* for the movies he had deleted any dialogue that was purely expository in favor of portraying directly on the screen events that must take place offstage in the play: "We can stage a crap game for the camera. We don't have to have someone talking about it afterward. But what we have to do in shooting this crap game is to make the choice of dramatic focus. We cannot rely on the beautiful Williams writing to describe it."

The crap game in a smoke-filled gambling room at Moon Lake Casino is deftly intercut in the film with a meeting of Alma's cultural club in the rectory parlor in order to demonstrate graphically the difference between John's life style and Alma's at this moment in their lives: a shot of John taking a swig of whiskey straight from the bottle is followed by one of Alma daintily pouring lemonade into a glass. Alma, who had invited John to the meeting, nervously fumbles with her watch as the camera cuts back to the clock on the wall behind John which indicates that he is long overdue at the cultural meeting. John gets into a scuffle with another gambler and sustains a knife wound on his arm. Rosa helps him out of the room through the beaded curtain that covers the doorway. There is a slow dissolve from the gaudy curtain to the drab bedroom in which Alma lies atop her bed with a book in her lap, waiting for John to return home. For a moment the two shots overlap on the screen, underscoring once again the difference between the two worlds in which Alma and John move.

It was this bedroom scene which Schumach observed Glenville shooting at Paramount. "The problem here," Glenville explained as technicians were adjusting the lights on the set for a shot, "is that we must, particularly, try to see inside the woman to understand how the apparent clutterings of her provincial culture conflict with her not-so-apparent smothered sensuality. The camera, it is true, has the advantage of being able to capture nuances of expression. . . . In this scene, for instance, where we do not have the benefit of beautiful Williams dialogue, we can hold a shot much longer with the camera than we could in the theater," where the audience depends more on dialogue to grasp the meaning of the action because of their distance from the stage.

In the scene in question Geraldine Page was to convey wordlessly Alma's jealous frustration and pain at John's affair with Rosa Gonzales by walking to her bedroom window when she hears his car arriving next door in order to spy on them. Glenville had the set lit so that Alma would be standing in a shadow to give her a furtive look as she pulls back the curtain to look down—literally and figuratively—on John and Rosa whom she feels are in every sense beneath her.

Though this particular scene happened to be played without dialogue, Glenville added that in general much of Williams's dialogue had been preserved in the script. "Williams does not work from situations and then find words to describe each situation. He works from character. The core of a Williams script is the delineation of characters and beautiful dialogue." This is manifestly true of *Summer and Smoke,* and so the screenplay preserves some of the long but thematically crucial dialogue passages from the play, such as Alma's speech comparing the human spirit to the spire of a Gothic cathedral and John's anatomy lecture to Alma. The film even restored the prologue in which John and Alma meet as children beneath the stone Angel, which Williams trimmed away from the Off Broadway production of the play.

Geraldine Page and Peter Glenville had a disagreement, however, about one line of dialogue that the director cut from the script and which the star wanted reinstated. In the play, when Nellie tells Alma that John believes that his

Laurence Harvey and Rita Moreno in *Summer and Smoke*.

regeneration was due mostly to Alma's angelic inspiration, she pounds the stone Angel with her fist and cynically spits out the words, "This is the only angel in Glorious Hill. Her body is stone and her blood is mineral water!" To Ms. Page this speech marks the turning point in the story because it is the first signal that Alma is finally fed up with her suffocating existence and is going to rebel against her Puritan past. Hence Ms. Page demanded that it be used in the film, though Glenville contended that the bitter expression on Alma's face in close-up rendered the verbal articulation of her seething emotions superfluous.

The director finally agreed to shoot the scene both ways and to choose the take that seemed to work better when the film was edited. Months later, when producer Hal Wallis hosted a private screening of the finished film at his home, Ms. Page was exhilarated to find that Glenville had used the take which she had favored. She impulsively leapt up in the middle of the gathering and shouted to Glenville, "You needed it! I was right!"

Although only a single line of dialogue was at issue, the disagreement over its inclusion in the film brings into relief the fundamental diversity between stage and screen. Consequently, when I recounted this story to Glenville, his comments on it were very detailed and are well worth relaying in their entirety:

"The anecdote that Geraldine Page tells about our discussion over cutting her line by the fountain in the film of *Summer and Smoke* is amusing and true. Certainly less dialogue is needed on the screen to carry the inner meaning of a scene than on the stage because certain subtleties and nuances of look or inflection defy the *optique du théâtre*. The film close-up allows for transmittal of thought on the most intimate basis. As I mentioned in the *Times* interview, in the theater you simply cannot have long passages of time without dialogue since the audience depends much more on dialogue to sustain the tension because they are seeing the play in one continual long shot, as it were. Since the camera brings the audience so much closer to the action in a film, one can allow subtle gestures and facial expressions to carry a scene more than is possible on the stage. That is the general rule, but rules are made to be disproved.

"Geraldine Page is a fine actress (she got an Oscar nomination for *Summer and Smoke*) and she spoke the line in question with such tact and truth that she brought it off beautifully; and I realized that it was helpful to the scene. It was essential, however, to do the shot both with and without the line of dialogue because a poetic line addressed to a statue can work on the stage but might well draw a laugh if the tone of it is not delicately understated on the screen. If for some reason the line hadn't worked in the scene as filmed, it would have been difficult to cut away from the shot, and we would have had to take it out altogether; and hence this crucial moment in the story—which Geraldine Page calls the turning point of the play—would have been lost altogether!

"A Tennessee Williams play is really a piece of chamber music, as it were, with a very lyrical vocabulary; and this must be kept in mind when one is trying to make the play accessible to the mass audience of the cinema." Glenville implemented his goal of making *Summer and Smoke* accessible to the mass movie audience mainly by turning the play's expository dialogue into immediate action on the screen whenever possible, as he said he would in his *Times* interview while shooting the picture.

Hence the film includes scenes in Moon Lake Casino and in the brothel managed by Nellie's mother Sally Ewell, who does not appear at all in the play. Episodes like John's knife fight and his escorting Alma to Moon Lake Casino add varying degrees of color and excitement to the script without straying from the main plot line. In the Moon Lake Casino segment John brings Alma to the pleasure palace to show her another side of life. Rosa's jealousy at Alma's being with John is expressed in a fiery dance which she does to the beat of a throbbing guitar. During her number she dances over to their table and glares at both of them. That Rosa is in her element and Alma decidedly is not becomes still more evident when John makes Alma watch a cock fight which is part of the evening's festivities at the Casino. Alma, painfully obtrusive in her sedate outfit, manages to watch the distasteful spectacle until her immaculate blouse is splattered with a few drops of blood; whereupon she screams and retreats from the scene.

The sequence shot in Sally Ewell's brothel has its source in Nellie's speech in the play about how John Buchanan persuaded her mother to send her away to the more sheltered milieu of a boarding school in order to escape the sordid ambience of a "good time" house. John chats with Nellie in her antiseptically plain room which is decorated very simply with pale wallpaper. Then he goes out into the corridor where he and Sally stand in front of blazing red wallpaper so different from that of Nellie's room as he warns Sally against her daughter's growing up in an unsuitable environment. The visual touch of the contrasting decor of the brothel corridor and of Nellie's room implies that Sally is trying (according to her lights) to create an insulated atmosphere in which her daughter can grow up. But John convinces her that this gesture of concern for Nellie is not enough; and she takes his advice by packing Nellie off to a finishing school, from which she returns a mature young lady.

The movie furthermore utilizes cinematic techniques to exploit the full dramatic intensity of incidents that had to be dramatized somewhat sketchily in the theater in order to involve the movie audience more in the movie's action. The shooting of John's father by Rosa's father is enhanced by carefully executed camerawork: Just before the elder Buchanan arrives on the scene, Rosa's father drunkenly shoots off his revolver at the gilt-edged mirror majestically hanging over the mantlepiece in the Buchanan living room to demonstrate his contempt for upperclass refinement. Outside, an empty whiskey bottle rolls off the front porch and the camera follows it as it bounces down the steps and into the gutter just as Dr. Buchanan's car pulls up to the curb. He goes inside and angrily belabors Rosa's father with his cane. A shot rings out and Dr. Buchanan's image is reflected in the cracked mirror as he slowly sinks to the floor. Glenville has here symbolized visually how John's consorting with Rosa and her gangster father has shattered his own father's hopes that his son would live up to the traditions of the Buchanan family as represented in the now smashed glass of the family heirloom.

A third method by which Glenville has increased the play's accessibility to the moviegoing public is by making more emphatic in the film some of the symbols already embedded in the play. One such symbol is the plumed hat which had been stolen from a millinery shop by Alma's neurotic mother, who is prematurely advanced in her second childhood. As far back as "The Yellow

Geraldine Page, without a plumed hat, and Laurence Harvey before the stone angel in *Summer and Smoke.*

Bird," Williams employed the plumed hat image as a reminder of the French Cavaliers' blood which runs in the veins of Alma's family just as much as the Puritans' blood does. To emphasize that this other branch of the Winemiller family tree is going to assert itself eventually in Alma's behavior as well as to imply that Alma is subconsciouly attracted to the cavalier John Buchanan, Alma's mother says in the film as she waves to John, "Hello, Cavalier!" and then to Alma, "He's dashing. He should carry a sword and rescue young ladies."

Alma secretly hopes that he will rescue her and is abashed when he tells her that she should wear a plumed hat as they sit beneath the stone Angel; for she is forced to admit that her plain wardrobe does not include such a fancy item. Later she irritably tries to possess herself of her mother's plumed hat. As she frantically engages in a tug of war with her mother over the handsome article, she accuses Mrs. Winemiller of having robbed her of her youth by forcing her to be the lady of the house in her mother's stead. It seems as if Alma subconsciously feels that her mother has stolen the youthful looking chapeau not from the hat shop but from her: Alma, after all, is the one who should be wearing fetching clothes to attract a beau instead of dressing like a middle-aged woman so that she can look the part of the hostess of her father's rectory. The scene ends with Alma muttering, "I have behaved badly over a hat with a plume," and the camera pans down to the battered hat with its wilted plume which she holds in her hand.

The plumed hat metaphor is brought to fruition in the scene in which Alma makes her final plea to John that they can forge a compatible marriage. She has finally bought a plumed hat of her own and she is wearing it during this last interview with John; and she is still wearing it when she goes off to Moon Lake Casino with the drummer whom she picked up by the stone Angel in the film's

Geraldine Page and Una Merkle as daughter and mother fighting over a plumed hat in *Summer and Smoke*.

Geraldine Page with a plumed hat, Laurence Harvey in *Summer and Smoke.*

closing moments. Her Cavalier ancestors have finally superceded her Puritan forebears as the chief influence on her character.

Unfortunately, in opting to switch her allegiance from one side of her family. tree to the other (from the ascendency of the spirit in her life to that of the flesh), she has still not succeeded in making herself an integral person. The camera pans from the retreating figures of Alma and her salesman to the symbol of her old life, the stone Angel atop the fountain whose cupped hands are shown to be empty. Alma's past singleminded dedication to the angelic cult of the soul (to the exclusion of the body) has left her empty too; but her present equally singleminded dedication to the cult of the body (to the exclusion of the soul) surely will be just as unfulfilling for her. A balanced personality lies somewhere between these two extreme forms of behavior and therefore Alma will remain an incomplete human being.

The genius of Geraldine Page's performance was that she envisaged Alma as a young woman who had a ration of spunk as well as more than her share of inhibitions; and Glenville very much agreed with this interpretation of the role. As he says, "Alma is not a passive individual. Indeed, she seems to be the young Blanche DuBois fighting for her place in life. And, of course, the indications at the end of the play are that she will develop into the same kind of woman that Blanche became. I sometimes wonder what Alma might have been like had the young doctor married her. Both of them perhaps would have been better for it—but less interesting!"

Williams, too, thought that Ms. Page possessed a witchery by which she was able to suggest that, in spite of Alma's self-conscious mannerisms, high-pitched voice, and diffidence, she was a potentially attractive young woman and wife. The aching feeling that one experiences in viewing her story on stage or screen is rooted in the awareness that she need not have been doomed to either spinsterhood on the one hand or prostitution on the other had she met a man who could have helped her bring her hidden good qualities to the surface before they atrophied. Ms. Page's portrayal was as impeccable in the movie as it had been in the theater, but Laurence Harvey was not satisfactory as John Buchanan.

Part of the blame must be laid at Williams's door for creating a character that he, too, feels is wooden. But Harvey was also at fault in playing John as a trifle too cold and remote, instead of as the more hot-blooded type that he should be in order to provide a sufficiently sharp contrast with Alma's frigidity. As a result Alma and John, instead of appearing as the opposites that they were designed to be, seemed too much alike to generate the kind of dramatic electricity that their conflicting personalities are supposed to ignite in the story; and Harvey's performance is the reason why.

Geraldine Page has since said that she always regretted that the film script was not based on the slightly revised version of the play which Williams prepared for the Circle-in-the-Square production in which he dropped the prologue and added a scene between Alma and old Dr. Buchanan which she maintains wove the exposition more integrally into the main body of the play. These revisions appear in the acting edition published for non-professionals, and after looking them over I must disagree with Ms. Page. I have always found the prologue, which is used as a pre-credit sequence in the film, to be haunting and touching, because it establishes that Alma's awkwardly expressed affection for John dates back to their childhood, and that he was as able to hurt the vulnerable young girl in the past when she tried to manifest her feelings for him just as much as he is able to hurt the young woman that Alma has become in the present when she makes her poignant attempts to articulate her emotional attachment for him; an attachment which has grown from childish puppy love into a pitifully thwarted adult passon.

As for the additional scene between the senior Dr. Buchanan and Alma that Ms. Page finds so effective, it really boils down to a shifting around of material that Williams had already incorporated elsewhere in the play more effectively. Thus Williams gives to the elder Buchanan in the revised text some lines that young John delivers to Alma in both the Broadway version of the play and in the film, expressing his concern for her lonesomeness. To me it is more moving to have John, Jr., speak these lines because it suggests the possibility of a more tender side to John's personality that gives some grounds for hope that he may yet respond to Alma with a degree of love somewhat akin to that which she has cherished for him since childhood, and thereby keeps the viewer from seeing their ultimate separation as a foregone conclusion.

Nonetheless I asked Peter Glenville if at any time he had considered using the revised text of *Summer and Smoke* when he was preparing the film and he responded, "Tennessee Williams often revises his work, not only while a play is in production but afterwards when it is published in an acting edition. But the play as originally presented professionally on the stage is the version that one must consider as the definitive one, and not the subsequent rewrites, which may or may not be improvements on the original. This is especially true when one is comparing the play to the film version of it. The play as originally mounted is what the film studio contracts for filming, and that is the source of the screenplay."

Besides the minor revisions that Williams made in *Summer and Smoke*, he also composed a substantially different version of the play entitled *The Eccentricities of a Nightengale* which departs as much from the basic text of *Summer and Smoke* as *Orpheus Descending* differs from *Battle of Angels*. Since this alternate version of *Summer and Smoke* has recently received a professional New York production and also has been seen on national television, it deserves consideration here.

Williams's reasons for recasting *Battle of Angels* as *Orpheus Descending* were sound because the earlier version represented the maiden voyage of an inexperienced playwright in the professional theater. But his motive for rewriting *Smoke* is frankly not as compelling since the latter play is the work of a mature dramatist. Williams says that he was dissatisfied with *Summer and Smoke* because he had introduced into the plot some scenes of conventional melodrama which obscure the more essential story of Alma's fight to find her place in life.

When a London production of the play was arranged for the fall of 1951, therefore, he decided to spend his summer in Rome working against time to rewrite the play in time for the London production. "I arrived in London with what I considered, quite correctly I think, was practically a new work excavated from the moldering debris of its predecessor," he recalls. He was met at the airport by Maria Britneva (later Lady St. Just), a young actress and close friend of his who was participating in the production. He announced that he had brought with him "a work purified of all but its humor, poetry, and passion," but she deflated his euphoria by telling him that the London company was already deep into rehearsals. She offered to save the rewrite for him until some later, more appropriate occasion arose when the alternate version of *Summer and Smoke* could be unveiled. Peter Glenville, who directed the London production of *Smoke*, says that the playwright never mentioned the possibility of another version of the play to him, but that he would have seriously considered it if rehearsals of *Summer and Smoke* had not already commenced.

Some ten years or more later, Maria Britneva returned the play to Williams and he read through it the same evening. He was still convinced that it was a better work than the one from which it was derived, and arranged to have it produced at a summer theater in Nyack, New York, in June, 1964, so that he could take a look at it. He then published the text of *The Eccentricities of a Nightengale* that same year hoping that publication would lead to a Broadway production.

It was not until the Buffalo Studio Arena Theater production of the play was transferred to Broadway in November of 1976, however, that Williams's wish for a New York production of *Nightengale* came true. In a *New York Times* article prior to the New York opening, Williams explained that he was convinced that he had purified *Nightengale* of all of the distracting, extraneous, and incredible elements which had cluttered the plot of *Smoke*. He accomplished his radical surgery by excising inessential characters and plot devices until he came up, he said, with a play that has fewer characters and a more straightforward story line. "Away went the shooting of the elder Dr. John by Papa Gonzales, and the abrupt revolution of the young Dr. John's character as an act of redemption for his involvement in the aforementioned melodramatic events." In point of fact, no trace of either Rosa, her father, or of Nellie Ewell remains in *Nightengale*. What, then, is left?

The Eccentricities of a Nightengale is a play in three acts which bear the individual titles of "The Feeling of a Singer," "The Tenderness of a Mother," and "A Cavalier's Plume." The second act title signals the fact that, although John's father does not appear in the play, his mother does; and she is the garden variety Williams matriarch that has become familiar in his work: a domineering woman cast in the same mold as the archetypical Amanda Wingfield. For this reason, and because he has in general softened the tone of the play, it almost seems as if the author was trying to convert *Summer and Smoke* into another *Glass Menagerie*, with Alma as the shy heroine and John doubling as her Gentleman Caller and the mother-dominated hero. It would have been better for him to start from scratch and write another play rather than to try to make over *Summer and Smoke*, since he succeeded only in making *Nightengale* a pallid imitation of both *Smoke* and of *Menagerie*.

Doubtlessly *Nightengale* has its felicitous moments—what Williams play does not?—and some of them merit honorable mention. In partial compensation for all of the material which Williams cut away from the reworked play, he has added a notorious event from the family's past to which Alma and her parents often refer. It is the recollection of this event that prompts Alma, after her loss of John, to renounce her Puritanical existence in favor of a dissolute life. This episode from her family's past history centers on Alma's Aunt Albertine, a minister's daughter who deserted the rectory to elope with a bigamist, Mr. Schwarzkopf, the proprietor of a "mechanical museum," an exhibition of elaborately constructed life-size mechanical dolls. Among them was a mechanical bird-girl, from whose mouth a tin nightengale periodically flew out and whistled three times. The bird-girl could also smile, nod, and lift her arms as if to embrace a lover. Mr. Schwarzkopf became so enchanted with his own creation that when his museum went bankrupt, he madly burned it to the ground rather than allow his bird-girl to be auctioned off by his creditors the following day with the other mechanical gimmicks which he had made.

Aunt Albertine rushed into the fire to save her obsessed paramour from dying with his bird-girl, but when she was dragged from the flames she was clutching nothing more than a button torn from his coat sleeve. "Some people," she whispered, "don't even die empty-handed!" She may not have saved her lover's life or her own, but she at least died with a memento of the man she loved in her hand. (In *Summer and Smoke* Alma speaks to John of her fear of dying "empty-handed," and resolves to make sure that in death her hand will hold some token which proves that her life was not totally void of love; and the message of the Aunt Albertine anecdote comes to the same thing.)

With Aunt Albertine as her inspiration, Alma coaxes John in *Nightengale* to take her to a "good time" house where they can spend one hour together which she will be able to cherish ever after as dearly as Albertine cherished the souvenir of her lover. To their place of assignation Alma wears a hat with a cavalier's plume, which is as important symbolically here as it was in *Smoke*. John fails to start a fire in their chilly room and Alma impulsively tears the plume from her hat and throws it in the fireplace to ignite the damp logs, almost as if she were imploring her French ancestors to enkindle the flames of ardor between John and her. Just when they have almost despaired of getting the fire started, the flickering embers miraculously burst into flame—a visual equivalent of the heat of the moment now being shared by John and Alma.

In *Summer and Smoke* the couple never consummate their abortive love relationship as they do in *Nightengale*, but Alma's destiny in the latter play is exactly the same as in the earlier play. As she picks up a stranger in the epilogue of *Nightengale*, she is apparently trying to relive yet again the single hour which she once spent with John. The upshot of both plays is the same, consequently, with Alma losing John for good, whether her rival is Nellie in *Smoke* or John's mother in *Nightengale*. Why, then, does Williams's predilection for the rewrite go so far as to allow him quite unfairly to denigrate *Summer and Smoke* as the "moldering debris" from which he salvaged *The Eccentricities of a Nightengale?*

My guess is that in *Nightengale* he articulated more explicitly than in *Smoke* or in any other play he has ever written his compassion for the misfits of this world. After John visits her literary club one evening, Alma taunts him for his condescension to the group in words that make her the champion of all of the misfits in the world of Tennessee Williams: "Oh, you put us in our place tonight, my little collection of eccentrics! . . . I suppose you're right to despise us, my little company of the faded and frightened and different and odd and lonely. You don't belong to that club but I hold an office in it!" Later she adds, "Well, I may be eccentric but not so eccentric that I don't have the ordinary human need for love. I have that need, and I must satisfy it, in whatever way my good or bad fortune will make possible for me."

As Catharine Hughes writes in the preface of this book, referring to the lines just quoted above, Williams offers us his outsiders, not as victims of their private illusions, but as victims of that world in which normality, triumphant, leaves no room for people who in any way depart from the established norm. And though Williams does not cover over their eccentricities, he endows his pathetic little people with tragic dignity. "I write so often of people with no magnitude, at least on the surface," he has said. "But are there 'little people'? I sometimes think there are only little conceptions of people," since whatever is living and feeling with intensity, when examined sympathetically and in depth, is not little at all. "And what about Miss Alma? Was she a 'little person'? Certainly not. Her passion gave stature to the drama."

Williams has without a doubt articulated his compassion for the outsiders of this world more explicitly in *Nightengale* than perhaps anywhere else, but he has done so at the price of systematically stripping away from the parent work characters and episodes that contributed to the fabric of the play as a whole. Clive Barnes, in reviewing the 1976 *Nightengale* production in New York, is virtually alone in choosing this simplified version of *Smoke* as superior to the earlier work:

"The new work effectively knocks *Summer and Smoke* off the map, except as a literary curiosity. . . . The new play is a straightforward conflict of two people—one hot and one cold—a woman at base nervously confident and a man at base confidently nervous." Barnes went on to say that the resolution of their conflict is far neater and more satisfying in this version than in the previous one. "It is as if a rather suaver Gentleman Caller from *The Glass Menagerie* had met a rather younger Blanche DuBois before she finally became Blanche DuBois."

But what Barnes characterized as a compassionate play filled with the simple poetry of the heart, the majority of theater critics viewed as a diluted oversimplification of *Summer and Smoke*. Walter Kerr, also writing in *The New York Times*, thought that Williams had "disembowelled a fine play and stuffed the cavities with sawdust." Whereas the original Alma tried to suppress and sublimate her sexual drives in her struggle toward fulfilling her rigorous spiritual aspirations, the other Alma is less a vulnerable battleground of conflicting desires than an aggressive flirt with extravagant mannerisms bent on seducing John Buchanan, a passive mama's boy. Because John in *Nightengale* is totally dominated by his mother and therefore makes it plain from the outset that he does not intend to fall in love with Alma, there is no contest between them. By removing Alma's conflicting urges and emasculating John, Williams has unwittingly undramatized *Summer and Smoke* and erased the tensions which keep that play alive. "Small wonder," Kerr concludes, "that *Nightengale*, even with something of the original lyricism retained, goes flat. But it really doesn't matter. We still have *Summer and Smoke*."

Indeed we do, and for my money it is *Nightengale* and not *Smoke* that is the literary curiosity of the pair, since the original play boasts a more touching heroine and a more aggressive hero, and in sum has a texture that is richer in both character and incident. The New York production of *Nightengale* closed in less than a month, having failed to supercede *Smoke* in the affections of most reviewers and theatergoers. A much greater audience saw it, however, when it was telecast on the Public Broadcasting System the June before the New York production of the play.

The TV version is really a transcription of the play as produced by the San Diego Globe Theater company with the kind of fluid and unobtrusive camerawork which has marked most of the television productions of Williams's plays. The opening shot of the first scene parallels the opening shot of the last scene: the first shows Alma, the eccentric nightengale of Glorious Hill, singing at a park band concert, while the corresponding shot shows a different girl in her place on the bandstand because Alma by this time has taken to picking up drummers near the stone Angel where she customarily stations herself.

Director Glenn Jordan also parallels the last shot of the second act with the last shot of the third act in the same contrasting fashion. Both acts end with a freeze frame of Alma: the second act ends with Alma smiling ecstatically in the expectation of her date with John; and the third act ends with Alma smiling wryly and wearily in anticipation of an hour with another in the endless series of anonymous strangers who have replaced John in her life.

But Alma does not elicit our sympathy at the conclusion of *Nightengale* in the way that she does in the other play, even though the final scenes of both are so similar. The radical difference is that in *Smoke* Alma is taking her first pathetic, tentative step toward soliciting a man, while in the corresponding scene in *Nightengale* she is already practiced in her trade, even hardened to it. We recognize so little of the former Alma in this transmogrified Alma that even the two parallel freeze frames which are meant to remind us, like two snapshots of the same person taken over a long period of time, that she is in fact the same person, are not enough to make the audience respond to observing the deterioration that has taken place in her in the intervening months. The calloused creature who has replaced her more vulnerable and sensitive counterpart is too remote from the earlier self to make us care very much about her any longer.

The flaws in the teleplay, then, lie in the original script of *Nightengale* and not in the production, which is well directed and photographed. Jordan points up visually the way that the characters are locked in their little cells of isolation by frequently photographing them looking through their windows at the seemingly inaccessible world that lies beyond their reach. Thus Alma's mother, just as batty here as she was in *Smoke*, peeks out at passers-by, and Alma spies on John next door. In one shot the camera moves from John being tucked in bed by his super-solicitous mother to his bedroom window, through the drawn curtains of which one can make out Alma looking wistfully out her window, across the bridgeless gap that separates them, toward John's window until his mother turns out his light.

The teleplay wisely begins each act with its title as given by Williams in the script, since this sets the tone for each segment. For example, the second act, in which Williams portrays how Alma's mother and John's mother both in their own way manipulate the lives of their respective offspring, is prefaced with the ironic heading, "The Tenderness of a Mother."

John Leonard, TV critic of *The New York Times*, sang the praises of the TV *Nightengale* in his column, stating that the sensitive acting of the principals (Blythe Danner as Alma, Frank Langella as John) compensated nicely for the admitted shortcomings of the rewrite. He singled out John and Alma's sole assignation as a scene which demonstrated simultaneously both the virtues and the flaws of the play. That one hour which these two timid souls spend together on a chilly New Year's Eve is so touching that "if you aren't moved, you need a bulldozer and other professional help. . . . It's a superb scene, and one which Mr. Williams almost wrecks by obliging the fire in the hearth to burst into flame at the perfect moment. Too much and too cute, as James M. Cain used to grumble. Such touches, fingerprints of an excessive theatrical squeeze, are all over various parts of *Nightengale*. Thanks be, the whole survives."

The whole does survive; but only, as I have said, as a curious offshoot of the more intricately plotted and better composed play by which it was spawned. Tennessee Williams has often acted as play doctor for the ailments which he diagnoses in his plays after their premieres; but I have rarely found his revisions to be an improvement on the work as originally produced, whether the "scene transplants" and "dialogue transfusions" are minor, as they were in the version of *Summer and Smoke* produced Off Broadway, or major, as they were in the metamorphosis of *Summer and Smoke* into *The Eccentricities of a Nightengale*. (Williams's admitted improvements in the third act of *Cat on a Hot Tin Roof* at the behest of Elia Kazan were made while the play was still in its pre-production, unpolished form.)

No play is perfect, even when it issues from the pen of our finest American playwright during the peak period of his career as *Smoke* did; but subsequent tinkering can further bruise rather than heal the work in question. The original text of *Summer and Smoke*, warts and all, is still the best version that Williams ever wrote; and to the extent that Glenville's film was faithful to that definitive version of the play, it was and is a fairly good movie (even though it lacked the superstar draw to make it a big box office hit).

But it just may be that the media are not yet finished with Alma—at least with Alma Tutwiler if not Alma Winemiller. Williams has for a long time been contemplating a film of "The Yellow Bird," the embryo from which *Summer and Smoke* came to birth. He said in his autobiography and repeated when I talked with him in Cannes that he has encouraged Faye Dunaway's long-term interest in the project. Whenever they have discussed the possibility of the movie, she has played for him his own Caedmon recording of the story to reconfirm her belief in its viability as a screen venture.

Since "Yellow Bird" has a strong ingredient of fantasy, it will mark a departure from the more naturalistic kind of motion pictures usually associated with Williams's work. But two other films already have been made from his work which represent a departure of one kind or another from the usual Williams movie. Those two films are *The Roman Spring of Mrs. Stone* and *Period of Adjustment*.

Because Williams is a major dramatist and only a minor fiction writer, his fiction has never been taken as seriously as his plays, and only one of his works of fiction so far has served as the source of a movie, *The Roman Spring of Mrs. Stone*. Similarly, Williams has usually stayed within the realm of serious drama, though all of his plays have strong comic elements. He has written only one domestic comedy, *Period of Adjustment*, in which he reversed his customary recipe and created a comedy with serious undertones rather than the opposite. Let us take up these two movies, beginning with *The Roman Spring of Mrs. Stone*, which has the added distinction of being singled out by Williams as the best film ever made from his work.

José Quintero: *The Roman Spring of Mrs. Stone*
George Roy Hill: *Period of Adjustment*

IN HIS PREFACE to *Small Craft Warnings* in the fifth volume of *The Theater of Tennessee Williams,* Williams explains why an author must draw on his own life experience as a source of his creative writing. If his writing is to be genuine, and not appear manufactured and synthetic, it must express those things most involved in his own experience, Williams writes. But he must integrate his personal experience into his writing by refining and evaluating it in a way that gives it wider implications which transcend his own private life. In this way his audience can identify with the author's personal experiences, "can somehow manage to feel in themselves: 'This is true.' In all human experience there are parallels which permit common understanding in the telling and hearing, and it is the frightening responsibility of an artist to make what is directly or allusively close to his own being communicable and understandable, however disturbingly, to the hearts and minds of all whom he addresses."

I have had occasion to note several such parallels between episodes in Williams's personal life and dramatic situations in his work, starting with the way he used his family life in St. Louis as the substratum of *The Glass Menagerie*. In the present instance, Williams's novella, *The Roman Spring of Mrs. Stone,* grew out of his trip to Italy in January of 1948, just after the opening of *A Streetcar Named Desire*; and it is fascinating to see how he transmuted his essentially pleasant personal experience into the tragic story of Karen Stone. Mrs. Stone fled to Europe to escape facing up to failure in the New York theater, but Williams found his way there to escape the oppressive burden of overwhelming success.

Williams had gotten as far as Paris when he was stricken with an illness which he afterwards came to recognize as psychosomatic, but he did not know that at the time. Within ten days he moved from his Paris hotel to an American hospital where a very business-like young doctor casually informed his hapless patient that he was "threatened with hepatitis and mononucleosis." Williams had never heard of either of these formidably named diseases, and he recorded in his diary his morbid judgment that "the jig is up: they have some fancy names for it."

But the jig was not up. "I was simply suffering from an exaggerated form of that terrific shock of success that a young writer (I was thirty-six) is bound to experience when the privacy and natural joyfulness of his old way of working and living is interrupted like a forward pass in football," and he finds himself not being thought of any longer as a serious writer but as the latest sensation of the entertainment world; and nothing turns staler than the latest sensation after the superficial excitement about his new work has worn off. Williams had made friends with Mme. Lazareff, editor of the French journal *Elle,* who told him that he was overreacting to his illness and summarily checked him out of the hospital and put him on a train for the South. When Williams arrived in Rome, he rented a two room apartment just off the Via Veneto and immediately became entranced with the genial personality of the Italian people. His comments on the Italian temperament which I cited in connection with *The Rose Tattoo* are worth recalling here: "The Italians I began to meet showed a different side of human nature than any I had ever known. I think Italians are like Southerners without their inhibitions. They're poetic, but they don't have any Protestant repressions. Or if they do have any, their vitality is so strong, it crashes through them. They live from the heat."

All along the Via Veneto a lonely foreigner could find the sort of chance acquaintances who more than anyone else "live from the heat" and who are most willing to share their warm-blooded companionship for a price. On his second night in Rome, Williams encountered a young man whom he calls "Rafaello" in his *Memoirs,* and who was to serve as the model for not one but two young Italians in Williams's novella, *The Roman Spring of Mrs. Stone.* Mrs. Stone in the story is pursued by a shabbily dressed youth who seems satisfied to stare at her longingly from a distance. That is Rafaello as Williams first met him, dressed in a delapidated overcoat with his shoes tied to his feet with string. Once Williams took him in and outfitted him in new clothes, he suggested to the author a second character for the novella, the darkly handsome Paolo.

One morning Williams gave an interview to a lady journalist while Rafaello lounged in the background. When the newsstory appeared in her paper, it was entitled, "The Roman Spring of Tennessee Williams," and made reference to the young *giovane* who was sharing the writer's rooms. Williams duly changed the working title of his novella from *Moon of Pause* to *The Roman Spring of Mrs. Stone.* In *More Memoirs of an Aesthete* British writer Harold Acton gives an account of a party at Williams's new Roman apartment at which he met Rafaello (whom he calls "Pierino" in his book). Acton knew Italian and could engage Rafaello in conversation. He found that the young man felt neglected because neither Williams nor his American friends as yet could speak the language. But, according to Acton, Rafaello stayed on with Williams because he was eager to go to America; he was a calculating opportunist interested in using the rich contacts which he could make while circulating in the *dolce vita* world of Rome to further his future prospects, and Williams brings this side of the young man very much into relief in the character of Paolo in *Roman Spring*.

While composing the novella, Williams kept in mind the hope which he had long nurtured that he could one day write a screenplay that would entice Greta Garbo back to the screen. She had politely turned down a script called *The Pink Bedroom* which he had submitted to her just before he had left for Europe, so he wrote the novella "to organize material for a film for Great Garbo," he says in his autobiography. "It started out with that intention but she obviously wasn't interested."

That Williams wrote the novella with a view to eventually filming it comes across to the alert reader of the story, which amounts to a succession of dramatic scenes imagined by the novelist in a highly visual style. As often happens in his fiction, Williams gives free reign to his poetic penchant for extended metaphors. One such metaphor is implicitly contained in the title and is developed throughout the story. That is the ironic contrast between the warm, sunny Roman springtime which suggests rebirth and juvenation, and Mrs. Stone's gradual decay into the chilly, bleak autumn of middle age.

Karen Stone had had a successful career as an actress until she refused to allow the onset of middle age to dictate her abandoning roles meant for younger actresses. Her final fiasco was her appearance as Juliet at an age when even heavy makeup and muted stage lights could not create the illusion that Karen Stone was the teenage Juliet. Added to this theatrical debacle was the death of her adoring husband and the onslaught of menopause (to which the novella's earlier working title, *Moon of Pause*, referred), all of which contributed to her flight to Rome. But instead of embarking on a new life in new surroundings, Karen finds herself leading a posthumous existence among ruins of the past which only remind her of the ruins of her own past. Karen has become a mere relic of the toast of Broadway that she had once been; for her the Roman sun is not a warm, revivifying glow but a cold glare that exposes her to the natives for the lonely, rich, middle-aged widow that she really is.

Another extended metaphor which Williams weaves into the texture of the whole story is that of Karen's symbolic kinship with a predatory bird. From her childhood days at a boarding school when she finished first in every competition, Karen has functioned like a rapacious bird which spies out its prey and captures it with sharp talons. She had married a passive husband whom she could easily dominate and had obliterated every youthful leading man who threatened to overshadow her performance by upstaging him during the play and even seducing him in his dressing room between acts if that, too, was necessary to bring him under her sway.

With the onset of middle age this savage side of Karen's nature has become more pronounced. Examining her face in a mirror, she is obliged to confess that she has not weathered the critical period in her life just past as successfully as she had hoped. "Her body had flown like a powerful bird through and above the entangling branches of the past few years, but her face now exhibited the record of the flight."

It is poetic justice that age and retirement have at last rendered the heartless Mrs. Stone vulnerable to other, younger birds of prey. There are the two young men in the novella who have designs on her. The first is Paolo, a handsome young adventurer with even fewer scruples about using others than Karen ever possessed. She carries on an affair with Paolo until he grows tired of her and places his talents at the disposal of a younger and still successful actress who is between husbands, and who may be able to further his aspirations to go to Hollywood more effectively than Karen. The other is the shabby and dissolute young man who stalks Karen wherever she goes, appealing directly to her basest sexual instincts by stealthily exposing himself to her in the street more than once. When Paolo finally discards Karen, she succumbs to the sordid blandishments of this lewd lad whom Williams employs in the story as the index of Karen's decisive capitulation to total depravity.

Karen had sought to recapture her youth by coming to Rome in the springtime and cultivating youthful male companionship, just as she had previously attempted to stay young by playing roles for which she was really too old and by dominating her young co-stars. But her experiences in Rome have only made her more aware than ever that her youth is irretrievably lost to her; and she is now willing to accept the crude, potentially cruel kind of sexual partner who might just as easily murder her in her bed as make love to her—a fate which Paolo had warned her has befallen many a rich widow whose desperate search for excitement had ended exactly that way.

There is little question that by the end of the novella Karen Stone deserves whatever the fate that overtakes her. But Williams, as always, is able to extract some modicum of sympathy from the reader for Karen as he watches her fall victim to the same kind of traps which she was accustomed to set for others. One cannot totally withhold compassion from a woman who wakes up in middle age and is forced to realize that she has prostituted herself both as an actress and a wife all of her life. She had selfishly entered her barren union with Tom Stone because he was rich and also would not insist on having a family to interfere with her professional life. That constituted a kind of marital prostitution. She had ruthlessly pursued her career as an actress (even though her second-rate talent was compounded mostly of surface beauty and carefully concealed craftsmanship) because she was spurred on by a competitive ambition that dated back to her childhood. And that constituted a kind of artistic prostitution.

Without a doting husband to protect her any longer from facing these brutal revelations, Karen's carefully cultivated complacency is destroyed and her grand façade, like that of the old Roman monuments that surround her, crumbles into ruins. She then begins her desolate drift toward the ignominious degradation which she is in the process of accelerating when the book comes to a close. Never one to do things by halves, Karen will now masochistically pursue corruption and depravity with the same sort of relentless tenacity with which she once pursued fame.

Williams's novella is a harrowing parable of decadence and despair, and an excruciatingly moral one at that. Since he visits severe retribution on his anti-heroine for her cunningly self-centered life, Williams was surprised to find critics calling his book a shocking tale with almost no redeeming thematic value. In an essay on current American fiction written after Williams's "degenerate and vicious" little novel was published in 1950, Gore Vidal defended the novelist by pointing to the welter of war novels then in vogue in the wake of World War II and stated that these works really deserved the epithets with which Williams's novella was being excoriated. Reviewers used to the sadistic violence of an ill-written war novel were not prepared to appreciate Williams's delicate, elegiac work and therefore denounced it bitterly as decadent. "And why?" Vidal asked. "Because Williams had, with some sympathy, described an aging actress who turns to sexuality in order to stop the aimless 'drift of her days,' a situation which is hardly unique."

Still one must concede that fiction has never been Williams's strong suit, and his forays into that artistic form have never equalled his accomplishments in the drama. Most of his short stories are little more than dress rehearsals for the subsequent plays which he has mined from them such as *The Glass Menagerie* and *Cat on a Hot Tin Roof*. Taking *Roman Spring* as typical of Williams's fiction, one can say that Williams is more at home with the spoken word than the written word, and in fact he relies heavily on dialogue in his fiction. This novella is weak in structure, with flashbacks to scenes of Karen's marriage or stage performances inserted rather awkwardly and unexpectedly. At one point the author abruptly cuts from Karen moping in her sumptuous Roman apartment to the opening night of her ill-fated appearance as Juliet and back again, before the reader can get his bearings.

Nancy Tischler put it best in her book on Williams when she wrote that "the more stringent requirements of drama subject him to a control that failed him in the looser fictional form. Nor does the characterization have the power of which Williams showed himself capable in his plays." Although Karen Stone comes alive on the printed page, some of the other principal characters do not. One has a difficult time visualizing Paolo as more than a one-dimensional stud, rather than as a fully drawn young man on the make with drives and ambitions of his own.

I suspect that Williams cast Karen Stone's story in fictional rather than dramatic form because he was preoccupied with ultimately turning the story into a film script for Greta Garbo and, as I pointed out in the introductory chapter of this book, the motion picture medium has more in common with fiction than with drama. With this in mind, reading the novella strikes one as being very much like reading the preparatory treatment for a film script, the very sort of thing which would be submitted to a producer with a view to getting a commitment from him for a screenplay.

Ten years later movie producer Louis De Rochement read the novella with just this idea in mind, but he wondered if Williams's story, with its assortment of aging homosexuals, aristocratic procuresses and other decadent types was too hot to handle for the cinema of the Sixties. He was struck by the unmistakably cinematic quality of the story with its series of vividly dramatized short scenes, however, and decided to go ahead with producing the picture.

Though the hope that Garbo would play the lead in his proposed film had spurred Williams to write *Roman Spring* in the first place, it seems a little naïve that the author should have seriously entertained the possibility that a film actress whose career and beauty were in decline would ever have consented to play a stage actress whose career and beauty were equally in decline. (It is true that former silent film star Gloria Swanson did consent to make her film comeback playing a hasbeen movie queen in *Sunset Boulevard* in 1950; but Ms. Swanson was not dedicated to becoming a legend in her own time as Ms. Garbo was.)

In any event, the role of Karen Stone is a meaty one and, with or without Garbo, De Rochement engaged novelist Gavin Lambert to do the screenplay, stage director José Quintero (at Williams's suggestion) to direct the film, and the late Vivien Leigh to take the title role. It has often been said that novellas are the ideal fictional form to be adapted to the screen; novels must be condensed and short stories must be expanded, but a novella usually provides just the right amount of material for a screenplay and this is unquestionably true of *Roman Spring*. Hence just about every incident in the novella has found its way into the film along with most of the dialogue from the book. Consequently *The Roman Spring of Mrs. Stone* is undoubtedly the most faithful transcription of any Williams work to the screen and it is little wonder that the author holds it in such high repute.

Since Williams handled the flashbacks rather clumsily in the book by sprinkling them throughout the story, the film makers decided instead to place the incidents of Karen's past which were needed for plot exposition in chronological order near the beginning of the film. Karen is shown playing Shakespeare and later flying to Rome with her husband after she has retired from the theater when he dies of a heart attack en route. Then the movie settles down to examining Karen's plight as a rich and lonely widow in Rome.

The movie actually begins with a short prologue in which a narrator sketches Karen's background, personality, and outlook. As the camera surveys the modern city of Rome, using exposition taken directly from the novella, the narrator explains that Karen had come to Rome because the city had so many ties with the past and therefore seems the perfect place to take up her posthumous existence as a former actress and former wife. When the Spanish Steps come into view, the narrator introduces them as a favorite place for assignations for more than two centuries. As he says this a middle aged male tourist approaches a younger man and points to his watch to fix a time for a rendezvous and a dowager passes by with a gigolo in tow.

Karen looks down upon this scene from her balcony like some remote, inaccessible goddess gaining fresh evidence to prove "what fools these mortals be." But as she drifts dejectedly through her luxurious apartment one infers that she has a suppressed longing to descend from her pedestal and mix with the low life beneath her. As the camera picks up the handsome young tramp staring fixedly up at her, the narrator closes with this comment: "She wondered why she noticed him at all. But self-knowledge was something that this proud and arrogant woman had always been able to avoid. . . ."

This is the only genuinely unsympathetic remark about Karen that is made in the whole picture. Throughout the book the authorial voice of the narrator expresses disapproval of the calloused, self-aggrandizing behavior which had undeservedly brought Karen to the top of the acting profession, notably with the reoccurring comparison of Karen to a vulture or some other kind of predatory bird. But the film, while filling in the moviegoer about Karen's unexpected loss of her husband and the dismal failure of her last play, does not develop the savage side of her character. As a result the viewer is more sympathetic to Karen's being manipulated and victimized by Paolo (Warren Beatty) than was the reader of the novella. Paolo is goaded on by the Contessa (the late Lotte Lenya), the procuress who is his employer, to take maximum advantage of Karen; and we do pity her as we watch Paolo work his wiles on her.

The only time in the picture that Karen is described with the fowl imagery which the narrator of the novella uses is late in the movie when Karen overhears the vile Contessa ridiculing her as a chicken hawk, "an American species which preys exclusively on tender young chickens." Granted the abject level to which Karen has sunk in her efforts to hold on to Paolo, the Contessa's statement seems gratuitously cruel to this pathetic woman who has sacrificed the last shred of her dignity to salvage a doomed love affair with a young man many years her junior.

Paolo is much more fully realized as a character in the movie than he was in the novella, and this at first sight seems inexplicable since his part is brought over virtually intact from the book. Perhaps what accounts for the greater depth of his personality in the film is Quintero's tantalizing the audience with the hint that Paolo is capable of a feeling of genuine affection for Karen and that he is gradually falling in love with her, perhaps in spite of himself. He has Beatty deliver his protestations to Karen that his feelings for her run deeper than for any of her predecessors with more conviction than one senses in the book. The audience thus becomes involved with seeing whether or not this May-December relationship may yet blossom into something like true love—until Paolo grows more and more childish in his churlish periods of sulking, and Karen herself becomes more immature in her frantic efforts to pamper his whims and mollify his tantrums.

All through the movie Karen's anonymous "admirer" materializes at various junctures, presaging the day when she will have deteriorated to a depth low enough to take this wretched tramp willingly as her lover. Quintero more than once foreshadows this not-too-distant eventuality by juxtaposing a shot of Karen with Paolo with a shot of the young tramp intruding into the scene. At a cocktail party in Karen's flat Karen's old chum Meg (Coral Browne) points to Paolo and asks Karen, "Is this what you want to be?" She then points to the other young man at his post beneath Karen's balcony and asks, "Is this what you want to become?" In the scene in the haberdashery where Karen is outfitting Paolo with new clothes, the camera pans from Paolo preening himself in a mirror to the tramp staring into the shop window at them. Karen gasps as she looks from Paolo framed in the mirror to the tramp framed in the window, and one wonders if some day the latter will be accompanying Karen on a similar shopping spree.

Although Quintero had never shot a motion picture before, there are several more inventive cinematic touches which he brought to the film. The crudely primitive sexual appeal which the young tramp makes to Karen, devoid of the cultivated refinement of a Paolo, is implied by the phallic street lamp near to which he is pictured as standing in one scene, and by the foaming waters of a fountain spurting upward through which he is glimped in another. There is no doubt that the veiled sexual invitation which this handsome and well-built young man, unkempt though he be, is proferring to her has stirred an elemental response in her. The sexual imagery in these scenes is reinforced by that embodied in the shots of Karen galloping through the park astride a handsome stallion to sublimate her frustrated venereal urges. And of course it is during one such outing that Paolo, the superstud, arranges to encounter her for the first time to begin his seduction of her.

The film sticks so close to the progression of the story as outlined by Williams in the novella that sequence follows sequence almost in the order in which each occurs in the book as the burgeoning affair between Karen and Paolo unfolds on the screen after their first meeting in the park. Some of the visual transitions between scenes in the movie are particularly smooth and serve to quicken the pace of the film. The escalation of Karen's relationship with Paolo from casual

Vivien Leigh (center), with cinematographer Harry Waxman and Warren Beatty, *The Roman Spring of Mrs. Stone*.

Vivien Leigh and Warren Beatty, *The Roman Spring of Mrs. Stone*.

dalliance to a grand passion is depicted by cutting from a nightclub scene in which the Contessa forces an unpleasant confrontation with Karen to extort a larger commission from her, to a large wall poster advertising the current issue of a notorious gossip magazine on whose cover is a garishly unflattering photo of Karen leaving the nightclub with Paolo, and finally to Paolo proudly showing off the magazine to his barber as he boasts of his conquest of the wealthy American widow.

The beginning of the end of Paolo's interest in Karen occurs when the Contessa introduces Paolo to Ms. Bingham, the Hollywood actress, and Quintero wrings every ounce of dramatic electricity out of this climactic scene. Paolo openly insults Karen before their guests in order to disassociate himself from her before going off to join his new client. Paolo's strategy works and Karen hysterically denounces him, the Contessa, and everyone else present and throws them all out of her apartment.

Quite unaccountably Williams did not develop this sequence of events to its full dramatic potential in the novel. Gilbert Maxwell in his biography of Williams remembers criticizing Williams's handling of this passage when he discussed it with him. "You're a skilled dramatist," Maxwell told Williams, "yet in your penultimate scene you violate the first rule of dramatic fiction by telling the reader what's happening as Mrs. Stone throws out her parasitic guests. You don't show her or the guests in violent action, with the sort of unexpected, yet inevitably right dialogue you always have in your plays." Williams was forced to agree with him, as he should have. The novelists merely summarizes Karen's frenzied behavior without portraying it in detail.

In the film, on the other hand, Quintero directs this scene at full throttle. As Karen drives everyone out the door, home movies of Paolo and her cavorting about in happier times are flickering on a movie screen in the background. The film runs out just as Karen sinks to the floor, and for a moment she sits in a daze as the naked beam of the projector lamp reveals the pain on her haggard face.

A brief scene is added to the script at this point which presumably is meant to make Karen's later beckoning to the tawdry young tramp in the street below her window more plausible, if not any more palatable: Still in a state of turmoil, Karen walks the dark streets of Rome and by chance sees Paolo entering Ms. Bingham's hotel and asking for her room. Actually witnessing Paolo in the process of ditching her for another, younger woman is cataclysmic for Karen's pride. So when she brushes past her shabby sentinel on the way into her apartment building, her decision to invite him up is all but made. Once upstairs she crushes Paolo's picture in her clenched fist, then ever-so-decisively wraps her keys in an expensive handkerchief and tosses them to the waiting lad. It is herself, of course, that she is throwing at his feet, as he knew she would eventually do after her affair with the other young man had run its course.

He looks up to her beckoning to him from high above him on her balcony: a

Vivien Leigh and her "admirer" in *Roman Spring*.

grotesque parody of Romeo and Juliet, and an indication that Karen has fallen from her pedestal for good. Though she may tell herself that she is lifting this impoverished youth up to her level, they both know that in a truer sense she is really coming down to his. After he enters her living room, his shadow falls ominously across her face, perhaps as a warning that she will one day be found dead in bed, as Paolo had predicted, with a hair tonic stain on the pillow beside hers and no sign anywhere in the apartment of forced entry. On this chilling note the picture ends.

In the ten years after *Roman Spring* was published, Williams had turned down several offers to have it filmed; but he finally acceded to the late Louis De Rochement's offer on the condition that José Quintero, responsible for the enormously successful off-Broadway production of *Summer and Smoke*, be allowed to direct it as his first film project. "I was attracted to this subject by the Roman setting and by the fact that it is a mature and challenging one to film," said De Rochement. "When the first draft of the screenplay was ready, I went over it with Tennessee Williams at lunch and he liked it." But later, when he saw a rough cut of the film, he requested a spoken prologue to be shot in Rome in order to establish more firmly the mood of the movie.

De Rochement, famed for *The March of Time* series and other highly regarded documentaries, had also made some semi-documentary features based on actual F.B.I. case histories that were filmed on the sites of the real events. Hence from the beginning he had wanted to shoot the whole of *Roman Spring* on location in Rome to impart to the picture a greater flavor of authenticity and reality. But the Italian censors took one look at the story and advised him before shooting began that no work permits would be issued for the company to shoot in Rome because they saw the plot as picturing Rome as a sink of prostitution and vice. Hence all of the interiors were shot in a London studio.

But by the time Williams saw the rough cut, De Rochement had succeeded in persuading the Italian government that the movie would not give the impression that Rome was populated solely by pimps, call boys and girls, and their customers. "What happened to Karen Stone in Rome," he explained to the authorities, "might also happen in Paris, London, or in New York." So the producer was finally granted permission to shoot exteriors in Rome for two days, and De Rochement dispatched a film crew at once. "We thought we had permission to use an apartment that really overlooks the Spanish Steps," he recalled, "but when the owner saw the script he wouldn't let us use his place. So we had to find someone else. In the end we got enough exteriors in Rome to give a sense of locale to the picture."

The Italian government was only one obstacle that the producer had to face in the course of production. Casting was another. "The choice of director had been decided by Tennessee Williams and I couldn't get actors to accept roles in the picture because everyone knew that the director, although very experienced in the theater, had never done a film before," De Rochement has told me. Vivien Leigh at first declined to play Karen Stone, but changed her mind when she read the script. But the starting date was fast approaching and no one had been signed for the part of Paolo. One actor who looked the part had all but signed a contract; then his agent raised his asking price to an exorbitant fee when he discovered that his client was to co-star with Vivien Leigh. Warren Beatty had been considered for the role but was rejected because he simply did not look like a Latin. He accordingly flew to Puerto Rico where Williams was vacationing and convinced the playwright that he should be selected. With time running short, Williams and everyone else finally agreed on Beatty and production got under way in late 1960.

In his autobiography José Quintero recalls arriving at the studio for the first day's shooting petrified at the thought of embarking on his first motion picture. A viewfinder hung round his neck on a dark leather string which felt like a noose

Director José Quintero (right) on location in the Piazza Navona in Rome for *Roman Spring*.

that could be tightened at any time by cast or crew. When he walked onto the sound stage he found a crowd of extras milling around, plus a huge technical crew "hanging on scaffolds and maneuvering hundreds of brilliant moveable lights, as if looking for a criminal. Surely, I felt, I was the criminal they were looking for."

He was further unnerved when Vivien Leigh swept onto the set. She had not made a movie in five years and both of them could hear the whispered conjectures that maybe an actress who had been away so long would not do her best in the hands of an untried film director. Then suddenly, unexpectedly, a smattering of applause broke out among some of the technicians overhead and Ms. Leigh looked up and waved to them. The rest of the crew took up the applause and even the extras joined in. The ice had been broken.

Heartened by this show of good will, Quintero then made the opening day speech expected of every movie director on the first day of filming. He admitted what everyone present already knew, that he did not know which end of the camera to look through or when to call "action" and "cut." "I will need your help," he concluded. "I have a stack of pictures in my head, but I don't know exactly how to deal the deck. In short, I don't know the language of this game." Vivien Leigh responded in the name of everyone, "We are with you, aren't we all?" And a wave of affirmation engulfed Quintero.

In the ensuing six months of shooting he convinced himself that he was right in levelling with the cast and crew in his maiden speech, since not a single member of the British crew ever took advantage of his technical ignorance. "I didn't know about floating walls. If it came to my mind to shoot through a permanent wall it was removed in fifteen minutes." He said to interviewer Stephen Watts while shooting the film that he was learning a lot about movie making while directing *Roman Spring*: "I found that you can't draw back and look at the scene as a whole without loss—you must stay fairly close at least, or you lose it. On the other hand, the close-up is obviously convenient. On the stage you must somehow cause the audience to look at something particularly; on the screen you can force them to do so—you can focus for them. If I had never worked in theater-in-the-round it would have been much more of a jolt."

According to his memoirs, Quintero did have trouble in two sectors: with the producer and the male lead. "Out of what I can only imagine to be insecurity," writes Quintero, Beatty was arrogant with everyone, including his co-star. One morning when he was being made up, Beatty dropped a powder puff and the make-up man stooped to pick it up for him. "No, Warren," snapped Quintero. "You dropped it, and even if we have to stay here the whole day, I will not shoot the scene until you pick it up." Warren picked it up.

As for the producer, Quintero complains that De Rochement was generally uncooperative with him. At the end of one day's shooting the director instructed his assistant that for the following day's scene he wanted a wagon to break down as Vivian Leigh ran by it and four crates to fall open, releasing the pigeons contained inside. De Rochement balked, saying that it was well nigh impossible to make birds behave exactly the way that you want them to in front of a camera, and that the shot would cause needless delays in the shooting. The next morning everything was prepared for the scene, just as Quintero wanted it. On the first take the wagon collapsed on cue, but the pigeons refused to budge from their

Director José Quintero, *Roman Spring*.

cages after the crates fell open. The producer felt vindicated until on the second take the birds flew away on schedule.

De Rochement, for his part, did not feel that he was unreasonable with Quintero while the movie was being made. "Tennessee had provided me with a stage director. I was worried about going over budget and so I was against unnecessary delays. In the end we did go over budget, but then the budget wasn't very large to begin with. Still, as a man of the theater, Quintero was very good with actors. I don't see how he could have directed them any differently than he did, given the story he was working with, and Warren was a problem for him as well as for everybody else. He tried to upstage everyone and that caused more problems for the director than for me."

One of the production staff who worked on *Roman Spring* gave me recollections of the making of the movie which serve to clarify the nature of the tensions which often pervade the set when a motion picture is being created. According to this observer, on the one hand, De Rochement might have bolstered Quintero's confidence more than he did with more visible signs of support. On the other hand, although Quintero was open to suggestions about the technical aspects of film making, he would definitely not entertain suggestions about how to compose any of the shots. This member of the production staff points out that Lothan Wolff, who was associate producer of the film, had been De Rochement's right-hand man for years and had himself already directed one film, *Martin Luther*—all of which placed him ahead of Quintero in experience in movie making. Yet when Wolff tried to be helpful by tactfully suggesting that it might be good to shoot a reversal shot or a close-up in the event that the editor would require them when he was assembling the footage, Quintero invariably resented any such suggestions as intrusions on the director's domain.

Lothar Wolff, quite understandably, declined to comment on the above remarks about the producer and director of *The Roman Spring of Mrs. Stone*. When I talked with him he confined himself to pointing out factual inaccuracies in Quintero's autobiography touching on the making of the movie, and this seems to be the appropriate place to set the record straight. For starters, Quintero says that the movie was shot at "Elms Street" Studios, which is probably a reference to Elstree Studios in London where in fact no part of the film was shot. The picture was actually begun at the MGM studios at Borehamwood, which were used for the first few days of shooting because Associated British Studios across the road were not yet available.

The director complains that the producers had changed the shooting schedule without notifying him and he was therefore faced on the first day of filming with a restaurant scene which was "possibly the largest and most complex set in the entire picture." Aside from the 250 extras, as Quintero remembers it, there were another hundred technicians on hand. "There was definitely no change of schedule on the first day of shooting," Wolff replies. "A thoroughly professional British staff (Basil Summer and Jack King as production managers and Peter Yates, now a well-established director, as first assistant director) would never—not in a million years—let a director appear in the studio without informing him, at least the night before, if the shooting schedule had been changed. It would be suicidal to work in any other way. I am also sure that there were not 250 extras (it may have seemed that way to José). As I remember, the first scene to be shot was aboard a plane, of which a cross-section had been built, for the sequence in which Mrs. Stone travels to Rome. If there were a lot of extras there were twenty-five."

Given the clashes of temperament and other tensions involved in movie making which we have seen exemplified on the set of *Roman Spring* and in earlier chapters during the shooting of other Williams films like *The Fugitive Kind* and *Suddenly Last Summer*, it seems nothing short of miraculous that somehow films do get finished. Everyone connected with *Roman Spring* agrees, however, that the late Vivian Leigh was one of the stabilizing forces that helped the morale of the film unit throughout the months of shooting. Ms. Leigh registered only one objection during the production period and that was her demand to substitute a scene of Karen playing Rosalind in *As You Like It* for Williams's scene of her playing Juliet. "At forty-seven I would be mad to play Juliet at all," she explained to Stephen Watts on the set. Besides, Ms. Leigh saw Karen Stone's failure in Shakespeare to have been caused less by her age than by overextending her limited talents in trying to meet the severe demands of classic theater. When her youth and beauty are no longer potent enough to cover up her second-rate acting abilities, "she is lost," Ms. Leigh continued. "No husband, no career, fading beauty." Asked if this lost lady stirred any resonances of Blanche DuBois for her, Ms. Leigh replied, "None whatever. Blanche was sensitive about everything. Mrs. Stone is only sensitive within her newly found circle. And she is much more realistic than Blanche—in the end fatalistic."

Surprisingly, Vivien Leigh did not think of herself as an actress who was very much better at plying her trade than Karen Stone was supposed to be, although she had met with unqualified success in playing Shakespeare and other classical authors during her long career. Shortly before her death in 1967, she confided to Quintero, "What I had was a flare that lit up the sky for a short while and it was mistaken for genius. But it really had more to do with youth and beauty, and you know how fleeting youth and beauty are." This was true of Karen Stone, but hardly true of Vivien Leigh, as her two Williams films, *Streetcar* and *Roman Spring*, clearly testify. While the film was still in production, Williams paid Ms. Leigh this tribute: "At present she is appearing in a film based on my novel, *The Roman Spring of Mrs. Stone*, a part she accepted with no reluctance despite its being an aged actress. Vivien, above all else, is incomparably graceful, . . . and she has an instinct for doing and saying just the one right thing to put you at ease. . . . In other words, she is not only a stunning actress but a lady with the most important part of that intricate composition, which is kindness of heart."

One of the reasons, then, that *The Roman Spring of Mrs. Stone* is Williams's favorite among all of the films made from his work is that it was "the last important work" of Ms. Leigh. He gave me another reason why this picture is "my favorite of the lot," namely that it is the only film of his work that remained completely faithful to the spirit of his original creation and avoided the accomodations to censorship which even *Streetcar* did not escape. "I was very fortunate in the case of *The Roman Spring of Mrs. Stone* that neither José Quintero, the director, nor Vivien Leigh and Warren Beatty would accept the compromises that were judged indispensible to make the film a success. As a result we have a work which preserves even today its poetic power."

It is a pity that the film is not more widely known and appreciated, for it has considerable merit. Veteran cinematographer Harry Waxman's lush color photography provides a striking contrast to the somber atmosphere of the story; and Quintero's sensitive, searching, and imaginative direction of actors elicited superb performances from Vivian Leigh and Lotte Lenya in particular. As the Contessa, Ms. Lenya can suggest the whole breadth and depth of old world decadence by saying with a satanic leer that it will take a little longer than usual to find an aging count a male companion who will comply with his specific sexual propensities.

Yet Pauline Kael unfairly sneered at the movie for diffidently beating round the bush about the whole subject of middle-aged people renting sexual partners. "Anyone who has ever watched the middle-aged and elderly women going in for their Arthur Murray dancing lessons knows that you don't have to go to Rome to drift," she writes. She seems to have missed the point that a lot of the reticence which Karen displays about negotiating for a gigolo is rooted in her own diffidence about getting caught up in a kind of behavior to which she has never resorted before, and not in the film makers' shyness about the subject matter. Besides, purchased sex was a daring topic for a commercial film to tackle in 1961; and given the censorship problems which Williams films like *Baby Doll* and *Cat on a Hot Tin Roof* had run into before, some degree of circumspection was in order in treating the topic with discretion and artistic indirection. The movie may have been too tame for Ms. Kael, but the general run of less sophisticated moviegoers, unaccustomed to the treatment of such frank material in a Hollywood movie, found the picture a little too unpleasant to be altogether entertaining.

And so *Roman Spring* went largely unseen and undiscussed until it finally turned up on television in December, 1969. Even with his mother chattering away next to him as they watched it in her living room, Williams found that the movie's tragic grace and style hold up very well and that his affection for the picture had not diminished, nor has it from that day to this.

But no one, not even Tennessee Williams, has been able to muster much enthusiasm for his one domestic comedy, *Period of Adjustment*, although it is a competent work that yielded a better-than-average film. If Williams is not at home writing fiction, he is on even less solid ground when he tries to compose light-hearted comedy whether the genre be fiction or drama. His is the tragic muse and while there is always ample room in his work for passages of comic relief, his efforts at sustained comedy show a hint of strain. It is the melodramatic content of *The Seven Descents of Myrtle,* and not the attempts at knockabout farce, after all, that provides the strongest moments in that play; and Williams was correct in calling it his "funny melodrama" rather than a melodramatic comedy.

But *Period of Adjustment* is another matter, for it is short on melodrama and long on the kind of grotesque comedy which at times makes one a bit uncomfortable about laughing at other people's pain. The play and the subsequent film deserve our consideration, nevertheless, precisely because *Period of Adjustment* is something of a curiosity in the Williams canon. It is interesting to watch a practiced artist striking out to investigate what is for him new territory, even if his experiment turns out not to be wholly successful.

In his introduction to the play, called "Prelude to a Comedy," published in *The New York Times* before the New York opening, the dramatist said that in writing this play he had taught himself to take a lighter approach to his characters' problems that dictated his treating them, if not always with laughter, at least with the conviction that their problems did not affect "the whole future course of the world." Elsewhere he noted that he felt that he had too long limited himself to portraying man's destructive impulses in his work. "I am through with what have been called my 'black' plays," he declared. "From now on I want to be concerned with the kinder aspects of life. Maybe these non-black plays won't be all white, but I hope to cast a kinder shadow, with more concentration on the quieter elements of existence."

From its inception, *Period of Adjustment* had not been conceived as an "all-white" play by any means, any more than subsequent "non-black" plays like *Seven Descents of Myrtle,* which I took up in chapter six, can be called a light-hearted comedy. (In *Myrtle* the chief character is a pathetic transvestite homosexual dying of consumption—hardly a figure of fun around whom to build a frivolous farce.) When *Period of Adjustment* was being given its first trial run at the Coconut Grove Playhouse in Miami two years before its Broadway premiere, Williams dubbed it "a serious comedy" about two husbands discussing their married life. "What they talk about is serious but the way they do it is comedy," he explained. Even when Williams intends to write a comic play with serious undertones, it usually turns out to be the reverse, and this is pretty much the case with *Period.*

Williams went on to say in Miami that he could not bring himself to write a totally bright, hilarious comedy untouched by a serious tinge because he believed that mankind was living in one of the most dreadful periods of human history ever, when nations could not co-exist with even a semblance of harmony.

Time covered the Miami opening of the play, and its critic simply did not know what to make of Williams's brand of "serious comedy," beyond making the tentative statement that it seemed an uneasy amalgam of serious subject matter and humorous treatment which could only be called "grimly bizarre." Williams still looked upon the play as a work in progress, however, and was satisfied that the brief Miami run would be helpful to him when he turned to revising the play for its New York debut. He temporarily shelved it in favor of polishing *Sweet Bird of Youth* into its final form.

I should point out that it has always been Williams's custom to have more than one play on his workbench at any given time. "I could not have gone on readying *Sweet Bird* for Broadway if I had not completed a play beyond it," he said at the time. He has learned that he needs the assurance that, whatever the fate of his present project, there is always another work on the back burner waiting its turn for his attention. Being what he calls "a compulsive writer," he finds that when he stops writing on a given day, "the rest of the day is posthumous. I am only alive when I am writing." He has never succeeded in ridding himself of the fear that his creative powers will atrophy, and not even psychiatry has disspelled this phantom anxiety from his psyche. "I drink to enable me to live with it," he concluded.

Once *Sweet Bird* was part of theater history, then, *Period of Adjustment* moved to the front burner, and Williams went back to revising it in earnest. The full title of the play is *Period of Adjustment or High Point Over a Cavern*. The genesis of the subtitle is interesting, in the light of my considerations at the beginning of this chapter on how Williams draws on real life experiences for his plays. When his mother was living in a house on Wydown Boulevard in St. Louis, around the time that Williams was putting together ideas for this play, she noticed some cracks in the cellar and called in an engineer to investigate. He discovered that the house had been erected on a slope and that it was in the process of "sliding right down the street," as he informed her. That part of St. Louis, it seems, had been built over a cave and the houses in the area had to be stabilized by supports from time to time, whenever the foundations began to give way. Williams was to get a considerable amount of thematic and symbolic mileage out of this situation when he made use of it in *Period of Adjustment*. The implication of the phrase "high point over a cavern" connotes sexual intercourse in the context of the play, but other things as well.

The extraordinarily symmetrical plot of *Period* revolves around two married couples: George and Isabel Haverstick, newlyweds on their honeymoon; and Ralph and Dorothea Bates, who have been married for six years. Both couples are poised on a high point over a cavern because both marriages are on the rocks. Ralph and Dorothea are contemplating a divorce, and George and Isabel are considering an annulment of their as yet unconsummated marriage.

George and Isabel arrive on Christmas Eve to see Ralph, his old army buddy, and his wife; but Dorothea has already gone home to father earlier in the day and George, angry with Isabel, deposits her on Ralph's doorstep and drives on. That leaves Ralph and Isabel to trade long expository accounts of how they each have become alienated from their respective spouses, and they discover that they have much in common. "We both married into the shakes," exclaims Isabel. She refers to Ralph's revelation that Dorothea's frigidity causes her to shake whenever he touches her (although they somehow have managed to beget a son) and to her own admission that George's psychosomatic tremor has rendered him impotent.

Another parallel problem that the couples face is that both wives have remained "daddy's little girl" and are still dependent on their fathers rather than on their husbands for emotional support. This factor has created a psychological barrier between both husbands and wives which is exacerbated in the case of the Bateses by Dorothea's awareness that Ralph's attraction for such a plain, timid girl was facilitated by her father's offer of a good job with his firm.

A third parallel between the two couples is that both Ralph and George are in reality two immature adolescents who are no more grown up than their wives. (George, for example, drives a hearse because he thinks it is prestigious to own a Cadillac, even if it is a funeral limousine!) As Isabel comments in exasperation after listening to the two men boast to each other about their virility, "You're a pair of small boys. . . . Bragging, showing off to each other."

Finally, the last parallel between the two pairs of married people is that both men have irresponsibly quit their respective jobs without even consulting their wives beforehand. Ralph wanted to get out from under the thumb of Dorothea's father and George hoped returning home to Texas to raise cattle would be just the thing to cure his nervous affliction.

All of this carefully plotted parallelism between the two couples is just a little too artificial and tends to undercut the reality of the characters as human beings, making them appear at times to be chess pieces manipulated by the playwright rather than individuals working out their own destinies. It really is a bit much, then, to have George announce formally what is already all too explicit: "It's a parallel case," he says; Ralph and Dorothea "are going through a period of adjustment just like us."

Ralph becomes interested in George's plan to move to Texas and raise not just ordinary cattle, but Texas Longhorns, the most well bred and dignified of beasts, before they become extinct. It is typical of the immaturity of the two young men that their noble aspirations to rescue the Texas Longhorn from extinction are tainted with commercial considerations. They want to raise this special brand of cattle for sale at lucrative prices to TV networks for use on television Westerns as their way of inspiring viewers with a respect for the heritage of America's primitive past! Nor does Ralph detect an inconsistency in his connivance with his fellow citizens of High Point Housing Development to sell their houses to unsuspecting buyers who do not know that the dwellings are slowly sinking underground. "Disgusting but necessary," he terms their collusion.

Williams has made expert thematic use of the circumstance of the suburban community resting on shifting ground, for he makes it a metaphor for the difficulties of the two married couples in trying to establish their lives together on the firm foundation of a lasting relationship and also a more universal metaphor for the anxieties that everyone experiences in coping with the uncertainties of human existence. "This whole community," says Ralph, "is gradually sinking, inch by inch, year by year, into a subterranean cavern." Life itself is one long period of adjustment in which humanity as a whole is engaged in the day-to-day struggle to maintain its unsure footing in an indifferent world which Isabel calls one big neurological ward.

Isabel makes this remark near the end of the play, after each couple has bedded down for the night in the Bates home in order to seal their respective reconciliations, and another earth tremor shakes all of the inhabitants of the house. These tremors, she says, are reminders that everyone has got a nervous twitch of some kind, whether they show it the way George and Dorothea do or not. The image of the world as a gigantic mental ward may be reassuring for Isabel, but it is hardly an optimistic note on which to end a comedy, even a "serious comedy."

Yet there is some hope resident in the imagery of the play, which is by no coincidence set on Christmas Eve. This implicit religious dimension of the play culminates in the circumstance of both couples snug in their marriage beds hoping on the night of Christ's Nativity to make their marriages fruitful with the continuing sign of lasting love that the conception of a child represents. Only through such mutual love can they hope to keep from falling into the void that widens beneath them.

The network of poetic imagery is as carefully worked out in the play as the plot parallels, even down to minor items like the names of the characters. George, who is suffering from psychic impotence, is given the ironic last name of Haverstick with its evident phallic connotation; his wife Isabel is-a-(Southern)-belle; and Ralph Bates testily challenges, or baits, his father-in-law. When the play had its New York opening, therefore, many of the critics criticized the carefully crafted plot and accompanying symbolism as self-consciously artifical and pretentious.

But they were more upset by Williams's presenting four neurotic characters with deeply rooted psychological problems as the principals in what purported to be a domestic comedy. My own judgment is that Williams's intent in having apparently ordinary people manifest the same kind of emotional difficulties which afflict the characters in his more serious plays was his way of testifying to his conviction that anyone living in our age of anxiety suffers from neuroses of some kind, and that such traumas are not the exclusive property of the misfits and outcasts who populate his other works. To me his point is a valid one.

I am therefore less uneasy about the oil-and-water mixture of comedy and melodrama in the play than some other commentators have been. Rather I tend to agree with Claudia Cassidy when she writes that Williams knows that "tragedy clings to the precipice of comedy, so that some of his saddest people are the most endearingly absurd." I also mind less than most the overly tidy contrivances of both plot and symbolism, except that seven explicit references to the title and to the subtitle of the play in the dialogue seem to constitute belaboring the obvious. Blanche explained the significance of the title of *A Streetcar Named Desire* once in the course of that play, and that seemed to be quite enough.

On the whole *Period of Adjustment* is not a satisfying work of art, but it does, as I said before, deserve attention as an interesting experimental work by a playwright trying to bend the conventions of different dramatic genres to suit his purposes in order to avoid getting in a creative rut. Benjamin Nelson has neatly defined the anatomy of the play as a tragi-comedy in the sense I have explained in dealing with the tone of *The Rose Tattoo* (or, to use the term which Williams himself coined to crystallize his concept of his own particular mixture of comedy and drama, "slapstick tragedy.")

Are these four characters with their personal fears and frustrations fit subjects for comedy? After raising this question in his book on Williams, Nelson answers that the quartet of principals in *Period* are saddled with dilemmas which could have precipitated tragedy; but the point is that in this play they do not. Williams sympathizes with his befuddled characters and unfulfilled lives because they are worthy of such compassion; but he also quite thoroughly exposes his four characters for their foolishness, blindness, and refusal to grow up. The hope which he extends at the conclusion of the play lies in the reconciliation of each of the two couples, as one would expect at the denouement of a comedy. But the tragic element which persists in this tragi-comedy is that none of the four are cured of the fears, doubts, and insecurity which have plagued them throughout the play. *"Period of Adjustment,"* Nelson says in sum, "does not pretend to be more than it is. In it, Williams laughs at many of the imperfections in people which in previous plays he viewed as bases for catastrophe. Here, by reducing his characters in stature and their problems in intensity, he is able to create a comic situation. The comedy is rooted in a serious point of view, but it is nonetheless comedy." In Williams's own words, "the people at the end still have problems, but they have found each other, and maybe they can now solve their problems together."

Whatever the technical difficulties of the play, there is no doubt that Williams understood the pressures and tensions of married life, and few have faulted him on this score, despite the fact that as a homosexual he has no direct experience of married life. One can explain his genuine grasp of the dynamics of marriage, I think, in the same way that Joseph Epstein explains how E. M. Forster, another homosexual writer, was capable of writing convincing accounts of heterosexual love and marriage: "If imagination, intelligence, and refinement of culture are all brought into play, a better view of the game may be available from a seat in the stands than from down on the field." In his essay in *Gays and Film* on gay sensibility, Jack Babuscio similarly responds to Molly Haskell and other film critics who have questioned the validity of Williams's view of heterosexual love. "Those on the outside better understand the activities of the insider than vice versa," he writes; "the gay artist often speaks more frankly than the straight on such matters as the tedium of marriage, the horrors of family life, the lover's exploitation of personality, and the slow erosion of character in promiscuity." Williams's work reveals an aspect of love, he concludes, that is neither gay nor straight, but simply human. *Period* proves that Williams has been able to make some perceptive observations about married life from his seat in the stands, not the least of which occurs at the point where the anguished Isabel says, "I'm afraid that I have married a stranger," and Ralph responds consolingly, "Everybody marries a stranger."

After the New York production closed in the spring of 1961 after four months, Williams saw a summer stock production and conceded after a second glance at the play that instead of being his first "non-black" play it had turned out to be "as black as *Orpheus Descending*, except that there was more tenderness, perhaps less physical violence." Even the author was finally prepared to admit that his vision is a dark one and that there will always be as much shadow as sunlight in one of his works.

When MGM purchased the movie rights of the play, George Roy Hill was asked to direct the film because Williams had been very satisfied with his direction of the play on Broadway. Initially Elia Kazan had agreed to direct the New York production and Williams had visited Kazan while he was making *Wild River* on location in Cleveland, Tennessee, to discuss the premiere production of *Period* with him. But in April, 1960, Kazan announced that he would have to withdraw from the production, which was scheduled to open that November, because he was committed to directing another movie, *Splendor in the Grass*, which would occupy him into October. "I offered to do the play when I was through with my movie," Kazan elaborated to a *New York Times* reporter, "but Tennessee was not willing to wait till then. I consider him the greatest living playwright and would certainly like to work with him again, if he will ask me."

Williams was stunned by this unexpected reversal, and said so to the same journalist. To him Kazan's action spelled the end of a creative association which dated back to *Streetcar* on both stage and screen, the film of *Baby Doll*, and also included the original stage productions of *Camino Real, Cat on a Hot Tin Roof,* and *Sweet Bird of Youth*. The dramatist suspected that Kazan had decided against directing *Period* because of the criticism which he had received over the years for influencing Williams, especially for urging the playwright to rewrite the third act of *Cat*, an episode which I took up when treating that play and film in chapter four. Kazan had also drawn fire for staging *Sweet Bird* in too melodramatic a fashion—unjustly so, as far as Williams was concerned, because he felt that it was himself and not the director who was to blame for sometimes exceeding dignified limits in his preoccupation to hold an audience's attention for a whole evening. "My cornpone melodrama is all my own," he told the *Times* reporter. "I want excitement in the theater. . . . I have a tendency toward romanticism and a taste for the theatrical."

Williams did everything possible to persuade Kazan to stay with the production, but finally admitted defeat. "We met Monday night for drinks. He showed up looking rather shaky and gray in the face, and told me definitely he couldn't do my new play. I tried my best to change his mind, but he was adamant. His withdrawal has been shattering for me. I felt at home with him." But the show must go on, and so Williams closed his remarks to the *Times* by expressing his confidence in George Roy Hill, who was to replace Kazan as director of the play; and Hill later agreed to do the films as well, even though, like José Quintero, he had never directed a movie before.

Because of the enormous amount of exposition contained in *Period of Adjustment* about the case histories of both couples, Isobel Lennart's screenplay strove to open out the play more than it has been necessary to do for the majority of the other Williams plays that have been filmed. The movie begins by portraying directly much of the narration which had been given by Isabel to Ralph in expository dialogue in the play.

Behind the credit titles a shaky hand belonging to George Haverstick (Jim Hutton) is seen reaching out to push the call button for the nurse. Isabel (Jane Fonda) responds to the summons and rubs his back while George smiles contentedly. Then George is shown recounting his flying experiences to Isabel; as his hand makes a sweeping gesture like a plane, it soars near her and she enfolds his hand in hers. As the credits end George pushes the call button one last time after closing the lid of his suitcase to leave the hospital. This time Isabel goes to him in tears, and the prologue ends with them embracing after their wedding ceremony.

They climb into the hearse (which George insists is a limousine-station wagon and Isabel insists is a hearse) and drive off as a "Just Married" sign incongruously painted on the back of the vehicle comes into view. George reveals to Isabel that he has quit his job as ground mechanic at the airport just as they cross a bridge, a visual suggestion that he has equivalently "burned his bridges behind him" before embarking on the honeymoon. "Jingle Bells" twanged out in a Southern accent on their car radio drowns out their ensuing quarrel.

They drive up to a dingy motel in a brutal rainstorm and struggle through the mud to their delapidated cabin. This scene is much funnier in the acting than it

Tony Franciosa and director George Roy Hill, *Period of Adjustment*.

was in the telling in the play because Hill plays it as slapstick in the film. Isabel steps under a broken spouting as she slops her way into the cold cabin and is deluged with an additional flood of rain water which devastates her hairdo, corsage, and new outfit. She is so drenched, in fact, that one cannot distinguish the tears coursing down her cheeks from the raindrops dripping down on her face from her bedraggled hair. As she goes inside the cabin and dejectedly shuts the door, the camera pulls back to show the "Just Married" sign being washed off the trunk of the hearse, an image of grim foreboding for their wedding night.

Another method which the script adopts to keep the movie from becoming a static conversation piece besides opening out is to introduce Dorothea (Lois Nettleton) and her parents, the McGills, much earlier in the movie than in the play. In this way many of the tensions and problems that beset Ralph's marriage to Dorothea can be displayed through Ralph's confrontations with his wife and in-laws rather than merely relayed through expository dialogue to Isabel in the course of their long conversation. Even before the Haversticks arrive at the Bates home, Ralph has a quarrel with Mr. McGill (John McGiver) in which the camera cuts back and forth between their mutual recriminations about Ralph quitting his job.

Moreover, Ralph and Dorothea's little boy, who never appears at all in the play, becomes a character in the movie and this serves to concretize the Bates's marital difficulties a little better. After accusing Dorothea of turning their son into a mama's boy, Ralph hurls into the fireplace the doll which Dorothea still allows the lad to sleep with. As his parents continue to argue, the camera switches to the vantage point of inside the fireplace itself and photographs the boy gingerly reaching toward the flames to retrieve his beloved toy. Although the distracting camera angle (which in effect places the viewer inside the fireplace) is too pretentious, the moment is a poignant one, implying the self-centered

Jim Hutton and Jane Fonda, *Period of Adjustment*.

Tony Franciosa and Jane Fonda, *Period of Adjustment*.

attitude of the parents who are so absorbed in their argument that they fail to notice their son's danger.

The two parallel strands of plot, one dealing with the Haversticks, the other with the Bateses, converge when Ralph answers the phone and finds that George is calling him from a gas station where he has had his autombile repaired. Just as George finishes telling Ralph that he and Isabel's wedding night ended in disappointment and quarreling, the platform on which the car has been raised in the repair garage lowers into the frame and the unhappy Isabel is visible through the window.

There are other inventive visual touches in the picture such as the one just described. After George storms out of Ralph's house and drives off in his car, Isabel tells Ralph that her new husband has gone off to find himself another girl just to spite her. Her self-pitying prediction is followed by a shot of George sitting forlornly in a swing in a snowy playground. He observes a little girl give the cold shoulder to her little male companion and then stalk off without him. George almost cautions the tot not to go after the girl, but decides to sit by and let the boy go, shaking his head dejectedly that men of whatever age never seem to learn how to handle women. This mini-tableau emphasizes how childish the bickering of the two married couples is by juxtaposing it with a quarrel between two small children. The snow in this and all of the outdoor scenes, furthermore, is a visual reminder of the chill which has settled over the relationships of the two couples and which will have to be defrosted before they can be reconciled.

The only attempt to take the story outside the principal setting of the Bates home which does not come off is the trip to the police station late in the film. This sequence seems to be an example of superfluous change of location just to remind the audience that they are watching a motion picture and not a play, for it serves no discernible artistic function. The occasion for moving the action to the station house is the arrival of the policeman whom Mr. McGill summons to ensure that Ralph will not bar him from removing Dorothea's valuables from the house as he and his wife pack their daughter's belongings in preparation for her moving back with them.

In the play at this point, Dorothea recognizes her parents' meddling for what it is and packs them off without her. In the film, however, they all accompany the cop to the police station to continue their dispute there. It seems highly unlikely that a prominent businessman in a small town would be willing to air private family quarrels in a public forum of this kind, and so the scene fails in credibility.

Another false note struck in this scene is that McGill has an instant change of heart, something which Williams was realistic enough to deny him in the play. Incredibly, McGill congratulates Ralph for standing up to him in the manner in which he should have defied his own father-in-law years before. Then he seals his new resolve not to interfere in Dorothea's marriage any longer by yanking his wife out of the frame as she continues to plead with Dorothea to come home with them. Mr. McGill's gratuitous change of heart presages the quick healing of the other rifts, those between the Bateses and the Haversticks, at film's end. This optimistic ending marks a definite and unjustified departure from the sense of tentativeness that permeates the respective reconciliations of the two couples at play's end, and dilutes Williams's theme that the whole of life is a period of adjustment in which people who are close to each other must try to relate to each other in a meaningful manner. (The fact that Isabel's rueful remarks about the world as one big mental ward are left out of the film also points to a happier ending than Williams wants.)

A third note that rings false throughout the picture is that Dorothea is simply too beautiful and vibrant a character to convince the audience that she was ever the inhibited ugly duckling that Ralph claims to have married for her money. The explanation that is fabricated to account for her transformation into the lovely lady set before us in the film is that she has had her nose fixed and her teeth straightened! The fault in Dorothea's characterization lies as much with Williams as it does with Hill. While the director might have allowed Lois Nettleton to look too glamorous all through the film, the author is the guilty party who explains away the gap between the plain girl with the inferiority complex and the handsome and self-assurred young woman in so shallow and superficial a fashion.

In the final analysis *Period of Adjustment* is still a better movie than it was a play, mostly because the play's long passages of exposition about the past lives of the two couples have given way in the movie to actual dramatic presentation of these events which cried out to be acted out in the film. By the same token, bringing the McGills into the story sooner and introducing Ralph and Dorothea's son into the action keep the movie progressing forward at a fairly lively pace. Except for the few reservations which I have noted above, including the unwarranted optimism of the movie's ending about the ease with which the characters will work out their mutual adjustments, the movie's other flaws were already inherent in the play. Thus the uncertain swinging of the tone of the picture from seriousness to frivolity is grounded in the equally ambivalent mood of the film's source. Williams is really not at home in the genre of domestic comedy and as a result both play and motion picture evolved as somewhat tentative and unsatisfying works of art.

The film is particularly blessed in the exuberant performances of Jane Fonda and Jim Hutton as Isabel and George, and of John McGiver as Mr. McGill. The latter tries to prepare the audience for McGill's repentance and firm purpose of amendment by implying in his performance the hint that behind McGill's forbidding and blustering front there beats a real heart of flesh, if not of gold. Also to the film's credit is the principal setting, Ralph and Dorothea's home, which was designed with an eye to the theme of the film. "The house is filled with pseudo-smart furnishings reflecting the tastelessness of surface sophistication," Ed Fischer writes in *Film as Insight*. "There are things marked 'His' and 'Hers' that tend to become symbols of separateness as the story unfolds."

As for George Roy Hill, he established himself with his first film as a director of great promise. Hill handled the disconcerting shifts between comedy and melodrama as well as any director could, and he was deservedly lauded by Fischer for making a film in which "the laughter is internal; the bleeding is internal too. It makes one realize how close comedy and tragedy are: they are the opposite sides of a coin and a very thin coin at that."

After Hill made *Period of Adjustment* he went on to become a major film director, and has been responsible for such blockbusters as *Butch Cassidy and The Sundance Kid* and *The Sting*. Conversely, José Quintero, who was also directing his first film when he made *The Roman Spring of Mrs. Stone*, returned to the stage afterward and never made another movie. Unlike Hill, Quintero found the pressures of commercial film making, where much greater sums of money are at stake, to be inimical to creating the kind of artistic atmosphere in which he works best.

In the succeeding chapter the two films to be taken up were directed by John Huston and by Joseph Losey, both of whom had established international reputations as film makers of distinction before they each tackled their Williams assignments. Since Foster Hirsch and other commentators on Williams contend that any movie derived from a Williams work retains its identity as primarily a Williams work regardless of the influence exerted on the film by its director, let us see if this statement remains true even when the directors happen to be film makers of the caliber of John Huston and Joseph Losey.

John Huston: *The Night of the Iguana*
Joseph Losey: *Boom!*

THE FILM OF *The Night of the Iguana* begins with Richard Burton ascending the pulpit of an Episcopal church to give his weekly sermon; the film of *Boom!* ends with Richard Burton holding a jewel aloft over a goblet in the same way that a priest holds the host aloft over the chalice at the Communion time of the Mass. I juxtapose these two images from these two Williams films to bring into relief the fact that the Williams canon proliferates with religious themes and imagery; and it is therefore relevant to touch upon the religious element in his work before going on to discuss these two motion pictures and the plays from which they derive.

Even in so slight a play as *Period of Adjustment* Isabel admits to being bothered by three nagging questions, "Where do we come from? Why? And where, oh where, are we going?" Williams's concern for such eternal verities and his employment of religious symbolism in his plays date back to the deeply ingrained religious streak that he developed in spending his early years in the Episcopal rectory of his much admired and greatly loved grandfather. Williams's younger brother Dakin still tells a tale about his older brother Tom as a very young child digging a monstrous hole in the rectory garden. When his mother asked what he was doing, the lad replied, "I'm diggin' to de debbil." Dakin Williams comments, "Many of Tennessee's critics believe that he has never stopped doing this—digging to the devil, for he has been frequently accused of continuing his childhood occupation of toying with evil." Tennessee Williams's own comment on this anecdote is that he agrees that in his work he has sought to uncover the evil tendencies that lie within every human being. "But I am also digging for the opposite: for God."

Back in 1958 he slated in a TV interview with Mike Wallace that he had always been a religious man but that up to that time people had ignored this positive side of his work. "I would rather think of my characters in terms of their spiritual assets—courage, generosity, humor, honesty, sympathy—than in terms of their failings," he concluded.

Public interest in Williams's religious views was sparked in January, 1969, when he was converted to Roman Catholicism through the auspices of his brother Dakin, himself a convert to Catholicism, and the ministrations of Father Joseph LeRoy, S.J., a pastor at the church near Williams's home in Key West. Williams had just gotten over a serious bout with Hong Kong flu, the disease which had already claimed his old friend Tallulah Bankhead, and he accordingly decided to rejuvenate his religious convictions because, as he explained to Father LeRoy, "I want my goodness back."

Dakin Williams had joined the Catholic Church while serving in the army air force in India during World War II ("The jungle has affected his mind," his father commented when he heard). Coincidentally, the Williams family is descended directly from Valentine Xavier, the brother of St. Francis Xavier, known as the Apostle of India, whose missionary work Tennessee Williams terms "a valiant but quixotic undertaking." The Williamses trace their descent from the family of the Spanish Jesuit saint through the members of the Xavier clan who migrated to France where they became Protestants, and then to England and finally to the American South. The family name underwent several permutations before it finally emerged as Williams by the time that Thomas Lanier Williams was born in 1911. (He called the hero of *Battle of Angels* and *Orpheus Descending* Valentine Xavier and took Francis Xavier as his patron saint at the time of his conversion.)

"I have always loved the richness of the Catholic ritual, the aroma of incense, the splendor of the art," he has said. He still does, although he is no longer an active churchgoer, preferring an empty church in which to pray because large congregations disturb him. "I've always been religious," he said recently. "I was religious as an Episcopalian and I'm still religious as a Catholic. I pray a lot, especially when I'm scared." Elsewhere he has added, "I do believe that there is a God, and I don't believe He's dead like people say. But I don't know where He is, or what He's doing."

These last sentiments are very close to those expressed by Dr. T. Lawrence Shannon, the defrocked Episcopal priest who is the key character in *Night of the Iguana*. Looking about him, the despairing ex-cleric finds man as God made him struggling and dying in a world that God never made. He has been attempting, since he was forced to leave the official ministry, to attach meaningful religious significance to human suffering and death; and his present occupation as a commercial tour guide throughout "God's world" is connected with this religious quest through life.

Critic Donald Newlove sees Shannon as something of a "failed Christ figure," moreso than Val Xavier and some other Williams heroes to whom this thematic dimension has been attributed. Indeed, T. Lawrence Shannon's full name is a tip-off that this was very likely in Williams's mind because at least some of the allusions which it calls to mind are related to Christianity: T. for the Cross (for men were in fact crucified on T-shaped crosses in Christ's time); Lawrence for D. H. Lawrence, who was well nigh obsessed with the role of religion in man's psychic life in his later years, as well as for T. E. Lawrence, who aspired to be a saviour of sorts of the Arab world; "and Shannon for the River Shannon of Ireland, with its Catholic associations and which, mystically, is the river of death that the sufferer must cross in atonement." Shannon is in for quite a bit of atonement before the play is over; and it is of course no accident that the site of his psychological suffering is atop a Hill where the play takes place.

Shannon, who is the fulcrum of *The Night of the Iguana*, does not appear at all in the seminal 1946 short story of that name, from which the play was developed. But the setting is the same (Mexico in 1940) and the central symbol of the title is carried over into the play as well. Williams had first discovered Acapulco in 1940 when he was travelling around the continent waiting for *Battle of Angels*, his first play to be commercially produced, to go into rehearsal. "There were no high rises then," he reminisced recently. "I was living in the Hotel Costa Verde. The hotel rooms were little sweat boxes, facing a long veranda with a hammock in front of each cubicle. At first there were only myself and another young writer. He and I were living in our hammocks, drinking rum and cokes and waiting for our cubicles to cool off." These numbered cubicles were to become symbolic in the play of man's radical isolation from his fellow man.

"Then a bunch of Nazis arrived. Mexico was full of Nazis at the time, and these were just like the group in the play. They had shortwave radios and they were listening to the news of the fire bombing of London. Really Wagnerian, these creatures, quite frightening and quite awful." In the course of the various creative processes which *The Night of the Iguana* underwent in the years to come, Williams did not have room for the Nazis in the short story; but he introduced them into the play, from which all reference to them was expunged when the film script was composed. Conversely, Williams's remembrance of some Mexican boys catching an iguana and tying it under the verandah to be fattened for the table stayed with the story in all three of its incarnations, as a short story, a play, and a motion picture.

The one character who is carried over from page to stage is the heroine of the short fiction, Edith Jelkes, although her personality in the story changes radically when she becomes the Hannah Jelkes of the play. In both she is a sedate spinster who wants to make up for her years of seclusion by a life of "refined vagrancy"; but Hannah has come to terms with life with a serenity that has so far eluded Edith, whose unfulfilled sexual desires have driven her more than once to the brink of a crack-up. She has usually kept her emotions in check; but, like the iguana held captive under the porch, she is subconsciously straining to be released from her inhibitions. She becomes morbidly interested in the only other two Americans staying at her hotel, a pair of homosexual writers, and is even physically attracted to the older of the two.

She invades his cubicle one sultry evening, ostensibly to ask him to set the iguana free but really she wants him to release her pent-up passions. Intuiting her motives in coming to see him, he impulsively tries to possess her; but some "demon of virginity" resident within her wards him off, and he collapses beside her, sobbing helplessly. On the way back to her room she notices that someone has let the iguana go and she, too, feels a sense of liberation. The strangling rope of her own loneliness has been severed by her sudden realization that she prefers her inviolate, self-centered isolation to risking involvement of any kind with another human being—least of all a pathetic older man who was presumably trying to reassert his heterosexual identity and thus break out of his homosexual pattern of behavior by having sexual intercourse with her.

In the play Williams distributes some of the properties of Edith's personality to other characters. To Ms. Fellowes (the rightly named masculine Lesbian) she gives Edith's implacably smug virginity, her conviction that no mere man will ever be worthy to possess her. Williams bestows on Shannon Edith's abiding fear of once more going over the brink of sanity into yet another nervous breakdown. But aside from what the author was able to borrow from the story for use in the play, it is of rather slight importance or impact; and the play represents an enormous artistic advance beyond the original materials. (Charles Moorman in the critical anthology *Tennessee Williams: A Tribute* calls the short story the kind of embarrassing sketch English teachers submit to *The New Yorker*.)

In 1959 Williams was invited to contribute a short play to the Third Annual Festival of Two Worlds in Spoleto, Italy. He decided that there was enough material in this short story to yield a one-act play at least. As he set about converting fiction into drama, he began to expand his intended playlet with additional major characters and incidents. He dispatched more and more material to the director, Frank Corsaro, in Italy; and when the steady stream of his additions finally came to a halt, the play had reached a full hour and a half running time.

Williams was unable to get to Spoleto for the opening, but the subsequent production which he saw at the Actors Studio in New York the following winter convinced him that he had the makings of a full-scale dramatic work. He elaborated the action still further and took the full-length draft to the Coconut Grove Playhouse in Miami for a tryout in 1960, something he had done with *Period of Adjustment* and other plays-in-progress. After a two week run in

Florida, Williams followed his usual custom of putting the play away so that he could turn to the final preparations of a play closer to completion, in this case *Period of Adjustment*. By the time that *Iguana* was ready for its pre-Broadway tour in the fall of 1961, it had been subject to four drafts (and was at one interim point temporarily going by the working title of *Shannon*.)

"You see," Williams explains about his rather unorthodox way of piecing together a full-length play, "I don't work from the beginning to the end of a play. Usually I have a vision of the most dramatic scene, the central scene, and I then work around it for the approach and the denouement. . . . I think that subconsciously I know the story line before I start to work, but I have to go through many drafts before I know for sure. It comes out, it emerges like an apparition out of the mists." Williams's explanation of his working habits recalls Peter Glenville's statement in chapter seven that "Williams does not work from situations and then find words to describe each situation. He works from character. The core of a Williams script is the delineation of characters and beautiful dialogue."

In delineating the characters in the play Williams not only divided some of Edith Jelkes's characteristics in the short story among more than one character in the play but likewise used his Grandfather Dakin as the source of not one but two characters in the play. To Shannon he gave the Reverend Dakin's profession as an Episcopal priest and to Hannah Jelkes's grandfather, the aged poet Jonathan Coffin, whom she affectionately calls Nonno, he gave his own grandfather's gentle and generous personality. Writing of Rev. Dakin, Williams has said, "My grandfather was a kind man. He was soft spoken and gentle. Somehow he created about the whole house an atmosphere of sweetness and light. Everyone in the house seemed to be under his spell. It was a spell of perfect peace."

This description could have been penned with equal accuracy about Nonno, and Edwina Williams agrees that "the old man Nonno in *The Night of the Iguana* is a partially true picture of Father; I don't think anyone could draw a completely true one. He was an individualist of the first order. Unlike Nonno, Father never wrote poetry, although he composed sermons with a great amount of poetry in them. . . . Some are old at twenty; my father was young at ninety. He believed people should not allow themselves to deteriorate mentally, that there were far too many interesting things in life to see and enjoy. He proved you don't need to decline into dotage, for his intellect was as keen at ninety-seven as it ever had been." And this, too, is Nonno just as Williams envisages him in the play.

Williams's later works, like *Period of Adjustment*, and also *The Milk Train Doesn't Stop Here Anymore* (which I will take up later in this chapter), are preoccupied less and less with action and more and more with character analysis: a crisis situation develops in which the characters reveal themselves to each other and, more importantly, to themselves; and with this new self-knowledge they are better prepared to endure if not necessarily to prevail over their problems. *Night of the Iguana* is by far the best example of this kind of Williams play. The dramatist has brewed up just enough plot to keep the audience watching and listening to the delicate and painful interchanges between the characters, wherein lies the heart of the play.

Shannon commandeers his tour-busload of Texas school teachers who are supposed to be billeted in the local commercial hotel, and instead delivers them to a shabby hotel run by his sage and sympathetic old friend Fred Faulk and his wife Maxine. He had hoped to find temporary solace in talking with Fred for a while, but he learns upon arrival that Fred has recently died and Maxine would like him to stay on as her co-proprietor and resident lover. Shannon is put off by Maxine's advances because he already has two females preying upon him in different ways: the Lesbian tour host, Judith Fellowes, is trying to get him fired for seducing a very willing younger member of the group, Charlotte Goodall, to whom Ms. Fellowes is herself subconsciously attracted, while Charlotte pursues Shannon.

Into this hornets' nest come Hannah Jelkes and Nonno, who support themselves in their travels by Hannah drawing character sketches of hotel guests and Nonno reciting his poems. Both of them have a calming effect on Shannon who respects both of them for having coped so much better with disappointment and reversal in their lives than has he, "the man of God on vacation."

Shannon's ambiguous status as a clergyman is concretized by Williams in the gold pectoral cross which moves through the play as the sign of his erstwhile vocation. He redeems the cross from a pawn shop en route to the Faulk hotel in order to seal his determination to write to his bishop and be reinstated as a priest. Later Shannon dons the cross, along with his frayed clerical collar, in a pitiful attempt to convince Ms. Fellowes that a man of the cloth would not have gotten sexually involved with an underage girl like Charlotte. When Ms. Fellowes fails to be impressed and confirms her determination to press charges of statutory rape against Shannon, he masochistically tries to tear from his neck the chain on which the gold cross is suspended, but only succeeds in causing the chain to cut into the back of his neck.

Hannah interrupts this furious act of self-laceration by removing the chain for him. Shannon realizes that clothes—or crosses—do not make the man and that he will probably never return to the ministry; he consequently tells Hannah to pawn the cross and keep the money for her travel expenses. Characteristically, Hannah responds that she will accept the cross not as a gift but as a loan, with the understanding that she will hold it for him until the time comes when he will want it back.

Williams has always been handy in using extended metaphors of this kind in his plays; but in his later works, where, as I said above, his chief concern seems more than ever to be theme and character rather than plot, his partiality to manipulating intricate symbolic patterns is very prominent indeed. Another beautifully realized symbolic metaphor is Shannon's speaking of his proximity to another nervous breakdown in financial terms (something which F. Scott Fitzgerald was fond of doing): "I don't have a dime in my emotional bank account," Shannon tells Charlotte to dissuade her from becoming further involved with him. "I can't write a check on it now." He has, comments the author in the stage directions, definitely overdrawn his reserves.

Shannon, like the iguana tied under the porch, has reached the end of his rope, and the metaphorical figure of the captive iguana is the most beautifully realized symbol in the entire play. It develops naturally and logically from the action of the story and is not belabored as were the key symbols in *Period of Adjustment*. The titular symbol of the iguana reverberates throughout the play, for several of the characters are, in a variety of ways, living out a kind of captivity. Hannah is tied to her grandfather, Ms. Fellowes is shackled to her hopeless homosexual attachment to young girls like Charlotte, and Maxine is fettered to her remote tourist hotel because she knows it is too late for her to go somewhere else and start life anew.

But the most pronounced parallel to the captive iguana is Shannon, especially when he goes to pieces and has to be literally tied down to a hammock until his suicidal impulse subsides. When it does, with the help of Hannah's soothing conversation and poppy seed tea, Shannon repays her kindness by acceding to her request to set free the iguana so that one of God's creatures can be liberated, like Shannon, from its panic and pain and be allowed to scramble home safe and free because, as Shannon says, "God won't do it and we are going to play God here."

In discussing the imagery of the play Williams, like Hannah, admits that the iguana is an ugly creature not easily pitied, and as such stands for humanity itself. "I don't think humans are such pretty creatures once you get past the facile prettiness of youth. It is right and true to feel for them, to want to release them from their captivity. You may not admire them but you get to feel for them. I guess that's what I meant."

Williams singles out *Iguana* as one of the few plays in which a male character (in this case Shannon), rather than a female character, is the playwright's mouthpiece. "Playwrights always have somebody speak for them. I think that more often I have used a woman rather than a man to articulate my feelings." Shannon does seem at times to express the author's sentiments, for example, in rejecting the Puritanical concept of God as a ferocious judge devoid of compassion for the human condition, an "angry, petulant old man," as Shannon puts it. But I for one find much more evidence of Williams's personal vision in Hannah's speeches than in Shannon's. Her gentle criticism of the undeniably masochistic aspect of Shannon's "dark night of the soul" in the hammock comes across as the playwright's comment on Shannon's self-deception. She insinuates ever so tactfully that, while she accepts his dejection and melancholy pain as genuine, she is willing to bet that he secretly enjoys them, and that he never collapses unless someone like herself is around to comfort him:

"Who wouldn't like to suffer and atone for the sins of himself and the world if it could be done in a hammock with ropes instead of nails, on a hill that's so much lovelier than Golgotha, the Place of the Skull, Mr. Shannon? . . . No nails, no blood, no death. Isn't that a comparatively comfortable, almost voluptuous kind of crucifixion to suffer for the guilt of the world?"

Hannah comes closest to verbalizing sentiments that the playwright has elsewhere expressed as his own in the same scene when she articulates her firm conviction that love is usually too self-centered to be a permanent antidote to lonesomeness; even in permanent relationships the moments of truly mutual communication are fleeting and few, but are all that one can dare hope for in life. (Williams expressed himself precisely in these terms when he was interviewed by David Frost on television in 1970.) Here is the way that he has Hannah elaborate this concept in the play:

She begins by saying that the gates between people can be broken down so that they can reach each other for one night of communication, such as she and Shannon are experiencing on the verandah "outside their separate cubicles." She continues, "I'm a human being, and when a member of that fantastic species builds a nest in the heart of another, the question of permanence isn't the first or even the last thing that's considered." To prove her point she then recounts a painfully pathetic anecdote about a lady's underwear salesman whom she once met in Singapore who took her rowing in a sampan before bashfully requesting her to lend him an article of her clothing for a few moments. She acquiesced to his request because, as she explains to Shannon, she had never before known that loneliness could reach such depths. And she concludes with a remark that Williams has often made his own, and to me it clenches the fact that Hannah is really the dramatist's spokesman in the play: "Nothing human disgusts me unless it's unkind or violent."

The next morning Shannon's tourists depart without him and he submits to staying on with the domineering if fundamentally likeable Maxine because, as Hannah reminds him, at their age one has to settle for some compromises in life and to accept situations which he is powerless to improve. For her part, Hannah is about to continue on her journey with Nonno when she discovers that, having finished his last poem, he has quietly died in his sleep. (Sebastian Venable in *Suddenly Last Summer* did not live to finish his last poem because, unlike Nonno, his vile life had rendered his creative imagination sterile and his pen incapable of any further poetic utterance.) At this peaceful, silent moment, she looks heavenward and murmurs the prayer which closes the play: "Oh God, can't we stop now? Finally? Please let us. It's so quiet here, now." Man's solitary hope, her curtain line implies, consists in God's taking pity on each of us in the way that Shannon took pity on the iguana and His extending to us the peace of soul which we need to continue the struggle of human existence toward the ultimate release of death.

Referring to Hannah's prayer, Williams has summarized the play as a demonstration of how human beings come to transcend despair and go on living. "These people are learning to reach the point of utter despair and still go past it with courage. Hannah will go on, even though it means being alone. For there is no alternative to going on but death." Shannon will go on, too, now that Hannah and her grandfather have shown him that endurance is the key to salvation, both in this life and the next.

Esther Jackson writes that Williams's later works like *Orpheus Descending*, *Sweet Bird of Youth*, and especially *Night of the Iguana* have assumed more and more of the apparatus of the Christian search for God and His forgiveness. In the present play, then, the playwright poses human compassion and understanding, as represented by Hannah, as the sign of divine reconciliation for Shannon. In the course of the play Shannon thus passes from sin to expiation to redemption, and in so doing becomes the chief example of what Ms. Jackson calls Williams's "negative saint, the great sinner toiling up the steep ascent to God."

With the principal writing and rewriting of the play completed by the fall of 1961, the production took to the road for a pre-Broadway run which Williams calls in his memoirs "the longest and most appalling tour I've had with a play." It began badly in Rochester and went on to Detroit and Cleveland before settling down for a seemingly interminable five week run in Chicago. Because the *Tribune*'s Claudia Cassidy's championship of Williams's plays dated back to the tryout of *The Glass Menagerie* in Chicago in 1944, it was customary for Williams to include Chicago in the pre-New York trek of a new play. But even Ms. Cassidy lambasted *Iguana* as plotless rambling.

Williams was willing to do his usual amount of revising on the road, but he absolutely refused to diminish Hannah's part in order to build Maxine's part up for Bette Davis. In her autobiography, *The Lonely Life*, Ms. Davis says that when Williams offered her the role of Maxine she accepted it even though she was aware from the start that it was "certainly the tertiary part—but as I have said many times since, I would rather have the third part in a Tennessee Williams play than a lead in an ordinary play."

Williams, on the other hand, recalls that during the tryout period Bette Davis had second thoughts about playing second fiddle to Margaret Leighton's Hannah: "Ms. Davis thought she had the leading role in the play. I don't know whatever gave her that impression, because she's a very bright lady, and Maxine is a secondary character." After a performance in Chicago, Williams was in Ms. Davis's dressing room and she asked him, "When are you going to cut the limey's lines? Who's selling tickets, her or me?" He answered that when she read the play she must have noticed Hannah's long speeches in the last act. "Well," retorted Ms. Davis, "I assumed you would cut them." Williams won that battle with Bette Davis but lost another. She grew dissatisfied with the director, Frank Corsaro, who had been with the play from its inception in Spoleto, through the Actors Studio production in New York, and the Miami production. "When we reached Chicago, Frank Corsaro was fired by Ms. Davis," says Williams laconically. "Not only did he have to leave the theater. The next night she sensed he was still in Chicago and he had to leave town, too." Williams took a hand in directing the play at this point, though Corsaro quite justly received directorial billing when the show opened in New York.

Because of bad out-of-town reviews, everyone was apprehensive about the Broadway premiere. "I don't think there is a prayer," Margaret Leighton confessed to one of her fellow actors on opening night. She and the others could not have been more wrong. In fact her performance in particular was singled out for praise, with *Time* describing it as having "the purity of light." Ironically enough, Williams had written the role for Katharine Hepburn and the latter was flattered to hear it. But after studying the play thoroughly she replied to Williams that "it captures the wrong part of my imagination. I couldn't live in it." After seeing the New York production she persisted in this view, telling Williams, "You're lucky. I would have ruined it."

The New York Drama Critics gave Williams his fourth best American play award, and Hollywood beckoned as it had so many times before. But this time the screenplay and the direction were to be in the very capable hands of a first-class film maker, John Huston, known for such movie classics as *The Maltese Falcon*, *The Treasure of Sierra Madre*, and *The African Queen*. *The Night of the Iguana* was made to order for Huston in that his films have often been concerned with the ennobling valor with which man must struggle to endure the challenges of life in the face of the likelihood, if not the inevitability, of failure. Furthermore Huston has often probed the suppressed emotional conflicts of his characters (without falling into pretentious Sunday supplement psychology); and there was every reason to hope that he could explore the psychological problems of the inhabitants of the Costa Verde Hotel in *Iguana* with the same expertise.

Huston transported his cast and crew to the primitive Mexican village of Puerto Vallarta for an uncomfortable three month sojourn. His cast was a stellar one: Richard Burton as Shannon, Deborah Kerr as Hannah, Ave Gardner as Maxine, and Sue Lyon as Charlotte. Because Burton and Gardner were known to become difficult on the set and because Burton was accompanied by his equally temperamental wife Elizabeth Taylor, the international press fully expected the torrid location site to provide a field day for them. But very little of a notorious nature transpired during the taxing period of shooting, so the beleaguered journalists took to manufacturing lurid press reports to satisfy the public's curiosity. It was true, for instance, that Huston's first assistant director was a well-known Mexican director and actor, Emilio Fernandez, who was barred from getting work in the Mexican film industry at the time because he had shot a producer during a quarrel. But it was not true that he was Ava Gardner's "new Mexican flame," as *The Los Angeles Herald Examiner* announced.

Ms. Gardner was understandably upset when she read this gossip item just before having to do one of her longest and most difficult scenes. But Deborah Kerr records in the diary which she kept during production that her co-star got through the scene with "extraordinary spontaneity" all the same. In point of fact, Ava Gardner's work in this film is quite possibly the best of her entire career, in that she projects the tenderness and vulnerability which lies beneath Maxine's earthy exterior in a way that eluded Bette Davis in her stage performance.

Ms. Gardner's fine performance is especially noteworthy because Huston had a difficult time persuading her that she was capable of the kind of serious acting required for the part. He had even flown to her home in Spain to convince her that as far as he was concerned "there was nobody in the world who could play Maxine but Ava," as he said later. "I knew she had the random, gallant, wild openness of Maxine." Ms. Gardner's misgivings perdured even after her arrival in Puerto Vallarta and Huston again had to reassure her of her competency in the part. He also persuaded her to don the frumpy clothes that the role required and to eschew wearing make-up, something which Maxine would never bother with. He even got her to do the one scene which she was embarrassed about. In it Maxine has to frolic drunkenly just off shore in the moonlight with her two beach boys. Huston saved the situation by first giving Ms. Gardner a stiff drink and then stripping to his shorts and splashing about in the water as he wanted her to do. After watching Huston good-naturedly make a fool of himself for a while, Ms. Gardner waded into the water and took his place with Maxine's two gigolos.

Throughout the long and difficult shooting schedule Huston managed to handle his principals with a finesse and circumspection that gave the lie to the heavy-breathing exposés being churned out by gossip columnists about trouble on the set ("Short fuses of top stars sizzle under a jungle sun," proclaimed one Denver paper.) For one thing, he wisely never complained about Burton's steady drinking because the star was always prepared when the cameras were ready to turn and because Burton was, after all, playing a drunkard. The director did, however, have to bar Sue Lyon's fiancé from the set because their constant off-camera petting was distracting to the actors filming a take nearby.

But such incidents are a tempest in a tea cup compared to the two near-tragedies which occurred during shooting on the hazardous location sites. The principal hotel set was constructed on a mountain side which the film unit nicknamed the Rock, located about half an hour away from Puerto Vallarta and which could only be reached by precariously switching midway in the journey from canoe to motor launch. Huston had twenty-five cottages constructed for the use of the actors and technicians near the location site; and one night two of Huston's assistants fell to the ground when the balustrade of their little porch collapsed. One man was injured seriously and was flown to a Los Angeles hospital. "I think the accident serves to show up the basic quality of this location," Ms. Kerr wrote in her diary. "That the whole place seems to have been put together with chewing gum is all too obvious, and dangerous." And Huston was overheard to mutter, "We'd better get this damned thing finished before we're all covered with rubble."

How right he was to be apprehensive was borne out when the tour bus, with Burton and several other actors aboard, careened off a narrow road in the mountains and screeched to a halt on the edge of a cliff. The occupants had to evacuate the vehicle ever-so-cautiously so that the shifting balance of weight did not cause the vehicle to tip forward and roll down the side of the mountain before everyone could get out.

I recount these anecdotes about the troubles and tensions that harrassed the film crew working in the remote location where *Iguana* was shot to point up that despite irritating privations and agonizing crises, somehow a movie was made, and a very good one at that. The sequence which worried Huston the most in terms of calling forth all the artistry that actor and director could bring to it was the long dialogue passage in which Hannah helps Shannon get through the night by recounting experiences from her past life, among them her encounter with the travelling salesman in Singapore described above. Deborah Kerr was concerned about the demands of this delicate scene too and confided to her diary that "it's really the guts of my part. I am nervous and afraid much of it will end on the cutting room floor. Movie audiences are so accustomed and conditioned to action, action, action that it is hard to get them to sit and *listen*," as one can get a theater audience to do.

When the sequence was actually shot one evening a week later, Ms. Kerr was relieved that it was over. ("It was 10½ pages and at the end of shooting I felt I had been talking for a week.") But she was not satisfied with it and told her diary why. "I don't feel I have managed to get any variation in the scene to make it interesting. Not that it *isn't* interesting; in fact, it contains most of the riches of the play, really all that Tennessee is saying throughout the whole. But to talk for ten pages is one thing in the theater and quite another kettle of fish on the screen. John shot it very simply with a minimum of movement—perhaps too little. I hope most fervently it comes off as it should; but I was tired and distracted, and felt nervous and dissatisfied when I got to bed about 4 a.m."

The next night things went better when the sequence in which Shannon sets the iguana free was photographed, except that—irony of ironies—the iguana did not want its freedom at all! Ms. Kerr conjectured that since the reptile had been living in its comfortable cage for three months, it was no longer interested in returning to the uncertainties of jungle life, and had to be cajoled into bolting when its rope was untied.

A few days later when she saw the first cut of her long scene with Burton her initial apprehensions about its falling flat were vindicated. Huston therefore decided to redo it, and Ms. Kerr and Burton were both glad to be able to take another crack at it. "So often producers won't or can't spend the extra money," her journal entry reads, "and a scene goes out to the public that could have been twenty times better." This time it was after three more "hideous" nights of reshooting the scene that Ms. Kerr could jubilantly record that Huston had directed the scene this time with more changes of pace and mood and that she gave a better reading of her lines, that they were able to make the whole thing visually interesting and dramatically alive. When I recalled this and other episodes of the filming of *Iguana* to Huston and inquired about his approach to directing actors, he responded with this fine summary statement:

"I have no standard approach to actors. I try to guide each actor through his part without letting him know that, as director, I am really acting all of the parts myself. Futhermore I look upon the camera as another actor on the set. The relationship between the actors is important, but the relationship between the actors and the camera is also important. The camera can be as eloquent as the finest actor if you know how to use it. You have to be the right distance from an actor when he says a line, for example. Very rarely has my best camera work been remarked on by either an audience or the critics because good camera work should be unobtrusive. One camera set up should naturally lead to the next, without anyone noticing. It's like a ballet.

"A good scene tells how it should be shot. I begin by letting the actors sort themselves out; and often, as I found in directing my very first film, *The Maltese Falcon,* they do the scene fairly well without any suggestion from me at all, falling into some of the compositions quite naturally. I don't cast an actor for his technique but for his personality, and because of my vision of what he will do with his personality in a given part." This last point is obviously exemplified in the cast of *Iguana,* in which Burton, Kerr, and Gardner all had personalities well attuned to the roles that they were playing (even to Burton's tippling coinciding with Shannon's). "My faith in the actors in *Iguana,* I think, was justified," he said in conclusion, "They all turned in an extraordinary group of performances that amounted to ensemble acting."

When planning the production Huston had anticipated problems from another sector where, as things turned out, few difficulties were forthcoming: Tennessee Williams. The playwright arrived in Puerto Vallarta about ten days before shooting was to begin for script conferences with Huston about the adaptation which Huston and Anthony Veiller had prepared. By the end of their second meeting Williams had agreed to all of the minor adjustments which had been made in his play to make it screenworthy. He stayed around another week to contribute some additional dialogue and then departed for home.

The first thing that one notices in comparing the film scenario with the play script is that Huston completely excised the German tourists; but if Williams did not mind their absence from the film Deborah Kerr did. Hannah represents the author's own fight against violence and brutality in the world, she explained in a subsequent interview; and Hannah saw that violence and brutality epitomized in the Germans. For Ms. Kerr they were one of the strongest elements in the play. "This is what Hannah was against, and yet had to woo" in order to sell her sketches. She had to cultivate the very people who represented everything that she detested.

For myself, the Germans seem an expendable part of the play. Introducing them and the short wave broadcasts about the war in Europe to which they are constantly listening tends to dissipate the story's intense concentration on the claustrophobic atmosphere of the isolated hotel, in which the group of refugees from the outside world who comprise the main characters of the story confront their private psychological traumas.

Because the world of the play is a circumscribed one, Huston opens out the play very little for filming purposes and rightly stays close to the stifling confines of the hotel setting. He and his collaborator on the screenplay did devise a pre-credit sequence which functions as a prologue to the film. But it is based on expository dialogue of Shannon's later in the play and enables the viewer to witness first-hand Shannon's emotional collapse.

The camera pans down from the steeple of an Anglican church on a rainy Sunday morning, then cuts to Shannon mounting the pulpit to preach on the text, "He that does not rule his own spirit is like a city without walls." As the parishoners begin to whisper among themselves about his sexual indiscretions, he breaks off from his prepared text and blurts out, "You have come to see this city with its broken walls," and then launches into a tirade against "the senile delinquent" whom they worship as their image of God, an image which he does not share. Shannon leaves the pulpit and drives the congregation out into the storm, shouting, "Close your windows, your doors, and your hearts against the God of compassion and love!" With that the credits appear on the screen.

Huston was absolutely right to separate the prologue from the balance of the film by the credits so that once the movie proper begins the audience enters the steamy, suffocating tropical world of the shabby hotel and its environs, and stays there right to the finale. The first scene after the credits are over begins with a shot that parallels the opening shot of the prologue: the camera pans down from a church steeple, but this time it is a Mexican cathedral. Shannon is sleeping in the sun while his charges are inside the church because, as a failed priest, he morosely refuses to enter another ecclesiastical edifice.

The director uses these first moments of the film proper to establish more graphically than could be done of the stage Ms. Fellowes's pursuit of Charlotte,

Richard Burton in the prologue of *The Night of the Iguana*.

and Charlotte's campaign to win Shannon. The bus stalls along the shore and Shannon takes the opportunity to take a dip in the sea. He is dismayed when he is joined by Charlotte while Ms. Fellowes (Grayson Hall) frantically shouts imprecations from the beach and reminds Charlotte before bursting into tears, "You only got to come on this trip because of me!"—the pathetic recriminations of a lonely and frustrated woman who is not even aware of the implications of her possessive behavior.

Another sequence invented for the film, and played superbly by Grayson Hall, who received an Oscar nomination for her work, portrays Judith Fellowes lying beneath the netting over her bed and abjectly apologizing to Charlotte for her tantrum on the beach that afternoon. Ms. Fellowes steals a sheepish glance across at Charlotte's cot and finds it—empty. She then flies like an outraged vampire to Shannon's room and finds Charlotte there.

The finest addition to the script made by Huston and Veiller also involves Ms. Fellowes: Maxine loses her patience with Ms. Fellowes's unrelenting abuse of Shannon and all but accuses of her harboring unwholesome feelings for Charlotte. Shannon quickly intervenes and forces Maxine into silence with the hurried and quietly uttered explanation that "Ms. Fellowes is a highly moral person; if she ever realized the truth about herself it would destroy her." Maxine replies that Ms. Fellowes is bent on destroying him and deserves to be destroyed herself, to which Shannon responds, "Maxine, do not rob me of my little accomplishments." In the play Shannon is depicted as a man capable at times of the kindness and generosity of his calling; but there is nothing in the play that quite captures these qualities in Shannon in the manner in which this interchange with Maxine in the film does.

Richard Burton, Cyril Delevanti, Deborah Kerr, and Ava Gardner, *Night of the Iguana*.

Ava Gardner and Richard Burton, *Iguana*.

Huston is careful to indicate the better side of Shannon's character in order to foreshadow the fact that Shannon will stay on at the hotel not only to be Maxine's consort but also to assume Fred Faulk's role as sympathetic counselor to the outsiders and misfits who often fill its guest list. The verbal imagery about Shannon's filling Fred's shoes for Maxine is present in the play; but in the movie it is extended to encompass how the defrocked priest will also be the comforter of the lonesome and flawed people who happen upon Maxine's jungle outpost. Moreover, Huston makes this imagery visual as well as verbal in the motion picture by photographing Shannon wearing Fred's shoes (given to him by Maxine) with his feet in the foreground on a desk. In effect Shannon's new ministry will be to help others as Fred helped him.

It is understandable that Williams accepted the emendations and refinements which Huston made in the play when the screenplay was composed. Huston both as co-screenwriter and director showed enormous respect for Williams's text, allowing Hannah's virtual monologue about her past life to be acted out on the screen without the intrusion of flashbacks and allowing Nonno to recite his final poem without interruption before he expires. The minor changes which the director did make in the play blend smoothly with the literary source of the film script without causing a single jarring note.

I disagree completely with Stephen Taylor's contention in *Film Quarterly*, consequently, that the movie reflects a conflict between dialogue and visuals: "It is like watching one ball game on television and listening to another on radio. You need two minds to follow the action. . . . The talk and the cinematography move at different speeds." Indeed they do, but this is a virtue in the film and not a vice. What this means in practical terms is that Huston accelerates the tempo of the camera movement and the editing in the action sequences and slightly retards the pacing of the movie, relatively speaking, in the dialogue sequences in order not to distract the viewer from the crucial content of these verbal interchanges. This variety of tempo provides a healthy tension between word and image which captures and holds the filmgoer's attention.

Censorship reared its ugly head only rarely during the transition of *Iguana* from stage to screen, and the alterations prescribed by the MPAA Code Commission are all but imperceptible in the film. In her speech about the travelling salesman who is also a clothes fetishist, Hannah omits in the film that he took "satisfaction" in holding her garment; but it is feasible that the prim New England spinster narrating the story just might have omitted this frank detail. Also the impression is given in the film that Shannon and Charlotte did not progress very far in their amorous interlude in Shannon's room before Ms. Fellowes swooped down upon them, whereas there is no doubt that Shannon's seduction by the girl was consummated in the play. But, again, neither the text nor the texture of the play is marred by this alteration of the episode in the movie.

When the motion picture was finished and ready for distribution, Huston expressed his satisfaction with it to columnist Hedda Hopper. "Fastest picture I ever made," he chortled. "Everyone adored themselves and one another." It is extraordinary that a film that was made under the most trying location conditions with more than its share of touchy actors on hand had actually been brought in ahead of schedule; and the excellence of the movie is a tribute to all concerned, starting, of course, with director and co-writer John Huston. Asked whether he thinks of *Iguana* as a John Huston film or as a Tennessee Williams film, the film maker gave an answer which epitomizes his philosophy of doing screen adaptations of literary works:

"Critics have never been able to discover a unifying theme in my films, and for that matter neither have I. Of course, as a director I do interpret reality. Just pointing a camera at a certain reality means an interpretation of that reality. But I don't seek to interpret reality by placing my stamp on it. I try to be as faithful as I can to the material I have chosen to film. Everything technical and artistic in the picture is designed to depict that material for an audience. That, in the end, is all that really matters."

Huston's own view of his role as an adapter is backed up by critical evaluations of his work. As Tom Reck has written, the reputation of the literary source and Huston's personal respect for it decide the amount of changes that he will make in it when he adapts it to the screen. "He is less intimidated by his material than he is respectful of it," and *Night of the Iguana* is a case in point. Because of respect for Williams's play, Huston tended to be more loyal to the original work than he was to, say, Maxwell Anderson's *Key Largo* and to other stage plays which he has filmed.

Besides its considerable artistic merits, *Iguana* also proved itself a hit at the box office and became an international success. *Boom!*, based on Williams's *The Milk Train Doesn't Stop Here Anymore*, on the other hand, was equally faithful to its source and boasted an equally distinguished director and cast; but it failed to find either critical or popular approval. The fault must be laid in great degree at the door of the play itself, therefore, which is one of Williams's least accessible works. Like *Night of the Iguana*, *Milk Train* started out as a short story and was first produced in Spoleto before going on to Broadway. Williams penned the short story, entitled "Man Bring This Up Road," one summer while he was residing at the Hotel Miramare in Positano on the Divina Costiera (Divine Coast) of Italy while he was also contributing bits of dialogue for the Italian film *Senso* (1954), which I mentioned in chapter two.

The short story centers on a vagabond poet named Jimmy Dobyne, no younger or wiser than Williams's other itinerate artists such as Val Xavier. Jimmy stumbles on the luxurious villa of Flora Goforth on the Divina Costiera and requests one of the Italian servants to offer her one of the few remaining copies of his sole volume of poems as a calling card that he hopes will merit him a few days respite from his travels. The servant obligingly presents the slender book to Jimmy's prospective hostess while stammering in broken English, "Man bring this up road."

The elderly lady toys with the idea of keeping Jimmy at her disposal for a few days, but rejects the idea because she has been too often exploited by not-so-young men of Jimmy's stamp in the past. When she learns that he lied to her about his age, she sends him on his way immediately. As Jimmy starts back down the road the sun seems hotter and yellower than usual, and he knows that his struggle for success in the uncertain "career" that he has chosen for himself will get tougher as he gets older.

The focus of the story, though somewhat evenly divided between the two chief characters, is primarily with Jimmy, whom Williams presents as typical of the "flock of gifted, improvident young wanderers of summer," who fly to Europe each year with enough travelers checks to last them until they make the acquaintance of a Mrs. Goforth. In the story Jimmy seems no more than a bargain-basement version of Paolo in *The Roman Spring of Mrs. Stone;* but as Christopher Flanders in the play he becomes a much more imposing figure. Yet Flora Goforth, and not the erstwhile poet, is the most important character in the play, since Williams fills out the sketch of the aging dowager in the short story by creating a full-length portrait in depth of a retired actress who is reminiscent of, but older and far more neurotic than Karen Stone.

(Flora Goforth, in fact, is what Karen Stone would certainly become if she were to live long enough.)

Flora is obsessed with completing her memoirs before death overtakes her. She shares with her creator a fear of death that is Williams's case dates back to his youth when he had more than one serious illness, and this fear has been kept alive throughout his life every time that he has been stricken by a siege of one disease or another. (His conversion to Catholicism was precipitated by a critical dose of Hong Kong flu, as I pointed out earlier in this chapter.) Asked if he was afraid of death, the playwright rejoined flatly, "Who isn't?" Expanding on this reply to another interviewer, Williams conceded that his work at times definitely mirrors a preoccupation with man's mortality and that he became increasingly obsessed with death during the Sixties as he grew more despondent and suicidal and got deeper into drugs and alcohol. "I don't know what I was doing if I wasn't trying to find an easy way out," he reflected. *The Milk Train Doesn't Stop Here Anymore,* he now freely admits, painfully depicts "the deepening shadows of my life as man and artist" as he experienced them at the time of its composition in the early Sixties.

Flora superstitiously looks upon the writing of her autobiography as an assurance of longer life since she constantly reassures herself that she will meet her publisher's deadline, i.e., she will not die until she has finished it. Given her penchant for superstition, she is upset when she discovers that Christopher Flanders has earned the title of "Angel of Death" because he has assisted at the bedside of several dying women of Flora's age and station in life.

The play, consequently, is a much more serious inquiry into life—and death—than the story that triggered it; and because the death theme is so close to Williams he worked and reworked the play many times to bring out its thematic complexities to his satisfaction. The first production of the play was at the Spoleto Festival of Two Worlds, with Hermione Baddeley playing Flora under the direction of Herbert Machiz, who had done the original production of *Suddenly Last Summer.* The ecstatic audience brought the cast back for more than ten curtain calls and Claudia Cassidy, who covered the opening, joined in the euphoric reception of the play. Reminiscing about Williams's career, she recalled the Italian triumph of *Milk Train* this way:

"Tennessee could reach in a dark theater and catch you by the throat. Once in Spoleto he did it to me. I had gone to the high hill town to see the tryout of *The Milk Train Doesn't Stop Here Anymore*. There on that dreamlike little stage was another marvelous, terrible old woman, Flora Goforth, with a fierce passion for life, an uproarious voracity sprung from the same intuitive understanding that had created Amanda Wingfield. . . . On that little stage at Spoleto, with Hermione Baddeley as Flora, it was marvelous while it lasted."

Roger L. Stevens offered to bring the play to New York with the same director and most of the principal players. One evening Tallulah Bankhead phoned Williams in Key West and asked if she could play Flora in the upcoming Broadway production. "Tallulah, I wrote it for you, but it wasn't ready for you," Williams was forced to reply. "So I tried it out in Spoleto with an English actress, Hermione Baddeley, and she was so terrific that I staggered into her dressing room after the Spoleto opening and said, 'Hermione, this play will be yours if you want it next season on Broadway.'" Tallulah gallantly withdrew her request. "Well, darling," she said, "you did the right thing and that's that. But if it doesn't work because it isn't ready, well, you know me. And I know you wrote it for me and sometime I'm going to play it."

Stevens wanted Ms. Bankhead; but Williams stuck to his original agreement with Ms. Baddelely, who received better notices for her performance than Williams did for writing the play during the Boston and Philadelphia tryouts. When the production opened in New York in January, 1963, *Time* applauded the "blinding, blistering brilliance" of her acting. "As she coughs, groans, and rages about the stage, she is larger than death." Unfortunately the newspaper reviews were not published because of a newspaper strike, and the show closed after sixty-nine performances. Williams was certain that the play could have made it had Stevens been willing to ride out the newspaper blackout; and so another producer, David Merrick, made the unprecedented offer to re-present the play in New York the following season, with Tony Richardson directing and this time Tallulah Bankhead in the part that Williams had conceived for her. "It is very sad that Tallulah didn't play it about five years earlier. When it was ultimately given her, it was simply too late," says Williams today. "Tallulah's on-stage liquor and pills were the real thing," he says, indicating that he had not only written the role *for* Ms. Bankhead but *about* her. "She had great difficulty projecting clearly past the front of the house."

The production limped listlessly through several cities and Richardson deserted the company at its last road stop in Baltimore. Merrick considered closing the show out of town, but Williams insisted that it would hurt Ms. Bankhead too much to do so. Broadway once more rejected the play when it re-opened on New Years' Day, 1964. Since this second Broadway production was the one which was purchased for filming and appears as the definitive version in Williams's collected plays, it is this text of the play which I shall analyze before examining what the movies managed to make of it. Nonetheless, the most perceptive review ever written of the play was *Time's* treatment of the 1963 production; and since the points made in it refer equally well to the revised 1964 version, I would like to draw on that review.

Time warned even at that early juncture in the play's history that many playgoers would be severly disconcerted by any Broadway play, but especially one by Tennessee Williams, which asked them to contemplate the state of their souls at the moment of impending death. Audiences could, if they chose, overlook the religious implications of *The Night of the Iguana* since there were enough melodramatic elements in that play to hold their attention. But the thematic dimension of *Milk Train* is front and center from start to finish, and one must take or leave the play on that basis. Shannon had the makings of a kind of Christ figure, but was primarily a very human being with emotional problems of his own; whereas Christopher Flanders seems more symbolic than real. While Flora schemes to possess his admittedly beautiful body, Christopher is preoccupied with living up to his reputation as the Angel of Death by gambling to save her soul.

The religious aura that surrounds Christopher Flanders begins with his name: his given name means Christ-bearer, implying his role as a Christ figure, and his last name is a reference to Flanders Field, a World War I burial ground, recalling his function as Angel of Death. Flora's villa is situated on the Divine Coast, moreover, and Christopher climbs the steep mountainside leading to her estate bearing a heavy pack on his back which causes him to stumble several times en route, arriving battered and bloody after being attacked by Flora's watch dogs. The parallel with Christ's ascent of the Mount of Calvary to die for the sins of mankind is unmistakable. Chris comes to Flora as the bearer of Christ's compassion for a woman whose memoirs are a record of a lifetime of sin and whom he hopes to prepare to meet her Maker.

Williams sprinkles other references throughout the play which confirm Christopher's symbolic status. He is said to have "worked a miracle" in helping an elderly dowager with a broken hip to learn to walk again; and as *Time* points out, "during the play he banishes the heartsick depression of Flora's prim widowed young secretary with an open-handed touch." And when Chris speaks of leaving for Sicily, Flora inquires testily, "Can you walk on water?" (By the end of the play, one suspects that perhaps he can!) When Flora is ready to admit that the hour of her death is at hand she frantically implores Chris to bring God to her. "How do you bring Him? Whistle? Ring a bell for Him?" she asks as she tinkles the little bell on her desk which, in this religious context, recalls the bell rung at Mass to signal the presence of Christ in the Sacrament of the Eucharist. Then she asks him to help her to her deathbed because "I can't make it alone."

Chris does prepare Flora to go forth to meet death almost in spite of herself by preaching to her the message of Christian resignation, couched though it is in mystical Oriental imagery. "I've disappointed some people in what they wanted or thought they wanted from me," he explains. "Once in a while I've given them what they didn't know even if they didn't know what it was. I brought it up the road to them, and that's how I got the name that's made me unwelcome this summer." He says that the insight which he has received through silent contemplation is one of acceptance: "Such as how to live and die in a way that's more dignified than most of us know how to do it. And how not to be frightened of not knowing what isn't meant to be known, acceptance of not knowing *anything* but the moment of still existing, until we stop existing—and acceptance of that moment too."

In accepting Chris's aid in her final moments, Flora is accepting his message, too, and so dies peacefully. Yet even critics sympathetic to the play find the significance of Chris's beliefs undercut by his ambiguous position as a freeloader who befriends rich old women before they die. Can such a person's philosophy of life and death really be taken seriously? In my opinion there is little evidence in the play that Chris has any selfish ulterior motives for comforting these wealthy women in their hour of need. He continues to pursue what he sees as his vocation without any visible sign of much remuneration for his pains, and this factor strengthens his credibility. Despite rumors and cynical gossip to the contrary, the milk train has not stopped for Chris in a long, long time; and it does not stop at Flora Goforth's for him either. The only thing he requests from Flora is a glass of milk, symbol of childlike purity and innocence, which further negates the assumption that Chris is selfish rather than selfless in his ministrations to his chosen clientele. Herbert Machiz, who directed the play in Spoleto and in its first Broadway production, agrees with this benign interpretation of Chris's character. "In *Milk Train* Tennessee pits a rich woman against a poet (material versus spiritual), and Flora Goforth is made to realize that not everyone can be bought, just as the young doctor in *Suddenly Last Summer* couldn't be bought."

Nevertheless it was much easier for Williams to create the earthy and frenetic Flora than the unearthly and serene Chris. Hence Flora overshadows him in the play even though the logistics of their relative places in the drama demand that he be a figure sufficiently imposing to be able to influence this stubborn and egocentric woman. But Chris does not come across in any version of the play with enough dramatic intensity to make this seem plausible. Despite the care and craftsmanship which the author lavished on the play, then, it never really catches fire; and Williams remained dissastified with it. When Universal purchased the film rights, therefore, he accepted the studio's invitation to write the screenplay in order to revise his material once again, although he had not collaborated on a film script of one of his works since the failure of the film version of *Orpheus Descending* in 1960. He is glad that he accepted Universal's offer to do the script because he still feels that his script for *Boom!* was an improvement on his stage versions of the story. "I used to rewrite and revise more than was necessary," he says. "Like *The Milk Train Doesn't Stop Here Anymore*. I should have let it go. It didn't get better, it got worse. It only got better when I made it into a film, *Boom!*"

The production began to shape up in a very promising fashion, with Joseph Losey directing, and two superstars who had each triumphed in other Williams films, Elizabeth Taylor *(Cat on a Hot Tin Roof* and *Suddenly Last Summer)* and Richard Burton *(The Night of the Iguana)*. Their presence in the movie assured financing.

"I had the script of *Boom!* for a long time and was unable to finance it," Joseph Losey told me. "I had met both Richard and Elizabeth passingly over the years (I had directed Elizabeth in a screen test at age thirteen, which she didn't remember), but I had never thought of casting them in the picture. Then my producer at the time, John Heyman, who had once represented them, came to me when we had *Accident* at Cannes in 1967 and asked me to consider Elizabeth for the role of Mrs. Goforth in *Boom!*. I responded that I knew that she was a remarkable actress but that it would mean a slight distortion of the part because the play is about an older woman who is about to die. But then I thought that it might be even more interesting if it were about a relatively younger woman about to die.

"John said that he had just come from seeing Elizabeth and Richard on their yacht and she had said to him, 'Get me something by Tennessee Williams. I adore playing Williams and I have always had luck with his plays on the screen.' After a long time in which we had many discussions about whom to cast as the male lead she said to me, 'What about Richard?' My answer was, 'You're too young for Goforth and he's too old for Christopher Flanders. But yes, surely, if he wants to do it. It's a listening part and he's a superb listener.' And so we came together."

In rounding out the cast Losey made one other unusual choice. He asked the late Noel Coward to play the Witch of Capri who comes to visit Flora, and who had always been played by actresses on the stage. "My agent, as a kind of joke, suggested Noel Coward and I jumped at the idea," Losey explains. "Not only because Noel Coward was a marvelous, witty man, but also because when people get to the point of dying there is a kind of obliteration of the sexes. That is the only really marked change we made in the play when we filmed it. The only other changes were simply part of the process of cutting the play's dialogue for the screen." In actual fact Losey never read the play because he saw no point in being concerned about something that had not been successful on the stage, particularly when the playwright himself was doing the screenplay. "Tennessee Williams presented me with a screenplay which I tried to honor as much as possible. I did ask him for certain rewrites, most of which he managed. I made certain cuts, subject to his approval, and just before shooting began we went through the whole script together."

Before the company went on location to Sardinia to shoot exteriors, Losey warned Richard Burton and Elizabeth Taylor that "one set of critics would blast

Elizabeth Taylor and Richard Burton in *Boom!*.

Joseph Losey for selling out to the Burtons while another set would criticize the Burtons for getting involved with the arty Joseph Losey. Subsequently I did *Secret Ceremony* (1969) with Elizabeth and *The Assassination of Trotsky* (1972) with Richard, and I realized in retrospect that we had all suffered from working together on *Boom!*, although they liked working with me and I liked working with them. I don't make the kind of commercial films that their fans expected from them and at the same time people who follow my work would stay away from *Boom!* just because the Burtons were in it—they would simply prejudge the film.

"Admittedly there was a kind of aggressiveness about the way that the Burtons flaunted their wealth which brought them very damaging press. (They're no longer the Burtons, I realize, but they still are to me.) They tried to control this 'yachts and poodles and diamonds' publicity but that was their image at the time, and it didn't do them or me or the picture any good. (In point of fact both Richard and Elizabeth are very generous with their wealth and their help, but this is not generally known.)

"As far as directing them goes, I found that they worked better apart than they

Director Joseph Losey, *Boom!*. On location in Sardinia.

did together. They tended to play to each other in *Boom!*, and I as director could not give them the individual attention that they demanded when they were in the same film as I could when I directed them separately in *Ceremony* and in *Trotsky*." Losey sensed that when they played together they were involved with each other in all sorts of subconscious ways; and hence he never knew which way their feelings were going to bounce in a given scene. "I sometimes felt while we were doing a scene in *Boom!* that one might be playing me off against the other."

When I inquired why Losey took on the formidable task of directing this film, he answered without hesitation, "I made the film because I adore Williams's plays. The verbal images are so rich that they offer a challenge to any film maker. I tried to match his verbal poetry with images which would extend and illuminate it, and make the work more accessible to moviegoers. For instance the film begins with a shot of the sea while the camera pulls back to reveal that we are looking at the world beyond the insulated fortress where Mrs. Goforth has immured herself. This represents the broader horizon of which she becomes increasingly less aware in her narrow existence on her estate.

"It has been said that the houses in my films often take on a life of their own, as in the three films which I made from Harold Pinter scripts, *The Servant*, *Accident*, and *The Go-Between*. In this case we tried to figure out what kind of place this woman would live in and we designed a rather sterile house. She would have employed the best architects in the world to give her what they thought she wanted; and what they gave her was what they would like to build in order to show off their own expertise. So her house turns out to be an expensive fortress in which she has walled herself up against the world outside. It is also a tomb because she is warring against death. Ironically, then, in the midst of the most beautiful natural views, she has erected a kind of grotesque mausoleum, meant more to be looked at than to be lived in."

Inside the mansion Flora is having a luxurious back rub and listening to sensuous music that echoes through the house in a way that underscores the essential emptiness of the place, regardless of how crowded it is with the sort of expensive bric-a-brac with which lonely rich people fill up their domiciles to make them seem less vacant. Then Chris is seen swimming ashore at the foot of the cliff which Flora's home overlooks. He rises from the shimmering sea like an apparition materializing from the deep, thus establishing the otherworldly ambiance that clings to him from the very beginning of the movie.

The "Ascent of Calvary" symbolism is retained from the play at this point, as Chris staggers up the hillside and collapses after being attacked by the watch dogs presided over by Rudy, the watchman (Michael Dunne). Blackie, Flora's secretary (Joanna Shimkus) tends his wounds. She is a compassionate young widow, a misfit among the freakish types with which Flora surrounds herself,

Burton and Taylor, *Boom!*.

including Rudy, a sadistic dwarf, and her alcoholic physician. The Witch of Capri, warlock though he be, is one of the few sensible acquaintances that Flora has. She invites him to dinner to give her the lowdown on Chris's past, and he arrives impeccably attired in a tuxedo, full of repartee and kindness for his eccentric friend Flora. They have dinner on the terrace where the contrast between Flora's willfully circumscribed existence and the infinite expanse of the sea that lies beyond her balcony railing is again pointed up.

The sea has special meaning for Chris, who murmurs "Boom!" when he watches the waves breaking against the rocks on the shore below with a booming sound. To him this sound recalls "the shock of each moment, of still being alive," a reminder that one must make the most of the gift of life before it is snatched away, for "death is one moment, and life is so many of them." But to Flora the surf is only an incessant, inarticulate clamor that expresses her own restless emotional state as she paces around her balcony dictating her memoirs into a tape recorder.

The scene in which she recalls the death of her first husband Harlon is much more gripping in the film than it was in the play because we see Flora moving perilously close to the edge of her terrace overlooking the raging surf far below as she narrates how she fled the bedroom in which Harlon died in the act of love. The wind washes over her and the sound of the pulsating sea rises to a crescendo as she collapses on the balcony floor just before falling over the railing in a hysterical fit of grief and horror as she calls up the traumatic experience.

Although Williams and Losey tightened up the screenplay to make it less talky, a great deal of the religious imagery which I detailed in discussing the play survives in the motion picture. The references to Calvary, to Christ walking on water, etc., are all in the movie, and culminate in the final scene. As Losey describes it:

"The death of Mrs. Goforth at the end of *Boom!* is technically one of the best things I've ever done. It's certainly one of the most difficult scenes I have ever directed. Few people have noticed that the whole thing is one extended shot. Flanders leaves her bedroom where she has sunk into her last slumber and walks out onto the terrace" where he drinks wine from a goblet; "he holds up one of her diamonds over the chalice-like cup, drops it into the cup, and casts the cup into the sea below. As far as the meaning of this action is concerned, one must remember that, while Williams is not an orthodox believer, he is a very religious man. He is aware that the human animal requires some kind of ritual for various important occasions such as birth, marriage, death. If he is denied these rituals, man simply cannot cope with these terrible and wonderful realities in human existence."

Building on Losey's remarks about this last scene in the film, may I say that for me Chris's ritual action of drinking from the goblet and then holding the diamond aloft over it, in the same way that the priest elevates the host at the Communion service of the Mass, is redolent of Chris's celebrating his having finally established communion with Flora before she died. Flora had for so long held herself incommunicado (communicating with others through tape recorders and intercoms) that it was something of a triumph of Chris to be able to bring her to a resigned acceptance of the death which she feared so passionately. Moreover, as Maurice Yacowar mentions in his monograph *Tennessee Williams and Film*, Chris throws Mrs. Goforth's diamond into the sea in order to maintain the purity of his mission: he has given her understanding and consolation at the end of her life and has received no material remuneration in return.

The last two shots of the film are a juxtaposition of an image of death (Flora's corpse lying across her bed) and an image of life (the waves once more crashing relentlessly against the rocks as Chris's voice is heard on the sound track for the last time uttering his incantation-like "Boom!"). Since the thundering sea has been established as symbolic of the shock of living from moment to moment, the final shot of the splashing waves suggests that life goes on, and in so doing triumphs over death. But one cannot be any more precise than that in analyzing the misty, not to say confused, religious symbolism that brings the film to a close.

As Losey predicted, Burton-Taylor fans were totally bewildered by the movie while more serious moviegoers who would have appreciated the thought-provoking ambiguities of the picture stayed away because they assumed that *Boom!* was merely another commercial vehicle for the Burtons. But the picture in actual fact is as much a Tennessee Williams film as it is a Burton or a Losey film. In one sense the movie belongs very much to the playwright, whose personal vision of man's struggle to endure unto death the challenges of existence Losey sought to interpret as he shaped the motion picture. "It has been said that some people didn't like *Boom!* because it dealt with death, a subject many of us don't like to confront," the director comments. "In fact, death is a recurring theme in Williams's work. He is one of the few major dramatists of this century and yet some of his work is being overlooked; and I think this is one of the reasons."

What was Williams's own reaction to the film? "Unfortunately the female star was too young and too beautiful for the role of Flora Goforth, and the male star was much too old and overweight by about twenty-five pounds. I am devastated to have to describe Elizabeth Taylor and Richard Burton in that way, but as far as I am concerned as a playwright, they brought on the heaviest of disasters. But of course Noel Coward figured in the cast; he is a man whose wit and charm are capable of conquering almost all obstacles. And I would like to render homage to the great Joseph Losey, who brought a lot of flair to *Boom!* by his incomparable sense of style."

Losey has always been a firm believer in film making as a collaborative venture and is as quick to acknowledge the contribution of a writer like Williams to the film as Williams is to acknowledge Losey's contribution as director. "Everyone must be free and encouraged to make his own contribution within the overall framework and control and discipline which obviously comes from the director," says Losey. "There are in general two kinds of writers who work on films as far as I am concerned. One is very personal and contributive, like Harold Pinter; the other is less so." Tennessee Williams belongs to the first category.

The film directors who have been associated with the movies of Williams's works represent a cross section of film makers that ranges from first class artists like Kazan, Brooks, Huston, and Losey, to more pedestrian directors, relatively speaking, like Daniel Mann and Irving Rapper. The influence of these various directors on the Williams films which they made is undeniable since, as Losey maintains, the overall artistic unity, control, and discipline of the movie-making process must be attributed to the director. Nonetheless, it is a tribute to Williams as the ultimate source of all of these motion pictures that all of them are interesting and worth watching, regardless of the relative merits of each film or film maker involved, because something of Williams's original content and intent perdures in every case.

"The people Williams writes about," says Robert Haller in his seminal article on the Williams films, "are almost invariably captive creatures in a moment of crisis, sweating under the hot sun and the silent night sky. Alone on the stage, their passions and will struggle for some kind of resolution in hope if not truth. How they find it, usually in terms of sex, violence, or madness, has made some of the most powerful theater in recent decades. Motion pictures have been enriched to an equal extent."

Television, too, has turned to Williams's work for material, and so it would be worthwhile to survey the TV productions of Williams's work in order to ascertain whether big screen or little screen has been more felicitous in presenting his stories for the mass audience. Let us take a brief look, then, at Tennessee Williams and the tube.

Epilogue
Tennessee Williams and the TV Tube

From the earliest days of television Tennessee Williams's work found its way to the home screen. In the Fifties a number of his shorter plays were televised, including *The Purification; I Rise in Flame, Cried the Phoenix; The Lady of Larkspur Lotion;* and *Hello from Bertha.* The date of April 19, 1958, however, was something of an occasion, since on that night the Kraft Television Theater showcased three of his one-acters on the same bill, *Moony's Kid Don't Cry, The Last of My Solid Gold Watches,* and *This Property is Condemned,* the last of which was dealt with in chapter three in connection with the feature film derived from it. The Sunday before the telecast *The New York Times* reported in an interview with the dramatist speculation along Madison Avenue as to whether the Williams trio of plays would provoke a storm of controversy similar to that which greeted the opening of *Baby Doll* a year or so earlier if they had not been severely expurgated.

Williams replied that he had trimmed the three short plays a bit in order to make them fit the show's one hour format, but that he had otherwise not been required to tamper with them in order to make them acceptable for prime time TV viewing. He also countered that he found the excessive violence on television much more inappropriate for family viewing than anything in his three playlets. "Sometimes when I watch a Western where everybody is shooting up everybody else, it seems to make human life pretty cheap." He thought that some of his previous works would be suitable for TV. "I think *The Glass Menagerie* or *Summer and Smoke* could be done on TV. They wouldn't offend anyone. I might write another play like them some day."

Several plays by Williams were to be adapted for television in the years ahead, but many of them are no longer available for even private viewing—and therefore for comment and analysis. So I shall confine myself to the relatively recent TV productions which continue to be accessible for viewing as re-runs on television and/or through the 16mm channels of distribution.

The Glass Menagerie was given a major TV production in 1973 and *Summer and Smoke* in its revised version as *Eccentricities of a Nightengale* received full-scale TV treatment in 1976, as did *Cat on a Hot Tin Roof* the same year. All three of these teleplays have been taken up in the preceding pages in connection with the theatrical films associated with the same Williams works. But I would like to survey briefly these made-for-TV movies here to forecast tentatively what future Williams's work might have on the little screen.

All of the three teleplays just mentioned indicate how the television format can be made to accomodate the format of a stage play more easily than can the format of a theatrical film. Because the budget of a telefilm is smaller than that of a commercial motion picture, TV producers forego the chance of opening out a play for TV to the degree often employed in a theatrical movie, in favor of staying close to the few settings dictated by the original play. Furthermore, TV viewers do not seem to mind more scenes of straight dialogue than would be tolerated by a cinema audience, presumably because television watchers are used to being talked at by newcasters and participants on programs which are unabashedly called talk shows! In addition, because of the commercial interruptions (which are usually inserted at natural breaks in the action between the original play's acts and scenes) the teleplay does not have to flow continuously in a straight line of sustained action from beginning to end as a motion picture does. These pauses make it possible to build momentum slowly in concentrated blocks of action, and to include within each unit long speeches and dialogue exchanges which might seem tedious in a theatrical movie, there the action unfolds without interruption.

Hence, as British movie critic John Russell Taylor contends, "The slow, intense build-up, the really concentrated, concentration-demanding scene" just might play better on the home screen than in a cinema. He points to his experience of watching the Katharine Hepburn *Glass Menagerie* with a living room full of people who were almost wordlessly enthralled for the entire two hours the teleplay ran; and *Glass Menagerie* is "a classic of the slow build, where atmosphere is all and any isolated few moments would make little or no sense." Although TV is often accused of ruining the watcher's attention span because of the commercial interruptions, it seems that a worthy TV production of a good Williams play like *Glass*, in which the intermissions are spaced at reasonable intervals and placed at suitable breaks in the action, can still capture and retain a TV viewer's attention. And this experience has been confirmed by the TV *Cat* and *Nightengale*.

Another reason why Williams's play can be televised with fewer alterations than has been the case in several of the motion pictures discussed in the previous chapters of this book is that, although movie censorship today is not as severe as TV censorship, current policies of TV censorship are not as strict as movie censorship and Hollywood taboos were in the days when many of the Williams films were made. Thus in the 1973 TV *Glass*, it is not necessary to provide a happy ending for the play in the guise of a viable Gentleman Caller for Laura as it was for the earlier theatrical film version because of the Hollywood prohibition against down-beat endings at the time when the 1950 film was made. Nor was it necessary to expunge all reference to Brick's latent homosexuality in the TV *Cat* as it was in the MGM film, a factor that caused writer-director Richard Brooks endless problems in clarifying by other explanations the motivation of Brick's behavior in the 1958 film.

When we talked in Cannes, Williams wistfully expressed his wish that many of the films of his work could be remade now that censorship is no longer the problem for a serious writer that it once was. "Some of those old films should be put in storage and replaced with more honest versions," he said. "The public is no longer upset by truth about the things that concern ordinary life. The artists in the cinema today are now liberated from the hypocrisy that once ruled in the marketplace." I suggested to him that this was for all practical purposes true of television today as well, and cited the TV version of *Cat* which was then in production in London as an example of what I meant. Perhaps television will continue, therefore, to give us more honest adaptations of Williams's plays than it was possible for Hollywood to do when the original motion pictures were produced.

Nevertheless, I do not think that all of the original films will necessarily be superceded by contemporary remakes as teleplays, or even as commercial films for that matter; and, again, the TV *Cat* is a case in point. Even granted the censorship problems with which Brooks had to contend in making the movie, the definitive casting of Elizabeth Taylor, Paul Newman, and Burl Ives in Richard Brooks's film is simply not matched by their counterparts in the television version, Natalie Wood, Robert Wagner, and even Lord Laurence Olivier. In short, the absence or presence of adjustments in the original play dictated by censorship cannot alone make or break a Williams movie. Each Williams film and teleplay must be judged on its total merits, and I for one feel that, while Anthony Harvey's 1973 TV *Glass* is vastly superior on every level to the original Irving Rapper film, such motion pictures as Brooks's *Cat*, Kazan's *Streetcar*, Mankiewicz's *Suddenly Last Summer*, and Huston's *Night of the Iguana* will remain pretty hard to beat by any possible future TV version of the same work, as long as these films continue to be revived theatrically and on the Late Show.

There is still the possibility of fresh material being mined for telefilms from Williams's work, moreover, including several one-act plays and short stories. One example of a Williams work done only on TV is the made-for-television movie *The Migrants*, based on a story outline by Williams, adapted for TV by playwright Lanford Wilson, and first telecast in February 1974. In 1971 Williams took to the late producer-director Tom Gries his conception of a story about migrant workers who annually follow the harvest trail from Florida to New England. After a year of developing the plot line in various ways, the pair enlisted Wilson, and together they worked out the tele-treatment. Wilson then wrote the teleplay which was shot on location along the East coast in the summer of 1973.

Gries, who directed theatrical films as well as telefilms, counted his experience of developing the script for *Migrants* with Williams as one of the most satisfying of his career, and thought it significant that in Williams and Wilson he was collaborating with writers who normally worked outside of the television medium. "It's hard to get good work from most television writers," he said to journalist Bruce Cook. "Most of them turn in a mess that you have to work over yourself. Why is it? Well, television has such a constant demand for material that most writers are trying to grab as many assignments as they can. They spread themselves too thin, do sloppy work, and the whole medium suffers."

The only real flaw in *The Migrants* is that most of Wilson's dialogue is far more matter-of-fact and pedestrian than one usually associates with a Williams venture. Some of the spare, laconic lines work, as when a little girl says of the family shack in a camp, "This place is terrible," and her weary mother replies, "That means the next place will be better." But some of the lean dialogue falls flat, as when the girl's older brother promises his mother, "I'm gonna buy you a house so big you're never gonna have to pick another bean." As Elia Kazan said in chapter two of this book, genuine Williams dialogue represents a stylized, poetic kind of realism which enriches his work without making it seem artificial. One must chide the playwright, then, for not collaborating on the dialogue of *The Migrants* as well as on the story, so that the telefilm would have benefitted from the flavor of his customary dialogue.

Yet the shadow of Tennessee Williams is apparent in the development of character and plot throughout the telefilm. Mrs. Barlow (Cloris Leachman) is another strong-willed Williams matriarch, but for once she inspires and encourages more than she dominates her family, holding them together through the inevitable disappointments and hardships that blight the lives of itinerant farm workers and through personal crises as well. The latter include the birth of her illegitimate grandchild, her son-in-law's death from tuberculosis, and the decision of her oldest son (Ron Howard) to get off the frustrating treadmill of migrant existence and elope with his girl to a big city and find a steady job. "Don't be lessen your dream," she says in splendid generosity, despite her pain in losing the sole member of her family on whom she could rely. "That's all I want from you."

Williams's inspiration is evident too in the bittersweet irony of the ending.

The boy knows the situation from which he is liberating himself; but is the situation in which he is becoming immeshed really going to be an improvement on the past? His unpromising future is foretold in the interchange between the lad and the girl who has encouraged him to make the break, just as they are embarking on their new life together. As he listens to her talk about "us" and searches her face, he is almost afraid to admit even to himself his suspicion that he is extricating himself from one net only to be snared in another. It is still not too late for him to turn back, but we sense that he will take his chances with his shrewish fiancée rather than turn back. "It is a hard moment to achieve on a small screen," *The New York Times* commented; "but Howard does so."

Besides Ron Howard's performance as a harried son, Cloris Leachman's Mrs. Barlow represents the best acting of her career so far. That she is willing to appear as haggard and unlovely as the role requires is an index of the authenticity with which invests the part. Tom Gries directed the telefilm with an uncompromising naturalism that allowed the wretched lives of the farm workers to speak for themselves. *The Migrants* proved that the little screen could be as felicitous to Williams as the big screen, and one looks forward to further TV adaptations of his work, just as one hopes that Hollywood will continue to turn to him for material. Williams's plays continue to be more adaptable to the visual media than the work of many other playwrights because, as I emphasized in the prologue, they have melodramatic plots and highly emotional central characters which together engage the viewer's attention and generally hold on to it. At the same time, the episodic nature of his plots make it easy to adjust them to the needs of the big or little screens.

Now that both the TV and motion picture media are free enough from unreasonable censorship demands to present his works with something approaching the artistic integrity with which he has written them, Williams does not fear that the frankness of his stories will shock contemporary viewers. Quite the contrary. He recently remarked that both critics and audiences focused on the sexual aspect of some of his plays when they were first produced and missed all the more serious artistic elements which were also there. But from the vantage point of the Seventies, in which some novelists and playwrights have exhibited what drama critic Dan Sullivan calls "dirtier pictures than Tennessee Williams ever drew or would ever care to draw," it is now obvious that Williams was never a raunchy writer. "This playwright's basic interest has always been the human race's funny, sad attempts to signal to one another over the barricades—sex being one of them, but only one," Sullivan continues. "Modern audiences aren't uptight around these plays any more, meaning that now we can hear what they have been saying all the time." Williams has earned the right to smile just a bit when he finds works of his like *Streetcar* or *Cat* that were once thought to be decadent achieving in his own lifetime the status of classics. In his own words:

"I think some works of mine, like *Sweet Bird of Youth*, are now seen more for other values than the sensational. People today are more accustomed to scenes of sex and violence. They can see a play like *Sweet Bird* much more objectively. *Cat on a Hot Tin Roof* is another example of that; the subject of Brick's sexual confusion is no longer the sensation it once was, so that the real theme of the play—the general mendacity of our society—is seen more clearly."

Homosexuality is, of course, one of the once taboo subjects which the Williams films have helped to make "respectable" topics for screen treatment. And they have prepared the way, perhaps, for the filming of some of his short stories which represent more direct attempts to penetrate the homosexual mind and milieu, presenting the homosexual in his own environment and not just as a misfit in the heterosexual world. Williams mentions in his *Memoirs* his story "Two on a Party" as one which he would particularly like to see committed to film, and he would like to have the independent film maker Paul Morrissey make the movie. Morrissey would be a good choice since he has made the best feature-length American underground films to deal with homosexuality so far, *Flesh* (1968) and *Trash* (1970), which give an insight into the life of a male hustler and his customers unmatched by any other films of this kind.

Edward A. Sklepowich, in his article on the image of the homosexual in Williams's fiction in *Tennessee Williams: A Tribute*, agrees that Morrissey would be a good choice to direct a motion picture of "Two on a Party": "Certainly Morrissey's wasteland vision would find appropriate material in this story of the unusual *ménage à deux* between Billy, a thirty-five year old queen and male hustler, and the somewhat older prostitute Cora. Both blasted by life, yet sensitive to its promises and beauties, they begin to pal around together, encouraging and sustaining each other." Serious Williams films which present homosexuality not as a curiosity but as a part of the human condition can have the universal value of demonstrating as his stories have that homosexuals are sád and mixed up—like everyone else.

Williams says that the renewed interest in his work, with major new productions of his plays in the theater and on TV as well as continued revivals of his films, makes him feel as if he has been resurrected and come back to life: "Oh God, I guess it shows that if you live long enough, you're either totally forgotten or you're in the revival business." And more, an artist whose best work has survived in the way that Williams's has is also in line for prestigious recognition. When the 1976 edition of *Iguana* opened on Broadway, *Time* called for the inscrutable Stockholm judges at long last to make Tennessee Williams the second American playwright (after Eugene O'Neill) to win the Nobel Prize for Literature.

"It does not matter that every play is not his best," says stage director Herbert Machiz. "He is one of the rare playwrights in America who has written original works steadily for more than twenty-five years. What artist can perpetually turn out masterpieces? Any writer should have the right to experiment, to make

Tennessee Williams and stage director Herbert Machiz in a recent photograph.

mistakes. Tennessee Williams is American, a Southerner; and his world, his theater is his own. He is a genius who must never stop writing. I admire him for surviving the way he has." One can only add that if he never wrote another line, Williams has already incalcuably enriched American literature, as well as the motion picture and television media.

Taken as a whole, the films of Tennessee Williams's works, despite their admitted flaws, are as much a monument to him as are the original stories on which they are based. As I have said more than once in the preceding pages, no matter what the shortcomings of a given Williams film (or of the Williams work on which it is based), some trace of the Williams genius manages to shine through. No fairer verdict on the cinema of Tennessee Williams has ever been rendered than that of Foster Hirsch: "Adult, decorative, distinctive, acted and directed with occasional inspiration and unflagging energy, the Tennessee Williams films offer some of Hollywood's proudest moments. Faithful to the playwright's original concepts, the films have been designed to preserve the twists and kinks, the spectacular and fabled neuroses, of the Williams personality."

It is the Williams personality and personal vision which permeate these motion pictures just as they saturate the original sources on which the films are based. That vision reflects the author's abiding concern for the lack of communication between individuals, and the attendant emptiness of many people's lives, especially—but not exclusively—of the misfits and outsiders of this world. "The most magnificent thing in human nature is valor and endurance," he has said, and this endurance in turn is predicated in some measure on the understanding and tenderness which one receives from others. The tragic life experiences of many of his characters are rooted in their failure to receive the understanding and tenderness which they craved and needed to survive.

I emphasize the contribution of the creative writer to the films adapted from his works without prejudice to the contribution of the film director of a given movie since, as I have indicated all along the way, a film director's function is to so guide a production that the artistic unity and spirit of the script which he is directing will be preserved on the screen. Richard Brooks has described the relationship of the director to the source work which he is putting on film as well as any director ever has: "I think that directing is an extension of writing, except you're writing with film. . . . You have nothing to direct until you have a story, and you begin to take the story and put it on film. What you're doing is writing with film. With me the camera is in one specific place because that is what the story calls for at this point in the action; and it is always the story that matters. Just the same with editing. All of the factors are determined by the story."

Regardless of the number of works of fiction and drama which he has already penned and the resulting corpus of films which have been adapted from them, Williams continues to write, and may thereby provide yet further opportunities for film makers to bring his work to the movies, and to TV too. At sixty-six, an age when many creative artists would decide to retire to a life of ease, Williams produced yet another new play on Broadway in the spring of 1977, *Vieux Carre*. In it he returns to the French Quarter of the late Thirties, where he lived as a young writer in a shabby boarding house peopled with even shabbier tenants, as

I pointed out in sketching Williams early life in chapter one. "In my new play there is a boy who is living in a house that I lived in," says Williams, "and undergoing some of the experiences that I underwent as a young writer." The house, at 722 Toulouse Street, still stands today, "but it's vacant now. Just as the boy says at the end of the play: 'The house is empty now. . . . They're disappearing—going. . . .' "

Vieux Carre marks a return for Williams not only to the New Orleans which he once knew, but also to the kind of naturalistic style of playwriting that characterized his work up to and including *Night of the Iguana*. In addition, the episodic nature of *Vieux Carre* allows the author to summon up characters reminiscent of figures recognizable from earlier Williams plays. Among the residents of the rooming house in which the play is set is a stud who recalls Chance Wayne with a mistress who reminds one of Blanche DuBois. "Sightseers outside the house are visitors from *Night of the Iguana*," comments Martin Gottfried in *The New York Post*. "The young writer is Tom from *The Glass Menagerie*, even to the point of . . . speaking to the audience much as if this, too, were a memory play." And of course the landlady herself is the typical domineering Williams mother figure.

It is Gottfried, too, who has perhaps best summed up the significance of this recent Williams play in the context of his work as a whole. "Poetic naturalism is in Williams's blood. . . . His experiments in a presumably modern mode have occupied many years of his creative life. If he is now returning to what seems his natural dramatic language, *Vieux Carre* is but a beginning. Williams has always been frightfully honest, speaking from the heart with the unmistakable voice of an artist. We are lucky indeed to have so magnificent a poet in our midst."

Vieux Carre was indeed a new beginning for Williams, judging by the fact that he has premiered two additional plays in 1978, though not on Broadway. In January *Tiger Tail* was well received at its opening at the Alliance Theater in Atlanta. This play is in fact a stage adaptation of his screenplay for *Baby Doll*, which in turn was based on two of his one-act plays, as detailed in chapter two; so *Baby Doll* has come full circle. *Creve Coeur* had its premiere at the Spoleto USA arts festival in Charleston, South Carolina, in June. It had started out as a one-act play but eventually developed into a full-length work (re-titled *A Lovely Sunday for Creve Coeur*). The play has four female characters, the most central of which is Dorothea, a school teacher whose love for the calloused headmaster remains unrequited. But like many a Williams heroine, she refuses to despair and utters in the end a remark that permeates Williams's work: "We must go on. Just go on."

And so Williams too goes on. At the conclusion of his discussion with myself and some other journalists in Cannes, Williams explained why he continues to write even though he realizes that the lonely life of a writer does not get any less arduous as one grows older. "I have a lot more to say as a writer, and I wish I were just beginning my career. But that kind of thing is not in my power. I have always tried to tell the truth as I see it in my work and I shall continue to do so." Another reason that Williams has no immediate plans for retirement is that he has never been completely satisfied with anything that he has ever written because "everything I have done has fallen short of what I set out to do; and so I must keep trying. I once said to someone that I think I'm a minor artist who has somehow managed to create two or three major works. I'm not sure which they are."

I would prefer to say that Tennessee Williams is a major writer who happens to have written some minor works, and that there is no doubt whatever which of his plays are his major ones: *The Glass Menagerie, A Streetcar Named Desire, Cat on a Hot Tin Roof, Suddenly, Last Summer,* and *The Night of the Iguana,* to name only the very best, will last as long as plays are read and produced, and as long as somewhere there is a movie projector on which to run their respective film versions. This is no mean achievement for a man who has been plagued throughout his life with ill health, both physical and mental, and other personal crises that together would have crippled the creativity of a less enduring personality. Williams ends his memoirs with the thought that a "high station in life is earned by the gallantry with which appalling experiences are survived with grace."

Tennessee Williams has, by his own criterion, won a station in life that is very high indeed.

Selected Bibliography

Primary Sources: The Works of Tennessee Williams

Books

American Blues: Five Short Plays. New York: Dramatists Play Service, 1968.

Baby Doll: A Screenplay. New York: New Directions, 1956.

Dragon Country: A Book of Plays. New York: New Directions, 1970.

Hard Candy: A Book of Stories. New York: New Directions, 1967.

The Knightly Quest: A Novella and Four Short Stories. New York: New Directions, 1966.

Memoirs. New York: Doubleday, 1975.

Moise and the World of Reason: A Novel. New York: Simon and Schuster, 1975.

One Arm and Other Stories. New York: New Directions, 1967.

The Roman Spring of Mrs. Stone: A Novel. New York: New Directions, 1950.

Tennessee Williams's Letters to Donald Windham: 1940–65. Edited by Donald Windham. New York: Holt, Rinehart and Winston, 1977.

The Theater of Tennessee Williams. New York: New Directions, 1971-76.
> Volume I: *Battle of Angels* (1940), *The Glass Menagerie* (1945), and *A Streetcar Named Desire* (1947).
>
> Volume II: *The Eccentricities of a Nightengale* (1948), *Summer and Smoke* (1948), *The Rose Tattoo* (1951), and *Camino Real* (1953).
>
> Volume III: *Cat on a Hot Tin Roof* (1955), *Orpheus Descending* (1957), and *Suddenly Last Summer* (1958).
>
> Volume IV: *Sweet Bird of Youth* (1959), *Period of Adjustment* (1960), and *The Night of the Iguana* (1961).
>
> Volume V: *The Milk Train Doesn't Stop Here Anymore* (1964), *Kingdom of Earth* (*The Seven Descents of Myrtle*, 1968), *Small Craft Warnings* (1972), and *The Two-Character* (*Out Cry*, 1975).

Twenty-Seven Wagons Full of Cotton and Other Plays. New York: New Directions, 1966.

Where I Live: Selected Essays. Edited by Christine R. Day and Bob Woods. New York: New Directions, 1978.

Articles

"The Catastrophe of Success." *New York Times*, 30 November, 1947.

"Five Fiery Ladies." *Life*, 3 February 1961, pp. 84-88.

"Foreward to *Camino Real*." *New York Times*, 15 March 1953.

"Foreward to *Sweet Bird of Youth*." *New York Times*, 8 March 1959.

"I Have Written a Play for Artistic Purity." *New York Times*, 21 November, 1976.

"Introduction" to Carson McCullers, *Reflections in a Golden Eye*. New York: New Directions, 1950.

"Le Cinéma et Moi." *Figaro*, 14 May 1976.

"Let Me Hang It All Out." *New York Times*, 4 March 1973.

"The Past, Present, and Perhaps." *New York Times*, 17 March 1957.

"Prelude to a Comedy." *New York Times*, 6 November 1960.

"Questions Without Answers." *New York Times*, 3 October 1948.

"Tennessee Williams Presents His Point of View." *New York Times Magazine*, 12 June, 1960, pp. 19, 78.

"Tennessee Williams's view of Tallulah Bankhead." *New York Times*, 29 December 1963.

"The Timeless World of a Play." *New York Times*, 14 January 1951.

"Williams Reflects." *New York Times*, 8 May 1977.

"The World I Live In." *Observer* (London), 7 April 1957.

Interviews

"Angel of the Odd." *Time*, 9 March 1962, pp. 53-60.

Barnes, Clive. "Tennessee Williams." *American Way*, May 1975, pp. 21-25.

Barnett, Lincoln. "Tennessee Williams." *Life*, 16 February 1948, pp. 113-27.

Berkvist, Robert. "Broadway Discovers Tennessee Williams." *New York Times*, 21 December 1975.

Buckley, Tom. "Tennessee Williams." *Atlantic Monthly*, November, 1970, pp. 98-108.

Burroughs, William S. "Talk with Tennessee Williams." *Village Voice*, 16 May 1977.

Clarity, James F. "Williams Finds Cannes Festival a Crass Menagerie." *New York Times*, 24 May 1976.

Gaines, Jim. "A Talk About Life and Style with Tennessee Williams." *Saturday Review*, 29 April 1972, pp. 25-29.

Gelb, Arthur. "Tennessee Williams." *New York Times*, 8 December 1959.

———— "Williams and Kazan." *New York Times*, 1 May 1960.

Gussow, Mel. "Tennessee Williams on Art and Sex." *New York Times*, 3 November 1975.

Jennings, C. Robert. "Tennessee Williams." *Playboy*, April 1973.

Newlove, Donald. "A Dream of Tennessee Williams." *Esquire*, November 1969, pp. 64-80, 173-78.

O'Grady, Desmond. "Tennessee Williams and the General of the Jesuits," *Profile*, (Dublin), IV (January 1973), 38-50.

Rice, Robert. "A Man Named Tennessee." *New York Post,* 21-25 April, 27 April-4 May, 1958.

Ross, Don. "Williams on Art and Morals." *New York Herald Tribune,* 3 March 1957.

Shanley, John P. "Tennessee Williams on Television." *New York Times,* 13 April 1958.

Taylor, Robert. "Williams: A Playwright Named Desire." *Los Angeles Times,* 14 December 1975.

"Tennessee Williams," *Newsweek.* 1 April 1957.

Wager, Walter. "Tennessee Williams." In *The Playwrights Speak,* edited by Walter Wager, pp. 213-37. New York: Delacorte, 1967.

Secondary Sources

General Works

Barr, Charles. "Cinemascope: Before and After." In *Film: A Montage of Theories,* edited by Richard Dyer MacCann, pp. 318-28. New York: Dutton, 1966.

Bluestone, George. *Novels into Film.* Berkeley: University of California Press, 1961.

Brandt, George. "Cinematic Structure in the Work of Tennessee Williams." In *American Theater,* edited by John Russell Brown and Bernard Harris, pp. 163-87. Stratford-Upon-Avon Studies, vol. X. New York: St. Martin's Press, 1967.

Donahue, Francis. *The Dramatic World of Tennessee Williams.* New York: Ungar, 1964.

Falk, Signi. *Tennessee Williams.* 2nd ed. Boston: Twayne, 1978.

Fulton, A.R. *Motion Pictures: The Development of an Art from Silent Films to the Age of Television.* Norman: University of Oklahoma Press, 1970.

Gow, Gordon. *Hollywood in the Fifties.* New York: Barnes, 1971.

Greene, Graham. "Preface" to *Three Plays.* London: Mercury Books, 1961.

Hirsch, Foster. *Elizabeth Taylor.* New York: Pyramid Books, 1973.

———. "Tennessee Williams." *Cinema,* VIII (Spring 1973), pp. 2-8.

Hurt, James, ed. *Focus on Film and Theater.* Englewood Cliffs, N.J.: Prentice-Hall, 1974.

Jackson, Esther Merle. *The Broken World of Tennessee Williams.* Madison: University of Wisconsin Press, 1961.

Jordan, Rene. *Marlon Brando.* New York: Pyramid Books, 1973.

Kael, Pauline. *Going Steady.* New York: Bantam Books, 1971.

Kunkel, Francis. "Tennessee Williams and the Death of God." *Commonweal,* 23 February 1968, pp. 614-18.

Manvell, Roger. *New Cinema in the USA.* New York: Dutton, 1968.

Maxwell, Gilbert. *Tennessee Williams and His Friends.* New York: World, 1965.

Murray, Edward. *The Cinematic Imagination: Writers and the Motion Pictures.* New York: Ungar, 1972.

Nelson, Benjamin. *Tennessee Williams: The Man and His Work*. New York: Obolensky, 1961.

Nicoll, Allardyce. *Film and Theater*. New York: Crowell, 1936.

Reêd, Rex. *People are Crazy Here*. New York: Dell, 1974.

Schumach, Murray. *The Face on the Cutting Room Floor*. William Morrow, 1964.

Stanton, Stephen, ed. *Tennessee Williams: A Collection of Critical Essays*. Englewood Cliffs, N.J.: Prentice-Hall, 1977.

Steen, Mike. *A Look at Tennessee Williams*. New York: Hawthorn, 1969.

Tharpe, Jac, ed. *Tennessee Williams: A Tribute*. Jackson: University of Mississippi Press, 1977.

Thomas, Bob. *Marlon*. New York: Ballantine, 1975.

Tischler, Nancy M. *Tennessee Williams*. Austin: Steck-Vaughn, 1969.

―――. *Tennessee Williams: Rebellious Puritan*. New York: Citadel, 1965.

Von Sternberg, Josef. *Fun in a Chinese Laundry: An Autobiography*. New York: Collier Books, 1965.

Weales, Gerald. *Tennessee Williams*. Minneapolis: University of Minnesota Press, 1965.

Whitehall, Richard. "Poet―But Do We Know It?" *Films and Filming*, VI (August 1960), 8, 32.

Williams, Dakin. "Is Tennessee Williams a 'Catholic' Playwright?" *Information*, April 1960, pp. 2-7.

Williams, Edwina Dakin. *Remember Me to Tom*. New York: Putnam's, 1963.

Yacowar, Maurice. *Tennessee Williams and Film*. New York: Frederick Ungar, 1977.

Chapter 1: The Glass Menagerie

Brady, Thomas F. *"The Glass Menagerie* on Film." *New York Times*, 22 January 1950.

Higham, Charles. "Katharine Hepburn." *New York Times*, 9 December 1973.

MacMullan, Hugh. "Translating *The Glass Menagerie* to Film." *Hollywood Quarterly*, V (Fall 1950), 14-32.

Chapter 2: A Streetcar Named Desire *and* Baby Doll

Ciment, Michel. *Kazan on Kazan*. New York: Viking, 1974.

Esterow, Milton. *"Baby Doll* in Dixie and Flatbush." *New York Times*, 26 February 1956.

Hewes, Henry. "The Boundaries of Tennessee." *Saturday Review*, 29 December 1956, pp. 23-24.

Kantor, Bernard R., Irwin R. Blacker, and Anne Kramer. "Elia Kazan." In *Directors at Work*, pp. 149-73. New York: Funk and Wagnalls, 1970.

Kazan, Elia. "The Director's Notebook: *A Streetcar Named Desire*." In *Drama on Stage*, edited by Randolph Goodman, pp. 295-304. New York: Holt, 1961.

――― "A Streetcar Named Desire." *New York Times*, 21 October 1951.

Kerr, Walter. "Melodrama Isn't Always a Dirty Word." *New York Times*, 8 February 1976.

Knight, Arthur. "The Williams-Kazan Axis." *Saturday Review*, 29 December 1956, pp. 22-23.

Leigh, Vivien. "Blanche DuBois on Stage and Screen." In *Drama on Stage*, edited by Randolph Goodman, pp. 307-11. New York: Holt, 1961.

Miller, Jordan Y., ed. *A Streetcar Named Desire: A Collection of Critical Essays*. Englewood Cliffs, N.J.: Prentice-Hall, 1971.

Vidal, Gore. *Two Sisters: A Memoir in the Form of a Novel*. Boston: Little, Brown, 1970.

Vizzard, Jack. *See No Evil: Life Inside a Hollywood Censor*. New York: Pocket Books, 1971.

Wesleyan University Film Program. *Working with Kazan*. Middletown, Conn.: Wesleyan University, 1973.

Williams, Tennessee. *A Streetcar Named Desire*. In *Film Scripts One*, edited by George P. Garrett, O.B. Hardison, Jr., and Jane Gelfman, pp. 330-484. New York: Appelton-Century-Crofts, 1971.

Chapter 3: The Rose Tattoo *and* This Property is Condemned.

Brown, John Mason. *"Rose Tattoo." Saturday Review*, 10 March 1951, p. 23.

Erens, Patricia. "Sydney Pollack." *Film Comment*, XI (September-October 1975), 24-29.

Reed, Donald A. *Robert Redford*. New York: Popular Library, 1975.

Reed, Rex. "Tennessee Williams Took His Name Off It." In *Conversations in the Raw*, pp. 235-40. New York: World, 1969.

Sarris, Andrew. *Confessions of a Cultist: On the Cinema, 1955-69*. New York: Simon and Schuster, 1971.

Chapter 4: Cat on a Hot Tin Roof *and* Sweet Bird of Youth

Kantor, Bernard R., Irwin R. Blacker, and Anne Kramer. "Richard Brooks." In *Directors at Work*, pp. 3-58. New York: Funk and Wagnalls, 1970.

Kerbel, Michael. *Paul Newman*. New York: Pyramid, 1974.

Kerr, Walter. *"Cat* Revival." *New York Times*, 6 October 1974.

Novick, Julius. "A Vivid But Not-So-Hot *Cat*." *New York Times*, 28 July 1974.

Quirk, Lawrence J. *The Films of Paul Newman*. Secaucus, N.J.: Citadel, 1974.

Chapter 5: Suddenly Last Summer

Dick, Bernard F. *The Apostate Angel*. New York: Random House, 1974.

Higham, Charles. *Kate: The Life of Katharine Hepburn*. New York: Norton, 1975.

Tyler, Parker. *Screening the Sexes: Homosexuality in the Movies*. Garden City, N.Y.: Anchor, 1973.

Weinberg, Herman G. *Saint Cinema: Writings on the Film, 1929-70*. New York: Dover, 1973.

Chapter 6: The Fugitive Kind *and* The Last of the Mobile Hotshots

Flatley, Guy. "The Kid Actor Who Became a Director." *New York Times*, 20 January 1974.

Nason, Richard. *"Fugitive* is Shot." *New York Times*, 5 July 1959.

Reed, Rex. "Flint, Meet Georgy Girl." *New York Times*, 8 June 1969.

Roberts, Meade. "Williams and Me." *Films and Filming*, August 1960, pp. 7, 35.

Chapter 7: Summer and Smoke (Eccentricities of a Nightengale)

Kael, Pauline. *I Lost It at the Movies*. New York: Bantam, 1966.
Kerr, Walter. "Where There's *Smoke*, There's Fire and Ice." *New York Times*, 19 October 1975.

Leonard, John. "TV: Drama by Williams." *New York Times*, 16 June 1976.

Schumach, Murray. *"Summer and Smoke."* 29 January 1961.

Chapter 8: The Roman Spring of Mrs. Stone *and* Period of Adjustment

Dyer, Richard, ed. *Gays and Film*. London: British Film Institute, 1977.
Fischer, Edward. *Film as Insight*. Notre Dame: Fides, 1971.

Quintero, José. *If You Don't Dance They Beat You*. Boston: Little, Brown, 1974.

Chapter 9: Night of the Iguana *and* Boom!

Davis, Bette. *The Lonely Life*. New York: Putnam's, 1962.

Kaminsky, Stuart. *John Huston*. New York: Houghton, Mifflin, 1978.

Kanin, Garson. *Tracy and Hepburn*. New York: Bantam, 1972.

Kerr, Deborah. "The Days and Nights of the Iguana." *Esquire*, LXI (May 1964), 128-43.

Reck, Tom. "Huston Meets the Eye." *Film Comment*, IX (May 1973), 6-11.

Tozzi, Romano. *John Huston*. New York: Falcon Enterprises, 1971.

Trevelyan, John. *What the Censor Saw*. London: Michael Joseph, 1973.

Epilogue

Cook, Bruce. "Can Filmmakers Find Happiness on TV?" *American Film Institute Report*, V (Spring 1974), 38-46.

Cyclops. "The World of the Joads is Still with Us." *New York Times*, 3 February 1974.

O'Connor, John J. "TV: *Migrants*." *New York Times*, 1 February 1974.

Unpublished Material

Asral, Ertem. *Tennessee Williams on Stage and Screen*. Unpublished Dissertation. Philadelphia: University of Pennsylvania, 1961.

Flaherty, S. J., Kevin H. "A Psychological Study of Blanche DuBois." Unpublished Paper. Chicago: Loyola University, 1976.

Frost, Frank. *The Films of Richard Brooks*. Unpublished Dissertation. Los Angeles: University of Southern California, 1976.

Warren, Clifton L. *Tennessee Williams as a Cinematic Writer*. Unpublished Dissertation. Bloomington: Indiana University, 1963.

FILMOGRAPHY

The Glass Menagerie (1950). *Director:* Irving Rapper; *Screenplay:* adapted for screen by Tennessee Williams and Peter Berneis from the play by Tennessee Williams; *Producer:* Jerry Wald and Charles K. Feldman; *Photography:* Robert Burks; *Music:* Max Steiner; *Art Director:* Robert Haas; *Editor:* David Weisbart. Warner Brothers. 107 minutes. *Cast:* Jane Wyman (Laura), Kirk Douglas (Jim), Gertrude Lawrence (Amanda), Arthur Kennedy (Tom), Ralph Sanford (Mendoza), Ann Tyrrell (Clerk), John Compton (Young Man), Gertrude Graner (Woman Instructor), Sara Edwards (Mrs. Miller), Louise Lorrimer (Miss Porter), Cris Alcaide (Eddie), Perdita Chandler (A Girl).

A Streetcar Named Desire (1951). *Director:* Elia Kazan; *Screenplay:* Tennessee Williams, from the play by Tennessee Williams, adapted by Oscar Saul; *Producer:* Charles K. Feldman; *Photography:* Harry Stradling; *Musical Director:* Ray Heindorf; *Art Director:* Richard Day; *Editor:* David Weisbart. Warner Brothers. 125 minutes. *Cast:* Vivian Leigh (Blanche), Marlon Brando (Stanley), Kim Hunter (Stella), Karl Malden (Mitch), Rudy Bond (Steve), Nick Dennis (Pablo), Peg Hillias (Eunice), Wright King (A Collector), Richard Garrick (A Doctor), Anne Dere (The Matron), Edna Thomas (The Mexican Woman).

The Rose Tattoo (1955). *Director:* Daniel Mann; *Screenplay:* Tennessee Williams, based on his play, adapted by Hal Kanter; *Photography:* James Wong Howe; *Musical Director:* Alex North; *Art Directors:* Hal Pereira, Tambia Larsen; *Editor:* Warren Low, in Vista Vision. Paramount. 117 minutes. *Cast:* Anna Magnani (Serafina Della Rosa), Burt Lancaster (Alvaro Mangiacavallo), Marisa Pavan (Rosa Della Rose), Ben Cooper (Jack Hunter), Virginia Grey (Estelle Hohengarten), Jo Van Fleet (Bessie), Sandro Giglio (Father De Leo), Mimi Aguglia (Assunta), Florence Sundstrom (Flora), Dorrit Kelton (School Teacher), Rossana San Marco (Peppina), Augusta Merighi (Guiseppina), Rosa Rey (Mariella), Zolya Talma (Miss Mangiacavallo), George Humbert (Pop Mangiacavallo), Margherita Pasquero (Gram Mangiacavallo), May Lee (Mamma Shigura-Tatoo Artist), Lewis Charles (Taxi Driver).

Baby Doll (1956). *Director/Producer:* Elia Kazan; *Screenplay and story:* Tennessee Williams (From his "Twenty-seven Wagons Full of Cotton"): *Photography:* Boris Kaufman; *Music:* Kenyon Hopkins; *Art Director:* Richard Sylbert; *Assistant Director:* Charles H. Maguire; *Editor:* Gene Milford. A Newtown Production. Warner Brothers. 114 minutes. *Cast:* Karl Malden (Archie), Carroll Baker (Baby Doll), Eli Wallach (Silva Vacarro), Mildred Dunnock (Aunt Rose Comfort), Lonny Chapman (Rock), Eades Hogue (Town Marshall), Noah Williamson (Deputy), and some people of Benoit, Mississippi.

Cat On A Hot Tin Roof (1958). *Director:* Richard Brooks; *Screenplay:* Richard Brooks and James Poe, based on the play by Tennessee Williams. *Photography:* William Daniels; *Art Directors:* William A. Horning and Urie McCleary; *Assistant Director:* William Shanks; *Editor:* Ferris Webster. An Avon Production in Metrocolor. MGM. 108 minutes. *Cast:* Elizabeth Taylor (Maggie), Paul Newman (Brick), Burl Ives (Big Daddy), Jack Carson (Gooper), Judith Anderson (Big Mama), Madeleine Sherwood (Mae), Larry Gates (Dr. Bough), Vaughn Taylor (Deacon David).

Suddenly Last Summer (1959). *Director:* Joseph L. Mankiewicz; *Screenplay:* Tennessee Williams and Gore Vidal, adapted from the play by Tennessee Williams; *Producer:* Sam Spiegel; *Photography:* Jack Hildyard; *Musical Director:* Buxton Orr; *Music Composed by:* Buxton Orr and Malcolm Arnold; *Art Director:* William Kellner; *Photographic effects:* Tom Howard; *Editor:* Thomas G. Stanford. Columbia Pictures. 114 minutes. *Cast:* Elizabeth Taylor (Catherine Holly), Katharine Hepburn (Mrs. Venable), Montgomery Clift (Dr. Cukrowicz), Albert Dekker (Dr. Hockstader), Mercedes McCambridge (Mrs. Holly), Gary Raymond (George Holly), Mavis Villiers (Miss Foxhill), Patricia Marmont (Nurse Benson), Joan Young (Sister Felicity), Maria Britneva (Lucy), Sheilia Roberts (Dr. Hockstader's Secretary), David Cameron (Intern).

The Fugitive Kind (1960). *Director:* Sidney Lumet; *Screenplay:* Tennessee Williams and Meade Roberts, based on the play "Orpheus Descending," by Tennessee Williams; *Producer:* Martin Jurow and Richard A. Shepherd; *Assistant Producer:* George Justin; *Music:* Kenyon Hopkins; *Assistant Director:* Charles H. Maguire. A Jurow-Shepherd-Pennebaker Production. United Artists. 135 minutes. *Cast:* Marlon Brando (Val Xavier), Anna Magnani (Lady Torrance), Joanne Woodward (Carol Cutrere), Maureen Stapleton (Vee Talbott), Victor Jory (Jabe Torrance), R. G. Armstrong (Sheriff Talbott), Emory Richardson (Uncle Pleasant), Sally Gracie (Dolly Hamma), Joe Brown, Jr. (Pee Wee Binnings), Virginia Chew (Nurse Porter), Frank Borgman (Gas Station Attendant), Janice Mars (Attendant's Wife), Debbie Lynch (Lonely Girl).

Summer And Smoke (1961). *Director:* Peter Glenville; *Screenplay:* James Poe and Meade Roberts, from the play by Tennessee Williams; *Producer:* Hal Wallis; *Photography:* Charles Lang, Jr.; *Music:* Elmer Bernstein; *Art Director:* Walter Tyler; *Editor:* Warren Low. Panavision and Technicolor. Paramount. 118 minutes. *Cast:* Laurence Harvey (John Buchanan), Geraldine Page (Alma Winemiller), Rita Moreno (Rosa Zacharias), Una Merkel (Mrs. Winemiller), John McIntire (Dr. Buchanan), Malcolm Atterbury (Rev. Winemiller), Pamela Tiffen (Nellie Ewell), Casey Adams (Robert Doremus), Thomas Gomez (Zacharias), Earl Holliman (Traveling Salesman), Lee Patrick (Mrs. Ewell).

The Roman Spring of Mrs. Stone (1961). *Director:* José Quintero; *Screenplay:* Gavin Lambert, from the novel by Tennessee Williams; *Producer:* Louis de Rochemont; *Photography:* Harry Waxman. *Music composed by:* Richard Addinsell; *Music conducted by:* Douglas Gamley; *Art Director:* Herbert Smith; *Associate Producer:* Lothar Wolff; *Editor:* Ralph Kemplen. A Seven Arts Presentation in Technicolor. Warner Brothers. 104 minutes. *Cast:* Vivien Leigh (Karen Stone), Warren Beatty (Paolo), Coral Browne (Meg), Jill St. John (Barbara), Jeremy Spenser (Young Man), Stella Bonheur (Mrs. Jamison Walker), Josephine Brown (Lucia), Peter Dyneley (L. Greener), Carl Jaffee (Baron), Harold Kasket (Tailor), Viola Keats (Julia), Cleo Laine (Singer), Bessie Love (Bunny), Elspeth March (Mrs. Barrow), Henry McCarthy (Kennedy), Warren Mitchell (Giorgio), John Phillips (Tom Stone), Paul Stassino (The Barber), Ernest Thesiger (Stefano), Mavis Villiers (Mrs. Coogan), Thelma D'Aguir (Mita), Lotte Lenya (Contessa).

Sweet Bird of Youth (1962). *Director:* Richard Brooks; *Screenplay:* Richard Brooks, from the play by Tennessee Williams; *Producer:* Pandro S. Berman; *Photography:* Milton Krasner; *Music conducted by:* Robert Ambruster; *Music supervised by:* Harold Gerlman; *Art Directors:* George W. David and Urie McCleary; *Associate Producer:* Kathryn Hereford; *Editor:* Henry Berman. CinemaScope and Metrocolor. MGM. 120 minutes. *Cast:* Paul Newman (Chance Wayne), Geraldine Page (Alexandra Del Lago), Shirley Knight (Heavenly Finley), Ed Begley (Boss Finley), Rip Torn (Thomas J. Finley, Jr.), Mildred Dunnock (Aunt Nonnie), Madeleine Sherwood (Miss Lucy), Philip Abbott (Dr. George Scudder), Corey Allen (Scotty), Barney Cahill (Bud), Dub Taylor (Dan Hatcher), James Douglas (Leroy), Barry Atwater (Ben Jackson), Charles Arnt (Mayor Hendricks), Dorothy Konrad (Mrs. Maribelle Norris), James Chandler (Prof. Burtus Smith), Mike Steen (Deputy), Kelly Thordsen (Sheriff Clark).

Period of Adjustment (1962). *Director:* George Roy Hill; *Screenplay:* Isobel Lennart, from the play by Tennessee Williams; *Producer:* Lawrence Weingarten; *Photography:* Paul C. Vogel; *Music:* Lyn Murray; *Art Directors:* George W. Davis and Edward Carfagno; *Editor:* Fredric Steinkamp. Panavision. MGM. 112 minutes. *Cast:* Tony Franciosa (Ralph Bates), Jane Fonda (Isabel Haverstick), Jim Hutton (George Haverstick), Lois Nettleton (Dorothea Bates), John McGiver (Steward P. McGill), Mabel Albertson (Mrs. Alice McGill), Jack Albertson (Desk Sergeant).

Night Of The Iguana (1964). *Director:* John Huston; *Screenplay:* John Huston, Anthony Veiller, from the play by Tennessee Williams; *Producer:* Ray Stark; *Photography:* Gabriel Figueroa; *Art Director:* Stephen Grimes. A John Huston-Ray Stark Production presented by MGM and Seven Arts. 125 minutes. *Cast:* Richard Burton (Rev. T. L. Shannon), Ava Gardner (Maxine Faulk), Deborah Kerr (Hanna Jelks), Sue Lyon (Charlotte Goodall), James Ward (Hank Prosner), Grayson Hall (Judith Fellowes), Cyril Delevanti (Nonno).

This Property Is Condemned (1966). *Director:* Sidney Pollack; *Screenplay:* Francis Ford Coppola, Fred Coe, Edith Sommer. Suggested by Tennessee Williams's one-act play. *Producer:* John Houseman; *Photography:* James Wong Howe; *Music:* Kenyon Hopkins; *Songs:* Jay Livingston, Ray Evans, Sam Coslow, W. Franke Harling, Arthur Johnston, Mildred J. and Patty S. Hill; *Art Directors:* Hal Pereira, Stephen Grimes, Phil Jeffries; *Assistant Director:* Eddie Saeta; *Editor:* Ardienne Fazan. Presented in Technicolor by Seven Arts and Ray Stark. 110 minutes. *Cast:* Natalie Wood (Alva Starr), Robert Redford (Owen Legate), Charles Bronson (J. J. Nichols), Kate Reid (Hazel Starr), Mary Badham (Willie Starr), Alan Baxter (Knopke), Robert Blake (Sidney), John Harding (Johnson), Dabney Coleman (Salesman), Ray Hemphill (Jimmy Bell), Brett Pearson (Charlie Steinkamp), Jon Provost (Tom), Quentin Sondergaard (Hank), Michael Steen (Max), Bruce Watson (Lindsay Tate), Bob Random (Tiny).

Boom! (1968). *Director:* Joseph Losey; *Screenplay:* Tennessee Williams, based on his short story, and play, *The Milk Train Doesn't Stop Here Anymore; Producers:* John Heyman, Norman Priggen; *Photography:* Douglas Slocombe; *Music:* John Barry; *Associate Producer:* Lester Persky; *Art Director:* Richard MacDonald; *Editor:* Reginald Beck. Limites/World Film Services Limited Production in Technicolor. Universal. 110 minutes. *Cast:* Elizabeth Taylor (Mrs. Flora Goforth), Richard Burton (Chris Flanders), Noel Coward (Witch of Capri), Joanna Shimkus (Blackie), Michael Dunn (Rudy), Romolo Valli (Dr. Lullo), Fernando Piazza (Etti), Veronica Wells (Simonette), Claudye Ettori (Manicurist), Howard Taylor (Journalist).

Last Of The Mobile Hotshots (1970). *Director/Producer:* Sidney Lumet; *Screenplay:* Gore

Vidal, based on the play "The Seven Descents of Myrtle" by Tennessee Williams; *Photography:* James Wong Howe; *Music:* Quincey Jones; *Associate Producer:* Jim Digangi; *Editor:* Alan Heim. Technicolor. Warner Brothers/Seven Arts. 108 minutes. *Cast:* James Coburn (Jeb), Lynn Redgrave (Myrtle), Robert Hooks (Chicken), Perry Hayes (George), Reggie King (Rube).

TV Productions

Several of Williams's short plays were televised in the 1950's, including *The Purification; I Rise in Flame, Cried the Phoenix;* and most notably the Kraft Television Theater production of three of his one-acters, *Moony's Kid Don't Cry, The Last of My Solid Gold Watches,* and *This Property is Condemned,* on April 19, 1958, directed by Sidney Lumet and starring Ben Gazzara, Lee Grant, and Thomas Chalmers. In more recent years full-length works of Williams have been presented on television, and those principally dealt with in the text are listed below.

The Glass Menagerie. First telecast December 16, 1973. *Director:* Anthony Harvey; *Teleplay:* Tennessee Williams, based on his play; *Producer:* David Susskind. ABC-TV. 120 minutes. *Cast:* Katharine Hepburn, Sam Waterston, Michael Moriarity, and Joanna Miles.

The Migrants. First telecast February 3, 1974. *Director:* Tom Gries; *Teleplay:* Lanford Wilson, suggested by a story of Tennessee Williams; *Producer:* Tom Gries. CBS-TV. 90 minutes. *Cast:* Cloris Leachman, Ron Howard, Sissy Spacek, Ed Lauter, David Clennon, Lisa Lucas, and Dinah Englund.

The Eccentricities of a Nightengale. First telecast June 16, 1976. *Director:* Glenn Jordan; *Teleplay:* Tennessee Williams, based on his play; *Producer:* Lindsay Law and Glenn Jordan. PBS-TV. 120 minutes. *Cast:* Blythe Danner, Frank Langella, Neva Patterson, Louise Latham, and Tim O'Connor.

Cat on a Hot Tin Roof. First telecast December 6, 1976. *Director:* Robert Moore; *Teleplay:* Tennessee Williams, based on his play; *Producer:* Laurence Olivier and Derek Granger. Granada TV (Great Britain) in association with NBC-TV. 120 minutes. *Cast:* Laurence Olivier, Natalie Wood, Robert Wagner, Maureen Stapleton, Jack Hedley, Mary Peach, David Healy, Heidi Rundt, and Sean Saxon.

Index